ANGLICANISM
AND THE
CHRISTIAN
CHURCH

ANGLICANISM AND THE CHRISTIAN CHURCH

Theological Resources in Historical Perspective

PAUL AVIS

FORTRESS PRESS
Minneapolis

T & T Clark Ltd
59 George Street
Edinburgh EH2 2LQ
Scotland

This Edition Published under License from T & T Clark Ltd by
AUGSBURG FORTRESS
426 South 5th Street, Box 1209,
Minneapolis, MN 55440, U.S.A.

First published 1989

ISBN 0–8006–2416–5 1–2416

Library of Congress Cataloging in Publication Data

Avis, Paul D. L.
Anglicanism and the Christian church : theological resources in
historical perspective / Paul Avis.
p.   cm.
Bibliography: p.
Includes indexes.
ISBN 0-8006-2416-5
1. Church —— History of doctrines.   2. Anglican Communion —
— Doctrines —— History.   I. Title.
BV598.A92   1989
262'.03 —— dc20

Typeset by Buccleuch Printers Ltd, Hawick
Printed and bound in Great Britain by Billing & Sons Ltd, Worcester

We have a vast inheritance, but no inventory of our treasures. All is given us in profusion; it remains for us to catalogue, sort, distribute, select, harmonise and complete.

J. H. Newman,
The Prophetical Office of the Church,
1837, p. 30.

The study of past controversies of which the final outcome is known destroys the spirit of prejudice.

G. M. Trevelyan,
Clio, a Muse, p. 153.

Contents

Part One

THE SIXTEENTH CENTURY

The Erastian Paradigm and the Formation of
Anglican Ecclesiology

Part Two

THE SEVENTEENTH & EIGHTEENTH CENTURIES

Co-existence of the Erastian and Apostolic Paradigms

Part Three

THE NINETEENTH AND EARLY TWENTIETH CENTURIES

Resurgence of the Apostolic Paradigm and the Making of Modern Anglicanism

Preface

In this book I offer an interpretation of the Anglican understanding of the Christian church – its foundation in the preaching of the Christian gospel and the sacrament of holy baptism; its identity in history and today; its relations with the Roman Catholic church and the churches of the Reformation; its involvement with the state; its ministry and government; its authority and terms of communion. It may perhaps raise a few eyebrows that I say '*the* Anglican understanding' rather than 'understandings' in the plural. We have become accustomed to think of Anglicanism as a chronically pluralistic communion, without a unified and coherent approach to Christian doctrine, even such central doctrines as those of ecclesiology. But in this book I present the theological resources of Anglican ecclesiology in historical perspective and this enables me to bring out very clearly the fact of a coherent Anglican position, or consensus, on the nature of the church.

I am acutely aware, however, that this consensus was only achieved at the cost of amputating, in 1662, following the Restoration of the monarchy, many who, fundamentally predisposed to conform, had opposed the execution of Charles I and thus fulfilled Izaac Walton's essential condition of true Anglicans – that they should be 'passive, peaceable protestants'. Though presbyterian by conviction in church government, some would nevertheless have settled for a modified, 'primitive' episcopacy and flexibility in the rubrics governing worship. But, paradoxically, even the ejection supports the consensus theory; the presbyterians recognised, in a statement of 1660, that 'there is a firme agreement betweene our brethren and us in all doctrinall truths of ye Reformed Religion, and in the substantiall parts of Divine Worship; and that thes differences are only in some various conceptions about ye antient forme of Church Gover[n]ment, and some particulars about Liturgy and Ceremonies' (c. Whiteman in Nuttall and Chadwick, ed., p. 54n).

In the first part I show how the distinctive Anglican ecclesiology was formed through the work of the Anglican Reformers, followed by Hooker and Field, though it is complicated for us by the now anachronistic unity of church and society in a single Christian commonwealth. I call this 'the erastian paradigm'. In part two I trace the consolidation of Anglican ecclesiology in the seventeenth and eighteenth centuries, when, in spite of the emergence of distinct traditions within the Church of England, a consensus prevailed as to the character of Anglicanism as both catholic and reformed. At this time we see the erastian model beginning to fail and an alternative conceptuality for Anglicanism, based on an appeal to the apostolicity of the church, beginning to emerge. Bishops take the place of the sovereign as the sacred symbol of Anglicanism. I call this 'the apostolic paradigm'. In the third part, I trace the final demise of the erastian model and the development of the apostolic model by the various high church groups that we carelessly tend to lump together as 'the Tractarians'. Distinguishing between the faithful old high churchmen on the one hand and the innovative positions of the radical Tractarians on the other enables me to show that the latter, in setting out to 'unprotestantise' the Church of England, challenged the tacit consensus as to the nature of Anglicanism, to which all schools of churchmanship were party. This development was opposed not only by evangelicals (who have been studied by Peter Toon in his *Evangelical Theology*; I do not deal with them), but also by the liberal Anglicans and the old high churchmen. I show the instability of 'the apostolic paradigm' with reference to Newman and Manning, and in conclusion I offer some suggestions towards formulating what I believe would be a more authentic model for Anglicanism in an ecumenical context, based on the common baptismal faith of all professing Christians.

The third section of the book, then, highlights the conflict of interpretations within modern Anglicanism as to the validity of the Reformation and its doctrine of the church. In focusing on this neglected aspect of nineteenth-century religious thought I hope to make a contribution to our historical understanding of both the Oxford movement and liberal Anglicanism, as well as to Anglican ecclesiology more broadly considered. But the subject is very far from being of merely antiquarian interest. Never has Anglican engagement with the heritage of the Reformation been so topical. This book has been more than ten years in the making but the third part was undertaken during 1983 – the year of the one hundred and fiftieth anniversary of the inception of the Oxford movement and the five hundredth anniversary of the birth of Martin Luther. I attended the celebratory conference on the Oxford movement at Keble College, Oxford, not as a partisan of Anglo-catholicism, but as a sympathetic, though obviously not uncritical student of the movement. Though I was relieved to find that the note of triumphalism was muted (see Rowell, ed., *Tradition Renewed*), I wondered how many of those present would have been prepared to support a conference on the work and influence of Luther.

It is due to the radical Tractarians that Luther's work impinges so minimally on the Anglican consciousness. When the Tractarians set out to 'unprotestantise' the Church of England they did so as men largely ignorant of the thought of the Reformers. For Newman, protestantism was just not Christianity; for some of his disciples it was merely a 'deplorable schism'. Newman himself began the habit of caricaturing Luther which has left its mark on Anglicanism to this day.

The Tractarians successfully challenged an Anglican consensus on the reformed character of the English church and established a new consensus that is happy that Luther and his fellow Reformers should be forgotten. But what the Tractarians did not do was to *catholicise* the Church of England. Does not true catholicism involve some sense of how the church has lived through history (cf. Chadwick, 'Catholicism') and some appreciation of the diversities of the Christian tradition? Does it not involve a willingness to learn from traditions other than our own and is it not incompatible with the defensive narrowing of historical vision that the Tractarians evinced with regard to the Reformation?

But there is another, more positive, side to the coin. Recent years have seen an astonishing conjunction of confessional rapprochements. In 1983 the Archbishop of Canterbury devoted his presidential address to the Church of England's General Synod to a commemoration of Luther and to Anglican-Lutheran relations. He spoke of the debt of Anglicans to 'the living Luther of today' (contrast Newman's destructive dictum, 'The spirit of Luther is dead'). Secondly, following the fundamental agreement achieved in Lutheran-Episcopal dialogue in the United States between 1976 and 1980, the European Commission of Anglicans and Lutherans reported that no serious obstacles existed to full communion.

Meanwhile, enormous advances were being made in relations between Anglicans and Roman Catholics and between Lutherans and Roman Catholics; the former marked by the Pope's visit to Canterbury and the publication of the Final Report of the AnglicanRoman Catholic International Commission in 1982, and the latter by a joint Lutheran-Roman Catholic statement 'Martin Luther – Witness to Jesus Christ' which attempted to overcome confessional barriers and present a Luther who belongs to the whole church. Pope John Paul II, having already stated in 1980 that the Lutheran Augsburg Confession reflected *a full accord on fundamental and central truths* with catholic doctrine, took the historic step of preaching in a Lutheran church in Rome.

While the Pope and the Archbishop have been directing the attention of their respective communions to the significance of Luther, scholars can do much to break down the barriers of inherited ignorance and prejudice. In the case of the Oxford movement this is precisely what we are up against. Now that the celebrations and congratulations of the one hundred and fiftieth anniversary have died down, perhaps we may hope for a willingness to redress the profit and loss account and to take a cool critical look at one negative aspect of the legacy of the movement. But my intention is that this should be done in the spirit of the motto from G. M. Trevelyan that stands at the beginning of the book.

It is unhistorical to be partisan about the Reformation. We can well appreciate that the spoilation of the English church under Henry VIII must have seemed to many like the destruction of Christianity itself – it still does! (cf. Scarisbrick, *The Reformation and the English People*). Most writers treated in the present work were protagonists or antagonists of the Reformation. A few, such as Bramhall, sought more objective assessment. That is the ideal that I wish to embrace for myself. It seems to me that the Reformation – or for that matter, the Counter Reformation or any other formative episode in the history of the Christian church – is not something that it is incumbent on us to take sides over. There is no reason for Anglicans to speak with either shame or pride of their Reformation, any more than Roman Catholics should be expected to respond with pride or shame to their own equally mixed history. These things were what they were, for reasons that were sufficient to account for them at the time. As I argue in 'The Authority of Scholarship' in chapter 17, it is vital for us to attempt an informed and dispassionate assessment of those developments that have made us what we are. That does not mean that, as Anglicans, we can sit lightly to our theological inheritance, or play fast and loose with received theological positions – regarding infallibility or primacy, for example – that were worked out with a good deal more learning and acumen than we seem to be able to muster, on the whole, today. It would seem to be a precondition of ecumenical progress that before we can know where we are going, we need to be clear about where we have come from and what has made us what we are.

It is also unhistorical to be partisan about the Oxford movement: we are all children of the Tractarians now. The Oxford movement was the Church of England's deferred Counter Reformation, an upsurge of consecrated energy through the channels of catholicism. In the realms of worship, discipline, the sacramental life and the cure of souls, the Tractarians had a prophetic message for the church. Through their sheer sense of God they may have saved the Church of England. Their emphasis on the role of the bishop as the channel of sacramental grace (easily derided by liberals such as Arnold and Hare as 'episcopolatry') contributed to the birth of Anglican Communion as a fellowship of autonomous provinces. But we need to be far more discriminating than we have been in our assessment of the Oxford movement. I attempt to make a contribution to such a reassessment in three ways. First, by distinguishing the three main groups: the old high churchmen, the radical Tractarians who went over to Rome, and those such as Keble and Pusey who rejected the Anglican consensus and worked to transform the Church of England from within. Second, by showing how and why Newman and Manning forced the apostolic paradigm of ecclesiology to breaking point and fell into the embrace of Rome. Third, by tracing in my penultimate chapter, the implications of Tractarian innovations for the area of authority in theology.

I want to be quite clear about the specific aims of this book. It is obviously not intended to be a history of the Church of England. First because there are considerable gaps in the 'narrative' – puritanism, the late eighteenth century, evangelicalism, for example. Second, because the history of the Church of England could only be written nowadays within the chastening frame of reference provided by social and economic history – a dimension that is patently absent from this work – and which has brought about an alternative, revisionist, interpretation of the English Reformation that sees it not as the outworking of theological principles in response to widespread demands for reform, but as an exploitation of the legacy of English catholicism, engineered from above and legitimated theologically in arrears (see Haigh, ed.). Rather, *Anglicanism and the Christian Church* is a study of Anglican identity, Anglican self-definition and Anglican apologetic. It provides some of the resources or raw materials for an Anglican doctrine of the church.

I agree with Professor Stephen Sykes when he inists that there is (at least implicitly) an Anglican doctrine of the church and that it is incumbent upon us to articulate this (in Wright, ed., and Draper, ed.). The present work confirms that there is indeed a tacit Anglican ecclesiology – though it is not static and needs to be disentangled from various specific historical frameworks, particularly those that I have designated the 'erastian' and the 'apostolic' paradigms. It brings to light some of the principles that need to be incorporated in an Anglican ecumenical ecclesiology. We owe it both to ourselves and to our partners in ecumenical dialogue to attempt this task. Such an Anglican ecclesiology would have to be the product of research and discussion through the Anglican Communion – a task perhaps for the Inter-Anglican Theological and Doctrinal Commission – and its materials could no longer be drawn from the writings of English divines from Richard Hooker to Michael Ramsey. An Anglican ecclesiology for today should not attempt to perpetuate what John Pobee has called 'the Anglo-Saxon captivity of Ecclesia Anglicana' (Sykes & Booty, ed., p.395). However, the roots of such an Anglican ecclesiology would inevitably have to be discovered in the 'theological resources in historical perspective' that I have presented from the first four centuries of the thought of the reformed English church – resources that now belong to a world-wide communion that can make of them what it wills. The question raised by Dr Gareth Bennett in his ill-fated Crockford's preface of 1987 (pp. 59f) still awaits an answer: Is the ecclesiology worked out by Jewel, Hooker and their successors, in the formative years of Anglican self-definition, understood, accepted or wanted today?

This book takes its place in a programme of research and writing that has occupied me for the past fifteen years or so. The first part presupposes and partly overlaps with the concerns of my book *The Church in the Theology of the Reformers* (Marshall Pickering 1982). I have not repeated the bibliography of secondary literature in the bibliography of this book: the earlier work and its bibliography should be consulted for substantiation of some of my assertions in part one. The latter part of the story covered here merges into the areas covered in my *Gore: Construction and Conflict* (Churchman Publishing 1988) and once again I have not repeated the material. Again, I have stopped short of discussing Anglican involvement in ecumenical discussions as I have written about aspects of this in my *Ecumenical Theology* (SPCK 1986). The present work substantiates with a wealth of historical reference the interpretation of Anglicanism that I deployed in *Ecumenical Theology*.

It is my hope that *Anglicanism and the Christian Church* will find a useful place as a resource work in theological education and in ecumenical discussion. The question of Anglican identity, as I suggest in my first chapter, has been emerging into prominence over the past ten years. To help in resolving that question would be to perform a service not only to Anglicans but to other branches of the Christian church, who sometimes find themselves baffled and frustrated when they ask what Anglicanism stands for. I would like to think that this book will contribute to progress in mutual understanding in the context of total mutual acceptance between Christians of (at present) separated communions.

I am extremely grateful to His Grace the Archbishop of Canterbury for commending this book to the Anglican Communion and to Dr David Newsome, the Revd Dr Perry Butler and Canon John Thurmer for reading parts of the typescript at an earlier stage. But they must not be held responsible for any weaknesses of the whole book in its final form. I am also most grateful to Dr Peter Nockles and the Revd Dr John Rowlands for generously giving permission for me to quote from their unpublished dissertations and the Revd M. G. Smith for pointing me to several obscure references. Finally I would like to pay tribute once again to the dedication and skill of my typist Mrs Gillian Piper.

Some material has already appeared in my articles 'Richard Hooker and John Calvin' (*Journal of Ecclesiastical History*), 'The Shaking of the Seven Hills' (*Scottish Journal of Theology*), 'The Tractarian Challenge to Consensus and the Identity of Anglicanism' (*King's Theological Review*), 'Coleridge on Luther' (*Charles Lamb Bulletin*), and 'The Church's One Foundation' (*Theology*).

PAUL AVIS
Stoke Canon Vicarage   *August, 1988*

I

In Search of
Anglican Identity

A Crisis of Identity?

This book aims to contribute historical perspectives and theological resources to the ongoing discussion of Anglican identity, in the context of the search for unity between separated branches of the Christian church. 'Identity' is a word whose time has come. It has been central in psychological theory and clinical practice and in sociological studies since the war. Now theologians and particularly ecclesiologists are taking it up – though not always with much care for the philosophical, psychological and sociological background. Stephen Sykes has written on *The Identity of Christianity* and Richard and Anthony Hanson have published *The Identity of the Church*. In the United States Hans Frei has given us *The Identity of Jesus Christ* and Robert Jenson has offered trinitarian doctrine under the title *The Triune Identity*. 'Identity' is one of those blessed words we latch on to when we know what we mean but cannot quite pin it down.

My identity is my sense of who I am and where I belong. Our identity is our conviction that we are part of the meaning of things. It is where we fit in. Identity contains a dynamic of stability and change, sameness and development, continuity and adaptation. It is a dynamic that is found in all organisms, societies and individuals. Identity operates in the world of symbols: symbolism constitutes the currency of identity–formation. So the locus of identity formation is where symbols are created and recognised, namely the human imagination, the intuitive level of perception and creation, rather than logical or discursive thinking. In the whole question of identity there is more going on beneath the surface than above the surface. Durkheim defined the identity of a society as 'the idea which it forms of itself'. It would acknowledge the role of symbolism if we adapted this to read 'the image which it has of itself'. To be preoccupied with one's identity is often a sign of impending neurosis, or at least of the loss of direction. The quest for identity can become introverted and morbid. But a number of factors are now compelling Anglicanism to look to its identity: the continuing Anglican-Roman Catholic discussions and the request of the Roman magisterium for a clear Anglican profile to engage with, the uncertainty over the authority of a Christian Church to undertake autonomously such reforms as the ordination of women to the priesthood, defections to Rome in search of strong authority, a conservative backlash against liberal theological opinions in high places in the church, and the decline of institutional religion in a secular environment, among others.

If sociologists and psychotherapists detect a crisis of identity in modern society, it is not surprising that theologians should be able to point to a similar problem within the church. J. B. Metz has asserted that 'the widely discussed crisis of identity in Christianity is not primarily a crisis of the Christian message, but rather a crisis of its subjects and institutions' (p.ix). I suspect that this is a false antithesis and that the source of the problem lies in our perception of the identity of the gospel and the nature of the church. George Stroup in particular has alleged that we have an 'ecclesiastical and theological crisis' on our hands, one that is 'more insidious, more elusive' than many of the crises that have confronted the church in the past, such as persecution and conflict with other religions, because it arises from 'a pervasive uncertainty about the identity of the Christian community'. And Stroup insists that this crisis is 'at its root theological and must be treated as such' (pp. 21, 24).

Stroup singles out four symptoms of this theological and spiritual malaise (pp.24–38). It is not difficult to see the relevance of these to Anglicanism.

(a) *The Bible*. The Scriptures have lost their impact and remain strangely silent in the church. Biblical criticism reveals the original context and meaning of scripture but leaves us cold and unsatisfied. Fundamentalist preaching claims biblical authority for its message but pays scant regard to the integrity of the text. But who can span the almost unbridgeable chasm between the revelatory events of so long ago and the needs of humanity today and make the Bible live? Here is a problem of authority and of the role of scholarship within it.

(b) *Tradition*. Tradition is the corporate memory of a community. When Christian communities lose touch with their roots in tradition they suffer a form of religious 'amnesia' leading to loss of identity, for 'the tradition provides the hermeneutical categories by which the community reconstructs and reinterprets its identity.' As Anglicans, our knowledge of our roots in the tradition is both impoverished and distorted.

(c) *Theology*. There is a widespread failure of theological reflection. 'It is the ability to think theologically which enables the church to engage the world by means of the resources of the past.' Where academics lose touch with the pastoral concerns of the church and pastors give up on theology the church will become confused and incoherent in its utterances and aimless in its activity. Anglicans least of all have grounds for complacency on this score.

(d) *Personal identity*. The problems of scripture, tradition and theology come to a head in the problem of our personal identity as Christians. Identity is formed through many sources, but what part does our Christian profession, our baptism, membership of a church and participation in its activities, play in this formation? Our relationship to Christ and through him to God the creator and to the church is surely the ultimate factor in construing our personal identity. As Stroup puts it:

> The crisis in the church is that the personal identity of many Christians is no longer shaped by Christian faith and the narratives that articulate that faith but by other communities and other narratives ... neither the language of Christian faith nor the fact of participation in the Christian community seem to play prominent roles in those identity narratives ... [that] Christians recite in order to explain who they are and what kind of people they think they are (pp. 36f).

Stroup's book is an attempt to examine the structure and the formation of Christian identity in general by means of the concepts of revelation and narrative. In fundamental theology, or to be more precise, fundamental ecclesiology, the importance of uncovering the springs of the identity of Christianity is becoming increasingly recognised – Edward Farley's *Ecclesial Reflection* and Stephen Sykes' *The Identity of Christianity* being notable examples of recent work in this realm. In the area of personal spirituality the insights of psychological studies of identity-formation are being increasingly appropriated. But in the whole sphere of ecclesiastical policy, the institutional aspect of church life, there seems to be a woeful disregard of the dynamics of identity-formation and identity-maintenance with its apparatus of sacred symbolism. I hope to make a modest contribution that will help to remedy that neglect in future publications. The present work is not intended as a contribution to that 'fundamental' (ie methodological) enquiry. It is an attempt to provide historical perspectives and theological resources for the rediscovery and reconstruction of the identity of Anglicanism.

The Relevance of Anglican Identity

Anglicanism is one of the least self-conscious of Christian professions. This is true of both its spirituality and its ecclesiology. It neither wears its heart on its sleeve nor flaunts its theological position. This does not mean, however, that Anglicanism does not possess either a genuine spirituality or rich theological resources – though it may mean that both spirituality and theology remain at the present time in a state of potentiality, largely unmobilised, in fact unidentified. Beneath the surface Anglicanism has a developing identity problem.

Self-conscious identity has not been required where Anglicanism has been the norm, as it has until recently in English society where it could be said without arrogance that more self-conscious nonconformist churches and a resurgent Roman Catholicism seeking to raise its profile, could neither hope nor intend to challenge the indelibly Anglican substratum of English society. The position today has changed not because non-conformity has become stronger (like all institutional religion it has declined) or because Roman Catholicism has begun in any measure to supplant Anglicanism as the faith of the English people (individual conversions to Rome are still exceptional), but because all institutional forms of Christianity have suffered an erosion of their authority, identity and numerical support in the process of secularisation. But is the identity of Anglicanism important? Who cares about it? The bishops of the Church of England and the wider Anglican Communion? The members of the General Synod, not to mention diocesan and deanery synods? The Anglican representatives on ARCIC II? Certainly the rural congregations to whom I minister have never had to bother their heads about the question of Anglican identity. For them the parish church is the undisputed, unrivalled focus of their Christian lives and of the deepest dimension of the life of the community. Neither, I believe, do urban Anglicans trouble themselves about the identity of Anglicanism. In their situation of a plurality of Christian and non-Christian religious traditions confronting massive secular indifference to all religious values, it may well be that urban Anglicans are motivated to think about the identity of the Christian faith as such – and what could be more important than that? – but not about the Anglican version or versions of it in particular. As far as the young Christians of university and college chaplaincies are concerned, among whom the future clergy and many of the articulate lay members of the Church of England are presumably to be found, the nature of Anglican identity is, I would guess, furthest from their thoughts and would, I imagine, be regarded as a comparatively trivial question. The ordinands in our theological colleges who apparently can complete their training without acquainting themselves with the Book of Common Prayer or making a study of church history will hardly be either motivated or equipped to think intelligently about the identity of the church that they are going forth to minister in.

I would like to hope that all that is an over-pessimistic assessment; there are signs that the question of Anglican identity is beginning to be taken seriously. But I am bound to conclude from these preliminary considerations, even allowing for some overstatement, that attempts to upgrade or push to the forefront the question of the identity of Anglicanism are likely to meet with a disappointing response, while on the other hand, the question of the identity of Christianity itself has an uncontroverted and urgent importance. Beyond that, of course, the question of the identity of Jesus Christ – who he was and who he is for us today – will necessarily have first call on the energies and efforts of theologians. Only if Anglicanism can be justified by reference to Christianity as such, and ultimately in relation to Jesus Christ, can its identity concern us. This is, needless to say, precisely what motivates those of us who are currently raising the question of Anglican theological integrity.

Nevertheless, the question of Anglican identity, though it cannot claim a place at the top of the theological agenda, remains a valid one. It asks, what is distinctive about Anglicanism? What is its peculiar contribution to world Christianity? What can its particular way of being the church teach us? Can it teach us anything about how to respond constructively to the questions that face the church today? What are its prospects for the future? I believe that these questions are important for several reasons. These are my reasons for disagreeing with John Howe's claim that 'There is no separate Anglican identity. To search for one, as some ecumenists feel they must, is an unprofitable exercise' (p. 28).

First, there is the domestic matter of Anglicanism's *integrity*, both as a way of living the Christian life together in the church, and as a tradition and style of Christian theology. In this sense, the quest for Anglican identity is no complacent and narcissistic contemplation of existing perfections, but a painful and abrasive journey into greater reality, a *via purgationis*. Alongside theological critiques such as Stephen Sykes' *The Integrity of Anglicanism*, sociological assessments can also spur us to look at our integrity. For example, A. D. Gilbert has described Anglicanism (in England) as 'a religion demanding minimum commitment, and requiring neither deviation from the generally accepted ethical and social standards of the wider society nor burdensome donations of time, money or energy' (p. 112). In defence of Anglican integrity, Gilbert, whose book was published in 1980, could be answered in terms of the transposition theory of Christian values which sees those values tacitly permeating society, thus obviating in many cases a direct clash between Christian and secular ethics (Gill, ch. 3), and secondly by pointing to the stewardship movement of the past twenty years or so, which has certainly called members of the Church of England to a greater degree of commitment expressed in terms of increased contributions (if not yet 'burdensome' ones – and why should they ever be?) of time, money and effort. But Gilbert is right to stress that being an Anglican, at least in England, is not too arduous! The conditions for membership are minimal, the requirement for membership of the church electoral roll being merely baptism, and for full communicating membership, confirmation and communion three times a year, of which one occasion shall be Easter Day. As Stephen

Neill says, 'To be a bad Anglican is the easiest thing in the world; the amount of effort required in minimum Anglican conformity is so infinitesimal that it is hardly to be measured.' He adds, however, 'To be a good Anglican is an exceedingly exacting business' (p. 423).

Increased commitment cannot of course be achieved by legislation – dedication cannot be produced to order – but depends on pastoral effectiveness. But it is also conditioned by the model of the church with which one is operating and that in turn depends on theology. It was with regard to the current state of theology within the Church of England that Sykes was particularly caustic. This is where the quest for integrity, and thence ultimately of identity, must begin.

The second factor that makes the issue of Anglican identity both legitimate and urgent is the requirement of *ecumenical dialogue* that each side needs to know what the other stands for. To put it in a form that reflects my own expressed dissatisfaction with the results of the first series of Anglican-Roman Catholic conversations (ARCIC I), each side needs to know what it itself stands for! The authorities of the Roman Catholic Church have asked for more explicit reference to the authoritative documents of the Anglican tradition. As I have commented elsewhere, this is not as simple as the apparently ingenuous request makes it sound – and no doubt that is why astute Roman Catholic defenders of the faith like Cardinal Ratzinger insist that we try it! (see Avis, *Ecum. Theol.*, p. x).

Thirdly, the question of Anglican identity is raised in an acute form in the context of the church's *mission*, whether that mission takes the form of the evangelisation of the unconverted, or the pastoral care of the faithful. What is the faith of the Church of England and of the sister churches of the Anglican communion? What is the faith that we proclaim, teach, defend? Although Anglicans have liked to pretend that it is 'mere Christianity', that unlike other traditions, Anglicanism has no axe to grind, there is no such thing as undifferentiated Christianity and to imagine that it exists in the Church of England is precisely a symptom of our unselfcritical complacency. So what exactly is the version of Christianity into which we attempt to incorporate new members? Once again, in this sense, the quest for identity is not self-indulgence but a necessary and salutary exercise that looks to the world beyond the church in the fulfilment of the Lord's Great Commission (Matthew 28.18ff).

'Sociological Catholicism'

Its largely unselfconscious, unreflective quality, in which the assertion of identity is not an issue, seems to mark Anglicanism, as we have known it especially in the Church of England, as belonging to a particular type of Christianity – which I call the 'catholic' type, using that denominator in a primarily sociological sense. Catholicism seems to express a deep, unquestioned, implicit integration of life and faith, world and church, nature and spirit. It seems to rest on a set of fundamental assumptions about reality that do not need to be continually articulated, but can be taken for granted while life goes on. Catholicism in this sense does not have a problem of identity: it is the norm. The integrated, harmonious and symmetrical character of catholicism (as we find it classically expressed in St. Thomas Aquinas, for example) is a reflection of social conditions – of the ordered, hierarchical, stable, geocentric and anthropo-centric world of the high middle ages – just as the fragmented, discordant and unbalanced theology of the early Karl Barth reflects the catastrophic upheavals of the First World War and its accompanying revolutions. Today, the age of catholicism in this sociological sense is over. Through the process of advancing secularisation those traditions that once enjoyed a position of unchallenged integration with their social environment, find themselves increasingly out on a limb – marginalised ideologically and alienated socially. The question of ecclesial identity emerges out of the collapse of sociological catholicism. It is rapidly becoming acute for all traditions.

My sociological use of 'catholicism' might be objected to on purist grounds as serving to confuse what we mean by the third credal note of the church. It is admittedly merely an heuristic device. It may not fit every case, but perhaps it is at least an advance on the present invidious practice of using 'catholic' as synonymous with Rome and 'protestant' for the traditions that emanated from Wittenberg and Geneva. For one thing, that usage finds it difficult to accommodate Anglicanism itself.

On this sociological definition of catholicism, not only Anglicanism but also territorial Lutheranism, Calvinism, Orthodox Christianity and Roman Catholicism are included. The emphasis is on indigenous and territorial churches with deep national or cultural roots. Exclusive, sectarian, marginalised groups, both protestant and Roman would be excluded in so far as they evince a basically dualistic approach to life, to the surrounding society and to the world at large. In other words, catholicism in my sociological sense can be predicated of territorial churches, but not of transplanted traditions that lack a secure, territorial, social basis in a culture and the life of a people. Without that they tend inevitably to be self-conscious, inward looking and sensitive as to their identity. Thus Anglican churches in former British colonial territories that are rooted in the way of life of a people and retain strong cultural links and affinities with their originating cultural tradition would qualify as belonging to the catholic type of Christianity, while Anglican churches in other parts of the world, where ties with the mother country or church are weaker and effective indigenisation has not taken place, would not qualify. Such churches would presumably already have a strong sense of their identity over against both other churches and the socio-cultural milieu.

If unassimilated churches, in a missionary situation or undergoing persecution, for example, do not enjoy a sociological catholicity, they do certainly possess a strong sense of identity. Territorial or established churches – and here we come very close to home – can, however, undergo the same process of having their sense of identity heightened when, through advancing secularisation, they find themselves becoming marginalised ideologically and no longer fully integrated socially. In this way the question of identity is becoming acute for all churches, especially the Church of England. As a territorial church, with a parochial structure which has a church in every community, cathedrals in the county towns and a role in civic life, chaplaincies in schools, colleges and the armed services, and a prestigious constitutional role, the Church of England is beginning to suffer the same pangs of identity crisis as a persecuted, minority, missionary church struggling to consolidate its foothold in an alien culture. It is only when identity is threatened that we become self-conscious about it. The situation is then ripe for the critic and reformer to ask, 'What is our spirituality?' (as David Martin and C. H. Sisson have asked with regard to the introduction of the alternative services) and 'What is our theological position?' (as Stephen Sykes has asked with regard to the dearth of Anglican systematic theology).

The Structure of Corporate Identity
The concept of identity incorporates, as we have seen, the twin themes of continuity and individuality (or, as Baumeister prefers, differentiation). These attributes, which exist in tension, constitute the identity of a society just as they do the identity of an individual. McDougall and Freud have sketched the anatomy of corporate identity. In his classical exposition of corporate identity *The Group Mind* (1920) McDougall enumerated five principal conditions for sustaining group identity without generating the pathological symptoms of mass consciousness and the submergence of the individual. McDougall's ideas were immediately adopted by Freud in his *Massenpsychologie und Ich-Analyse* (1921).

The first condition of corporate identity is naturally *continuity*, either of individuals or of office. The second is that each member of the group should have a definite *idea* of the nature, composition, functions and capacities of the group. Durkheim defined the identity of a society as 'the idea which it forms of itself'. The third requirement is *interaction* – especially in the form of conflict or rivalry – of the group with other similar groups 'animated by different ideals and purposes and swayed by different traditions and customs.' Fourthly, the group needs *traditions*, customs or habits, that delineate the role of the individual in the group. And finally, group identity demands a definite *structure* expressed in 'the differentiation and specialisation of the functions of its constituents' (McDougall, pp.49f; Freud, XII, pp.114f). It is significant that Freud takes the Christian church, together with the army, as a paradigm of group identity. Are these five conditions met in the Anglican church today? Do they shed any light on the alleged crisis of identity in the church?

1. *Continuity*. While the church has maintained the obvious continuity of personnel – the apostolic succession of bishops and the clergy they ordain – together with the more elemental continuity of place in the parish structure and parish churches that, at least in the mother country of Anglicanism, go back to time immemorial, it seems to me that it has patently broken the vital continuity of the liturgy in its modern, multi-choice service books. Here the church faces a dilemma. Unless the liturgy expresses a Christian's sense of identity, it leaves him or her cold, and fails in its function. But that very sense of identity is, in part, created through the repetition of familiar words and images, the participation in something that can be taken for granted, that is second nature. As David Martin has written:

> Repetitions are ways of freeing the attention by making a lower hierarchy of habit purely automatic. An absolutely familiar sequence allows the mind to stand outside for a moment: in suspension, in recollection, in interpretation, or in ecstacy. At one level the saying of a collect can be somnambulistic. The ancient syllables are part of a waking dream. At another level the collect touches a profound level of recollection . . . The words have acted like a tuning fork to bring all the disparate modes of being into a unifying harmonious world (p. 87).

The present stage of liturgical disturbance and confusion is producing a marked break in the continuity of the *teaching* of the church. For teaching is received not only explicitly through sermons and lessons, but tacitly and subliminally through the whole liturgy. The message subliminally received from the recent alternative services is more than subtly different from the message absorbed from the old Book of Common Prayer. The images of God, creation, providence, humanity, salvation, and community are certainly different in emphasis and sometimes irreconcilable. The standard transcendental model of Christian belief is giving way to an immanental model. The standard paradigm of Christian doctrine is transcendental. It postulates a monarchical deity, operating transcendentally through an all-embracing providence and intermittent miraculous interventions in nature or history; making his will known through positive law and ensuring infallible means, through pope or scripture, of its communication to men. This paradigm's conception of truth and meaning is dominantly literalistic. Its strength and persistence can hardly be over-estimated even today, though it has been subjected to criticism and modification on scientific grounds since the Enlightenment, and on grounds of a felt inappropriateness since the Romantic movement. What then is taking its place? The alternative paradigm of Christian theology is immanental. Within Anglicanism it began to take shape with the publication of *Lux Mundi* in 1889. Evolutionary philosophical ideas derived from German idealism fostered a distate for an 'interventionist' model of divine agency in the world and postulated an immanent deity realising his purposes through the emergence of human spirituality crowned by the emergence of Jesus of Nazareth. This second paradigm is of a God who 'lets be', whose transcendence is evidenced in the fact that there is no unequivocal embodiment of his mind, whether in written texts, unchanging dogma, an authoritative, charismatic persona in the papacy, or guaranteed grace-bestowing structures in the historic episcopate; while his immanence is disclosed in the aspirations of the social reformer, the vision of the artist and the compassion of the good samaritan wherever there is suffering to be assuaged. Its concept of truth leans heavily on metaphor and symbol (Avis, 'The Church's One Foundation', pp.259f).

This is not the place to comment critically on these alternatives, nor to explore the possibility of a 'third way' which attempts to do justice to the seriousness, definiteness and transcendental claims of the first paradigm, while at the same time incorporating the liberty, humanity and compassion of the second. My point here is simply concerned with the role of the liturgy in the formation of Christian and ecclesial identity. The immanental paradigm that we find emerging strongly if inchoately in the modern alternative services is one that is still in the making. It is not at the stage when it can lend itself to liturgical formulation, for it is the nature of liturgy to short-cut conscious reflection and reach back through multiple reference and unimpeded association to the unconscious recesses of the self where the springs of vitality are to be found. To throw hallowed symbols such as the traditional wording of the Lord's Prayer, the General Confession and the Creed precipitately into the melting pot, is to invite identity problems. It is asking for trouble in the realm of identity-formation if the received symbols and constellations of meaning are disposed of with scant regard for what the social and human sciences can tell us about the logic of symbolism in personal and corporate life.

2. *Idea of the Group*. The second requirement was for members of a group to have a clear conception of the nature, composition, function and capabilities of the group. Can it be said that the members, particularly the laity but probably the clergy too, of the Anglican church have a clear idea of what the Christian church is, what their own branch of it stands for, why it exists and what it has to offer? The grasp of the laity is notoriously deficient and we the clergy are often troubled about our role. In the Church of England, the Tiller report has challenged the laity to take over some of the traditional roles of the clergy. The question of the ordination of women to the priesthood remains unsettled in parts of the Anglican Communion at the time of writing. If suitably qualified women were

given to understand that their services were not permitted in the sanctuary, at the same time that the laity were being stirred up to engage more fully in the ministry of the church, confusion would reign over the nature of the church and its ministry, and over the distinction between lay and ordained Christians.

3. *Interaction.* The third requirement was for *interaction* with similar but not identical groups. Do we see this happening in the church? It is the aim of all ecumenical endeavour to promote such interaction, to explore what various ecclesial bodies have in common without abandoning their own identity. Psychotherapy emphasises the importance of genuine interaction between the client and the therapist, producing feedback and leading to the enrichment of one's identity through introjection. There is no reason why this process cannot be extrapolated on to the corporate scale of interchurch dialogue. But for the process to be beneficial, for it to produce a psychological payoff in terms of enhanced identity and self-understanding, there has to be mutual unreserved acceptance. Can it be said that this climate of mutual and unreserved acceptance of the other partner in dialogue obtains between churches in the present ecumenical state of play? Can there really be genuine interaction at a fundamental level without intercommunion? Surely the basic condition of such interaction, unreserved mutual acceptance, is unfulfilled. Churches do not know where they stand in relation to each other. Is their 'church' a true church? Are their ministries holy orders? Are their sacramental acts valid sacraments? Are their 'bishops' truly the recognised successors of the apostles? Where these questions do not yet receive a clear and affirmative answer, a problem of ecclesial identity is inevitable.

4 and 5. *Tradition and Structure.* Freud and McDougall's fourth and fifth points emphasise the need for clear expectations regarding the role of the individual within the group and for customs, habits and traditions to guide him or her along. As we have already commented, tradition has been significantly undermined in the church and structures are coming under increasing threat. Symptomatic of this in the Church of England are the proposals recently under discussion for a new strategy for the church's ministry, in the Tiller report, which would change the face of the church over the next generation by removing many of the landmarks of the Church of England as we know it – the full-time professional ministry in many areas, the parson's freehold and patronage in particular – centralising the direction of pastoral strategy in the hands of the diocesan bishop. Tiller's aim is an admirable one both theologically and psychologically: a shared ministry of the whole priestly body of the church. But it is questionable on grounds of identity theory whether, in order to achieve this, it is necessary or desirable to make every congregation or group of congregations responsible for its own ministry in the first instance, with outside help, in the form of the services of one of a

reservoir of 'diocesan priests' available for a limited period only in the last resort. The identity of the church and its members, which requires tradition and structure, would be threatened by radical change to a 'congregational' rather than territorial model. On the other hand, it would be safeguarded and, I believe, enhanced if the ideal of a shared ministry of the whole priestly body of the church were to be fostered through existing structures as far as possible. Tradition and structure have already suffered severe erosion.

Identity requires local forms and fixed boundaries. Most people cannot relate to abstract ideals like 'the priesthood of all believers'; they need close parameters. The sacralisation of traditions and structures not only protects identity and modifies or obstructs change; it can also mediate and legitimate change, provided that the sacred symbols are treated with due respect. Identity, it is true, is on the side of consolidation and permanence. It is indeed antithetical to change or differentiation. However, a healthy system of sacred symbols contains the dynamic for salutary change. But identity is fragile and needs careful handling. Symbols need to be respected and 'serviced'. Upheaval damages identity: but a shared commitment to allow changes to evolve naturally towards agreed goals can mobilise the resources of identity and strengthen it in the long run (cf. Mol. pp. 6, 10, 85f).

In *The Group Mind* McDougall made the now classical division into natural and artificial groups. Building on this, Eric Erikson speaks of natural and artificial identity. *Natural* or collective identity is a genuine, given, spontaneous identity – an identity of class, nation or culture, for example. *Artificial*, synthetic, or contrived identity is a defensive, reactive, ideological identity – nationalism, racism, class hatred, for example (Mol, pp. 57f; McDougall, pp. 89f). Is there anything corresponding to this in Christian identity? It might be salutary to ask whether contemporary developments in the church – the denigration of 'folk religion', the eclipse of parochial boundaries by eclectic congregations, the break with traditional liturgies, for example – represent the triumph of natural or artificial identity.

It would seem that belonging to a parish or congregation, a communion of the Christian church and one of the great traditions of Christianity falls into the category of natural identity. But for many Christians the sense of identity that this gives is not enough. It is abstract, impersonal, remote. They need closer and more tangible boundaries of identity. The need to belong to a greater whole is one of our most elementary human needs, along with the need for food, shelter, security, sexual satisfaction, etc. Strong commitment brings an enhanced sense of identity. An artificial identity comes on the cheap and is quickly assumed.

For some Christians it is not enough to belong to a parish, a diocese and a communion of the Christian church. They want to throw in their lot with some more narrowly identified group – a church party or pressure group that will sustain their identity through its own lines of communication, newspapers, journals, conferences, etc. It makes us feel good like few things do to be accepted in a fellowship of kindred spirits, a confraternity of the elect.

This belongs to Erikson's second category, that of artificial or contrived identity. It is defensive not expansive, it thrives on a them-and-us mentality and cultivates an adversarial outlook. It stereotypes both the opposition and its own cause, overlooking the contingent, ideological determinants of both. Although the intention is a positive one – to uphold truth, to safeguard certain values and to provide mutual support and encouragement, thus promoting the very intensification of identity that the more diffuse collectivities could not offer – the unintended results are not so attractive. These side effects include narrowness of outlook, bigotry in beliefs, and fanaticism in putting them into practice. In this way the sincere quest for identity can become the mere propagation of ideology. In their more extreme manifestations, these phenomena belong to what Horkheimer and Adorno call 'the paranoiac forms of conscious-ness'. They generate alliances, parties and cliques because, as Horkheimer and Adorno put it, 'their members are afraid of believing in their delusion on their own. Projecting their madness they see conspiracy and proselytism everywhere' (p. 197).

The Pathology of Ecclesial Identity

Theorists of psycho-social identity point to several pathological aberra-tions of identity formation. *Identity diffusion* is excessive directedness towards others. *Identity dislocation* is caused by fixing on an inappropriate model or ideal. *Identity foreclosure* is an unnatural attempt to call a halt to further development, a refusal to integrate new events and experiences into the self (Mol, pp. 57f). Have these phenomena any application to the identity of the church?

Perhaps when sixteenth-century puritans continually looked over their shoulder to Geneva and insisted that the Church of England should be further reformed on the model of 'the best reformed churches', they were exhibiting *identity diffusion*. When Anglo-Catholics of recent times aped Italian baroque spirituality, ecclesiastical ornamentation and clerical dress, they were likewise exhibiting diffusion of identity. England is not Switzerland or Italy; Canterbury is not Geneva or Rome; each must seek its identity in a way that is true to itself, to its environment, opportunities and tradition. When in ecumenical debate today it is insisted that the Anglican church cannot act – for example in ordaining women – until Rome and the Orthodox have given approval, we have once again, in my opinion, a sad case of identity diffusion. 'To thine own self be true!'

Identity dislocation is diagnosed when the subject has fixed on an inappropriate model of behaviour and attempted unsuccessfully to incorporate it into himself. It may be that the model of consensus is a case in point. The Anglican church is currently exploring the consensus model for policy formation both domestically, through its synodical structure, and ecumenically, in the Anglican-Roman Catholic International Commission's blueprint for resolving differences within a united church. Both levels of consensus government in the church have come in for heavy criticism recently (Moore, ed.; Avis, *Ecum. Theol.*, ch.4). Consensus can easily become a formula for paralysis – for marginalising prophetic voices, for concocting unprincipled compromise and for failing to face genuine conflicts. The expressions of consensus will inevitably reflect a lowest common denominator; they will be bland, safe, platitudinous. Consensus weakens identity. It is not an appropriate model for the church. Healthy conflict, rigorous argument, freedom to experiment, liberty of prophecying (with safeguards for conscientious objectors) is surely a healthier recipe for the strengthening of Christian identity – provided, however, that there is an environment of unreserved mutual acceptance, based on our common baptismal faith and expressed in the church by intercommunion.

Identity foreclosure is the refusal to integrate new events and experiences. Interpreted ideologically, this is an attribute of extreme conservatism. Stroup calls this 'ecclesiastical nostalgia' (p.22). In the church we find it in evangelical and catholic forms of fundamentalism and reaction, both of which refuse to face the questions that the most alert and perceptive Christian voices are asking. It is not that they merely insist on traditional answers: they do not admit the legitimacy of the questions. In the Church of England, the organised protest against the mildly radical views (albeit provocatively expressed) of David Jenkins the bishop of Durham illustrates the point. The predominantly populist and pragmatic character of the agitation, majoring on the discomforting of the faithful and the danger of their withdrawing financial support from the church, reveals (quite apart from its low moral tone) an intellectual weakness in the more articulate sector of the right wing of conservative evangelicalism. It tends to be heavy on biblical exegesis – though often a precritical form – but weak on systematic theology, strong in conviction but weak in judgement. Of those accustomed to assert it may excusably be inferred that they are not equipped to argue. This is not a sin, but it perhaps betrays a reluctance to face new challenges and to move with the logic of development – in other words, in the jargon of identity-theory, it is a case of 'identity foreclosure'.

Symbols are the currency of identity-formation. Symbols are not within our control; they emerge from the unconscious in response to some unconsciously felt need, crisis or inadequacy. There can be a 'rebirth of images' as new symbols draw numinous power into themselves and regenerate the whole symbolic world. But it is possible to resist the emergence of new symbols. The Christian feminist movement is producing new symbols of the sacred, immanental rather than transcendental symbols. But the persistent blocking of women's ordination is a case of resistance to new symbols, and of the failure of the received symbol-systems to evolve in order to incorporate new meanings in response to the changing demands of human identity (see Avis, *Eros and the Sacred*).

In his recent study, *Identity*, Baumeister has usefully distinguished three basic functions of identity. First, a sense of identity relates to the need to make *choices*. Our identity concerns our personal values and priorities. Second, identity has to do with *relationships*. Our identity concerns our social roles and our personal reputation. Third, identity is a function of *character*. It refers to our inner resources, our individual potentiality, our ability to attain our goals and fulfil ourselves (p. 19). By extrapolation we might say that the identity of a church or of a religion is revealed in the values and priorities that it manifests, in its ability to relate to other churches or the outside world, and in the moral strength and resourcefulness that it brings to the fulfilment of its objectives in relation to those other parties.

Baumeister also points to two principal causes of the undermining of identity. Identity may suffer through *destabilisation* or *trivialisation*. Destabilisation is caused by the failure of the unifying functions of the components of identity. It represents a weakening of continuity and its source is change or the threat of change. 'Actual change separates the present and future self from the past self. Possible change . . . separates the present and past self from the future self' (p. 122). (The self concerned may of course equally well be a corporate self, a society). Trivialisation, on the other hand, comes about through failure of the differentiating function of the components of identity, when there is a weakening or a breakdown of the distinction between the self and others, when people have ceased to regard some traditional point of differentiation as important. The example Baumeister cites, of Roman Catholics and protestants (though not in Ireland) is pertinent and suggestive. A moment's reflection will confirm that the Christian churches are currently suffering both the destabilisation and the trivialisation of their identity. Whether they are aware of that situation and have a policy to meet it is another matter.

Both destabilisation and trivialisation are forms of what Baumeister calls *identity deficit*. This is the condition of the inadequately defined self with its lack of commitment to positive goals and values. In the individual, identity deficit is a problem of adolescence and the 'mid-life crisis'; in institutions it occurs at the corresponding stages: during the period of vigorous growth when the society or institution is finding its feet and establishing its orientation, and when it has passed its peak of strength and success and the symptoms of decline become apparent. Then, both for the individual and society, identity has to be reborn, with reaffirmed values and new goals; new relationships have to be established and fresh resources discovered. I surely do not need to labour the application to the church. Its identity problems are not terminal but provide the opportunity for renewal and rebirth.

The opposite of identity deficit is *identity conflict*. This condition arises where identity is strong, where there is, so to speak, an excess of identity, but where two or more components of identity conflict. A parent might experience a conflict between home and career, a theologian between pastoral and academic roles. 'The essential pre-requisite for an identity conflict is a strong personal and emotional commitment to two distinct identity components that become incompatible' (ib., p. 211). A Christian church such as the Church of England might experience a sort of diffused identity conflict between its commitment to being a territorial church of all the people and its aspiration to ideals of Christian discipleship that could only be realised among the dedicated few. It might suffer conflict between its desire for rapprochement with Rome and its growing awareness of common ground with the churches of the Reformation. No doubt the Church of England could be said to be undergoing mild conflicts of identity in both these areas but they are certainly not traumatic. No one is going to suggest that the churches are suffering from an excess of identity. That is hardly their problem.

Identity and Integrity

The current debate on the nature and identity of Anglicanism was generated by the publication of Stephen Sykes' book *The Integrity of Anglicanism* a decade ago. In this book Sykes castigated complacent appeals to the comprehensiveness of Anglicanism as merely an excuse for morally reprehensible theological laziness and evasiveness. He asked whether Anglicanism could be said to possess integrity if no one seemed to know what it stood for. He claimed that for a church integrity is equivalent to 'coherent identity' (p. 4). Personally I would be reluctant to make this equation between identity and integrity. As my discussion of 'sociological catholicism' indicates, I think that there are situations where there can be integrity without a strong awareness of identity. In that state of ideological prelapsarian innocence the church just gets on with being the church – believing, worshipping, celebrating, serving – without bothering its head about its identity. Furthermore, a distinct identity does not necessarily guarantee integrity. Identity can be contrived by various dubious means, including the manipulation of people's perceptions through the media, as we have seen in every general election campaign. A strong sense of identity, a sharp social profile, may be induced by methods that are theologically and psychologically dubious – by the totalitarian assertion of authority in suppressing dissent, for example. Alternatively, the same effect – the enhancement of identity – can be achieved by a deliberate strategy of withdrawal into a sectarian form of Christianity, with clear-cut beliefs, rigidly enforced, and a tight-knit social structure. Both these moves may strengthen identity and hold secular relativising influences at bay, but they sacrifice the priceless privilege of catholicity, that fundamentally unchallenged integration of Christianity with civilisation. But there is no short cut to integrity. It is a state of moral probity in belief and practice, one that we aspire to but never fully attain: *ecclesia reformata semper reformanda*, the reformed church must be continually reforming itself. Identity is merely the reflex of integrity, not its substance. Pursue integrity and identity will take care of itself.

It is only when the church becomes relativised by the emergence of rival churches, secular belief systems and profane ways of life, that identity becomes an issue. The days of sociological catholicism are numbered and in the new relativistic situation of a secular society it is certainly true that there will be no integrity without identity.

The question of identity arises then when formerly unquestioned assumptions are forced to become explicit. This process in itself serves to relativise them: they then have to co-exist in the market place of ideas with alternative views. The quest for identity, as psychological and sociological studies would confirm, indicates a crisis, a threat, a new set of problems to be confronted. A glance at church history supports this interpretation.

Anglican identity began to be forged in the sixteenth century in the work of Jewel, Whitgift and Hooker in response to internal political changes and an external political threat. Anglican identity was inseparable from the birth of national identity. In the middle and late seventeenth century there was a renewal of Anglican identity and a resurgence of theology in response to the puritan threat embodied in the Commonwealth. Similarly the quest for the identity of Anglicanism was urgently renewed in the 1830s in the Tractarian movement which was the defensive response of old high church Anglicanism to the threat of an emerging secular state reflected in Whig legislation, for removal of the Church's privileges and monopolies. In our own time, Christianity has become further marginalised by the advance of the complex and disputed phenomenon that we call secularisation, forcing the Church of England, among others, to bring into the open, and make explicit the assumptions by which it has lived.

The language of the new alternative liturgies is a case in point. While the Book of Common Prayer takes for granted the central realities of the Christian faith and merely alludes to them as the unquestioned presuppositions of worship (for example in the collect form), the new liturgies choose to spell it all out to the extent of labouring the point, reminding both God and ourselves of the various affirmations of Christian doctrine. ('The Lord is here' and 'You are God' being particularly crass examples). This is neither appropriate to the worship of God, since he does not need to have his memory jogged, nor pedagogically effective, since it serves to relativise the doctrinal content of the liturgy by tacitly acknowledging that it cannot be taken for granted as the unquestioned presupposition of a Christian life grounded indeed in worship but lived out amid the challenges and opportunities of the secular world. To the psychologically and sociologically sensitive eye, this phenomenon reveals a sense of uncertainty, a crisis of identity (cf. Davies). If as I have suggested, attempts to convince ourselves and to suppress anxiety as to our Christian identity are actually counter-productive, what is the alternative? Can identity be reborn?

Anglican Identity: Singular or Plural?

Before looking at the possibility of the rebirth of identity we need to face one more question. Is it possible to speak of a single identity for Anglicanism as a diverse worldwide movement? There are two ways of looking at this question. First, there is the theological question: is there a distinct Anglican version of Christianity, and if so what is essential to it? To answer this requires a considerable effort of historical research. We would need to look at the unfolding of the Anglican tradition since the Reformation. I hope that this book will be a useful contribution to that project. Second there is the sociological question: are there recognisable characteristics that are common to all the manifold expressions of the Anglican tradition in the world today? To tackle this is a largely descriptive, phenomenological and comparative study of the outward identifying marks of the churches of the Anglican Communion, of what they have in common but do not share with other non-Anglican churches. It is not within the scope of this book.

We would I think certainly expect that world Anglicanism would have a recognisable identity. The historical and cultural links, the practice of intercommunion and exchange of ministers, the various procedures of consultation such as the Lambeth Conference, the Anglican Consultative Council and the primates' meetings, the presiding role of the Archbishop of Canterbury, the theological traditions of the Anglican heritage, and the family resemblances of its liturgies, all create the necessary conditions for both a common spirit and a shared identity. But we should not imagine that these are stronger than they are, or that they are not becoming more fragile and tenuous as traditions acquire a momentum and dynamic of their own, as originally daughter churches grow in confidence and in resources, both theological and liturgical and in terms of spirituality and church government. Both the indigenous cultural input and progressing relations with churches of other traditions would appear to make for a weakening of explicit ties within the Anglican communion, while they at the same time serve to strengthen immensely world Christianity. Anglicanism is not a federation of churches nor is it an *ad hoc* fellowship for a particular purpose. In its dependence on historical, cultural and tacit constitutional links it bears comparison with the British Commonwealth of Nations: like the Commonwealth, it ought to be able to sustain conflicts, disagreements and antipathies and to provide a supportive and constructive context for trying to resolve them.

Anglican identity is developing and diversifying. As the Lambeth Conference of 1988 showed, this development and diversification can proceed within the context of communion. There is no *a priori* reason why the member churches of the Anglican Communion should grow closer together; no imperative for the links to become tighter and more formal; no reason why the Church of England should continue to be dominant; no reason (except domestic reasons confined to the Church of England and its relationship with the Crown) why – to put it symbolically – the Archbishop of Canterbury should always be English, any more than the Pope has to be Italian. We would expect the sister churches of our communion to go their own way and to pursue their own integrity without the sacrifice of communion. Anglicanism has been receptive to the notion of development. In its practice of toleration or comprehensiveness it has tacitly acknowledged it. In the working of the Anglican Communion sufficient scope is given for it. While the Church of England itself, in its consistent resistance to the challenge of new spiritual movements – notably ecumenism and the Christian feminist movement – has seemed to foreclose against development and to harden its position in favour of tradition, the younger churches of the same communion have acquired the initiative. They have succeeded in creating schemes of church unity, entered into relations of intercommunion with non-episcopal churches, and ordained women to the priesthood. The torch of necessary and legitimate development has passed to them.

Identity Reborn

In conclusion I would like to return to the analogy between individual and corporate identity. Just as individuals experience the birth, growth, crisis and renewal of their identity at different stages of their lives, so too societies pass through comparable stages. It is not fanciful to speak of the emergence of a group's sense of identity, its development, decline and perhaps renewal. The turning point of western civilisation over the past two millennia was the rebirth or 'renaissance' of learning that began in the twelfth century, and had its ultimate payoff as far as Christian theology is concerned in the Reformation of the sixteenth. Both the Renaissance and the Reformation were a return to the springs and sources of western culture and the church's theology. By drawing on the classical expressions of humane learning and Christian theology respectively, these movements brought about a rebirth of Christian identity in the west.

The rebirth of identity comes about through returning to our origins and applying the strength there derived to the problems of the present. Many forms of psychotherapy take us back to childhood and infancy, allowing us to see where our later development went wrong and releasing hitherto unconscious resources to enable us to tackle the present situation constructively. The return to origins and its consequences is often a painful process. It is a stripping down, a way of purgation, a making vulnerable and weak once again. But this is the inescapable prerequisite of renewal and rebirth. The rebirth of identity comes through death and resurrection and there is no road to resurrection except by dying first. Like all forms of identity it is expressed in symbols and its renewal depends on what Austin Farrer called 'the rebirth of images'. But the dynamics of ecclesial identity and its symbolic structure is a subject for another occasion.

The principle of death and resurrection suggests that Anglicanism may have to go deeper into the painful process of self-examination and heart-searching, that much more may have to go into the melting pot, more difficult problems faced, more awkward questions no longer evaded, before her identity can be reborn. She may need to make a journey back to her origins, yet without disowning any stage of her development. It is precisely to facilitate that process that the following study of Anglicanism and the Christian Church, with its combination of historical perspectives on Anglican development and its making available of neglected theological resources, is offered.

Christian identity – and derivatively Anglican identity – is not fixed and unchanging. Like personal and social identity it is fluid, dynamic, vulnerable. It cannot be created at will, it cannot be guaranteed, it does not need to be defended by ideology, it is not in the church's possession. The church's identity is eschatological. The identity of the church is a grace given to her by God and received dynamically as she beholds the glory of God in the face of Jesus Christ.

Part One

THE SIXTEENTH CENTURY
The Erastian Paradigm and the Formation of Anglican Ecclesiology

2

The English Reformers
and the Christian Church

The English Reformers' View of the Church of Rome
Like their continental counterparts, the English Reformers evaluated the
visible church by its outward marks. In the debate with Rome these
marks were the true preaching of the word of God and the right
administration of the sacraments. In the debate with the anabaptists, it
was necessary to add a reference to church polity, the outward order and
government of the church, its ministry (c.f. Avis, *CTR*, pt 1). How did
the church of Rome measure up to the two criteria of the preaching of the
word and the administration of the sacraments?

In the view of the English Reformers, Rome retained the essential word
but had overlaid it with human traditions. She retained the essential
sacraments of baptism and the Lord's Supper, but had corrupted the latter
by withholding the cup from laity, and by the doctrine of transubstantiation
and the sacrifice of the mass. In the Roman church the word was not pure
nor the sacraments correctly administered. Furthermore, Rome not only
imposed her errors on the consciences of individuals as terms of
communion, but she refused all calls to reform them. In that case, the
English Reformers believed, separation from her communion was a duty.
Rome could not be regarded as a true church.

Jewel wrote: 'We truly have renounced that church wherein we could
neither have the word of God sincerely taught nor the sacraments rightly
administered, nor the name of God duly called upon' (PS, III, pp. 91f).
Hooper observed: 'These two marks, the true preaching of God's word
and the right use of the sacraments, declare what and where the true
church is . . . Where the doctrine is sound and no idolatry defended, that
church is of God, as far as mortal man can judge. And where this doctrine
and right use of the sacraments be not, there is no church of Christ'
(PS, II, p. 87). Preaching at St. Paul's Cross, Bancroft asserted that the
church 'which maintaineth without error the faith of Christ, which

23

holdeth the true doctrine of the gospel in matters necessary to salvation, and preacheth the same: which retaineth the lawful use of those sacraments only which Christ hath appointed . . . is a true church' (c. Woodhouse, p. 61).

Rome's persecution of the Reformers and their followers throughout Europe produced a rather paranoid strain of anti-Roman polemic. For Cranmer Rome is the 'true natural mother of anti-Christ' and our 'most cruel stepmother' (c. Woodhouse, p. 143). For Fulke and Bradford Rome is anti-Christ because she denies Christ's redemption and refuses the word of God (PS, Fulke, II, p. 392; Bradford, I, p. 395). For Philpott Rome is Babylon and for Bale her practices and corruptions are blasphemous (PS, Philpott, p. 428; Bale, p. 431). For all the English Reformers Rome is simply not the catholic church (PS, Tyndale, III, pp. 39ff; Hooper, II, p. 532; Whitgift, III, p. 622). It is important to bear in mind that at this stage the Reformers are still working with the assumption that there could be only one church, the true church, the catholic church. If Rome was the church, the Church of England and her reformed sisters on the continent were not, and vice versa. As we shall see, Hooker and Field would break out of this ecclesiology and offer a concept of a visible church that could suffer heresy and schism within its confines. In doing so they would be employing concepts embodied in official formularies of Henry's reign: 'The Bishop's Book' (1537) and 'The King's Book' (1543) presented the Christian church as a mixed society, parts of which could err and go into schism without ceasing to be the church, and Rome was just such a part.

In the Reformers' evaluation of the Roman Catholic Church, the entire focus was on the papacy and its power. Their quarrel was not with the great mass of faithful misguided followers of the hierarchy. The question of the salvation of 'our fathers' came to concern a later generation: Hooker and Field had to deal with it. The Reformers saw catholic Christendom as suffering a Babylonian captivity (as Luther had put it) to the doctrinal and canonical authority of the papacy. The act extinguishing the authority of the bishop of Rome (1536) rejected 'the foreign pretended power and usurped authority' – both temporal and spiritual – 'of the bishop of Rome, by some called the pope'. It is significant that it is under article 37 'Of the Civil Magistrates' that the Thirty-nine Articles insist that 'The bishop of Rome hath no jurisdiction in this realm of England'. While the Henrician legislation to abolish Roman jurisdiction could claim that 'this realm of England is an empire', the Reformers for their part appealed to the ancient British church which antedated the mission of Augustine of Canterbury – Archbishop Parker's *De Antiquitate Britannicae Ecclesiae* being the classic exposition of this claim (c.f. Brook, pp. 322ff). This ancient church had been planted by Joseph of Arimathea or St. Paul. It was independent of the papacy and had its own ministry and martyrs. The English Reformers took pride in this pedigree (e.g. PS, Bale, p. 188). But the church of Rome had departed even from the sounder doctrine of St. Augustine of Canterbury (PS, Fulke, II, pp. 7, 20).

However, like the continental Reformers, the English divines wished to leave open the door to eventual reconciliation with Rome provided she would reform herself and return to apostolic purity of doctrine and life. Jewel undertook that the English church 'would be willing to yield to Rome all the honour Irenaeus gave her if she would return to the doctrine and traditions of the apostles' (PS, I, p. 365). Field gave a similar pledge and it was to recur constantly in the writings of the seventeenth century Anglican divines. King James I, in his first speech to Parliament said, 'I acknowledge the Roman church to be our mother church, although defiled with some infirmities and corruptions' and elsewhere indicated his willingness, when those corruptions were amended, to give due precedence to the historic patriarch of the west (c. Pawley, p. 25).

Continental Influences on Emergent Anglicanism
The question of the cross-fertilisation of the English Reformation by ideas from the continent continues to be the subject of research. While Luther himself was made to take the blame for the reforming notions that were circulating in the early 1520s, it is likely that the theological influence of Luther has been exaggerated and that much of the inspiration of the first generation of English Reformers – men such as Tyndale and Barnes – derived firstly from diffused reforming ideas stemming from Wycliffe, Colet and Hus, and secondly from the contemporary writings of Erasmus. In 1520 Luther's works were judicially burned in Cambridge and in the following year archbishop Warham, as chancellor of Oxford University, complained to Wolsey that 'divers of that university be infected with the heresies of Luther and others of that sort, having among them a great number of books of the said perverse doctrine'. 1521 also saw the ceremonial – almost liturgical – incineration of Luther's works at St. Paul's Cross, London, in the presence of the two primates and with the sermon preached by Fisher, bishop of Rochester. The bonfire was repeated in 1526 on a grand scale in the presence of Wolsey and thirty-six dignitaries, with Fisher again preaching: denouncing faith as *fiducia* – faith was 'the faith of the church' (Hall, p. 113; Clebsch, *Earliest Protestants*, pp. 27ff).

Tjernagel has claimed that Luther was the dominant influence on the Henrician Reformation and that his influence continued into the formularies and liturgy that became the lasting fruits of the sixteenth-century Reformation in England. The English Reformation, writes Tjernagel, 'was a Lutheran Reformation in its origins, and it left a Lutheran imprint on the Church of England that developed and matured in the reigns of the son and daughters of Henry VIII . . . During the reign of Henry VIII, the formative and determining influence was that of Martin Luther and German Lutheranism'. Though Henry was not drawn to Lutheran principles on their own intrinsic merits, he needed Lutheran support against the pope and the emperor. However, Lutheran views on civil government were congenial since Henry could have countenanced neither anabaptist anarchy nor Zwinglian theocracy. Tjernagel also points out that, with the exception of the doctrine of the Lord's Supper, the Forty-two Articles of Edward VI and the Thirty-nine Articles of Elizabeth 'were and remain Lutheran. Their view of scripture, the church, church-state relations, justification, good works, election and other fundamental doctrines is Lutheran' (pp. 250, 253). In all this, the influence of Philip Melanchthon, though not precisely quantifiable, was enormous (Meyer).

Against this thesis we need to set several factors. First there is the broadly consistent hostility of Henry himself to Lutheran theology. Henry had received from the pope the title *Fidei Defensor* for his attack on Luther's sacramental teaching and had engaged in a bitter exchange of polemic with the Reformer. The official formularies of Henry's reign gave little comfort to those looking for a reform on Lutheran principles. Henry's opposition inhibited the penetration of Lutheran theology on the scale of the entry of Swiss theology during the reign of Edward. Until 1526 when Tyndale published his introduction to the epistle to the Romans, which was Luther in disguise, Luther's teaching was available only in the original Latin or, occasionally, German.

Second, we need to note the argument (presented for example by J. S. Marshall, ch. 1) that Henry's Reformation was intended to be moderate, limited and Erasmian in its inspiration – a reform of church life and structures, not of doctrine, and one that reflected the pervasive influence of the English humanists with their lay mentality and aversion to dogma (McConica, pp. 199, 280f). Humanist notions of reform provided a perfect excuse for the transfer of the church's assets to the state.

Third, there is the evidence brought forward by W. A. Clebsch that the dominant influence on the English Reformers of the first generation was actually Erasmian and moralistic rather than Lutheran and libertarian. 'Luther's thought by no means determined the theology and religious character of the Englishmen's writings ... they yet remained more enamoured of Erasmus than Luther ever was, and they owed much of their programme for church reform to the Hollander' (*Earliest Protestants*, p. 311). Their emphasis was on the four gospels and the epistles rather than, with Luther, on 'the gospel'. Their thought focused on the future life rather than justification, Christian morals rather than Christian liberty. For example, Barnes moved from the general reformatory ethos of 'Little Germany' at the White Horse tavern in Cambridge, where the ideas circulating were common to Wycliffe, Hus, Colet and Erasmus, to a Lutheran theology, after his flight to Wittenberg in 1528 (see Anderson). While Barnes progressed to Lutheran theology and became an intermediary between the court of Henry and the Lutheran Reformers, Tyndale moved from a position that virtually parroted Lutheran tenets, to one verging on the later puritan moralistic covenant theology. Tyndale's later emphasis on the law as gospel was the antithesis of Luther's. As Clebsch has pointed out, the early exiles from the English Reformation held views that were to form the basis of the puritan opposition to the establishment of the Tudor church. 'Their biblical, convenantal, moral Christianity logically and actually conflicted with the royal, hierarchical, liturgical Christianity that Ecclesia Anglicana, even under Henry, adopted' (*Earliest Protestants*, p. 317).

In assessing the conflicting accounts of the dominant influence – either Lutheran or Erasmian – on the English Reformation, we need to distinguish between (a) the public policy of Henry or Elizabeth, (b) the convictions of those such as Cranmer or Parker who had the opportunity to shape the theological position of the reformed English church through liturgies and articles of belief, and (c) the predilections of those such as Barnes, Tyndale and Foxe (whose martyrology took Luther as its central and heroic figure), who made their contribution indirectly and from the sidelines. In that perspective, the picture emerges of a national church whose independence, integrity and unity were the first concern of its royal supreme governors and of liturgical and doctrinal reforms that were shaped by these constraints. It seems that, as far as Henry and Elizabeth were concerned, doctrinal reform and liturgical change were acceptable only so far as they served overiding considerations of Tudor statecraft. In Henry's case, these took the form of foreign policy considerations and covetousness with regard to the wealth of the church; in Elizabeth's of national cohesion and consensus in the face of the internal and external threats. As Clebsch has pointed out, Tudor monarchs, especially Elizabeth, 'wrought their religious inclinations into actualities not so much by doctrines as by liturgies and not so much by liturgies as by their choices of bishops who gave sacred representation to the royal presence throughout the realm' ('The Elizabethans', p. 106). Those reforms dictated by the sovereign were in the external forum, having to do with the outward polity and government of the church, and consisted in abolishing papal jurisdiction, dissolving the religious orders with their property and privilege, and asserting the role of the sovereign, together with parliament, as the defender of the church's integrity and the final court of appeal in place of the pope. Along with these reforms, went eventually a vernacular liturgy, communion in both kinds and a married ministry. In support, appeal was made to the ancient indefeasible rights of the British nation under the government and protection of the sovereign.

These changes went beyond the Erasmian platform for the reformation of the catholic church, but were consistent with Lutheran principles.

In those areas where the archbishops and their advisors had an opportunity to reform the liturgical and doctrinal life of the church, Lutheran influence was more explicitly at work. The formularies resulting from Anglo-Lutheran negotiations during the reign of Henry VIII were employed in the construction of the Forty-two Articles and hence subsequently of the Thirty-nine. The Book of Common Prayer drew on Lutheran catechisms, litanies and liturgies. Tyndale provided a Lutheran Bible. With the exception of eucharistic doctrine and the influence of Bullinger's *Decades* – officially commended to the clergy – Swiss theology never had the chance to make the same impact. Elizabeth frustrated the attempts to Swiss-inspired reformists in the Convocation of 1563 to undertake further liturgical, disciplinary and doctrinal reform.

These putative reforms, as Haugaard has indicated, were an attempt to make the Church of England a confessing church on the lines of 'the best Reformed churches'. Not only would doctrinal, liturgical and disciplinary loopholes and ambiguities have been tidied up in the interests of theological purism, but the bishops would have been empowered to require *lay persons* of doctrinally suspect views to subscribe to the Thirty-nine Articles. The decision of the Church of England at this time – imposed by the royal lay supreme governor of the church – not to make doctrinal precision and uniformity the key factor in ecclesial integrity had enormous implications for the subsequent Anglican tradition. Haugaard pertinently warns against mistaking identical wording in English and continental doctrinal formularies for identity of purpose and character (p. 233). The scale of values was not the same. As Haugaard comments:

> Had progress in doctrine been made in 1563 as the zealous reformers anticipated, it is difficult to see how the Church of England could have provided fruitful soil for the growth of its distinctive comprehensiveness. In an age when ecclesiastical guards were busy shutting doors to theological alternatives, the Elizabethan Reformers left a remarkable number of doors ajar (p. 290).

'In the first years of Elizabeth's reign the attempt to make the Church of England a "confessional" church was decisively repudiated' (p. 338).

The Church of England went its own way. It drew on the resources of Lutheran and Reformed theology from the continent according to its merits, without slavishly following any particular school. The appreciative but critical attitude of the English Reformers towards the persons of their continental counterparts was reflected in their assessment of their theology. Though congenial perhaps to time-honoured English intellectual habits, this theological independence was secured above all by the policy of queen Elizabeth herself. Doctrinal uniformity did not interest her; uniformity of outward profession of faith and unity of national purpose did. As Haugaard has aptly commented: 'The effective governorship of the church by a monarch is distasteful to the twentieth century, but the consequences of Elizabeth's role are much more congenial to modern tastes and values' (p. 341).

The Reformers of the Reformation

Though the doctrine of the reformed English church was not regarded as differing in essentials from that of the other reformed churches, the attitude of the English Reformers to their continental counterparts is not one of deference or subservience. They are prepared to be critical where necessary. They see themselves as colleagues working in the same cause, not as disciples propagating their masters' teaching. They are selective in what they adopt – justification by faith but not Luther's sacramental doctrine, the freedom of a Christian man, but not Luther's pervasive dialectic of law and gospel. There is little in their writings to substantiate the charge levelled at them by catholic controversialists that Luther was to them 'a patriarch' or even 'a god' (PS, Cooper, pp. 39, 23; Jewel, I, p. 214).

It goes without saying that the English Reformers stand by the necessity of Reformation. It was light in the darkness, new life springing forth in the desert, an awakening after the deep sleep of ignorance and error. As Jewel puts it: 'In the midst of the darkness of that age first began to spring and to give shine some one glimmering beam of truth'. When reproached by his adversary Harding that 'before Luther's time all Christian people came together peaceably into one church, under one head, as sheep into one fold under one shepherd,' Jewel replies: 'Before the time that God's holy will was that Doctor Luther should begin, after so long time of ignorance, to publish the gospel of Christ, there was a general quietness, I grant, such as in the night season, when folk are asleep' (PS, IV, p. 666; III, p. 174). In the midst of this death-like slumber of the church, Luther and Zwingli 'being most excellent men', were 'sent of God to give light to the whole world'. Like the Old Testament prophets they were raised up to awaken the people of God and reform the church. Their credentials may not always have been impressive. Harding objects that the new teaching came, not from Jerusalem or Rome but from obscure Wittenberg. To which Jewel replies that Wittenberg was 'not more simple than was the town of Nazareth', adding, 'Christian modesty would not distain the truth of God in respect of place' (PS, IV, p. 666; c.f. Fulke, p. 245; Philpott, p. 386; Jewel, III, pp. 193f).

The first Reformers did not intend to set up a new church but to reform and purify the one church of Christ. 'These worthy and learned fathers Luther and Zwinglius,' writes Jewel, 'and other like godly and zealous men, were appointed of God not to erect a new church but to reform the old – whereof you have made a cave of thieves – to kindle again the light that you had quenched and to bear witness to the truth of God' (PS, III, p. 213). The church was *reformed* not *transformed*, claims Whitgift, retaining the good, refusing the evil (PS, II, p. 439). The Reformers, Jewel points out, departed not so much from the church as from 'the errors thereof' and, moreover, did so not 'disorderly or wickedly but quietly and soberly' (PS, III, p. 79). Like Luther they insisted that they had departed from Rome not because of the evil life of its rulers, but because of false doctrine (PS, Fulke, II, p. 175).

The later English Reformers actually regarded some manifestations of Lutheranism as a menace. Grindal commented in 1562 that though the Lutherans regarded Luther as all but a god, they took issue with Reformed theologians, Bucer, Calvin and Peter Martyr, on the doctrine of predestination, when Luther himself had taught an equally uncompromising doctrine in *The Bondage of the Will* (PS, *Zurich Letters*, II, p. 73). Lutheranism, with its continual internal and external disputes was a 'great disturber of Christianity' wrote Robert Horn, bishop of Winchester in 1576 (ib., I, p. 321). The English Reformers held no brief for the Lutheran version of Reformation theology. 'God be thanked' wrote Whitgift, having the Lutherans with their images, 'popish apparel' and doctrine of the real presence in mind, 'religion is wholly reformed, even to the quick, in this church' (PS, III, p. 530). Other reformed churches could not hold a candle to the Church of England in respect of reformation: her doctrine and practice were as pure as ever in the church since the apostles, or any other reformed church (ib., I, p. 3).

The Reformers' attitude to Luther himself, though always more respectful, could be equally critical. Hooper, writing to Bucer in 1548, two years after Luther's death, sets the tone: 'I readily acknowledge with thankfulness the gifts of God in him who is now no more, yet he was not without his faults'. Hooper mentions some, including the 'calumnies and reproaches' with which he 'attacked even the dead', adding, 'I do not write thus by way of reproach of a most learned man, but that no one may swear by his opinions, as if whatever he wrote were an oracle of Apollo or a leaf of the Sibyl' (PS, *Zurich Letters*, III, pp. 46f). Clebsch has asserted that no English tract claimed outright to espouse Luther's teaching as such; none praised his life or leadership. 'Neither his doctrine, narrowly understood, nor his person greatly appealed to the English Reformers' ('The Elizabethans', pp. 104, 117). It was Henry VIII and Sir Thomas More who thrust Luther himself into the limelight in their writings.

When pressed by catholic critics, the Reformers were not prepared to undertake a wholesale defence of Luther. 'I will not take upon me to defend him in all points', remarks Latimer. 'I will not stand to it that all that he wrote was true; I think he would not so himself: for there is no man but he may err. He came to further and further knowledge.' But surely, Latimer concludes, he was a 'goodly instrument' (PS, I, p. 212). Luther, writes Grindal, 'has indeed deserved exceeding well of the church and is worthy of being celebrated by all posterity'. But his disciples are sometimes the worst enemies of his cause. 'He would be more eminent in my eyes,' Grindal adds, 'if these Canaans were not always discovering the nakedness of their father, which all godly persons desire to be concealed' (PS, *Zurich Letters*, II, p. 73).

While Whitgift ordered Calvin's *Institutes* to be studied at Oxford (along with Bullinger's *Catechism*), he reserved his position: 'I reverence M. Calvin as a singular man and worthy instrument in Christ's church; but I am not so wholly addicted unto him that I will condemn other men's judgements that in divers points agree not fully with him' (PS, I, p. 436).

Reformation Ecumenicity

Historians of the modern ecumenical movement (and not just Anglicans!) have detected significant ecumenical potential in the position of the English church in the mid-sixteenth century, as a church which had accepted the principles of the Reformation yet had attempted to maintain an essential continuity of pastoral and liturgical ministry together with the uninterrupted episcopal line of continuity in the government of the church. As R. W. Dixon put it, the English reformation was revolutionary in spirit but not in form: 'A revolution was effected, first in property, then in religion, but none in polity, none in the ancient constitution of the Church of England. It was effected within the constitution, not by the subversion of the constitution' (I, p. 6).

J. T. McNeill writes: 'Thus the reformed Church of England held a strategic position in ecumenical matters. It carried forward more that was medieval than the continental churches, while it acknowledged a fraternity with both Lutheran and Reformed protestantism' (Rouse and Neill, ed., p. 54). In his work *Unitive Protestantism*, McNeill has traced the ecumenical aspirations and efforts of the Reformers, not least of Thomas Cranmer, significantly setting them in the context of the tradition of conciliar, as opposed to monarchical catholicism. The conciliar movement had reached its peak with the councils of Constance and Basle in the first half of the fifteenth century, when calls for the reform of the church and of the (fragmented) papacy had provided the motive. The council of Constance (1414–17) asserted its authority above that of the pope(s), but condemned the teachings of Wycliffe and Hus, handing over the latter to the secular authority for execution. The council of Basle had seen the boldest attempts to assert the authority of a general council over the pope in its early sessions (1531–), but it failed to pull this off and its status is disputed. The failure of the conciliar movement gave impetus to less constitutional and more radical movements towards the reformation of the church. R. W. Dixon (writing in the 1870s) called it 'the most mournful event of modern history', commenting: 'The defeat of this attempted reformation by councils, which was effected by the intrigues of Rome, and above all by the skill of the last of the great popes, Martin V ... caused despair: it gave weight to the clamour that no reformation was to be expected from the church herself: and thus it opened the way for the invasion of the temporal power, and for the doctrinal revolution which presently overswept northern Europe' (I, pp. 23f).

We fail to understand the nature of the Reformation unless we see it as both a reaction to the failure of conciliarism and a continuation of the conciliar movement. Luther first appealed to a general council in 1518 and continued to press for a free council – not one packed by the pope with his own supporters – for the next quarter of a century (Pelikan, *Obedient Rebels*, ch. 4). Cranmer similarly insisted that a general council be called, not by the pope or by one prince, but with the general consent of Christian princes. It is in line with the aims and principles of the conciliar movement of the early fifteenth century that article 21 of the Thirty-nine Articles insists that 'general councils may not be gathered together with the commandment and will of princes'. When he suffered degradation from his office under Mary, Cranmer presented a formal appeal from the authority of the pope to that of 'a free general council', for such a council, 'lawfully gathered together in the Holy Ghost, and representing the holy catholic church, is above the pope' (c. McNeill, in Rouse and Neill, ed., p. 56).

Before the death of king Henry, Cranmer was in correspondence with Philip Melanchthon about a possible conference of protestant theologians to be held in England. For Melanchthon, Cranmer suggested, this would be an opportunity to draw up a pan-protestant confession of faith. Between 1547 and 1549 a number of distinguished foreign Reformers sought refuge in England – Peter Martyr Vermigli, Bernardino Ochino, John à Lasco and Martin Bucer. As the Council of Trent continued to condemn Reformation doctrines Cranmer pressed Bullinger and Calvin himself to lend their support to a protestant council. Calvin, in reply, paid tribute to Cranmer's concern for the Christian *oecumene* and vowed that he would if necessary cross ten seas to bring about such a council. Regrettably, the death of Edward VI in 1553 put an end to Cranmer's hopes (McNeill, *Unitive Protestantism*, ch. 6; ib., in Rouse and Neill, ed., pp. 56ff).

Cranmer was motivated not only by the need to respond to Trent, but also by distress at protestant divisions, especially over eucharistic doctrine. 'It cannot be told how greatly this so bloody controversy has impeded the full course of the gospel both throughout the whole Christian world and especially among ourselves.' Cranmer's vision is that the various reformed churches 'may with united strength extend as widely as possible one sound, pure evangelical doctrine, conformable to the discipline of the primitive church' (PS, *Original Letters*, p. 14). He wrote to à Lasco of his plan to seek 'the assistance of learned men who, having compared their opinions together with us, may do away with all doctrinal controversies and build up an entire system of true doctrine' (ib., p. 17). To Calvin, Cranmer expounded his dream of a great reformed confession of faith to answer and counteract the decrees of the council of Trent:

> I have often wished, and still continue to do so, that learned and godly men who are eminent for erudition and judgement might meet together and, comparing their respective opinions, they might handle all the heads of ecclesiastical doctrine and hand down to posterity, under the weight of their authority, some work not only upon the subjects themselves but also upon the forms of expressing them (ib., pp. 24f).

A concept of conciliarity was one aspect of emergent Anglican ecclesiology, but it was by no means unique to the English church among the churches of the Reformation. In once sense, it represented a line of continuity with the church catholic of pre-Reformation Christendom, in that the aspirations of the conciliar movement were inherited by the Reformers. In another sense, there is a significant break with tradition, for just as Luther had severed one link with the medieval catholic consensus when he had asserted that councils could err (the council of Constance had erred in condemning the reforming views of John Hus), so too the Anglican formularies asserted that general councils 'may err, and sometimes have erred, even in things pertaining unto God', since they are gatherings of human beings not all of whom are 'governed with the spirit and word of God' (Thirty-nine Articles, art. 21).

Episcopacy and Catholicity

While the historic episcopate was preserved in the English Reformation it was not regarded as of the essence of the church or as constitutive of her catholicity. The English Reformers shared the view of Luther, Melanchthon and the mainstream of the continental Reformation that ecclesiastical polity belonged to the external form of the church (*externa forma ecclesiae*), whereas the preaching of the gospel and the administration of the sacraments, which were the proper work of the church, belonged to her inward essence. They alone, not the ministry, whether episcopal or not, showed where the church was to be found. For Luther, the threefold ministry of bishops, priests and deacons was a purely human arrangement. Bishops might by all means be retained if they acted as fathers in God and did not oppose the reform, but there was no compulsion, and the church lost nothing in losing its bishops, provided the essential ministry of word and sacrament was carried on (see Avis, *CTR*, pp. 109ff). The outward polity of the church belonged to the sphere of *adiaphora,* things indifferent. The test in this sphere was not that of biblical warrant or divine right, for no such mandate was forthcoming in the case of bishops, but the pragmatic test of edification, good order and decency.

Calvin's view of episcopacy was by no means inflexible and he did not share the position of his successor Beza that a purported scriptural pattern of presbyterian government was binding on the church for all time. Even Beza was willing to tolerate a reformed episcopate though he believed that reformation was incomplete until presbyterianism was established in its place (see Avis, *CTR,* pp. 114f, 123f). The champion of divine-right presbyterianism in England, Thomas Cartwright, however, maintained that far from belonging to the sphere of things indifferent, ecclesiastical polity was of the essence of Christianity and had a direct bearing on the salvation of souls. 'The want of eldership is the cause of all evil,' Cartwright asserted, 'it is not to be hoped that any commonwealth can flourish without it . . . it is no small part of the gospel, yea the substance of it' (c. Usher, p. 8n2).

Cartwright's opponents, Whitgift and Hooker, were not to be manoeuvred into making a counter claim for the divine right of bishops, Though he held episcopacy to be 'apostolical and divine' (Strype, II, p. 170), Whitgift retorted that the notion of biblically prescribed divine-right polity was 'very popish'. Circumstances changed and the church had the right to adapt its outward forms to meet them provided the broad principles of scripture were followed:

> The substance and the matter of government must indeed be taken out of the word of God and consisteth in these points, that the word be truly taught, the sacraments rightly administered, virtue furthered, vice repressed and the church kept in quietness and order. The offices in the church whereby this government is wrought be not namely and particularly expressed in the scriptures but in some points left to the discretions and liberty of the church, to be disposed according to the state of times, places and persons (PS, Whitgift, I, p. 6).

Although the 1590s saw an escalation of Anglican claims for episcopacy in response to the presbyterian challenge, such writers as Bancroft, Savaria and Bilson did not break with the consensus of the Elizabethan church that, while scripture did not lay down any binding form of church government, episcopacy was an ancient, venerable form and was consonant with the teaching of scripture. Moreover, it was the form ordained by the magistrate (Henry or Elizabeth) from whom the bishops held their territorial jurisdiction (see Avis, *CTR,* pp. 115ff and references; Somerville).

The catholicity of the church for the English Reformers did not reside in the succession of its bishops but in continuity of true doctrine. Jewel insists that the integrity of the English church does not depend on its bishops; if not one were left alive, the Church of England would not undertake a wholesale emigration to Louvain to receive orders from Rome (PS, III, p. 335). Pilkington asserts that 'Succession of good bishops is a great blessing of God, but because God and his truth hangs not on man nor place, we rather hang on the undeceivable truth of God's word in all doubts than on any bishops, place or man' (PS, pp. 599f). Hooker too envisages an extreme situation in which a corrupt hierarchy might be suppressed and the church make a fresh start with a godly and reformed ministry without benefit of episcopal ordination. Needless to say, any doubt as to the catholicity of the Lutheran and Reformed churches abroad and the validity of their non-episcopal orders, did not occur to the English Reformers.

'The King's Book' of Henry's reign, while far from endorsing Reformation theology, detached catholicity from communion with Rome. The unity of catholic Christendom does not depend on the pope but is 'conserved and kept by the help and assistance of the Holy Spirit of God in retaining and maintaining of such doctrine and profession of Christian faith, and the true obedience of the same, as is taught by the scripture and doctrine apostolic'. Particular (i.e. national) churches are catholic when they 'profess and teach the faith and religion of Christ according to the scripture and apostolic doctrine'. This is precisely the position that the English Reformers defended. Catholics, claimed Whitaker, are those who profess sound, solid and pure doctrine (PS, p. 668). The Reformers assumed a uniformitarian conception of truth that prevailed in Anglican and Roman Catholic theology alike until the notion of development began to emerge in the early nineteenth century. Catholic truth was for the English Reformers what it was for Vincent of Lerins – what had been held everywhere, always and by all. 'Catholicism is what has been, is, and shall be', says Philpott (PS, p. 37). Catholicity is the state of being in agreement in catholic truth. 'Unity must be in verity' (PS, Bradford, *Sermons*, p. 394; see further, Avis, *CTR*, p. 130).

3
Authority in Theology and Church

Authority in Early Anglicanism

The early Anglican conception of authority in doctrine and practice was forged in the fires of controversy. The sixteenth-century divines were fighting on two fronts: firstly against Rome and secondly against radical protestantism. Against Rome they invoked the authority of scripture and the primitive church; against incipient puritanism they added reason to the appeal to scripture and tradition. The lines of the debate with Rome were well established before Elizabeth came to the throne, but soon after her accession John Jewel (1522–71) transformed the situation of Anglican theology by turning what had been a largely defensive action against Roman Catholic claims into an offensive campaign. In a series of sermons of which the first and last were preached at St. Paul's Cross (1559–60), Jewel carried the attack into the enemy camp. Listing twenty-seven significant Roman Catholic beliefs and practices, mostly relating to the eucharist, he offered to convert to Rome 'if any learned man of all our adversaries or if all the learned men that be alive, be able to bring any one sufficient sentence out of any old catholic doctor or father, or out of any old general council, or out of the holy scriptures of God, or any one example of the primitive church' to prove that such had been held or done during the first six centuries of the Christian church (Southgate, p. 50). Jewel's backers held their breath, fearing that he had gone too far, but their fears were unfounded. Jewel was sure of his ground; his challenge could not be refuted. It was to provide the pattern of Anglican argument against Rome for the next two or three centuries – until defenders of Roman Catholicism, such as Newman, introduced the notion of development and so changed the ground rules of the debate. No longer would it be necessary to establish that controverted aspects of Roman Catholicism were apostolic and primitive: catholicity implied development and change.

Jewel was rewarded with the bishopric of Salisbury and proved an admirable bishop. He followed his triumph with his *Apologia Ecclesiae Anglicanae* (1562). The *Apology* and its successive vindications comprise 'one of the most complete pieces of controversy in the world' (Dixon, V, p. 320). These writings 'constitute the first thoroughgoing attempt to prove to the world the catholicity of English doctrine, to demonstrate that the teachings of the English church at no point departed from the church of the apostles and the fathers' (Southgate, p. 120). Jewel's appeal was to the scriptures as containing all things necessary to salvation and to the consensus of antiquity in disputed points. His tactics were effective: with inexhaustible learning, infinite labour and enormous polemical skill 'he succeeded time and again in placing his opponent in the position of having directly contravened patristic authority' (ib., p. 87). No wonder archbishop Parker wanted the *Apology* appended to the Articles of Religion! It is a classical document of Anglican self-definition.

For the explicit appeal to reason we have to wait for Jewel's protegé Richard Hooker, but the appeal is implicit in Jewel himself: 'Let reason lead thee,' he urges, 'let authority move thee; let truth enforce thee' (PS, III, pp. 122f). Jewel's approach both presupposed and significantly developed the established Anglican method of appeal to scripture and antiquity, informed by reason.

The Anglican Reformers did not set out to make changes in the substance of Christian truth. Indeed their aim was to recover and preserve the truth once for all delivered to the saints. Christian doctrine was unchanging; it was what had been, is and always would be (PS, Philpott, p. 37). In this insistence the Anglican Reformers were appealing to the famous canon of Vincent of Lerins: *semper, ubique et ab omnibus*. The legislation of the 1530s to secure the independence of the English church from Roman jurisdiction took pains to point out that no change of doctrine was involved. The Dispensations Act of 1534 included the caveat that nothing in it should be interpreted to mean that the English church, under her earthly governor and protector, the king, intended 'to decline or vary from the congregation of Christ's church in any things concerning the very articles of the catholic faith or Christendom; or in any other things declared by holy scripture and the word of God' as necessary for salvation (Elton, p. 354).

For the Anglican Reformers the true doctrine of Christianity was to be found only in the scriptures. They contained everything necessary to be believed for salvation. The church therefore had no power to insist on any conditions as necessary to salvation (such as absolution by a priest, the performing of satisfactions for sin committed, being in communion with the pope, etc) that were not found clearly taught in scripture. The message of salvation, the Christian gospel, was clearly revealed on the page of scripture and needed no interpretation. But there were other teachings of scripture that it was incumbent on the church to follow, such as the christological and trinitarian dogmas and aspects of the ministry and the means of grace, that were not clear without assistance. Here the English church appealed to the guidance of the consent of antiquity and the general councils of the undivided church. Thus the Act of Supremacy (1559) laid it down that any charge of heresy must be proven by scripture or the first four general councils or any one of them, or any other general council where such views were expressly condemned by the words of scripture (Elton, p. 368).

The Authority of the Supreme Governor of the Church

In all matters of authority, the nascent reformed Church of England appealed from the jurisdiction of the pope to the only available alternative source of ecclesiastical jurisdiction, that of its 'supreme head in earth, so far as the law of Christ allows' (Henry VIII) or 'supreme governor' (Elizabeth I). Henry, while repudiating any claim to headship in the mystical body of the church – his role, he insisted, was confined to the government of its outward order and to the headship of all estates of the realm, including the clerical estate – had certainly taken it upon himself to promulgate doctrine in consultation with his spiritual advisors. He had been encouraged in his theological ambitions not only by the civil lawyers but by Cranmer himself (c.f. Scarisbrick, *Henry*, pp. 364f, 521–543).

Elizabeth, on the other hand, exhibited some diffidence – either out of conscience or political astuteness – about her supremacy in the church. Ostensibly at least, she declined any 'superiority . . . to define decide or determine any article or point of the Christian faith and religion' (c. Haugaard, p. 237). Appended to the queen's Injunctions of 1559 was an Admonition drawn up by Cecil, which denied that 'the kings and queens of this realm may challenge authority and power of ministry of divine offices in the church,' and added: 'Certainly her majesty neither doth, nor ever will challenge any other authority.' Her claim was only 'under God to have the sovereignty and rule over all manner of persons born within her realms . . . of which estate, either ecclesiastical or temporal . . . so as no other foreign power shall or ought to have any superiority over them.' Article 37 of the Thirty-nine refers to these Injunctions when it says, 'Where we attribute to the queen's majesty the chief government, by which titles we understand the minds of some slanderous folk to be offended, we give not to our princes the ministering either of God's word or of the sacraments . . . but only that prerogative which we see to have been given always to all godly princes in holy scriptures by God himself; that is, that they should rule all estates and degrees committed to their charge by God, whether they be ecclesiastical or temporal.' As we shall see, Hooker and Field reinforced this restricted interpretation of the royal supremacy. But, as Claire Cross has pointed out, while apologists made much of the distinction between jurisdiction and doctrine, 'the complexities of Tudor politics did not allow a monarch's actions to fit into these neat categories' (*Supremacy*, p.18; c.f. 69). The 'intuitive flashes of sagacity or caprice' which dictated Elizabeth's conduct of affairs (Dixon, VI, p.3) baffled the theorists of the Elizabethan settlement.

However, by the end of Elizabeth's reign it had been established that the supremacy lay in the-queen-in-parliament. Although James I had something of Henry VIII's self-confidence when it came to the finer points of theology, there could no longer be any question of the supreme governorship of the Church of England entailing any decisive voice in the definition of Christian doctrine. As the seventeenth century progressed, it became abundantly clear that parliament was the dominant partner within the lay governorship of the church. Just as the 1530s had seen an appeal from pope to king, a later generation appealed from king to parliament. It is significant that the Act of Supremacy of 1559, which referred to the scriptures and general councils as the criteria of orthodoxy and heresy, went on to give parliament, as the lay synod of the church, power to determine what was heretical 'with the assent of the clergy in their convocation' (Elton, p.368). This took the determination of right and wrong doctrine out of their hands not only of the pope, but also of the queen and her successors.

In the twentieth century, the Church of England would turn from a parliament which had long ceased to be in any meaningful sense the lay synod of the Church of England, to her own decision making bodies, with competence in the spheres of doctrine and worship. While, as we shall see in our discussion of Hooker, a Reformation principle of the theological competence of the laity was carried forward from the sixteenth century as a permanent feature of the Anglican faith, there is nothing in the Church of England of today, or in her sister churches of the Anglican Communion, that corresponds even remotely to the theological office that Henry VIII appropriated for himself.

The Authority of Scripture

The Reformation principle *sola scriptura* was interpreted in various ways. For Luther it was a critical principle to cut back radically the claims of the church to elaborate the conditions of salvation and to impose heavy burdens on the consciences of Christian folk. Scripture clearly taught the way of salvation; its central message of justification by faith alone without meritorious works was the criterion of all Christian doctrine. For Luther it was also the criterion of canonicity and led him to disqualify certain New Testament books as not sufficiently Christological and evangelical. Luther's emphasis was taken up by Hooker in his teaching that scripture is adequate to its divinely given purpose, namely to show the way of salvation, but not to prescribe for all aspects of life, as the puritans insisted. Here the puritans were the heirs of the Swiss Reformation which had tended to take the Bible (both Testaments equally) as a body of prescriptive truths legislating for every aspect of Christian worship and discipline. Luther sat lightly to such matters, emphasising evangelical freedom and categorising large areas as things indifferent – provided always that conscience was not imposed upon.

Some English Reformers seem to countenance the puritan approach. 'Scripture is the rule by which we must try all things,' asserted Whitaker. 'Thus, whatever disagrees with scripture should be rejected; whatever agrees with it, received' (PS, p. 660). Whatever the sympathies of some individual English Reformers may have been, the official formularies of the English Reformation commit the Church of England only to the limited sense of *sola scriptura* advocated in their different ways by Luther and Hooker. Their whole emphasis is on things necessary for salvation – on the mission and purpose of the revelation given through the prophets, apostles and evangelists of the Bible. The Anglican formularies contain no definition of the nature of biblical inspiration or the extent of biblical authority – statements which would undoubtedly have embarrassed the church in a later, critical, age. The distinction between things necessary to salvation and things not necessary but nevertheless prudent and edifying to be followed, was made in the Ten Articles of Henry's reign (Dixon, I, pp. 409ff; Burnet, *Reformation*, I, pp. 332ff). The 'Bishops' Book' (1537) prepared the ground for the subsequent doctrinal reformation by asserting the supremacy of scripture. The notion of truths necessary for salvation was perpetuated in the ordinal of Cranmer's second prayer book (1552):

> Be you persuaded that the holy scriptures contain sufficiently all doctrine required of necessity for eternal salvation? And are you determined with the said scriptures to instruct the people committed to your charge, and to teach nothing (as required of necessity to eternal salvation) but that you shall be persuaded may be concluded and proved by the scripture?

The First Book of Homilies, written under Henry but published under Edward, proclaims that 'there is no truth of doctrine necessary for our justification and everlasting salvation, but that is or may be drawn out of that fountain and well of truth', the holy scriptures. The Second Book of Homilies, promulgated under Elizabeth, contends that the holy scriptures contain 'all things needful for us to see, to hear, to learn and to believe, necessary for the attaining of eternal life'.

In his *Apology* for the reformed Church of England, Jewel expounds the same principle. The English church holds concerning the scriptures:

> That they may be the very might and strength of God to attain to salvation; that they be the foundations of the prophets and apostles whereupon is built the church of God; that they be the very sure and infallible rule,

whereby may be tried whether the church doth stagger or err, and whereunto all ecclesiastical doctrine ought to be called to account; and that against these scriptures neither law nor ordinance nor any custom ought to be heard (PS, III, p. 62).

Like the Homilies, Jewel's *Apology*, together with his *Defence* had quasi-official status in the sixteenth century, both sets of writings residing in parish churches and available for settling parish-pump theological arguments.

However, the Anglican Reformers were not crass literalists: like their continental counterparts they had enjoyed a humanist training; they were not merely engaged in bandying proof-texts taken out of context. That is why Whitgift, reiterating the standard Anglican position on the authority of scripture says that nothing may be put forward as necessary to salvation or as an article of faith which it is incumbent on Christians to believe 'except it be expressly contained in the word of God, *or may manifestly thereof be gathered*' (PS, I, p. 180, my emphasis). A similar nuance may be detected in the Thirty-nine Articles' reference to proving or testing claims by the scriptures:

Holy scripture containeth all things necessary to salvation: so that whatsoever is not read therein, *nor may be proved thereby*, is not to be required of any man, that it should be believed as an article of the faith, or be thought requisite or necessary to salvation (Article 6, my emphasis).

As we shall see, the Articles also make the scriptures the rule whereby all other forms of authority in the church are themselves to be assessed.

The Authority of Fathers and Councils

The arguments of the Reformation were fought out, not only on the battleground of the interpretation of scripture, but also on that of the authority of the early fathers of the church. Controversialists on both sides set about proving, with immense labour, the agreement of their respective churches' positions with the teaching of the primitive church. The Reformers were not content to appeal to the authority of scripture, though scripture was indeed the paramount and ultimate arbiter. Had they been setting out to create a church *de novo* rather than, as Calvin put it, to renew the face of the catholic church, they could have ignored tradition. Had they believed, with the radical spirits of the Reformation, that the church had apostatised from the truth after the death of the last apostle, the teaching of the fathers would have been irrelevant.

In fact the appeal to patristic tradition was not merely *ad hominem*, to counter such an appeal by Roman Catholics, nor merely tactical, to undermine such radical innovations as the rejection of infant baptism. The Reformers' appeal to patristic tradition was integral to their theological position. It was an extension and practical application of the *sola scriptura* principle, for the fathers were revered as biblical theologians who themselves deferred to the paramount and ultimate authority of scripture. The Reformers acknowledged that the guidance of the fathers was needed, for while the message of salvation was clear to all on the surface of the biblical text, not all the teachings of scripture were equally perspicuous.

Cranmer had appealed to 'the consent of all the old doctors of the Church' (PS, II, p. 360). For bishop Jewel, the apologist of the reformed Church of England under Elizabeth, a consensus of antiquity was to be sought where the scriptures were obscure. The first six hundred years of Christian history were normative; they provided a safeguard against the accretions of tradition and untrammelled private judgement alike. But the fathers were not to be awarded greater authority than they sought for themselves; it was as faithful and privileged interpreters of scripture that their guidance was to be valued. 'We despise them not, we read them, we reverence them' Jewel insisted. 'Yet may they not be compared with the word of God. We may not build upon them; we may not make them the foundation and warrant of our conscience; we may not put our trust in them' (PS, VI, p. 1173; c.f. Booty, *Jewel*, pp. 130ff, 147).

The reformed English church inherited the substance of the Christian faith in its integrity. It received, affirmed, preserved and defended the trinitarian and christological dogmas formulated by the early ecumenical councils and embodied in the Niceno-Constantinopolitan and 'Athanasian' creeds (*Quicunque vult*). These doctrines and the creeds that express them are inculcated assiduously in the Book of Common Prayer and upheld in the Thirty-nine Articles with the significant comment that 'they may be proved by most certain warrants of holy scripture.' The English Reformers, like their continental counterparts, presupposed the catholic faith and, in a sense, took it for granted. Their writings were on the whole devoted to controversial matters arising from later, medieval, developments, which they maintained not to be of the catholic faith. The Reformers were, however, over optimistic in supposing that aspects of medieval religion such as prayers for the faithful departed, veneration of saints, the historic episcopate, the religious life, a form of eucharistic sacrifice, and so on, could not be justified by appeal to primitive Christianity. When this became apparent through the post-tridentine resurgence of Roman Catholic patristic scholarship, Lutheran and Reformed use of the fathers became more critical and selective, while the Anglican response was to make a limited accommodation to such usages.

The Church of England did not set out to make new doctrines. It did not claim to have its own version of the Christian faith. It held that the message of salvation and the form of Christian life that was its appropriate response were clearly revealed in scripture. The formulation and defence of the catholic faith at the hands of the fathers and first four (or six) general councils was to be received as consonant with scripture.

The English Reformers discuss councils at great length (the general index entry of the Parker Society edition runs to thirty columns of small print), but they do so not to discuss the doctrines of the first ecumenical councils, but to rebut polemically the claims of their Roman Catholic adversaries that councils were dependent on the pope and were authoritative sources of teachings not found in scripture. Jewel claimed on the basis of his patristic research that Rome had 'forsaken the fellowship of the holy fathers' (PS, IV, p.901).

Cranmer summarises the purpose of councils as being 'to declare the faith and reform errors' (PS, II, pp.76f). Jewel gives them a similar declaratory function: 'a council may testify the truth to be truth'; but he adds, 'it cannot make falsehood to be truth' (PS, II, p.996). Councils acknowledged themselves to be subject to scripture and are still to be evaluated by the same standard. They appealed to scripture and so should we (PS, Whitaker, pp.434f; Becon, III, pp.391f; Rogers, p.210). Their role is to articulate and defend the faith once for all delivered, not to make new articles of faith to be imposed on the consciences of Christians (PS, Cranmer, II, p.36).

The negative tenor of some of the English Reformers' comments on councils should not blind us to the underlying fact of their respect for and acceptance of the early ecumenical councils. And as we have already seen, they deplored the failure of the reforming councils of Constance and Basle in the early fifteenth century. Jewel in particular appealed from the conciliar principle in general to the early normative councils. However, for the Reformers only the scriptures were infallible guides: councils were fallible and had erred in matters of substance. Cranmer insisted that 'general councils have erred, as well in the judgement of the scriptures as also in necessary articles of our faith' (PS, II, p.39; c.f. pp.11, 53; Fulke, II, p.231; Jewel, III, pp.176f, IV, p.1109; Ridley, pp.129f, 134; Rogers, pp.207f).

The Thirty-nine Articles express the unanimous view of the English Reformers (and of the German and Swiss Reformers for that matter) when they assert (article 21) that Councils 'may err, and sometimes have erred, even in things pertaining unto God.' The Latin text of the Articles (1563) makes it clear that the expression 'things pertaining unto God' is a way of speaking about the substance or essence of Christianity as contained in the church's traditional rule of faith (*in hijs quae ad normam pietatis pertinent*) – though it is imperative to note at this point that this does not mean that the Reformers had no doctrine of the indefectibility of the church: they did indeed believe that the church would not perish from the earth nor the true faith be lost; if councils, popes and bishops failed or went astray, the faith would be preserved in a part of the church, even if by a persecuted remnant. Jewel asserted that 'the church of God hath been ever from the beginning, and shall continue unto the end' (PS, III,

p. 190; see further Avis, *Ecum. Theol.*, pp. 96ff). Article 21 concludes by once again insisting that councils do not have an authority superior to, or complementary to scripture, but 'things ordained by them as necessary to salvation have neither strength nor authority unless it may be declared that they be taken out of holy scripture.'

The Authority of the Church

'Every particular or national church (*quaelibet ecclesia particularis siue nationalis*) hath authority to ordain, change and abolish ceremonies or rites of the church, ordained only by man's authority, so that all things be done to edifying.' In asserting the right of a church to make laws to regulate its worship, government and life, article 34 of the Thirty-nine cuts two ways, against Rome, which insisted on uniformity of order directed from the centre and resisted the claims of national churches to reform themselves, and against the extreme reformists who believed in a biblical blueprint for every aspect of life and that this blueprint was embodied in 'the best reformed churches', i.e. Geneva. Against both, the Church of England in its official formularies maintained the right and duty of a particular national church to govern itself. True, there must be uniformity within the realm, but a uniformity imposed from Rome or Geneva is rejected, 'It is not necessary that traditions and ceremonies be in all places one, or utterly like, for at all times they have been diverse, and may be changed according to the diversity of countries, times, and men's manners, [yet] so that nothing be ordained against God's word.'

It was a fundamental plank of the English Reformation that, just as a particular, national church had the right and duty to undertake reformation without prejudicing its catholicity, so too a diversity of ceremonies and outward order between particular churches did not betoken a breach of unity. The Henrician formularies declared that the unity of the 'one catholic church is a mere spiritual unity', consisting in 'the unity which is in one God, one faith, one doctrine of Christ and his sacraments' (here we clearly have a precedent for Hooker's famous 'one Lord, one faith, one baptism'). This essential spiritual unity is not destroyed by the various 'outward rites, ceremonies, traditions and ordinancies' instituted by proper local authority. The churches of England, Spain, Italy and Poland 'be not separate from the unity, but be one church in God, notwithstanding that among them there is a great distance of place, diversity of traditions, not in all things unity of opinions, alteration in rites, ceremonies and ordinancies' (c. Verkamp, p. 139).

Cranmer concluded his first (1549) and prefaced his second prayer book (1552) with a statement 'Of Ceremonies' which maintained that matters of 'discipline and order . . . upon just causes may be altered and changed and therefore are not to be esteemed equal with God's law'. And Cranmer added, 'In these our doings we condemn no other nations, nor prescribe anything but to our own people only.' For Cranmer, as Marshall has argued, the corporate principle was supreme: 'He stressed in every possible manner the communal use of the Bible and the liturgy.' His stress was on the common good; communal action was the highest good for man (p.14). Once again we see the continuity between the Henrichean and Edwardian conception of the national church and the Christian political philosophy of Richard Hooker. It would be left to Hooker to provide the philosophical principles underlying Anglican claims for the power of the church to make laws, in his distinction between mutable and immutable positive law in the third book of the *Ecclesiastical Polity*.

In asserting the power of the church to make laws, the articles had Calvin on their side against the extreme protestants. While Zwingli, Bucer and German-speaking Swiss theology laid the foundations of the puritan legalism that appealed to the Bible – and to both testaments equally – as a book of laws and precedents, Calvin himself exhibited a humanistic reasonableness in this matter and operated with a tacit concept of *adiaphora*, things indifferent (on adiaphorism see Verkamp). In his treatment in the *Institutes* (IV, ch.x) of the church's power to make laws, Calvin employs the distinction, so crucial to all Reformation theology between things necessary to salvation and things indifferent, of merely human origin, which cannot bind the conscience. Calvin's attack is directed against laws of the church enforcing rites, ceremonies and observances as an obligation of conscience and necessary to salvation, so laying burdens on Christian folk that are more than they can bear. He specifically excludes the 'sacred and useful constitutions of the church which tend to preserve discipline, decency or peace.' Hooker was able to make considerable play of the fact that Calvin had upheld the right of the church to make laws to regulate its life, in upholding the prerogatives of the Church of England against the radical reformers such as Cartwright who would have permitted nothing not explicitly laid down in scripture. Calvin holds that while 'the whole sum of righteousness, and all the parts of divine worship, and everything necessary to salvation' is clearly revealed in scripture, 'in external discipline and ceremonies' the Lord has not prescribed what should be done, foreseeing that this would vary with times and circumstances: 'in them we must have recourse to the general rules which he has given, employing them to test whatever the necessity of the church may require to be enjoined for order and decency.' The church has the freedom to change and abolish old forms and to introduce new to meet a changed situation. Calvin is impatient with the scrupulous legalism that continually intrudes on Christian liberty. 'What, is religion placed in a woman's bonnet . . .? Is her silence fixed by a decree which cannot be violated . . .?' In such matters, custom, humanity and modesty should be our guide (*Inst.* vol. II, pp. 413ff, 434ff).

The Thirty-nine articles also maintained that, besides her power to decree rites or ceremonies, the church has 'authority in controversies of faith' – though she cannot ordain anything contrary to scripture or enforce any such decrees as necessary for salvation (article 20). The English Reformers in their writings support this claim. The church not only has authority in rites, ceremonies and things indifferent, (PS, Rogers, p. 184; Whitaker, p. 507; Whitgift, I, pp. 180, 222), but also has authority in controversies of faith (PS, Whitaker, p. 190). But she has no authority to make new articles of faith (PS, Coverdale, II, pp. 338, 418; c.f. 422) and cannot bind things left free by the gospel. Nothing can be enforced that is not grounded in the word of God, and the church cannot forbid what the apostles permitted (PS, Philpott, p. 344, 379; Rogers, p. 201).

To sum up, if there are liberties and privileges of the individual Christian, there are also liberties and privileges of the Christian church. It can regulate its life where the scriptures do not prescribe the pattern, and adjudicate in theological debate where the scriptures are unclear. But this power is subject to two constraints: the individual conscience is answerable to its maker alone (in Luther's phrase *coram Deo*); and in all essential matters affecting salvation, the scriptures speak with a decisive voice. There is a principle of moderation at work here, which is opposed to every form of absolutism, and a principle of reticence in the matter of Christian dogma. The Thirty-nine Articles (1563) reflect these aspects of the Anglican philosophy. They emerged from a continual process of replication and revision going back to the formularies of Henry's reign. As such they incorporated both the corporate, conservative principle that characterised the English Reformation and the progressive, critical principle without which there could have been no Reformation. They carried forward the gains of the past while constantly adapting them to the needs of a new situation. The Articles are generally reserved in their assertions, speaking out sharply only when necessary to correct some blatant error. Dixon claimed that they stood on a higher level than the argumentative confessions of the continent (though he could not have intended to include the Augsburg Confession) or the anathematising of Trent. 'They dogmatise without arguing; they affirm without offering proof; they deal neither in expostulation nor rebuke. They are not apologetic. Completeness of form is their character' (V, pp. 394f).

4

Architects of Anglican Ecclesiology: Richard Hooker

Richard Hooker (1554–1600) is unquestionably the greatest Anglican theologian. It is significant that his writings are concerned, almost without exception, with ecclesiology. Together with his friend Richard Field, Hooker laid the foundations of Anglican ecclesiology. Not that he had to begin *de novo*, for he built on the work of Jewel, Whitgift and others, but their ecclesiological principles had been embedded in tortuous works of polemic. It could be argued that they were operating with merely a latent ecclesiology. Hooker's writings were no less polemical, in fact they were all the more effectively polemical for being couched in a vein of studied moderation, calm reasonableness and unfeigned charity. But Hooker's method of referring the issues back to first principles of philosophy and theology gives his thought a lasting value that the cut and thrust of most sixteenth-century works of polemical divinity does not possess. Hooker's writings are not without their elements of misrepresentation, special pleading and casuistry, as he defends the Elizabethan establishment of religion against the agitation of the theological purists who were demanding further radical reform. Every book of the *Laws of Ecclesiastical Polity* is directed against some tenet of radical protestantism, but his method of handling the issues of the moment illuminates for later generations the foundation principles of Anglican ecclesiology. In what follows we are not concerned to set out the structure of Hooker's argument, grounded as it is in the nature of God and what he has communicated of his nature through reason and revelation. Nor are we going to trace the steps by which Hooker disposes of the objections of the reformists to the liturgy, discipline and ceremonies of the Church of England as by law established. What interests us is Hooker's teaching about the nature of the Christian church and the position of the Church of England within it.

The Church Visible and Mystical

The Christian church is both a 'politic society' and a 'supernatural society'. While every politic society professes some religion, the church is distinguished from other politic societies by the nature of its fellowship and the profession of its distinctive faith. In other politic societies we associate with 'men simply considered as men' but in the church our fellowship is with 'God, angels and holy men' (I, p. 273). This supernatural society is distinguished from others and united in itself by its profession of the essential Christian faith: it consists of all 'them which call upon the name of our Lord Jesus Christ' (II, p. 369). It is 'a community of men sanctified through the profession of that truth which God hath taught the world by his Son' (III, p. 495).

Within this supernatural society, however, we have to distinguish between the mystical and the visible church. The mystical church (Hooker studiously seems to avoid the term 'invisible' as liable to misunderstanding) is known only to God: it is the mystical body of Christ because it must be affirmed of its members that 'the mystery of their conjunction is removed altogether from sense' (I, p. 338). The mystical church has no need of an ecclesiastical polity (I, p. 406). The visible church, on the other hand, is the company that God has called out to himself from the beginning of the world and consists of the Jewish church before the coming of Christ and the Christian church afterwards. Just as the oceans of the world are contiguous and form together one 'main body of the sea', 'so the catholic church is in like sort divided into a number of distinct societies, every one of which is termed a church within itself' (I, p. 351).

The Christian church has its identity in its baptismal faith, for through baptism we are made members of one body.

> The unity of which visible body and church of Christ consisteth in that uniformity which all several persons thereunto belonging have, by reason of that *one Lord* whose servants they all profess themselves, that *one faith* which they all acknowledge, that *one baptism* wherewith they are all initiated. The visible church of Jesus Christ is therefore one in outward profession of those things which supernaturally appertain to the very essence of Christianity and are necessarily required in every particular Christian man (I, p. 339).

This passage is the key to Hooker's ecclesiology and the Anglican tradition that takes its direction from him. It identifies the church, not by the marks of word, sacrament and discipline, as the Reformers did, nor by the notes of antiquity, unity, universality, etc., as Roman Catholic ecclesiology did, but by its outward profession of faith taken at face value. Hooker's complaint about Roman Catholic definitions is that 'they define not the church by that which the church essentially is, but by that wherein they imagine their own more perfect than the rest are'. Hooker's use of the concept of the essence of Christianity here serves as an identifying rather than as a critical principle. It denotes the 'outward profession' of 'that vital substance of truth which maketh Christian religion to differ from theirs which acknowledge not our Lord Jesus Christ the blessed Saviour of mankind, give no credit to his glorious gospel, and have his sacraments the seals of eternal life in derision' (II, p. 369).

On Hooker's criteria, only Moslems, Jews and atheists are excluded from the Christian church as a visible divine society. Heretics, schismatics and excommunicated persons are still in a sense members of the visible church, though they must be regarded as 'imps and limbs of Satan' unless they repent (I, p. 342). Only 'plain apostacy, direct denial, utter rejection of the whole Christian faith' can exclude a (formerly) professing Christian from the visible church (II, p. 371). Hooker points out that failure to distinguish, firstly between the church mystical and the church visible, and secondly between the sound visible church and the corrupted visible church, is the root of much error and confusion in ecclesiology (I, p. 343). For 'many things exclude from the kingdom of God although from the church they separate not' (II, p. 369). Even heretics remain a part, though a maimed part of the visible church (I, p. 347; II, p. 370). Is it then possible, asks Hooker, conscious of the tension and paradox inherent in this position, 'that the selfsame men should belong both to the synagogue of Satan and to the church of Jesus Christ?' Not to the church which is Christ's mystical body, Hooker answers, but 'Of the visible body and church of Jesus Christ those may be and oftentimes are, in respect of the main parts of their outward profession, who in regard of their inward disposition of mind, yea, of external conversation, yea, even of some parts of their very profession' are condemned both by God and by the sounder part of the visible church (I, p. 342). The consequences of this doctrine for Hooker's view of the church of Rome are not far to seek.

The Foundation of Christianity

Hooker does not provide a systematic account of the fundamental articles of Christianity, but in his debate with Travers, his colleague at the Temple Church, over the destiny of those ancestors who lived and died within the Roman communion, he does clarify the concept of fundamentals – though Hooker prefers to speak of 'the foundation' of faith. If this is taken as meaning 'the general ground whereupon we rest when we do believe', it must consist of the New Testament gospels and epistles (III, p. 501). But Hooker takes the foundation of faith to be generally understood as 'the principle thing which is believed' (ib.). This, for Hooker, is simply the person and work of Jesus Christ. Again and again in the great and seminal sermon 'Of Justification, Works and how the Foundation of Faith is overthrown' he recurs to this with radical simplicity and evangelical passion. The foundation, the crucial thing in Christianity is:

> 'Christ crucified for the salvation of the world' (p. 502)
> 'salvation by Christ alone' (p. 505)
> 'salvation purchased by the death of Christ' (p. 512)
> 'salvation only by Christ' (p. 528)
> 'Salvation . . . by Christ' (p. 532)

In his fullest statement, Hooker pronounces:

> This is then the foundation, whereupon the frame of the gospel is erected: that very Jesus whom the Virgin conceived of the Holy Ghost, whom Simeon embraced in his arms, whom Pilate condemned, whom the Jews crucified, whom the apostles preached, he is Christ, the only Saviour of the world: 'other foundation can no man lay' (p. 513).

This 'precious' doctrine, this 'inestimable treasure' is the 'rock' which forms the foundation of the church (pp. 500, 502). So long as a church professes and acknowledges it, it remains a branch of the visible church. However, the foundation may be denied directly or indirectly (p. 514). No Christian church can directly deny the foundation without ceasing to be such. Only unbelievers can directly deny the foundation of the faith. To those who directly deny it there can be no salvation (p. 504). But a church may (and often does) deny the foundation indirectly, by implication or 'by a consequent'. Some may hold the foundation 'weakly and as it were by a slender thread'; others may continue to hold it though 'they frame many base and unsuitable things upon it' (p. 500). Those who overthrow it indirectly must be condemned as erroneous, 'although for holding the foundation, we do and must hold them Christian' (p. 515).

How then does Hooker assess the status of the church of Rome? If Rome, by its teaching that works are necessary to salvation, *directly* denies the foundation, it is no more a Christian church than are the assemblies of Turks and Jews (p. 510). But it is Hooker's judgement that Rome does not deny the foundation directly. She errs 'not in the work of redemption itself . . . but in the application of this inestimable treasure'. She certainly does overthrow the foundation – 'they teach indeed so many things pernicious to Christian faith . . . that the very foundation which they hold is thereby plainly overthrown and the force of the blood of Jesus Christ extinguished' – but not directly or intentionally (p. 502). However, if there are any voices within the Roman Catholic Church maintaining that we cannot be saved by Christ alone without the addition of meritorious human works, 'they do not only by a circle of consequence, but directly, deny the foundation of faith; they hold it not, no not so much as by a slender thread' (p. 505). But Hooker is confident that it is not merely his private opinion, but the considered judgement of the consensus of protestant Reformers, that Rome does not directly deny the foundation of faith (p. 525).

The Fate of 'Our Fathers'

In his defence of the reformed Church of England, Hooker had to deal with the argument of the English reformists that nothing should be retained in a reformed church that was tainted with popery. For Cartwright, the antagonist of Whitgift as well as of Hooker, 'papists' were 'neither the people of God nor our forefathers' (I, p. 425). Hooker, however, insisted (with Whitgift, and later Field) that those who had 'lived and died' in the Roman communion in the centuries before the Reformation were to be regarded as 'not papists, but our fathers' (I, p. 64). If Rome were to be judged to be no Christian church wherein the means of salvation were provided, there could clearly be no hope for the eternal state of 'thousands of our fathers living in popish superstitions' (I, p. 501).

In his sermon 'Of Justification', Hooker acknowledges that where the truth of salvation by the unmerited grace of God, through the saving work of Christ, received by faith, is lost or denied, the foundation of the Christian faith is overthrown and there is no true Christian church. But his judgement is that, though Rome perverts the gospel and misleads her followers in teaching justification through the divine infusion of inherent righteousness by the merits of Christ with its entailed doctrine of the necessity of good works (III, p. 489, 491, 495), nevertheless she errs not in the substance of saving truth, but in its interpretation or application. If she can be said to overthrow the foundation, it is only 'by a consequent' (III, p. 489).

While Travers insisted that those in error would be saved if they repented and came to a knowledge of the truth before death – hence the Anglican divines' repeated use of the significant phrase 'lived and died' – Hooker was convinced that they would not be condemned for their invincible ignorance but would enjoy the benefit of a general repentance and a general confession in casting themselves on the mercy of God (III, pp. 503). The puritan rigour in this matter provokes Hooker to one of his rare outbursts of personal moral passion: 'Let me die if ever it be proved that simply an error doth exclude ... utterly from hope of life. Surely I must confess unto you, if it be an error to think that God may be merciful to save men even when they err, my greatest comfort is my error; were it not for the love I bear unto this error, I would neither wish to speak nor to live' (III, p. 543).

Hooker's assessment of Rome was informed by intellectual discrimination and fraternal charity. He was unswayed by the understandable anti-papal paranoia of a time when Roman Catholicism stood for treason as well as heresy: the excommunication of Elizabeth in 1570 and the appearance on the horizon of the Spanish Armada in 1588 meant that no one could afford to underestimate the Roman threat to the precarious integrity of the nascent English state. It was boldness in the cause of truth that led Hooker to affirm:

> Notwithstanding so far as lawfully we may, we have held and do hold fellowship with them. For even as the apostle doth say of Israel that they are in one respect enemies but in another beloved of God; in like sort with Rome we dare not communicate concerning sundry her gross and grievous abominations, yet touching those main parts of Christian truth wherein they constantly still persist, we gladly acknowledge them to be of the family of Jesus Christ (I, p. 347).

Hooker on the Reformation

Before Luther arose in Germany and Henry VIII took in hand the reform of the church in England, writes Hooker, 'the ruins of the house of God' had become so notorious that even superstition itself could not hide a blush (I, p. 487). Though Reformation was imperative, it was carried on in different ways in different places. In Scotland and Switzerland its course was 'extreme and rigorous'; in England moderate and cautious, thanks to the restraining hand of divine providence (I, pp. 486f). Henry VIII, remarks Hooker in an unfortunate phrase, set about restoring the decay of the church by 'beheading superstition'. Edward 'the Saint' opened up the promised land, but darkness descended again under Mary 'till such time as that God, whose property is to show his mercies then greatest when they are nearest to be utterly despaired of, caused in the depth of discomfort and darkness a most glorious star to arise [Elizabeth I], and on her head settled the crown, whom himself had kept as a lamb from the slaughter of those bloody times'. Through 'that glorious and sacred instrument' of the purposes of God, the reformed religion had been 'even raised as it were by miracle from the dead' (I, p. 487f).

Yet the Reformation made no new church. Hooker holds with all catholic and protestant ecclesiology the doctrine of the indefectibility of the church: 'God hath had ever and ever shall have some church visible upon earth' (I, p. 343). Roman Catholics ask 'where our church did lurk, in what cave of the earth it slept for so many hundreds of years together before the birth of Martin Luther?'

> As if we were of opinion that Luther did erect a new church of Christ. No, the church of Christ which was from the beginning is and continueth unto the end: of which church all parts have not been always equally sincere and sound. . . . We hope therefore that to reform ourselves if at any time we have done amiss, is not to sever ourselves from the church we were of before. In the church we were, and we are so still (I, pp. 346f).

Protestant purists are under the same illusion 'that we have erected of late a frame of some new religion' and have borrowed the furniture from the church of Rome. But the customs and ceremonies that we have retained, replies Hooker, are not the property of the church of Rome, but have been handed down to us by our fathers in the faith who had them from the ancient church. For our Reformers, aiming at the glory of God and the good of his church, retained whatever seemed necessary to that end, 'not rejecting any good or convenient things only because the church of Rome might perhaps like it' (I, pp. 445, 447). We neither follow Rome in her errors nor reject what is sound simply because it is hers. Not everything that idolaters have done is to be abhorred, but what they have done idolatrously. 'For of that which is good even in evil things God is author' (II, p. 49). 'The indisposition of the church of Rome to reform herself must be no stay unto us from performing our duty to God; even as desire of retaining conformity with them could be no excuse if we did not perform that duty' (I, p. 447).

Hooker's view of the continental Reformers is discriminating. Often they had proceeded with reckless zeal, attempting to outdo one another in their ambition to be as unlike the church of Rome as possible. While Hooker allows for the urgency of their situation, what he finds most open to censure is that they claimed for their local platforms of reform the authority of God's word against which there could be no appeal and no dissent (I, pp. 129f). But these criticisms, together with his critique of Calvin's work at Geneva, to which we turn next, are made in the context of Hooker's acknowledgement that 'all the reformed churches . . . are of our confession in doctrine' (I, p. 478).

Hooker on Calvin

Hooker was compelled by the pressure of puritan argument to come to terms with Calvin's theological legacy and the Genevan experiment in theocracy – upheld by the English reformists as the perfect model of a reformed church. Hooker himself had been schooled in Calvinism: his nineteenth-century editor, John Keble, suggested that Hooker's earliest work revealed the influence of those puritan divines who looked to Calvin and his successor Beza for their inspiration (I, p. xlviii). F. D. Maurice noted that Hooker not merely reverenced but trembled at the name of Calvin (*MMP*, II, p. 191). That is an exaggeration, but it makes the point that Hooker's attitude to the Genevan Reformer was one of deep, though not uncritical respect.

Hooker's critique of Calvin and Calvin's Geneva in the preface to the *Laws of Ecclesiastical Polity* represents a distancing exercise. Hooker attempts to stand back and make a critical assessment of an episode in recent history that was often regarded with uncritical admiration by his contemporaries. He successfully evacuates it of its aura of unquestionable authority, and thus undermines one of the most powerful weapons in the armoury of his opponents – the personal prestige of Calvin. Hooker will not have Calvin set on a pedestal of solitary eminence: even when praising him he sets him alongside others. He was 'incomparably the wisest man' that the French church had possessed then or since and was 'among the best learned in our profession' (I, p. 127; II, p. 525). Calvin's greatness, industry and influence he does not attempt to deny:

> Two things of principal moment there are which have deservedly procured him honour throughout the world: the one his exceeding pains in composing the Institutions of Christian religion; the other his no less industrious travails for exposition of holy scripture according to the same Institutions.

(Is there an implication here that Calvin tended to impose a rigid doctrinal scheme on the scriptures?) With a view to the Calvin cult among his contemporaries Hooker mischievously adds: 'In which two things whosoever they were that after him bestowed their labour, he gained the advantage of prejudice against them if they gainsayed and of glory above them if they consented' (I, p. 139).

Hooker credits Calvin for being self-taught, or rather divinely taught, in theology, commenting: 'Though thousands were debtors to him as touching knowledge in that kind, yet he to none but only to God, the author of that most blessed fountain, the book of life, and of the admirable dexterity of wit together with the helps of other learning which were his guides' (I, p. 128).

In a marginal note to the so-called 'Christian Letter' in which the puritan party remonstrated with Hooker for his criticism of Calvin, he makes a fascinating comparison between Calvin himself and his successor Theodore Beza: 'How different they were in natural disposition and yet how linked in amity and concord: Calvin being of a stiff nature, Beza of a pliable; the one stern and severe, the other tractable and gentle. Both wise and discreet men ... Beza was one whom no man would displease, Calvin one whom no man durst' (I, p. 134n).

But Hooker is deeply suspicious of the unquestioning acceptance accorded to Calvin's teaching among the puritans. His utterances have all the authority of papal decretals. Three lines from Calvin were enough to damn a man throughout Europe. His works are now classical texts for commentary and interpretation like Peter Lombard's in the church of Rome. 'The perfectest divines were judged they which were skilfullest in Calvin's writings. His books almost the very canon to judge both doctrine and discipline by.' The authority of Calvin carries more weight than ten thousand Augustines, Jeromes, Chrysostoms, Cyprians or what have you (I, pp. 124n, 139). Shortly before his death, Hooker's exasperation seems to have become obsessive. 'Two things there are which trouble greatly these later times: one that the church of Rome cannot, another that Geneva will not, err.' Hooker ruefully concludes: 'Safer to discuss all the saints in heaven than M. Calvin' (I, pp. 139n, 133n).

In several places Hooker is able to strengthen his hand against the puritans by showing that Calvin is on his side. When his opponent

Cartwright claims that scripture lays down precept or precedent for every eventuality, however trivial, Hooker refers him to Calvin's teaching on the power of the church to make laws to regulate its own life (I, pp. 403f). Against the puritans' demand that the outward order of the Church of England should conform to the pattern of 'the best reformed churches' (i.e. Geneva), Hooker can quote Calvin to the effect that variation in outward ceremonies is desirable (I, p. 473). When he is accused by his rival at the Temple, Walter Travers, of employing irrelevant subtleties and scholastic distinctions, Hooker can reply that 'these school implements are acknowledged by grave and wise men [here he cites Calvin, *Institutes*, I, xvi, 9] not unprofitable to have been invented', for 'the most approved for learning and judgement [i.e. Calvin himself] do use them without blame' (III, p. 586). Again, Calvin lends his support to Hooker's assertion that Rome has not ceased to be a church – though, in Calvin's own words, 'a church crazed, or if you will, broken quite in pieces, forlorn, misshapen, yet a church'. For the English reformists, however, it was doubtful whether even the Church of England, let alone the church of Rome, was a true church (III, p. 525). Finally, Hooker knows that the puritans do not have Calvin entirely on their side when they claim divine right for presbyterian church government, since exclusive claims for presbytery originated not with Calvin but with Beza. Calvin's own view of episcopacy is remarkably open and dispassionate. Hooker observes that Calvin himself, 'though an enemy unto regiment by bishops' admits that in the early church they were elected by the clergy to exercise supervision (III, p. 175).

What the authors of the 'Christian Letter' objected to was Hooker's way of discussing the Genevan system purely on its merits and not with the reverence due to a divinely-revealed scheme. To speak of Calvin acting wisely or correctly in the circumstances was, as far as they were concerned, to damn with faint praise. For the puritan reformists the system of lay elders was 'simply propounded as out of the scriptures of God' (I, p. 133n). But in sketching the progress of events at Geneva Hooker gave due weight to the part played by expediency, calculation and self-interest.

The citizens of Geneva, having first submitted themselves to the evangelical preachers Farel and Calvin, began to have second thoughts, 'to repent them of what they had done and irefully to champ upon the bit they had taken into their mouths'. Calvin and his colleagues, 'stiffly refusing' to compromise, were banished and Calvin went to join Bucer at Strasburg. But, Hooker resumes, 'a few years after (such was the levity of that people) . . . they were not before so willing to be rid of their learned pastor, as now importunate to obtain him again'. Moreover, they saw that Calvin's reputation was increasing and that 'together with his fame, their infamy was spread which had so rashly and childishly ejected him'. It dawned on them that their former pastor might again lend lustre to a city that had little else to boast of – 'Calvin's foreign estimation' being 'the best stake in their hedge' (I, p. 135. Here, no doubt, as Mark Pattison drily remarked in an essay of 1858, Hooker is moralising in a strain borrowed from the Latin classics over 'the levity of popular humour' ('Calvin at Geneva', p. 20).

Hooker goes on, in the vein so offensive to the puritans, to attribute merely pragmatic, prudential motives to Calvin in establishing his regime in Geneva for the second time. 'He ripely considered how gross a thing it were for men of his quality, wise and grave men, to live with such a multitude and to be tenants at will under them,' and made acceptance of the discipline a condition of his return (I, p. 135). On the form of church order proposed Hooker comments: 'This device I see not how the wisest at that time living could have bettered, if we duly consider what the present estate of Geneva did then require.' Now this is precisely the sort of tacit reductionism that so irritated the authors of the 'Christian Letter' (ib.). When further opposition arose, the city fathers had to choose, as Hooker puts it, 'whether they would to their endless disgrace with ridiculous lightness dismiss him whose restitution they had in so impotent manner desired' or let Calvin have his way. In the event, 'they thought it better to be somewhat hardly yoked at home than for ever abroad discredited' (ib.).

Hooker's most telling point is the claim that it was only after Calvin had decided that his form of government was called for by the circumstances that he sought scriptural justification for it. His reasons for doing it are more impressive than his defence of it when done. 'That which by wisdom he saw to be requisite for that people was by as great wisdom compassed. But wise men are men and the truth is truth. That which Calvin did for establishment of his discipline seemeth more commendable than that which he taught for the countenancing of it established.' But this is perfectly natural: 'nature worketh in us all a love to our own counsels' and opposition only makes us dig our heels in.

> Wherefore a marvel it were if a man of so great capacity, having such incitements to make him desirous of all kinds of furtherances unto his cause, could espy in the whole scripture of God nothing which might breed at the least a probable opinion of likelihood that divine authority itself was the same way somewhat inclinable (I, p. 138).

Here Hooker excels himself as a controversialist. His apparent admission that there might be something, somewhere in the entire sacred volume that might perhaps be capable of being developed into 'a probable opinion of likelihood' that the will of God might be 'somewhat inclinable' to the presbyterian programme, is crushing – it implies that the puritan view was at least ten times removed from the truth!

While he has a profound respect for Calvin, Hooker is prepared to treat his system as a human construction and Calvin (like Luther) as a great but fallible human being, pointing out that among the many 'admirable patterns of virtue' that scripture sets before us, there is not one without some fault or failing. God allowed those 'worthy vessels of his glory' to be in some respects 'blemished with the stain of human frailty', lest we esteem any human being more than we should (I, p. 163).

Bishops by Divine Right?

Hooker's view of episcopacy is one that is unpalatable to liberal protestants and high catholics alike. While he holds episcopacy to have been ordained by God in the period of the church's infancy, he does not accept the inference that it is therefore binding on the church for all time. The external government of the church is a thing indifferent or 'accessory' to the essentials of the Christian faith, an area in which the church has the freedom to make changes to meet fresh circumstances. Happily, however, the Church of England is not in the position of some of the reformed churches on the continent who were compelled to abolish a corrupt hierarchy that opposed the reform. The English church means to preserve and defend its episcopate as a channel of God's blessing for the church.

For Hooker, as for his eighteenth-century exponent Edmund Burke, what was established and had stood the test of time merited a presumption in its favour. This was pre-eminently the case with the episcopate:

> A thousand five hundred years and upward the church of Christ hath now continued under the sacred regiment of bishops. Neither for so long hath Christianity been ever planted in any kingdom throughout the world but with this kind of government alone; which to have been ordained of God, I am for mine own part even as resolutely persuaded, as that any other kind of government in the world whatsoever is of God (III, p. 143).

In the face of the presbyterian challenge Hooker is not afraid 'to be herein bold and peremptory, that if any thing in the church's government, surely the first institution of bishops was from heaven, was even of God, the Holy Ghost was the author of it' (III, p. 168). What could have possessed the nation, Hooker demands, to forsake episcopacy, 'the use whereof universal experience hath for so many years approved' and betake itself to a system of lay elders, etc., neither appointed by God nor even heard of until yesterday? (III, p. 144).

But for all his emphasis on the divine institution of episcopacy, Hooker is not departing from the consensus of the Elizabethan divines which did not go so far as to claim that bishops were the sole permitted form of church government. Two fundamental principles served to restrain Hooker's argument at this point: the distinction between faith and order, which he shared with his predecessors, and the distinction between mutable and immutable positive law, which he made very much his own, though it had been injected into the philosophy of the Henricean Reformation by Thomas Starkey who may have drawn it from Melanchthon (Zeeveld, pp. 129ff; cf. also Mayer).

First, Hooker takes up the distinction, employed by the Anglican Reformers following Melanchthon, between things necessary to salvation ('whatsoever is unto salvation termed *necessary* by way of excellency, whatsoever it standeth all men upon to know or do that they may be saved . . . of which sort the articles of Christian faith and the sacraments of the church of Christ are': I, p. 356) and things indifferent (adiaphora). But in place of the term 'indifferent' Hooker employs 'accessory', for he would not endorse the view that the customs, ceremonies and forms of government that belonged to the external life of the church were 'indifferent' in the sense that they were of little value and that one was under no kind of obligation to follow them. Rather they were accessory to the word and sacraments – enshrining, applying, protecting and hallowing them. They are merely the surface on the path of salvation: a gravel, grass or paved surface may be used at the church's discretion, provided it serves to keep the path from being overgrown with brambles and thorns. Sound theology 'putteth a difference between things of external regiment in the church and things necessary unto salvation' (III, pp. 356f). For the radical protestants, however, 'matters of discipline and kind of government' were 'matters necessary to salvation and of faith'. Cartwright had been bold to claim, 'We offer to shew the discipline [i.e. rule by lay elders, etc.] to be a part of the gospel' (I, pp. 354f, nn). This disastrously unreformed doctrine of course followed inevitably from the puritan view of scripture as the absolute authority prescribing for every area of life (I, pp. 287f).

Second, episcopacy belongs to the category of positive law and may be changed if the circumstances it was designed to meet themselves change. In his first book, Hooker describes, with unrivalled profundity and eloquence, the world of law (which for him is the sphere of reason), with its source and fountain in the nature of God and its manifold manifestations as natural or positive law. Natural law belongs to the nature of things and is universal and unchangeable. Positive law is decreed by proper authority (whether God or man) and makes things right or wrong for a particular purpose, though they remain neither good nor bad in themselves. Positive law is designed to fit a particular situation; if the situation changes, positive law must be adapted. Scripture contains positive as well as natural law, and divine positive laws are no exception to their kind – they may be changed by proper authority. 'Although no laws but positive be mutable, yet all are not mutable which be positive. Positive laws are either permanent or else changeable, according as the matter itself is concerning which they were first made. Whether God or man be the maker of them, alteration they so far forth admit, as the matter doth exact' (I, p. 273; cf. 244, 248, 384). All supernatural laws are positive laws. Some are immutable, because their 'matter' does not vary: for example, the sacraments. Some are mutable because their 'matter' alters with circumstances: for example, the outward government of the church.

> Laws which the church from the beginning universally hath observed were some delivered by Christ himself, with a charge to keep them to the world's end, as the law of baptizing and administering the holy eucharist; some brought in afterwards by the apostles, yet not without the special direction of the Holy Ghost, as occasions did arise.

It follows that the church 'hath power to alter, with general consent and upon necessary occasions, even the positive law of the apostles, if there be no command to the contrary, and it manifestly appears to her that change of times have clearly taken away the very reasons of God's first institution' (III, p. 164).

Hooker brings these two points – the distinction between faith and order, and between mutable and immutable laws – together when he says:

> The church being a body which dieth not hath always power, as occasion requireth, no less to ordain that which never was, than to ratify what hath been before . . . The church hath authority to establish that for an order at one time which at another time it may abolish, and in both may do well . . . Laws touching matter of order are changeable, by the power of the church; articles concerning doctrine not so (II, p. 33).

Consequently, though bishops may justly claim apostolic descent, 'yet the absolute and everlasting continuance of it they cannot say that any commandment of the Lord doth enjoin; and therefore must acknowledge that the church hath power by universal consent upon urgent cause to take it away, if thereunto she be constrained through the proud, tyrannical, and unreformable dealings of her bishops' (III, pp. 165).

Furthermore, where bishops are not available, the church has power to create a ministry *de novo*:

> Where the church must needs have some ordained, and neither hath nor can have possibly a bishop to ordain; in case of such necessity, the ordinary institution of God hath given oftentimes, and may give, place. And therefore we are not simply without exception to urge a lineal descent of power from the apostles by continued succession of bishops in every effectual ordination (III, p. 232).

Hooker's assessment of the ministries of foreign reformed churches is in line with these principles. Though they do not enjoy that form of church government that 'best agreeth with the sacred scripture', and cannot remedy it now, Hooker would rather lament than condemn this 'defect and imperfection', 'considering that men oftentimes without any fault of their own may be driven to want that kind of polity or regiment which is best, and to content themselves with that which either the irremediable error of former times or the necessity of the present hath cast upon them' (I, p. 409).

The Liberation of the Laity

The Reformation of the sixteenth century could be said to represent the coming of age and liberation of the Christian laity. Luther had called upon the nobility of the German nation to undertake the reform of the church: his doctrine of the universal priesthood entitled them so to do. But the role of the laity was particularly decisive in the English Reformation. The *devotio moderna* had signalled the awakening of the laity. Henry VIII's ambitions and policies were informed by a consuming anticlericalism. G. R. Elton has characterised the progress of the English Reformation as 'the unquestioned triumph of the laity over the clergy' (p. 336). Writing more than a century ago, the Anglican historian of the English Reformation, R. W. Dixon, deplored the fact that necessary reform was managed by bad instruments, being taken out of the hands of the clergy and left to the tender mercies of the laity (I, pp. 7f). But Dixon overlooked the point that any scheme of reform emanating from the clergy would have been futile since it would have required authorisation by the pope. The only alternative source of jurisdiction was the lay one of the sovereign – and to this the Reformers turned (cf. Avis, *CTR*, pp. 133f). The Elizabethan settlement was forced through by parliament against the resistance of convocation (the Marian bishops could hardly be expected to support it). As another older writer on the settlement put it:

> The shaping of the national church is largely, nay mainly, the outcome of the work of laymen. Indeed ... churchmen of the Old Learning strenuously opposed its formation from first to last, and it had taken definite shape before any single churchman of the New Learning had gained place or power to exercise influence or control over its development (Birt, p. 43).

Scarisbrick has pointed out that this is not the whole picture. The abolition of lay guilds and fraternities, employers of chaplains and mass priests, reduced the power of lay patrons and transferred it to the hierarchy (*Reformation & English People*, pp. 39, 43, 165ff). But against this needs to be set the points made by Claire Cross who subtitles her history of the period 'The Triumph of the Laity in the English Church'. Cross points out that the emancipation of the laity was symbolised in the 1530s by the right to own and study a Bible in the vernacular (*Church and People*, p. 71). It is also significant that the Elizabethan Act of Supremacy gave parliament the authority to judge heresy (with the convocations assenting). Cross comments: 'To the limits of their capacity, laymen were trying to ensure that never again would the clerical estate have the power to enquire into religious beliefs in the way it had done during the Marian persecutions' (p. 130). That this lay ascendency would not again be reversed is clear from the failure of the Laudian reforms. Laud's downfall and the destruction of his programme is largely attributable to lay opposition (p. 175). Under the impress of the Reformation and its aftermath, the Church of England became – what it remains to this day – very much a layperson's church.

While Hooker's writings provided theoretical foundations for this redistribution of power in the church, from clergy to laity, he did not intend to support lay domination of the church. Rather he sought, with his characteristic abhorrence of all forms of absolutism, to describe a balance and coherence of clergy and laity, convocation and parliament, within the Christian commonwealth, with the sovereign presiding over and mediating between them. The unity of church and commonwealth is indeed the key to Hooker's view of the royal supremacy together with the role of parliament as the lay synod of the church and the involvement of the laity in making laws for the church. It remained the presupposition of Anglican ecclesiastical polity through the next century until the emergence of the incipiently secular and pluralist state in the early eighteenth century when parliament began to decline the role of guarantor of the established church's privileges. But that is to anticipate. For Hooker, 'there is not any man of the Church of England but the same man is also a member of the commonwealth; nor any man a member of the commonwealth which is not also of the Church of England' (III, p. 330). The church is that politic society that maintains the Christian religion (III, p. 329). Temporal and spiritual affairs are two separate functions of one and the same community. The king and parliament are responsible not only for the temporal but also the spiritual well-being of the people: 'pure and unstained religion ought to be the highest of all cares appertaining to public regiment' (II, pp. 13f; III, pp. 333, 363).

Hooker continues the process of tightening the restraints on the royal supremacy in the church. Henry VIII had demanded a blank cheque in spiritual matters and Cranmer had willingly given it. Jewel and others had begun the process of retrenchment. Hooker gives the prince merely 'supreme authority in the outward government which disposeth the affairs of religion so far forth as the same are disposable by human authority' (III, p. 363). Hooker rejects as 'absurd' the suggestion that princes may prescribe how God may be served in the church ('how the word shall be taught, how sacraments administered') or adjudicate in matters of faith, or exercise excommunication (III, p. 431). Even in the appointment of bishops, where the royal prerogative might seem most in evidence, Hooker excludes the prince not only (and obviously) from the bestowal of the bishop's power of order but also from his power of episcopal jurisdiction, leaving only the granting of the worldly appurtenances of his office – 'the place of his seat or throne, together with the profits, preeminences, honours thereunto belonging' (III, p. 419).

While Roman Catholicism restricted the power of making ecclesiastical law to the clergy – what Thomas More objected to in the supreme headship of Henry was its lay character – Hooker gave the laity and the supreme layperson, the sovereign, a significant place. In all politic societies (of which the church is one) the power of making laws resides in the whole body politic and the validity of law derives from the consent of the whole body, either directly or through its representatives. So in the church: 'Till it be proved that some special law of Christ hath for ever annexed unto the clergy alone the power to make ecclesiastical laws, we are to hold it a thing most consonant with equity and reason, that no ecclesiastical law be made in a Christian commonwealth without consent as well of the laity as of the clergy, but least of all without consent of the highest power' (III, p. 404). The king, 'the common parent' of all estates of the realm, both temporal and spiritual, has the role of preserving 'an even balance' between them (III, p. 405).

The polemical purpose of Hooker's argument is to prove that the laws for the establishment of religion 'do take originally their essence from the power of the whole realm and church of England' and as such deserve the deference, not the criticism, of the radical reformers (III, p. 412). But his argument embodies principles of constitutional balance, representation and consent that are of abiding validity and provide a justification – in political theory, not just in theology – for the Reformation's liberation of the laity in the church.

The reward of the laymen who played such a determinative part in shaping the reformed Church of England was to see her emerge from the struggles of the sixteenth century as a church in which lay persons, as well as clergy, of diverse views might stand side by side in their parish church and kneel together at the communion rail, united by a required minimum of outward conformity. Hooker stressed that the identity of the Christian church was to be found in its profession of the fundamental baptismal faith – 'one Lord, one faith, one baptism'. He pointed out that religious belief could not be legislated for: 'As opinions do cleave to the understanding, and are in heart assented unto, it is not in the power of any human law to command them, because to precribe what men shall think belongeth only unto God' (III, p. 401). Elizabeth reassured her subjects that she would force no one's conscience nor 'make windows into men's hearts and secret thoughts'. She forbade that 'any of our subjects should be molested by examination or inquisition, in any matter, either of faith, so long as they shall profess the Christian faith, not gainsaying the authority of the holy scriptures and the articles of our faith, contained in the creeds . . . ; or for matters of ceremonies, or any other external matters appertaining the Christian religion, as long as they shall in their outward conversation show themselves quiet and comfortable'. Only an Anabaptist for whom a national church was a contradiction in terms and the Church of England apostate, or a convinced Romanist for whom Elizabeth was an excommunicate heretic, would find himself excluded from full participation in the Church of England of Elizabeth, Whitgift and Hooker. 'The doctrinal limits of the church were as wide as it is possible to imagine them in the sixteenth century' (Haugaard, *Elizabeth*, p. 247; see further on the theme of this section Avis, *CTR*, pp. 135–144, 151–163 and bibliography).

Scripture, Reason and Tradition

In refuting the puritan contention that scripture alone was the rule governing all the things that might be done by humankind (I, p. 334), Hooker clarifies the Anglican view of prescriptive authority in matters of doctrine and practice. He shows the proper place of scripture, reason and tradition, that famous 'threefold cord not quickly broken' which was to become the hall mark of classical Anglicanism. But Hooker defines each of these discriminatingly and distinctively. Moreover, he sets them within a perspective created by aesthetic and moral judgement, a cultivated sense of what is fitting in particular circumstances. Finally, he takes away all illusions of infallible certainty and stresses that probability is our guide. R. W. Church aptly designated Hooker's view of authority as 'the concurrence and co-operation, each in its due place, of all possible means of knowledge for man's direction'.

(1) *Scripture.* Hooker operates with the Thomistic and late medieval distinction between two sources of knowledge for man's earthly life: the light of nature and the light of revelation, both interpreted by reason. Nature follows its ordered course according to natural laws ordained by its creator. When these natural laws are recognised, interpreted and followed by humanity we have the law of reason. Though nature and reason cannot show us the way of salvation, they overlap with the revealed scriptures. Scripture and nature are neither mutually exclusive nor fundamentally opposed. 'The scripture is fraught even with the laws of nature' (I, p. 262). But the proper office of scripture is to teach those things 'required as necessary unto salvation . . . so that without performance of them we cannot by ordinary course be saved, nor by any means be excluded from life observing them. In actions of this kind our chiefest direction is from scripture, for nature is no sufficient teacher what we should do that we may attain unto life everlasting. The unsufficiency of the light of nature is by the light of scripture so fully and so perfectly herein supplied, that further light than this hath added there doth not need unto that end' (I, pp. 331f; cf. 356, 261f, 267; III, p. 213). In things necessary to salvation, Hooker affirms, following the Reformers, the scriptures possess a perspicuity that makes their message available even to the simple (I, p. 143).

While the radical protestants claimed that one required scriptural warrant for the meanest action, Hooker insisted that to consult the Bible about 'vain and childish trifles . . . were to derogate from the reverend authority and dignity of the scripture' (I, p. 275). The immutable part of the teaching of the apostles is not concerned with such secondary and in-different matters as ecclesiastical ceremonies and government, where we have the light of reason and experience to guide us and can exercise our sense of what is appropriate to changing circumstances. Just as every book of the Bible was written for a particular purpose (I, p. 270), so the whole scripture is given to serve the purpose of God in leading humanity to salvation.

> The testimonies of God are true, the testimonies of God are perfect, the testimonies of God are all sufficient unto that end for which they were given. Therefore accordingly we do receive them, we do not think that in them God hath omitted any thing needful unto his purpose, and left his intent to be accomplished by our devisings. What the scripture purposeth, the same in all points it doth perform. Howbeit that here we swerve not in judgement, one thing especially we must observe, namely that the absolute perfection of scripture is seen by relation unto that end whereto it tendeth (I, p. 333).

Except in its fundamental gospel, scripture is not self-explanatory; it requires the application of reason. In defending himself against the charge of Walter Travers at the Temple Church that he had introduced scholastic distinctions and rational subtleties into the exposition of scripture, Hooker explained that by reason he meant not his own individual reasoning capacity, but 'true, sound, divine reason . . . reason proper to that science whereby the things of God are known; theological reason, which out of principles in scripture that are plain, soundly deduceth more doubtful inferences' and brings to light the true meaning of the 'darker places' of scripture (III, p. 594f). Hooker contributed to the Anglican conception of authority in religion not only by clarifying the scope and purpose of the biblical mandate, but also by injecting an appeal to reason into the earlier Anglican appeal to scripture and antiquity.

(2) *Reason.* For Hooker, as for all the Reformers, scripture holds the place of paramount authority, but second place he gives not to tradition but to reason. In matters of doctrine and practice alike, he writes, 'what scripture doth plainly deliver, to that the first place both of credit and obedience is due; the next whereunto is whatsoever any man can necessarily conclude by force of reason'. 'After these,' he adds, 'the voice of the church succeedeth' (III, p. 34). Like Augustine and Aquinas before him, Hooker is drawing on scripture, tradition and philosophy to create a synthesis (Marshall, pp. 66ff). The role of reason is not only to provide one of the components (the material constituent of philosophy), but also to serve as the formal principle whereby the synthesis is constructed.

Reason has its function in the world of law, that ordered world that derives from the God whose being is a law unto his working. The vocation of reason is to bring human existence into conformity with the order and harmony in the nature of things. 'All good laws are the voices of right reason, which is the instrument wherewith God will have the world guided' (II, p. 40). 'The laws of well doing are the dictates of right reason' (I, p. 222). Reason for Hooker is therefore not autonomous or individualistic or secular. His concept of reason is the antithesis of that of the Englightenment. Reason is a divinely implanted faculty for apprehending the truth revealed by God in nature or scripture. It seeks the good for humanity and moderates between appetite and will. 'The object of appetite is whatsoever sensible good may be wished for; the object of will is that good which reason doth lead us to seek.' 'To will is to bend our souls to the having or doing of that which they see to be good. Goodness is seen with the eye of the understanding. And the light of that eye is reason' (I, p. 220f).

Reason alone, considered as the study of the light of nature, has manifest limits. It cannot reveal the ultimate destination of faith, hope and charity: *faith* 'the principal object whereof is that eternal Verity which hath discovered the treasures of hidden wisdom in Christ' and that conduces to 'the intuitive vision of God in the world to come'; *hope* 'the highest object whereof is that everlasting Goodness which in Christ doth quicken the dead' and which, beginning with a 'trembling expectation' in this life, 'endeth with real and actual fruition of that which no tongue can express'; *charity* 'the final object whereof is that incomprehensible Beauty which shineth in the countenance of Christ the Son of the living God' and which, 'beginning here with a weak inclination of heart towards him unto whom we are not able to approach . . . endeth with endless union, the mystery whereof is higher than the reach of the thoughts of men'. These matters are the sole prerogative of revelation: 'There is not in the world a syllable muttered with certain truth concerning any of these three, more than hath been supernaturally received from the mouth of the eternal God' (I, pp. 261f).

Hooker's is a proto-Butlerian probabilistic doctrine of reason. Against both the Roman Catholics with their appeal to the infallibility of the church and the pope, and the puritans with their biblical absolutism, Hooker insisted that the highest form of certainty we enjoy is that of 'probable persuasions'. Though the human mind craves 'the most infallible certainty which the nature of things can yield', assent must always be proportionate to the evidence. Neither direct intuition of the truth nor demonstrative proof are given to humanity in its earthly pilgrimage (I, pp. 322f). Hooker is no rationalist. 'His theory is divided from the rationalism of later days not only by the maintenance of the traditional theological background and the limits which he is careful to assign to the independence or autonomy of human reason, but also by his idea that rational constructs must stand the test of history and may not contradict the evidence of tradition and historical development' (d'Entrèves, p. 120). To this latter aspect of Hooker's conception of authority we now turn.

(3) *Tradition*. The term tradition will serve to designate this third component of Hooker's synthesis, though practice, experience and consent are all involved. They constitute the third and final test or touchstone of religious truth. 'Where neither the evidence of any law divine, nor the strength of any invincible argument otherwise found out by the light of reason, nor any notable public inconvenience' are decisive, 'the very authority of the church itself . . . may give so much credit to her own laws, as to make their sentence touching fitness and conveniency weightier than any bare and naked conceit to the contrary' (II, pp. 35f).

There is a fundamental conservative principle underlying Hooker's thought at this point and it belongs to the uniformitarian presupposition that he shared with all European culture before the eighteenth century. Truth was eternal. What was right was right for all times and places. Universal consent was equivalent to nature itself, and the voice of nature was as the voice of God (I, p. 227). Let us be loath 'to change, without very urgent necessity, the ancient ordinances, rites and long approved customs of our venerable predecessors . . . antiquity, custom and consent in the church of God, making with that which law doth establish, are themselves most sufficent reasons to uphold the same, unless some notable public inconvenience enforce the contrary'. If and when it does, Hooker immediately goes on, the church has authority to respond by altering its practice (II, pp. 32f).

Hooker's appeal to Christian antiquity is largely pragmatic, born of respect and prudence. 'Neither may we . . . lightly esteem what hath been allowed as fit in the judgement of antiquity, and by the long continued practice of the whole church; from which unnecessarily to swerve, experience hath never as yet found it safe' (II, p. 30). Hooker has already established with the utmost clarity and definiteness the principle that matters regarding the outward government of the church come within the category of mutable positive law. There is then no question of antiquity and tradition legislating for all future situations. Respect for what has gone before is the fruit of wisdom not obedience. Moreover, the authority that Hooker does accord to tradition is subject to the restrictions provided by scripture and reason: first, tradition cannot deliver 'supernatural necessary truth', which belongs only to scripture; second, 'the authority of men' should not 'prevail with men either against or above reason' (II, p. 325).

It is in the context of the foregoing principles that Hooker's idealisation of general councils should be set – 'those reverend, religious and sacred consultations . . . whereof God's own blessed Spirit was the author', which were 'never otherwise than most highly esteemed of, till pride, ambition, and tyranny began by factious and vile endeavours to abuse that divine intention unto the furtherance of wicked purposes'. Hooker shows himself an exponent of the conciliar catholicism which antedated the Reformation and which the Reformers, both English and foreign, reappropriated to fit their situation, when he prays that 'so gracious a thing may again be reduced to that first perfection' that it enjoyed in the time of the apostles (I, p. 252).

What became in later Anglican thought an appeal to antiquity as legislative for the later church, in Hooker remains a prudent regard for well-tried human practice – 'that which the habit of sound experience plainly delivereth' (II, p. 31). His version of the threefold cord is 'nature, scripture and experience itself' (I, p. 166).

What distinguishes Hooker's use of authority in matters of religion is the absence of literalism and legalism. Neither scripture nor tradition contains a set of binding prescriptions and precedents for the life of the church. Underlying his teaching on this question is the assumption that there is an intuitive moral and aesthetic discernment that judges what is appropriate in the circumstances, a sense of what is fitting, what is becoming (cf. Marshall, pp. 24, 81). In all outward aspects of the church's corporate life, what interests Hooker is the discernment of the 'conveniency and fitness in regard of the use for which they should serve' (II, p. 28). 'Signs must resemble the things they signify.' The outward deportment of the church in all its offices, ceremonies and discipline must be such as to convey and reveal the inward realities of worship and holiness. Though subject to the test of scripture and reason, in the senses defined above, Hooker's characteristic requirement is that 'in the external form of religion such things as are apparently, or can be sufficiently proved, effectual and generally fit to set forward godliness, either as betokening the greatness of God, or as beseeming the dignity of religion, or as concurring with celestial impressions in the minds of men, may be reverently thought of; some few, rare, casual and tolerable, or otherwise curable inconveniences notwithstanding' (II, p. 30).

5
Architects of Anglican Ecclesiology: Richard Field

Richard Field (1561–1616) was one of the most stupendously learned of Anglican theologians in an age when Anglican clerical scholarship was the wonder of the world (*clerus Britannicus stupor mundi*). Field was preferred to the deanery of Gloucester in 1610; when he died six years later, King James I, who had intended him for the bishopric of Salisbury or Oxford, confessed, 'I should have done more for that man'. Together with his friend Richard Hooker, Field is the architect of Anglican ecclesiology. His great work was his voluminous treatise *Of the Church*. It is marked by an underlying irenicism and moderation and a broad appeal to the fathers and (notably) to medieval theology. But Field is roused to implacable polemicising by what he regards as the corruptions or pretensions of the Tridentine Roman Church. His arguments are indeed exhaustive and definitive. 'I will so write', he said, 'as they shall have no great mind to answer me'. At the time of his death Field was working on a book intended to clarify the points of contention between Rome and the Church of England.

The Church Visible and Invisible
Field's starting point in his ecclesiology is not the threefold *notae ecclesiae* that had been developed by second generation protestantism (c.f. Avis, *CTR*, pt 1), but, as with Hooker, the visible church as a divine society upon earth to which all branches of Christian profession belong, even though they fall into error or schism. The church is made up 'of very divers sorts' who share the calling of God to be his people, make the outward Christian profession and enjoy the means of grace.

> All they must needs be of the church whom the grace of God in any sort calleth out from the profane and the wicked of the world, to the participation of eternal happiness, by the excellent knowledge of divine, supernatural and revealed verity and the use of the good, happy and precious means of salvation (I, pp. 26f).

This includes those who do not belong by election to the orthodox, catholic and invisible church which is the mystical body of Christ.

> For there are some that profess the truth delivered by Christ the Son of God, but not *wholly* and *entirely*, as heretics: some that profess the whole saving truth, but not in *unity*, as schismatics; some that profess the whole saving truth in unity but not in *sincerity* and singleness of a good and sanctified mind, as hypocrites and wicked men, not outwardly divided from the people of God.

Only those who 'profess the whole truth in unity' are 'perfectly and fully members of the visible church' (I, pp. 25f).

This visible society is distinguished from other human societies and other religions of the world by three marks: doctrine ('the entire profession of those supernatural verities which God hath revealed in Christ his Son'), sacraments ('the use of such holy ceremonies and sacraments as he hath instituted'), and the ministry ('lawful pastors and guides, appointed, authorised and sanctified') (I, p. 65). Field marks an advance on the Reformation concept of the *notae ecclesiae* and begins to develop a distinctive Anglican ecclesiology, in that these three notes are not marks of the *true* church against the false, but of the whole Christian society over against the world. It is clear that this approach will have important consequences for his view of the Roman church.

Heretics and schismatics bear these three marks and so are to be counted as within the visible church. Heretics belong to the church as to outward order, but not as to spiritual truth. They are not 'right believing Christians' and so are not of the *catholic* church, which 'consisteth of them only that without addition, diminution, alteration or innovation in matter of doctrine, hold the common faith once delivered to the saints; and without all particular or private division or faction, retain the unity of the spirit in the bond of peace' (I, pp. 43f). Schismatics likewise, 'notwithstanding their separation, remain still conjoined with the rest of God's people in respect of the profession of the whole saving truth of God, all outward acts of religion and divine worship, power or order and holy sacraments' (I, p. 42). 'Damnable schism' only arises when 'whole churches . . . out of the pride and pharisaical conceit of fancied perfection and absolute holiness' break communion with the rest of the body (I, p. 163). Field thus presents the notion, important for later ecumenical theology, of division, on account of doctrine or communion, *within* the church.

Where Hooker speaks of the visible church and the mystical church, Field retains the distinction of visible and invisible, but denies that he teaches that there are two distinct churches as Roman controversialists often claimed. He also defends Luther against the same charge. The one church 'will be visible in respect of the profession of supernatural verities revealed in Christ, use of holy sacraments, order of ministry, and due obedience yielded thereunto, and they discernible that do communicate therein', but invisible 'in respect of those most precious effects and happy benefits of saving grace, wherein only the elect do communicate . . . and they that in so happy, gracious and desirable things have communion among themselves, are not discernible from others to whom this fellowship is denied, but are known only unto God' (I, pp. 31f).

The Catholic Church and the Roman Church

In his assessment of the Roman Catholic Church, Field employs a two-fold distinction. First he distinguishes, as we have seen, between the whole visible church of Christendom, comprising the protestant, Orthodox and Roman churches, and the orthodox, catholic church within it, from which Rome, according to Field, has departed by her considered rejection of the Reformation. Second, in the West, he distinguishes between the Latin church, in which all 'our fathers' lived and died, and the Tridentine Roman church which, Field holds, is merely a schismatic faction within the church.

Field's doctrine of the indefectibility of the church, which he shared with all the Reformers, does not allow him to condemn the Latin church of the West before the Reformation. 'We hold it impossible that the church should ever, by apostacy and misbelief, wholly depart from God' (II, p. 396). Though individuals and particular churches may from time to time 'err damnably', 'the whole church at one time cannot so err', for that would be end of the church; it would destroy its catholicity and Christ would be sometimes without his church. 'Yet that errors, not prejudicing the salvation of them that err, may be found in the church that is at one time in the world, we make no doubt; only the whole symbolical and catholic church, which is and was, being wholly free from error' (II, p. 406).

Furthermore, like Hooker and unlike the radical protestants of the Church of England, Field regards it as intolerable to suggest that the Christian faithful who lived and died in the communion of the unreformed Latin church, were deprived of salvation. 'For we most firmly believe all the churches in the world, wherein our fathers lived and died, to have been the true church of God, in which undoubtedly salvation was to be found' (I, p. 171). Field claims that Luther, Calvin, Bucer, Melanchthon and Beza held the same opinion (IV, pp. 520ff). Until Trent, none of the errors attacked by Luther 'ever found general, uniform and full approbation'; the abuses reformed by Luther had long been deplored by all good men and a reformation desired (I, p. 171). But Field detected a significant change in the Roman church as it reacted to the Reformation.

> None of those points of false doctrine and error which they now maintain and we condemn, were the doctrines of the church constantly delivered or generally received by all them that were of it; but doubtfully broached and

devised without all certain resolution, or factiously defended by some certain only who, as a dangerous faction, adulterated the sincerity of the Christian verity and brought the church into miserable bondage (I, p. 166).

A great deal of Field's work is taken up with substantiating, from scholastic and late medieval theologians, his contention that the errors attacked by the Reformers were not the official doctrine of the Latin church before the Reformation and that true doctrine, even in such vexed questions as justification and merit, was taught by the church.

As a result of the reaction to the Reformers, Field concludes, 'the present Roman church is still in some sort a part of the visible church of God, but no otherwise than other societies of heretics are, in that it retaineth the profession of some parts of heavenly truth and ministereth the true sacrament of baptism to the salvation of the souls of many thousand infants that die after they are baptised before she have poisoned them with her errors' (IV, p. 527). The last words of Field's treatise are an implacable denunciation of the errors of the Roman hierarchy. Rome is 'an erring, heretical and apostatical church . . . defiled . . . with intolerable superstition and idolatry' (IV, p. 572).

Field rejects the 'glorious pretences of antiquity, unity, universality, succession and the like' that were adduced (for example by Bellarmine) in support of the claims of the Roman church. Field questions the pedigree of Tridentine catholicism: 'All those things wherein they dissent from us are nothing else but novelties and uncertainties . . . the things they now publish as articles of faith to be believed by all that will be saved, are so far from being catholic, that they were not the doctrines of that church wherein they and we sometime lived together in one communion' (I, p. xxi). The name of 'catholic' cannot be employed as a note of one branch of the church over against another, since the church has long been divided (I, p. 88f).

Here Field is thinking not of the Reformation but of the separation of East and West. Like so many protestant controversialists he makes great play of the fact that the Orthodox churches do not accept Roman claims. But the Church of England accepts the Orthodox as among the churches of God: 'we . . . doubt not but that innumerable living and dying in them, notwithstanding their sundry defects, imperfections and wants, are and have been saved' (I, p. 164). Again, 'though distracted and dissevered by reason of diversity of ceremonies and outward observations, different manner of delivering certain points of faith, mistaking one another, or variety in opinion touching things not fundamental,' the Orthodox churches 'agree in one substance of faith and are so far forth orthodox that they retain a saving profession of all divine verities absolutely necessary to salvation and are all members of the true catholic church of Christ' (I, p. 151). It is not the least of Rome's errors to reject the Orthodox 'from the unity of the catholic church and to cast into hell so many millions of souls of poor distressed Christians, for many hundreds of years enduring so many bitter things for Christ's sake, in the midst of the proudest enemies that ever the name of Christ had' – i.e. Islam (IV, p. 289).

Field's position on the papacy is firm but discriminating: while condemning the papacy in its present form as antichrist because it exalts itself above all earthly authority and condemns to damnation the greater part of Christian folk in the protestant and Orthodox churches (I, p. 153), Field gladly accords to a reformed papacy its ancient prerogatives and points out that Luther does the same (IV, p. 382). Christ did not give Peter power in the commonwealth (the temporal sword) but merely a fatherly office in the church, and even there not unlimited power to command, or infallible judgement, or a unique exemption from heresy, or the plenitude of ecclesiastical power of order or jurisdiction, which belongs to the college of bishops throughout the world, but a primacy of order and honour (IV, p. 1; III, pp. 433–479).

> We deny not therefore to the Roman bishop his due place among the prime bishops of the world, if therewith he will rest contented; but universal bishop . . . we dare by no means admit him to be, knowing right well that every bishop hath in his place, and keeping his own standing, power and authority immediately from Christ, which is not to be restrained or limited by any but the company of bishops (III, pp. 264f).

Field grants the pope the presidency of general councils, but not the power of veto or direction (IV, p. 33).

The Reformers and the Reformation

To the standard Roman Catholic challenge, 'Where was your church before Luther?', Field gives the standard protestant reply: 'It was where now it is. If they ask us, which? we answer, it was the known and apparent church in the world, wherein all our fathers lived and died, wherein Luther and the rest were baptised, received their Christianity, ordination and power of ministry' (I, p. 165). To the further question, 'Then why did you separate?' Field replies, in words that echo Jewel:

> Seeing we could no longer have peace with our adversaries but by approving these impieties, we had just cause to divide ourselves from them, or (to speak more properly) to suffer ourselves to be accursed, anathematised and rejected by them, rather than to subscribe to so many errors and heresies contrary to the Christian and catholic verity (I, p. 170).

Luther, Calvin and 'other worthy servants of God' had obtained the support of Christian states to reform the errors, superstitions and other 'grievous abominations' that the medieval church had come to tolerate (I, p. 93). We honour them for this. 'Master Calvin' is 'worthy of eternal honour' (IV, p. 339). Field defends him against the attempts of Roman polemicists to drive a wedge between his theology and that of the fathers

(I, pp. 194–). Luther 'was a most worthy divine' and 'all succeeding ages shall ever be bound to honour his happy memory' for disentangling the essentials of Christianity from the 'intricate disputes of the schoolmen and Romish sophisters' (I, p. 342). But Field makes no attempt to gloss over Luther's crudities:

> That he was of a violent spirit we deny not; nay himself glorified in it, that he had an heroical spirit, made to contemn the fury and folly of the Romanists: neither had he been fit to oppose against enemies of this kind, if he had been of another spirit. That he was carried too much with the violent stream of his passions, we impute it to the infirmity of flesh and blood, and the perverseness of the manifold adversaries he found in those times (I, pp. 371f).

Against the charge that protestants were fragmented and divided, Field argues that 'protestants have no real and essential differences in matters of faith and doctrine' (IV, p. 417). While this assertion would find support in later scholarship (c.f. Avis, *CTR*, pp. 215f), it must be admitted that on the question of sacramental doctrine Field tends to play down the insuperable differences between Luther and Zwingli. Luther misunderstood the Reformer of Zurich: there was 'no difference in judgement between them who, out of human frailty, are too much divided in affection' (IV, p. 410; c.f. I, p. 341). In Field's judgement – and this is the important point for ecumenical theology – any real differences were not such as to prevent Lutherans and Swiss being 'of one church, faith and religion' (IV, p. 420).

Against the charge that protestants admitted sectarians and heretics into their communion, Field insists that 'we admit none into the communion of our churches but such as receive all the lawful general councils that ever were holden touching any question of faith, the three creeds ... and whatsoever is found to have been believed and practised by all ... at all times and in all places' (IV, p. 289). There is a common orthodoxy that unites the Anglican, Lutheran and Reformed churches, their differences being either imaginary or trivial (ib.).

Bishop and King

On the question of holy orders Field maintains a mediating position between the Calvinist and presbyterian principle of parity of ministers and the later high church platform of monarchical episcopacy. From the beginning there had been an inequality between the chief pastors of the church in each city (bishops) and their assistants (presbyters). But just as presbyters could do nothing without the bishop, so the bishop could not act without the support of his presbyters. 'It is evident that the power of ecclesiastical jurisdiction resteth not in bishops alone but in presbyters also' (IV, pp. 1f).

With regard to the notion of episcopal succession, Field stands firmly with the Reformers, yet without abandoning the principle of transmitted authority. 'The ministry of pastors and teachers is absolutely and essentially necessary to the being of the church . . . an inseparable and perpetual note of a true church . . . For how should there be a church gathered, guided and governed, without a ministry?' But not so succession, unless in the sense of continuity of sound doctrine. 'Not a bare and naked succession, but true and lawful, wherein no new or strange doctrine is brought into the church, but the ancient religiously preserved, is a mark, note or character of the new church' (I, pp. 82ff).

With regard to the authority of the sovereign in ecclesiastical matters, Field rebuts the charge that the Church of England makes the prince the chief bishop. He distinguishes between power of order and power of jurisdiction (as Hooker does): under the power of jurisdiction, princes have the duty to defend the church and to take measures to reform it when bishops and pastors fail to do so; but they are absolutely prohibited from exercising any power of order (i.e. in the sacramental sphere) (IV, pp. 91ff). As Field expands the point elsewhere:

> The kings and queens of England neither do, nor have the power to do, any ministerial act, or act of sacred order; as to preach, administer sacraments, and the like: but the power and authority which we ascribe unto them is that they may, by their princely right, take notice of matters of religion, and the exercise of it, in their kingdoms.

They are duty bound to see that true religion is practised and God rightly worshipped and to punish offences against true religion, even by bishops and priests (I, p. 278).

Authority in Doctrine: Councils

The doctrine of the indefectibility of the church of Christ leads Field to postulate an ideal 'essential church', comprising the whole body of true believers since Christ and subsisting within the visible church, and which is 'absolutely free from all error and ignorance of divine things that are to be known by revelation' and 'absolutely led into the knowledge of all truth' (II, pp. 292f). It enjoys this mystical indwelling of the truth not through some intuitive vision but by adhering to the rule of faith which is itself derived from scripture which is the church's sole authority in matters of necessary doctrine:

> The rule of faith . . . delivered to us from hand to hand by the guides of God's church, containeth nothing in it but that which is found in scripture, either expressly or by necessary implication, so that although we admit another guide in the interpretation of scripture besides the bare letter, yet we admit no other but that form of Christian doctrine which all right-believing Christians, taught by the apostles and apostolic men, have ever received as contained in the scriptures and thence collected (IV, p. 484).

This scriptural rule of faith contains the fundamentals of Christianity – 'those things which every one is bound expressly to know and believe, and wherein no man can err without note of heresy' and 'upon peril of eternal damnation' (I, p. 158). They comprise the trinitarian nature of God; the creation, fall and moral government of the world; the Incarnation and atonement of Christ; the election of the church, the means of grace and the last things. These, and only these, constitute 'the whole platform of all Christian religion' (I, pp. 158ff, 161).

It falls to general councils to formulate controverted doctrines on the basis of scripture guided by the rule of faith. A lawful general council, at which all the patriarchs are present or represented and which agrees 'with unanimous consent' is entitled to our acceptance and obedience. The first six general councils meet these criteria. If doubts remain we may privately search the scriptures and the records of antiquity, but not publicly challenge the conclusions of such a council. 'We may safely conclude that no man can certainly pronounce that whatsoever the greater part of bishops assembled in a general council agree on is undoubtedly true.' Probability remains our guide, for we have no grounds for supposing that general councils have a unique degree of divine assistance, 'beyond the general influence that is required to the performance of every good work', nor do they enjoy any more privileged guidance than patriarchal, national or provincial synods (IV, pp. 51–61).

Part Two

THE SEVENTEENTH AND EIGHTEENTH CENTURIES
Co-existence of the Erastian and Apostolic Paradigms

6

An Anglican Consensus

Between Rome and Reformation

'In the reign of James I,' writes Hugh Trevor-Roper, 'the Church of England had pretensions to be an ecumenical church, a third force, competing with the international Church of Rome and international Calvinism. It attracted French Huguenots like Casaubon, Dutch Arminians like Grotius, dissident Italian Catholics like Paolo Sarpi and Marcantonio de Dominis, Greek patriarchs like Cyril Lucaris' (p. ix).

It would be a massive task to attempt to trace the paths taken by Anglican scholars throughout the seventeenth and eighteenth centuries as they attempted to establish and interpret the identity of their church, interact polemically or irenically with Roman Catholicism on the one hand and the churches of the Reformation on the other. In subsequent chapters the emergence of liberal, moderate and high church traditions within an overall Anglican consensus will be illustrated by a series of case-studies. But first some general features may be sketched.

An Anglican was a 'passive peaceable protestant', as Izaak Walton puts it (p. 183) – the royalism and the anti-Romanism going hand in hand. The Anglican attitude to Rome continued to be implacably hostile. Rome was the enemy for Anglicans as much as for Lutherans or Reformed or English dissenters. There is little to choose between the attitudes of the sixteenth century and those of the seventeenth in this respect. There is no perceptible rise in the ecumenical temperature. In such writings as Laud's *Relation of a Conference*, Hammond's *Of Schism*, Bramhall's *Vindication of the Church of England*, Jeremy Taylor's *Dissuasive from Popery*, Stillingfleet's *Rational Account of the Grounds of the Protestant Religion*, and Isaac Barrow's *Treatise of the Pope's Supremacy* (to mention only a sample) Anglican objections are rehearsed – objections to the claim of the pope's universal jurisdiction and to pretensions to infallibility; to the claim to make new articles of faith, necessary for salvation, setting tradition over the sufficiency of scripture; to the sacrifice of the mass and withholding the cup from the laity; to transubstantiation, penance, indulgences, purgatory and so on. It would be tedious to enumerate the charges and counter-charges, refutations, vindications, replies to replies and answers to answers that were the stock in trade of seventeenth century theological polemic. Some of the more concise examples are conveniently available in More and Cross's *Anglicanism* (MC, pp. 53–72).

The argument was relentless but discriminating. The church of Rome might be sorely corrupted yet she remained a Christian church and her people remained within the ark of salvation. Though the pope might be antichrist (a moot point and a pointer to Calvinistic views, this tenet lost ground under the influence of Laud and the Laudians: see Hill), a primacy of the bishop of Rome, by human right, was not ruled out. The Church of England and the church of Rome, wrote John Cosin bishop of Durham, agree in acknowledging the bishop of Rome 'by right of ecclesiastical and imperial constitution, in such places where the kings and governors of those places had received him, and found it behooveful for them to make use of his jurisdiction, without any necessary dependence upon him by divine right' (c. MC, p. 55). Cosin was intimate at the court of Charles I and chaplain to his Roman Catholic queen's English entourage in exile. He was an accomplished liturgist, composing collects and drafting rubrics for the 1662 Book of Common Prayer, and lover of extravagant ritual. In his writings during the Commonwealth he defended the catholicity of the Church of England. She was catholic in her retention of the apostolic faith, ministry and sacraments, but protestant in her rejection of Roman innovations. At the same time, Cosin fraternised with Huguenots, sought reconciliation with presbyterians at the Savoy Conference (1661), polemicised ferociously against Roman errors and disinherited his son when he turned Roman. Fuller wrote of Cosin: 'Whilst he remained in France he was the Atlas of the protestant religion, supporting the same with his piety and learning, confirming the wavering therein, yea, daily adding proselytes (not of the meanest rank) thereto' (c. *DNB*).

In his life of the diplomat and (subsequently) provost of Eton, Sir Henry Wotton, Izaak Walton records some amusing examples of Wotton's repartee that illustrate on the one hand an unwavering rejection of Roman claims and, on the other, a complete absence of bigotry. Walton, whose ideal of an Anglican was that he should be not only a passive (i.e. divine-right-of-kings royalist) but a *peaceable* protestant (p. 183), holds up his subject as 'a great enemy to wrangling disputes of religion'. When in Rome Wotton became acquainted with a 'pleasant priest', who invited him to vespers. 'The priest seeing Sir Henry stand obscurely in a corner, sends to him by a boy of the quire this question, writ in a small piece of paper, "where was your religion to be found before Luther?"' Refraining from making the usual answer to this old chestnut – 'Where was your face before you washed it?' – Wotton replied, 'My religion was to be found then, where yours is not to be found now, in the written Word of God.' But to a person who asked him his opinion, Whether a papist may be saved?, he replied, 'You may be saved without knowing that. Look to your self.' To another who was 'railing against the papists, he gave this advice, . . . Take heed of thinking, The further you go from the church of Rome the nearer you are to God.'

Wotton defended the learning, character and moderation of Arminius, though professing not to agree with him in some points. He believed in a modified universal atonement (Christ had made '*sufficient* satisfaction for the sins of the whole world, and *efficient* for his elect': my italics). Wotton planned to write the life of Luther with the history of the Reformation in Germany. In his decline at Eton he was often visited by John Hales who was of course a fellow of the college (Walton, pp. 131f, 140f, 149). Like Izaak Walton himself, Henry Wotton was a model Anglican layman (he received holy orders on being appointed to the provostship of Eton at the age of fifty-nine) combining firm convictions with moderation, charity and breadth of sympathy.

Fraternal relations continued between the Church of England and the Lutheran and Calvinist churches on the continent throughout the seventeenth century. In the protestant world the Church of England was held in high esteem as 'the chief and most flourishing of all the protestant churches' and 'the bulwark of protestantism'. The protestant churches' lack of the episcopate (in most cases) was not regarded as a bar to communion and the recognition of their ministries. It was the custom for visiting Lutherans or Calvinists to communicate at Anglican altars and for English churchmen abroad to worship, and frequently to communicate, with Lutherans or Calvinists (though Laud did not encourage this). Before 1662 there were no barriers to those canonically (but not episcopally) ordained among the Lutherans or Reformed being licensed to minister in the Church of England. Norman Sykes offers plenty of examples in his *Old Priest and New Presbyter*. An extraordinary case is that of Hadrian à Saravia (1531–1613), a Dutch Calvinist and professor of theology at Leyden who sought sanctuary in the Church of England and – without being reordained himself – became an apologist for episcopacy as of divine right, held a succession of livings and canonries, helped to translate the Authorised Version of the Bible and ministered to the dying Hooker. Saravia was apparently unaware of any significant differences between the Church of England and the continental Reformed churches (Nijenhuis, esp. pp. 111f).

These differences related primarily to church government. The seventeenth century saw a steadily increasing emphasis on the office of the bishop as a channel of sacramental grace. The Anglican exponents of episcopacy – even those who made the strongest claims for episcopacy by divine right – upheld the three-fold ministry as an ancient, honourable, reconciling, divinely-sanctioned form of polity for the church, but it did not occur to them to suggest that churches who for one reason or another lacked the episcopate were deficient in their enjoyment of divine grace, lacking in valid ministries and effective sacraments. Salvation was proclaimed, received and enjoyed. Christ was present among his people. The church was a reality. The sacred ministry, whatever form it might take, was there to serve, assist and facilitate these realities, not to make it possible for them to come about. No crude pipeline theory of divine grace as a tangible substance that required unique vehicles of conductivity to flow from source to recipient had emerged to confuse the issue. The men who formulated Anglican ecclesiology on the sixteenth and seventeenth centuries were seldom ivory-towered scholars, or naïve country curates. They were accomplished political operators and knew the realities of power-politics. They did not need to be reminded that the Reformation had not been immaculately conceived in the studies of Luther, Calvin and Cranmer. They had no illusions about the motives of Henry VIII. But they still believed in the sovereignty of God working his will in the counsels of men, and of the Spirit that blows where it wills. They recognised the continental Reformers and their churches as being of the same spirit as themselves, sister churches of the Church of England.

In the matter of orders, the English divines developed a view of Lutheran and Reformed ministries that was discriminating and critical, yet without at any time undermining the validity of those ministries. Charity, a sense of reality and a fundamental grasp of the essence of Christianity restrained even the most convinced episcopalian from pronouncing judgement on non-episcopal churches. Lancelot Andrewes insisted:

> Nevertheless, if our form be of divine right, it doth not follow from thence that there is no salvation without it, or that a church cannot consist without it. He is blind who does not see churches consisting without it; he is hard-hearted who denieth them salvation. We are none of those hard-hearted persons; we put a great difference between these things. There may be something absent in the exterior regiment, which is of divine right, and yet salvation be to be had (*MC*, p. 403).

It was vital to distinguish, Bramhall pointed out, 'between the true nature and essence of a church, which we do readily grant them, and the integrity or perfection of a church, which we cannot grant them without swerving from the judgement of the catholic church' (ib.). Cosin, advising that there was no obstacle to exiled Anglicans communicating with the French protestants, made a similar distinction;

> Though we may safely say, and maintain it, that their ministers are not so duly and rightly ordained, as they should be, by those prelates and bishops of the church, who since the apostles' time have only had the ordinary power

and authority to make and constitute a priest, yet that by reason of this defect there is a total nullity in their ordination, or that they be therefore no priests or ministers of the church at all . . . for my part I would loath to affirm and determine against them (ib., p. 398).

The Calvinist Component: Hall and Ussher

There existed also a genuine, though not slavish, theological affinity between the Anglican and continental theologies. As Owen Chadwick has pointed out, three out of the six archbishops of Canterbury from Parker to Laud (Grindal, Whitgift and Abbot) 'would not have disdained the theology of Switzerland' (*Mind*, pp. 19f). Anglican divines such as Field, Forbes the first bishop of Edinburgh and Joseph Hall, bishop successively of Exeter and Norwich, though they could not have fully subscribed to Calvinist orthodoxy, deployed the Reformers in their writings, treating them even-handedly along with the medieval school-men and the fathers. As Collinson has remarked with regard to Carleton, Downame and Hall: 'that Calvinism and *de jure divino* episcopacy should have been bedmates disturbs conventional categories and classifications' (p. 19).

In his *Episcopacy by Divine Right Asserted* (which was provoked by the bishop of Orkney's renouncing his episcopal function and craving pardon before the Edinburgh Assembly), Hall appealed to Calvin's teaching that godly, reformed bishops are not to be refused, reinforcing this by invoking the Augsburg Confession of the German Lutherans and even the authority of Bucer. Bishops are to be heard if they teach God's word. This was deployed as an *argumentum ad hominem*, but Hall and the English divines would have shared the principle implied: the word of God, not the existence of bishops, is the test of a true church. To the extent that Rome maintained 'the true principles of Christianity', she continued to be a visible church (c. Huntley, p. 113). Hall goes on to cite the testimony of Beza, Zanchius, Molinus, Casaubon and Saravia, as to the worth of the English episcopate, more than slightly extrapolating from their evidence to the conclusion that 'no church in the world comes so near to the apostolic form as the Church of England' – we can't imagine Beza ever saying that! (X, pp. 147ff).

In his *Humble Remonstrance to the High Court of Parliament* (1640–41) in defence of episcopacy, Hall clarified the mainstream Anglican view of the foreign reformed churches: 'We love and honour those sister-churches as the dear spouse of Christ. We bless God for them. Lacking the episcopate, they nevertheless lose nothing of the true essence of a church, though they miss something of their glory and perfection.' Hall is persuaded that they would jump at the chance of turning their superintendents into bishops. In insisting on government by bishops in the Church of England, the episcopalian position is 'only affirmative, implying the justifiableness and holiness of the episcopal calling, without any further implication' for those that lack it. When we invoke divine right, Hall explains, 'we mean not an express law of God, requiring it upon the absolute necessity of the being of a Church, what hindrances so ever may interpose; but a divine institution, warranting it where it is and requiring it where it may be had' (X, p. 282). As we shall see, Laud himself – though he had revised the manuscript of *Episcopacy by Divine Right* – was not content with these modest claims.

James Ussher (1581–1656), the first professor of divinity at Trinity College, Dublin, at the age of twenty-six and subsequently bishop of Meath and archbishop of Armagh, presents a combination of Calvinist theology, phenomenal scholarship and great moderation and charity of views (see B. Knox, and Trevor-Roper, pp. 120–165). In his ecclesiology, Ussher's starting point is the Hookerian one that the foundation of the church is 'Jesus Christ the Son of the living God' (II, p. 479). He distinguishes between the foundation – 'unity of the faith and the knowledge of the Son of God' – and the 'superstruction' of the church – 'a perfect man and the measure of the stature of the fulness of Christ'. In the foundation there is 'general unity' among Christians based on a few fundamental 'radical truths'. In the superstruction there exists a great deal of variety. 'Now as long as the church is subject to these ignorances and infirmities, it cannot be otherwise but there must be differences betwixt the members thereof ... Neither will it follow thereupon that these churches must be of different religions because they fully agree not in all things' (II, pp. 482ff; III, p. 28).

In his sermon before king James I in 1624, on the universality of the church and the unity of the catholic faith, Ussher expounds what later became known in Anglican theology as the 'branch theory' of the church. Following the Henricean formularies, the Thirty-nine Articles and Richard Hooker, Ussher states 'The catholic church is not to be sought for in any one angle or quarter of the world: but among "all that in every place call upon the name of Jesus Christ our Lord, both theirs and ours."'

> Thus must we conceive of the catholic church, as of one entire body, made up by the collection and aggregation of all the faithful unto the unity thereof: from which union there ariseth unto every one of them such a relation to, and a dependence upon the church catholic, as parts use to have in respect of their whole (II, pp. 475f).

Ussher differs from the radical protestants in that he includes Rome, and from the later extreme high churchmen, including the Tractarians, in that he includes the churches of the Reformation within the church catholic.

There is no reason for the reformed churches to 'disclaim all kindred with those in ancient times, because they have washed away some spots from themselves . . . It is not every spot that taketh away the beauty of a church, nor every sickness that taketh away the life thereof; and therefore though we should admit that the ancient church of Rome was somewhat impaired both in beauty and in health too . . . there is no necessity that hereupon presently she must cease to be our sister' (III, p. 28). Of 'our forefathers' who lived and died in the Roman communion, 'we have no reason to think otherwise but that they lived and died under the mercy of God' (II, p. 490). All Christian churches, including the Roman and the Eastern, retain enough truth for salvation (II, p. 494).

But by claiming universal jurisdiction for the pope and insisting on communion with the pope as a condition of salvation, Rome has created 'the most cruel schism that ever hath been seen in the church of God.' Not being content to be a branch of the catholic church 'which is the mother of us all', Rome claims to be the root, indeed the whole body of the church. She has 'confined the whole church of Christ within herself', condemning all outside the Roman obedience to be aliens from the commonwealth of Israel and strangers to the covenants of promise. But what, asks Ussher, of the Russian and Eastern Orthodox churches, the reformed churches, the Coptic church and those of India and Asia? 'Must these, because they are not the pope's subjects, be therefore denied to be Christ's subjects?' Ussher replies, in the same vein as Richard Field, 'We, who talk less of the universality of the church, but hold the truth of it, cannot find in our hearts to pass such a bloody sentence upon so many poor souls, that have given their names to Christ' (II, pp. 477ff).

To the standard question, 'Where was your church before Luther?', Ussher replies: 'Our church was even there where now it is . . . we bring in no new faith, nor no new church.' Again: 'If you demand then, Where was God's temple all this while? the answer is at hand: there where antichrist sat. Where was Christ's people? Even under antichrist's priests.'

> The field is the same: but weeded now, unweeded then: the grain the same; but winnowed now, unwinnowed then. We preach no new faith, but the same catholic faith that ever hath been preached: neither was it any part of our meaning to begin a new church in these latter days of the world, but to reform the old . . . neither is the church reformed in our days another church than that which was deformed in the days of our forefathers (II, pp. 493, 496f).

What the fathers accounted catholic, according to the Vincentian canon, 'is at this day entirely professed in our church' (II, p. 494).

On the question of episcopacy and communion, Ussher held that since bishops and presbyters were one order, the ministries of non-episcopal churches were not invalidated.

> I have declared my opinion to be that *episcopus et presbyter gradu tantum differunt, non ordine*, and consequently that in places where bishops cannot be had, the order of presbyters standeth valid: yet on the other side, holding as I do, that a bishop hath a superiority in degree over a presbyter, you may easily judge that the ordination made by such presbyters as have severed themselves from those bishops unto whom they had sworn canonical obedience, cannot possibly by me be excused from being schismatical.

The orders of such churches Ussher judged to be 'much defective' especially in the Dutch churches who, unlike the French, have not the excuse that they are under the power of the pope. Nevertheless that does not affect communion, for as Ussher insists elsewhere, the Christian church has consistently admitted to her communion on the basis of baptism and the baptismal faith, the creed (II, p. 485):

> Yet for testifying my communion with these churches (which I do love and honour as true members of the church universal), I do profess that with like affection I should receive the blessed sacrament at the hands of the Dutch ministers, if I were in Holland, as I should do at the hands of the French ministers if I were in Charentone (I, pp. 258f).

The 'hierarchy of truths' with which he was operating is further revealed in Ussher's proposal to Roman Catholic clergy in Ireland (since he believed ignorance of basic Christianity to be more harmful than 'the vulgar superstitions of popery') that they join forces to teach the fundamentals of the Christian faith, which both churches held in common as necessary to salvation (II, p. 499).

The Anglican Ethos

One of the most impressive features of seventeenth-century Anglicanism, as we look back at it from a perspective in which party groupings within the church are separated by mutual suspicion and an apartheid of personalities, theological colleges, journals and publishing imprints, is the almost total absence of such divisions. Anglicanism had external enemies enough: both papists and puritans were a threat to church and state together. Anglicanism itself exhibited a consensus of opinion as to the character of the Church of England – though we should not forget that this consensus was ultimately consolidated at the cost of the 'great ejection' of puritan clergy after the Restoration. She was a catholic church whose roots went back to the beginning of the Christian era. Before Augustine of Canterbury and his Roman mission there had been a vigorous Celtic church. Before that, Joseph of Arimathea or St. Paul had brought Christianity to these islands. She was a reformed church who, along with her sister churches of the Reformation, the Lutheran and Reformed, stood for the protestant principles of justification by the grace of God through faith, the supreme authority of holy scripture, a liturgy in the vernacular and a non-sacerdotal married ministry. She was a national church who looked to her supreme governor, a lay person, to defend her rights against foreign jurisdiction and her peace against domestic faction.

This consensus is clearly evident in the inter-action of personalities and the inter-penetration of groups with their different emphases. One of the constantly reiterated sub-themes of McAdoo's book on the Anglican thought of the period is this inter-action and the resulting cross-fertilisation of ideas. McAdoo brings to light a fundamental agreement of principles and a common spirit, comprising 'the centrality of scripture and the visibility and continuity of the church, both confirmed by antiquity, and illuminated by the freedom of reason and liberality of viewpoint' (p. 357; cf. 395).

There was no clear line of demarcation between the Laudians and the Great Tew circle, for example. Sheldon, Laudian archbishop of Canterbury in 1663, Hammond and Hyde (Clarendon), architect of the Restoration, were members of Falkland's perpetual seminar at Great Tew. Though Falkland attacked the bishops in the Lords, Chillingworth defended Laudian sentiments in the preface to *The Religion of Protestants*: out of a desire that God should be worshipped in the beauty of holiness, 'the governors of our church' – 'my friends' – 'have set themselves to adorn and beautify the places where God's honour dwells, and to make them as heaven-like as they can with earthly ornaments.' Chillingworth submitted the work for Laud's approval, who sent it out to censors, mindful that this brilliant young man might need to be restrained. Chillingworth was Laud's godson; John Hales and Jeremy Taylor his chaplains.

Henry Hammond, the most unbending high churchman of them all after Laud himself, was praised by the puritan Richard Baxter and the latitudinarian Gilbert Burnet. It was the Calvinist James Ussher who urged Hammond to bring his learning and eloquence to the defence of episcopacy, though Ussher, like Leighton and Baxter, actually favoured a modified 'primitive' episcopacy in which presbyters shared the rule. Hammond was the intellectual heir of Falkland and Chillingworth at Great Tew and defended Hugo Grotius's (then radical) New Testament criticism (though he could not accept his conclusions about pseudonymity) and wrote in defence of Falkland after his death at the battle of Newbury in 1643, publishing an edition of his *Discourse on the Infallibility of the Church*. The versatile Hammond wrote also on *The Reasonableness of Christianity*, and his treatise is a little known forerunner of similar works by the latitudinarians and the deistic John Locke. None other than John Milton came to the defence of Hammond when his scholarship was impugned by Salmasius.

There was a catholicity and breadth of reading that crossed 'party-lines' (though that expression is anachronistic applied to the seventeenth century). Though Hales 'bid John Calvin goodnight', he imputed the offending tenet of double predestination not to Calvin himself (though it is at least implicit in the *Institutes*) but to Calvin's successor Beza and the puritan William Perkins. Hales profoundly reverenced Hooker; in his last months John Aubrey found him reading Thomas à Kempis. Sanderson read both Calvin and Hooker, finding the latter a sound guide for a judicious perusal of the former. Hales' remains were edited by the high church divine and exponent of antiquity John Pearson who also published Falkland's writings on infallibility. Pearson's own remains were edited by the nonjuror Henry Dodwell. The non-juring archbishop Sancroft had been chaplain to John Cosin, bishop of Durham, the conciliator of presbyterians, and himself had a tender conscience for dissenters. The nonjuring bishop Ken had been chaplain to the Calvinistically inclined George Morley of Winchester in 1665. Morley, though a Calvinist in theology, was intimate with high church circles. He had been ejected from his living as a royalist in 1648 and lived in exile until the Restoration. Isaak Walton dedicated his life of Sanderson to him because he had introduced him (with remarkable even-handedness) to Hammond and Chillingworth as well as to Sanderson himself. Hall had the assistance of Laud in the first of his writings on episcopacy, and of Ussher in the second.

In the preface to his *Exposition* of the Thirty-nine Articles, Gilbert Burnet characteristically offers his opinion of other divines. It comes as no surprise that the liberal Burnet should praise Chillingworth: his *Religion of Protestants* was 'writ with so clear a thread of reason and in so lively a style that it was justly reckoned the best book that had been writ in our language.' But it is perhaps significant that he links with it Laud's *Relation of a Conference*: together they comprise 'two of the best books we yet have'. Burnet pays tribute to Hammond for his 'great learning and solid judgement' though he could not possibly have seen eye to eye with him on many matters of theology and policy. He welcomes Pearson on the creed which 'as far as it goes, is the perfectest work we have.'

In this complex situation it is impossible to play off high churchmen against latitudinarians or to try to trace a party line. The Cambridge Platonists were the original 'men of latitude' as Burnet puts it, and the fully fledged latitudinarians – Tillotson, Stillingfleet and Simon Patrick – 'were formed under those great men' (*HOT*, pp. 128f). Taylor enjoyed later the friendship of the Platonist Henry More. The latitudinarian bishop William Lloyd had the friendship of John Wilkins who was on the fringe of the Cambridge Platonist circle and an exponent of the new science, a supporter of Parliament during the Civil War and an advocate of toleration for dissenters as bishop of Chester from 1668, but balanced this theologically (as McAdoo puts it: p. 395) by his equally close friendship with the non-juring lay theologian Henry Dodwell. Joseph Mede is another remarkable for eclectic views and friendships. Though he believed the pope to be antichrist and was an exponent of the prophetic scheme of Christian history, he had Laudian views on the altar and was one of Laud's chaplains. His friends included both the Calvinist Ussher and the ritualistic Cosin.

John Sharp (1645–1714) is another ecclesiastic who muddles our anachronistic categories. His life admirably illustrates the conflicts and cross-currents of the time. Sharp's father was a puritan who indoctrinated him with Calvinism; his mother a royalist who taught him the Anglican liturgy. As rector of the London church of St. Giles-in-the-Fields he incurred the displeasure of James II for two sermons against Rome, preached in response to a wavering parishioner's appeal for guidance (Macaulay, I, p. 578), and in 1688 he refused to read James' Declaration of Indulgence in favour of Roman Catholics. But Sharp was no Whig: he upheld the doctrines of Caroline Anglicanism of the divine right of hereditary kingship and passive obedience even to tyrants. Preaching to the House of Commons at St. Margaret's Westminster after James had fled and the House had just declared the throne vacant, he courageously prayed for the king and denounced the doctrine that princes might be deposed by their subjects (ibid., II, p. 191). On the accession of William and Mary he took the oaths but declined to accept any see vacated by a non-juring bishop during the lifetime of the latter. His scruples were rewarded, for Lamplugh of York died a fortnight later and Sharp succeeded him. As archbishop he forbade pulpit diatribes against dissenters. A high churchman by conviction, he made it known that 'if he were abroad, he would willingly communicate with the protestant churches where he should happen to be'; and he carried on a considerable correspondence with Jablonski of Prussia about a possible union of the Lutheran and Reformed churches (N. Sykes, *Wake*, II, pp. 21, 61). Cultured in his sympathies, he was imbued with the works of Shakespeare and was fascinated by the new science, especially Newton. Sharp was latterly confessor and soul-brother to Queen Anne. His place in seventeenth and early eighteenth-century Anglicanism is indicated by Macaulay when he calls him 'the highest churchman that had been zealous for comprehension and the lowest that felt a scruple about succeeding a deprived prelate' (II, p. 799).

This perhaps tedious sample of the network of relationships that was both personal and theological, that transcended the gravitational pull of high church or liberal tendencies, is culled almost at random from a relatively superficial acquaintance with the period and its literature. As a phenomenon it is important as 'the best commentary on the fact that, in spite of varying views on different questions, parties had not yet emerged' (McAdoo, p. 395).

High Church Trends – The Nonjurors

As late as the early eighteenth century high churchmen were said to esteem the Lutherans as 'the best part of the reform'd religion' and as closest to the Church of England in doctrine, discipline and worship. One decided high churchman advanced that 'as they retain a considerable share in the divinely appointed form, without any schismatical opposition to it, so we may reasonably hope that a proportionable share of the divine blessings attends and vertuates their sacred ministrations.' The same writer (W. Hume) added: 'Of these protestants we cannot advisedly say that their sacraments are no sacraments, that their ministers are mere laymen, that their churches are no churches, but rather that they may be churches, tho' not so perfectly formed.' This, concludes George Every in his study of the emergence of the high church party after 1688, was 'the traditional high church view' (p. 145). The high church bishop of Exeter, Jonathan Trelawny, who abetted Atterbury in the convocation agitation of 1701, offered 'altar and pulpit fellowship' to Huguenot ministers though ordaining them first in accordance with canon law. As M. G. Smith writes, Trelawny 'hesitated to place the divine origin of episcopacy on the same level as the doctrine of the Trinity. A protestant church which lacked bishops was a true, though errant, branch of the true Catholic church' (*Trelawny*, pp. 129, 103).

But as we shall see, the view precisely that non-episcopal churches were no churches, their ministers mere laymen, and their sacraments no sacraments, was to be proposed by the theorists of the nonjuring schism in 1688 and adopted into the ecclesiology of the Tractarians a century and a half later. English churchmen had never been undiscriminating in their view of the foreign Reformers. But in the course of the seventeenth and eighteenth centuries a sense of distance from and reserve towards the continental churches of the Reformation was growing, affecting first the Reformed, in the seventeenth century, then the Lutherans in the eighteenth. As a result of the Civil War and Commonwealth, Calvinism became identified with disloyalty to the Church of England, a threat to both mitre and crown. A more discriminating attitude to the Reformation developed, which favoured the Lutherans as members of a sister church, at the expense of the Reformed. But as rationalising tendencies gathered pace within Lutheranism during the *Aufklarung* of the eighteenth century, English high churchmen looked on with dismay and a sense of increasing alienation.

It is paradoxical that while the Lutheran Jacob Serenius, who had been Rector of the Swedish congregation in London, was extolling the harmony of the Lutheran and Anglican churches in their common continuity with the primitive church, a common national character and a common opposition to both Rome and dissent, the nonjuror Thomas Brett was attacking the Lutherans as combining the worst features of Calvinism and popery. They lacked valid ordinations and so could not be regarded as true churches; they were more ready to join with the papists than the Calvinists whom they hated as much as the Turks; they had introduced theological monstrosities such as the ubiquity of Christ's body and the doctrine of consubstantiation; on the other hand they retained auricular confession and venerated relics. Brett's criticisms were directed at the German Lutherans: like Hugh James Rose after him, he saw their lack of the episcopate as a lack not only of sacramental grace but also of the safeguard of sound doctrine (Pinnington, p. 139).

But for all their suspicion of the continental protestants, the nonjurors were no friends of Rome. Though frequently accused of Romanising, the accusation was unfounded and arrived at by a process of elimination (as Overton suggests, pp. 143f) since the nonjurors seemed to fit into no other category. It is true that the pope was consulted about the first round of nonjuring consecrations in 1694, but this is to be attributed to James II in exile who sought the advice of the archbishop of Paris and Bossuet, who in turn consulted the Vatican. It is significant that while their principle of royal supremacy and passive obedience led the nonjurors to consult their lawful king, their principle of the spiritual independence of the church led them to resolve that, if James delayed his answer too long, they would consecrate 'without his majesty's consent than not at all'. Overton points out that 'though they were often absurdly charged with being papists at heart, they were in fact, as a body, protestant to the backbone. Rome had no sympathy with them nor they with Rome.' Leslie, Spinckes, Brett and above all Hickes had polemicised against Rome and in defence of the claims of the Church of England. Throughout his life, George Hickes 'was a very *malleus Romanensium*', asserts Overton (pp. 451, 391, 93f).

At the same time the nonjurors hardened opinion against dissent wherever they exerted influence – and after the first reconciliation with the established church in 1710, the nonjurors acted like leaven in the lump. Henry Dodwell (1641–1711) the influential lay theologian who led the return of the Shottesbrooke group in 1710, argued on the basis of the apostolic succession that non-conformist baptism was doubtful (needless to say, Dodwell did not accept the validity of lay baptism) and marriage between an Anglican and a nonconformist was a nullity and tantamount to adultery. (For Lawrence, foreign protestants and English dissenters were in the position of catechumens.) This view had consequences at home and abroad. If nonconformists were not baptised Christians they ought not to be admitted to occasional communion in their parish churches. Protestants abroad were in no better position and there was therefore no basis for fraternal dealings with them. Episcopal orders were valid even in schism: non-episcopal baptisms were invalid even in charity and unity. As George Every has put it:

> [Dodwell] could not and did not deny that these schismatics [the jurors] were bishops and priests in a true succession. They were in an altogether different position from Presbyterians, Independents and Quakers, for they had authority to give the seals of the covenant in baptism and communion,

even if their ministrations were irregular and doubtfully valid, on St. Cyprian's principles, while they were still separated from the remnant of the episcopal college. A schism between bishops, however terrible, was on another footing from a separation of churches from episcopal government. The occasional conformity of a non-juror who was weak enough to attend his parish church . . . was venial beside the admission of a nonconformist, whose baptism was doubtful, and had never been completed by the episcopal seal of the Spirit, to communion in the eucharistic sacrifice (p. 71).

In magnifying the episcopal office, Dodwell was a forerunner of the Tractarians. For him as for them, 'in comparison with the question of ministry all other differences between churches fade into insignificance, except questions concerning the Trinity' (ib., p. 72).

G. V. Bennett has observed that such ideas 'had an uncanny fascination for the Anglican priesthood' (*Tory Crisis*, p. 151). But Dodwell entertained more extreme and bizarre ideas than this (see Macaulay, II, p. 564ff). In 1706 he advanced the view that the soul was naturally mortal, being quickened to eternal life by the gift of the 'divine immortalising Spirit' by bishops alone standing in succession from the apostles. As Every explains, Dodwell's argument seemed to imply that those who had not been confirmed, whether protestant or pagan, had the benefits of mortality, but Dodwell went on to explain that while this indeed applies to German protestants, the English dissenters and Scottish presbyterians, who spurn the gift of confirmation where it may be had, sin against the Holy Ghost and are made immortal to their own damnation (ib., pp. 121f). This was certainly an extremely backhanded way of favouring the continental protestants over non-Anglicans at home! The distinction became more and more difficult to sustain.

An Instructive Episode

If there is one figure that symbolises extreme high church views in the first half of the eighteenth century, it is Francis Atterbury. Atterbury achieved notoriety for his agitation on behalf of the Lower House of Convocation against the latitudinarian bishops, and ended his life in the disgrace of exile for his Jacobite plotting for the sake, he believed, of the church (1732). It is all the more remarkable to find the young Atterbury emerging as the champion of Martin Luther. In the pamphlet war between papists and Anglicans at Oxford in 1687, a Roman Catholic propagandist put out an attack on 'the spirit of Martin Luther'. 'It was a crude vilification, utterly confused in argument, and barely literate. Luther was accused of sexual indecency, abusing the primitive fathers, and inventing new doctrines, such as justification by faith . . . Luther had had personal communication with the devil and had received his theology by direct diabolical revelation' (Bennett, *Tory Crisis*, p. 29). Atterbury immersed himself in the study of Luther. His reply when it came was 'devastating', a 'systematic destruction' of Luther's detractor. But while defending the Reformer as a man of conscience, the restorer of primitive Christianity, a skilled Bible commentator and learned patristic scholar, Atterbury made it clear that the theology of the Church of England was by no means identical with that of the Lutheran Reformation. 'How comes the Church of England to be so concerned in what Luther said or did?' he asked (ib.). Atterbury's mixture of admiration for the Reformer and appreciation of his achievement, with a critical reserve and reluctance to become the disciple of any human authority, is one that we have become familiar with already.

The Gap Widens

The embittering experiences of ejection and exile during the Commonwealth had an effect on Anglican assessments of non-episcopal ministries. Where presbyterian ordinations at home were filling the place of deposed episcopalians, it is not surprising that 'the old hostility deepened into hatred that was almost an obsession. It became a matter of faith with churchmen that the presbyterians were responsible for all their ills' (Bosher, p. 80). Anglicans could not forgive them for the twofold crime of martyring the king and abolishing the apostolic ministry. In both divine right had been flouted; nothing could be more heinous. As Henry Byam (prebendary of Wells in 1660) put it: 'To give these men the right hand of fellowship . . . were to partake of their sins and render ourselves guilty of that sacred blood their hands have spilt, to join with them were to justify all their infernal and unparalleled actions' (c. ib.). For Richard Watson (prebendary of Salisbury after the Restoration), non-episcopal ministers were 'lay-Reformed Calvinists (for ecclesiastics I dare not acknowledge those who they pretend to make such)' (c. ib., p. 84 &n).

This attitude to rebellious presbyterians at home rubbed off on their coreligionists abroad. They became tarred with the same brush. It was as though the rebellion had revealed Calvinism in its true colours. Outwardly Anglican spokesmen were still insisting that the Church of England did not judge other churches. Thus Clarendon wrote: 'The Church of England judged none but her own children, nor did determine the other protestant churches who were without ordination [sic]. It is a thing without her cognisance.' Morley was even more non-commital: we neither admit them to be true churches nor deny them to be such, he declared (c. ib., p. 83). This is a subtle departure from the attitude of Anglican divines at the beginning of the century, such as Hall, who while refraining from judging foreign reformed churches for their lack of the episcopate, insisted that nevertheless they were indeed true churches. While fraternal relations were to continue – with the primacy of William Wake witnessing an upsurge of ecumenical activity – damage had been done; the rot had set in. As Hensley Henson wrote: 'The Church of England had always been episcopal; it now became episcopalian – that is, what had been a matter of practical policy became the requirement of religious principle' (*Church of England*, p. 123).

The Church in Danger

The rigours of persecution and exile during the Commonwealth had served to temper the spirit of Anglicanism and to strengthen Anglican identity. The emergence of a high church party at this time represented an Anglicanism that would resist absorption into an undifferentiated protestantism. It was marked by uncompromising convictions and a new sense of the coherence and uniqueness of the Anglican faith. As Bosher has written, the Laudian movement 'had undeniably bred a new generation of clergy who believed passionately in the truth and rightness of their Anglican faith. The Church of England was for them no haphazard product of political compromise, but the one pure and authentic embodiment of primitive tradition.'

A comparison with the Marian exiles reveals a new spirit of Anglican self-confidence: 'Remembering those bishops-to-be who had sat humbly at the feet of Calvin, deprecated their prayer book and its minimum of ceremonial, and studied eagerly in Zurich, Basle and Geneva "the best models of the foreign Reformed churches", we may find it hard to recognise their spiritual descendents' (pp. 56f).

Henry Ferne was one who had fought through the troubles for the strengthening of Anglican identity. He wrote:

> Lest there be any mistake in names (because all the sects in this nation call themselves . . . Churches of England) . . . by the Church of England is understood the Church of Christ in this land established upon the Reformation, holding out her doctrine and government in the Thirty-nine Articles, her liturgy and public divine service in the Book of Common Prayer (c. ib., p. 32).

But the returning exiles of 1662 could not put the clock back to the reign of the first two Stuarts. Under the last two monarchs of that House, their authority was undermined by concessions to dissenters intended to aid the Roman Catholic cause. Then under William and Mary and under Anne, with foreign protestant interests hovering in the wings, the future of the reconstructed Church of England seemed insecure. Attendance at worship was no longer enforced; the clergy and their churchwardens found their position as the enforcers of Christian morals undermined; attacks on the church and its standards were unrestrained in a flood of subversive literature; poor, overtaxed, undermined, the parochial clergy began to look back to a supposed golden age of the Church of England, and to turn their backs on these first intimations of a pluralistic society. 'In the years following 1688, the clergy of the Church of England had to go through an agonising reappraisal of all that they had stood for theologically, morally and pastorally' (Smith, *Trelawny*, p.61; c.f., ib.,

'Toleration, etc'; Bennett, *Tory Crisis*, pp. 20ff). As William Turnbull put it, 'Whereas our former fears were of popery and arbitrary government, now it is of a commonwealth and the pressure of the church by the dissenters' (c. Bennett, 'William III and the Episcopate', p. 116).

A further strain was placed on the tacit consensus of Anglicanism, in which adherence to the fundamentals of a reformed catholicism left room for much diversity of opinion on secondary points, by the audacious challenge of the extreme latitudinarians to the fundamentals themselves. Symbolic of this development is the so-called Bangorian controversy, sparked off by the sermon preached before King George I by Benjamin Hoadly, bishop of Bangor, on the text, 'My kingdom is not of this world.' Hoadly challenged the very concept of ecclesiastical authority and doctrinal subscription, claiming that since Christ was head of the church, his kingdom, the individual conscience was answerable to him alone and not to any human authority:

> As the church of Christ is the kingdom of Christ, he himself is king; and in this it is implied that he is himself the sole lawgiver to his subjects and himself the sole judge of their behaviour in the affairs of conscience and eternal salvation. And in this sense, therefore, his kingdom is not of this world: that he hath in those points left behind him no visible human authority (p. 11).

However absurd the picture of a bishop of the church by law established ridiculing all ecclesiastical authority, there was a twofold motive behind Hoadly's provocation to the high churchmen: first political, for the house of Hanover's tenure of the British throne had been shaken by the Jacobite rising of 1715 and some high churchmen were believed to be implicated; and second theological, for Hoadly and his supporters were blatantly defending their right to hold heterodox, Arian, views that were certainly excluded by the terms of the church's subscription. It was for the political implications of his attack on the politically suspect hierarchy that Hoadly became the darling of the Whigs and of the court, being preferred to a series of well-endowed sees, culminating in Winchester, and so receiving a reward very much of this world. The government could not afford to have its champion condemned, so convocation was prorogued indefinitely by the king (not to be convened again until 1852). Hoadly challenged a tacit Anglican consensus by his extreme latitudinarianism as much as the nonjurors and their sympathisers did by their disproportionate appeal to antiquity. (See further Rupp, *Religion in England*, pp. 88–101.)

As many of the inferior clergy saw it, the remedy to the Whig threat of a secularised society and perhaps the submersion of the Church of England in a pan-protestant toleration that would include deists and unitarians, as well as Reformed Dutchmen and Lutheran Hanoverians, was to play down those aspects of Anglicanism that were common to all protestant churches and to emphasise those aspects that distinguished her from her protestant sisters on the continent. As the godliness of the godly prince became questionable, the episcopal office acquired new lustre (as Every puts it, p.73). In the thought of such as Dodwell, apostolic succession, not passive obedience was to be the distinct doctrine of the Church of England. Let the bishops magnify their office. If they will not act, let the Lower House of Convocation compel them to do so. The church is in danger; its heritage must be preserved, its identity protected. All through the eighteenth century the Church of England was on the defensive, and in the nineteenth the battle continued. The watchword of the high churchmen of the turn of the seventeenth century became the watchword also of their Tractarian successors a century and a half later: 'The Church in danger.'

7

The Anglican Liberal
Protestants

Lucius Cary, Lord Falkland
In his classic study of the development of religious toleration in England,
W. K. Jordan drew attention to the influence of lay opinion in the
religious controversies of the seventeenth century. Whereas religious
questions had been the monopoly of the clergy in the sixteenth century,
in the succeeding century lay voices made themselves increasingly heard
(II, p. 315). It might be more accurate to say that lay opinion in the
sixteenth century was embodied in the queen and her advisors, for in the
doctrine of the godly prince the Anglican Reformers had provided a
dominant lay role in the government of the Church of England (Avis,
CTR, chs 9 and 10; Claire Cross). But as the monarchs lost their grip on
the church, liberal opinion spread among the laity in reaction to religious
bigotry and conflict. The two most outstanding exponents of lay liberal
theology were Falkland in the first half and Locke in the second half of
the seventeenth century – though to these should be added Edward
Hyde, Earl of Clarendon, who had a considerable output as a lay divine
as well as an historian.

Lucius Cary, Lord Falkland (?1610–1643), gathered around him at the
family seat of Great Tew near Oxford a university in miniature, where
liberal clerics such as Hales and Chillingworth, high churchmen like
Sheldon, Hammond and Edward Hyde (Clarendon), together with an
admixture of poets and men of letters, gathered for discussion (see
Trevor-Roper, pp. 166–230; Clarendon, *Life*, I, 42–50, 104f, 201–4). The
Tew Circle was the hub of progressive theological exploration before the
Civil War. As Every and McAdoo have emphasised, high church and
liberal circles interpenetrated at Great Tew. It was here that the authority
of antiquity was challenged under the influence of the French reformed
theologian Jean Daillé's *Traité de l'emploi des saints pères* (1632) (see
Wormald, pp. 240–276). It was here that the claims of reason were

injected into the reformed Anglican appeal to scripture and the consent of antiquity (in the spirit of Hooker's appeal to rationality as law) to create the famous 'threefold cord not quickly broken' of the Anglican theological tradition.

Falkland was their host, catalyst and acknowledged mentor. His vast reading and brilliant mind earned him the respect of the fraternity. Falkland wrote two short treatises, published posthumously, on the infallibility of the Roman church, and expressed his views on episcopacy, the reformed character of the Church of England, and relations with other reformed churches in the two debates in the Lords in 1641 for the abolition of the hierarchy. Aubrey confidently retails the fact that Falkland was a Socinian, but without evidence. He also describes his wilful death at the battle of Newbury in 1643 to troubles with his mistress. Others at the time offered a nobler interpretation. As S. R. Gardiner put it in the *DNB:* 'By a death which is scarcely distinguishable from suicide Falkland closed his eyes to the horrors [of civil war] which he loathed'.

In his writings on infallibility, Falkland appeals to scripture and antiquity, both interpreted by reason. To humbly seek for truth is more acceptable to God than to blindly cling to dogma:

> To them who follow their reason in the interpretation of the scriptures, God will either give his grace for assistance to find the truth, or his pardon if they miss it. And then this supposed necessity of an infallible guide (with the supposed damnation for want of it) fall together to the ground (*Infallibility*).

Falkland detested the coercion of opinion and persecution of dissidents. True Christianity does not persecute. This is the deepest ground of his objections to Rome: 'To this certain and undoubted damning of all out of the church of Rome, which averteth me from it, comes their putting all to death that are so, where they have power . . . and that averteth me yet more' (*Infallibility*). He attributes the widespread dissaffection from Rome to her record of persecution.

> I confess this opinion of damning so many, and this custom of burning so many, this breeding up those who knew nothing else in any point of religion, yet to be in a readiness to cry, 'To the fire with him, to hell with him' . . . were chiefly the causes which made so many so suddenly leave the church of Rome (c. Jordan, p. 376).

Falkland makes a telling point when he comments on Roman claims: 'When there is fire for them that disagree, they need not brag of their uniformity who consent' (*Infallibility*).

On the question of the sources of authority in the church, Falkland places the consent of antiquity (the 'diffused' church) above the decisions of councils (the 'representative' church). It would be a greater heresy to challenge what was unanimously held for the first four hundred years than to deny any canon of a council. It is significant that Falkland does make this, admittedly qualified, appeal to antiquity, because it places him within the consensus of Anglican divinity that transcended emerging differences of churchmanship. On the question of fundamentals, he points out that one may err as much by holding something to be essential which is only profitable or probable as by insisting on what is actually false. When 'necessary' is used as equivalent to 'very convenient' it is a small step to 'absolutely necessary'. Episcopacy is a case in point: 'These things may have come, without much opposition from being thought profitable to be done and probable to be believed, to be thought necessary to be both' (*Infallibility*).

In his speeches against the Laudian hierarchy in 1641, Falkland spoke as the liberal protestant against those who 'have been the destruction of unity, under pretence of uniformity – [who] have brought in super-stition and scandal under the titles of reverence and decency – [who] have defiled our church by adorning our churches'; who insisted more on 'conforming to ceremonies' than 'conforming to Christianity'. Laud and his abettors have preached but one gospel: 'the *jus divinum* of bishops and tithes, the sacredness of the clergy, the sacrilege of impropriations, the demolishing of puritanism'. They have attempted to enforce a spiritual tyranny, 'an English though not a Roman popery; I mean not only the outside and dress of it, but equally absolute, a blind dependence of the people upon the clergy, and of the clergy upon themselves [the bishops], and have opposed the papacy beyond the seas that they might settle one beyond the water' (c. Tulloch, pp. 138f).

But if he attacked the pretensions and abuses of the Laudian hierarchy, Falkland drew the line at the abolition of episcopacy. He reminded the House that it was the bishops who had been the instruments of the English Reformation. Bishops had lasted from Christ to Calvin. As Tulloch aptly says, it was against all his instincts both as a scholar and a statesman to change overnight the face of the church. But Falkland made his position unequivocally clear. 'Mr Speaker,' he said, 'I do not believe them to be *jure divino* – nay, I believe them not to be *jure divino*.' He rejected Scottish presbyterianism on precisely the same grounds, because of its divine right pretensions and its tendency to destroy spiritual unity by imposing outward uniformity (Tulloch, pp. 140, 155).

One of Falkland's charges against the Laudians was that they had 'slackened the strictness of that union which was formerly between us and those of our religion beyond the sea: an action as impolitic as ungodly' (c. Tulloch, p. 138). In his treatise on infallibility, he suggested that this had been conducted for superficial reasons. If the reformed churches of the continent had thought 'bishops' as good a word as 'superintendents', many 'who understand nothing but names, would have missed that scandal they have now taken' (*Infallibility*).

Falkland's unnecessary death at the age of thirty-three symbolises the tragedy of the liberal school of seventeenth-century Anglican theology which put forward a charitable and spiritual approach to questions of doctrine and the nature of the church only to be overwhelmed by a tidal wave of religious bigotry and political conflict.

William Chillingworth

Chillingworth (1602–1644) and Hales are the two brightest stars in the galaxy of early liberal Anglicans. Their influence is extensive and is not confined to liberal thinkers. Chillingworth's reputation was not always crowned with lustre, however (c.f. Clarendon, *Life*, I, pp. 62–66). As Laud's godson, it was felt that he had disgraced his church by his conversion to Rome as a result of his rashly tackling a Jesuit in disputation. It appears that Chillingworth, who had scruples about subscribing the Thirty-nine Articles, had been persuaded that a climate of greater intellectual liberty existed in the Roman communion. He saw himself as following in the tradition of Erasmus and other Roman Catholic humanists who refused the Reformation and saw their calling as being to bring enlightenment to the church from within (Orr, pp. 15, 19). Chillingworth's experiences at Douai rapidly disillusioned him, but his abrupt return to the church of his baptism did his reputation little good either. Chillingworth redeemed himself, however, in the eyes of all Anglicans by his masterpiece of 1638 *The Religion of Protestants a Safe Way to Salvation*.

Despite the popular misconception of Chillingworth as a biblicist, based on his celebrated dictum about 'the Bible only', Chillingworth's view of the 'religion of protestants' is a more sophisticated one. He praises the 'great and heroical spirit of Luther' (v, 112; p. 387) and attributes the division of the western church to the persecution of Luther and his followers for serving God according to their consciences (v, 106; p. 382). It was Chillingworth's conviction that intellectual differences were not, in themselves, a legitimate cause of separation. The only proper cause of secession is a radical infringement of the moral and intellectual liberty of the individual. The protestants would therefore have been guilty of schism if they had departed the church of Rome solely because of doctrinal disagreements. For Chillingworth, the significance of the Reformation was not so much theological as moral (Orr, pp. 128f). The cause of schism was always doctrinal rigidity and intolerance, 'this deifying of our own interpretations, and tyrannous enforcing them upon others, this restraining of the word of God from that latitude and generality, and the understandings of men from that liberty, wherein Christ and the apostles left them' (iv, 16; p. 250). It was not the function of the church to obtain uniformity of belief. Essentials were few and clearly apparent on the surface of scripture. In the nature of the case, belief is not coercible.

Chillingworth's famous appeal to scripture is therefore to a scripture which plainly reveals the way of salvation and which everyone may freely interpret by the light of his own reason. Differences of interpretation should be settled by calm discussion and rational argument, not by mutual anathemas and excommunications. Chillingworth was aware that he was making drastic demands on human nature which was prone to bigotry. Even Luther 'had a pope in his belly' (ii, 82; p. 120). It is a sad irony that the dying Chillingworth had to suffer the zealous adjurations of a puritan divine who seems to have had a legion of popes in his belly.

Bearing in mind, then, these qualifications, the central statement of *The Religion of Protestants* deserves to be quoted extensively:

> By the 'religion of protestants', I do not understand the doctrine of Luther, or Calvin or Melanchthon; nor the confession of Augusta, or Geneva, nor the catechism of Heidelberg, nor the articles of the Church of England, no, nor the harmony of protestant confessions; but that wherein they all agree, and which they all subscribe with a greater harmony, as a perfect rule of their faith and actions; that is, the Bible. The Bible, I say, the Bible only, is the religion of protestants (vi, 56; p. 463).

The authority of the church and its traditions, on the other hand, is a shifting sand. 'I see plainly and with mine own eyes, that there are popes against popes, councils against councils, some fathers against others, the same fathers against themselves, a consent of fathers of one age against a consent of fathers of another age, the church of one age against the church of another age.' This was the passage that troubled Newman and to meet it he developed a notion of development that could impose order on the diversity of tradition. But for Newman the mere phenomenon of development of doctrine was not enough without an infallible defining authority to pronounce with certainty which developments were to be followed. Chillingworth had already disposed of that argument: an infallible interpreter is superfluous. 'So that those places [of scripture] which contain things necessary, and where no error was dangerous, need no infallible interpreter, because they are plain: and those that are obscure need none, because they contain not things necessary; neither is error in them dangerous' (c. Tulloch, p. 329). But this depends on Chillingworth's belief that individuals will not be damned for their errors, if they hold them in good faith and humbly seek for truth. 'They that err and they that do not err may both be saved.' Newman, however, with his celebrated 'dogmatical principle', did not share this generous view. But for Chillingworth, for the reasons adduced, holy scripture, bearing the good news of the way to salvation plainly for all to read, was the only sure foundation for faith. It was also the fundamental Reformation principle.

'I for my part, after a long and (as I verily believe and hope) impartial search of "the true way to eternal happiness", do profess plainly that I cannot find any rest for the sole of my foot but upon this rock only . . . This therefore, and this only, I have reason to believe: this I will profess, according to this I will live, and for this, if there be occasion, I will not only willingly, but even gladly, lose my life' (vi, 56; p. 463).

If Chillingworth is distinctive in the emphasis he places on the critical reason as the arbiter of religous truth, he is more truly representative in some of his other views. His *Letter Touching Infallibility*, published posthumously, attacks claims to papal infallibility. His tract *The Apostolical Institution of Episcopacy Demonstrated* sets out to defend the limited thesis that episcopacy 'is not repugnant' to the writings of the New Testament. As Tulloch observes, 'Any further claim for it as a positive *jus divinum* is inconsistent alike with his object in the tract, and with the whole tenor of his thought and reasoning' (p. 307).

Like the Reformers, Chillingworth believes in the indefectibility of the church of Christ, though not, needless to say, in the infallibility of any branch of it. Any particular church and any individual may err, even in fundamentals, but the whole church cannot forsake the fundamentals of the faith. 'The catholic church cannot perish, yet . . . she may and did err in points not fundamental' (iii, 11; p. 177). 'That there shall always be "a church infallible in fundamentals" we easily grant: for it comes to no more but this, "that there shall always be a church" (iii, 39: p. 194). A church may err, yet remain a true church; the gates of hell will not prevail against her, but she cannot err in fundamentals without ceasing to be a church (iii, 70; p. 216. iii, 55; p. 207). While Hooker in his controversy with Travers had resisted the assertion that Rome erred fundamentally ('in the foundation'), Chillingworth is more tentative: he 'hopes' she does not (Answer to the preface, 20; p. 42. iii, 56; p. 207). Like Hales, however, Chillingworth will not be drawn on what precisely the fundamentals are. Beliefs necessary to salvation may vary from one individual to another according to circumstances (iii, 13; p. 179). The Apostles' Creed contains all necessary beliefs, i.e. fundamentals, but Chillingworth noticeably does not commit himself to the corollary that all the propositions of the creed are fundamental (iv, 1ff; pp. 245ff).

In conclusion, it is appropriate to bring in here the views of that exquisitely cultured Anglican layman Sir Thomas Browne whose *Religio Medici* (1642) seems to contain an explicit echo of Chillingworth's words quoted earlier. Browne's credo is quintessentially Anglican and Hookerian in the critical distance that it preserves from all conflicting human authorities – 'neither believing this because Luther affirmed it or disproving that because Calvin hath disavouched it'. Browne's famous words could well serve as a motto for seventeenth-century Anglican theology:

I condemn not all things in the council of Trent, nor approve all in the synod of Dort. In brief, where the scripture is silent, the church is my text; where that speaks, 'tis but my comment; where there is a joint silence of both, I borrow not the rules of my religion from Rome or Geneva, but the dictates of my own reason (p. 8).

John Hales

John Hales (1584–1656) stands out as the most broadminded and liberal of seventeenth-century Anglicans (c.f. Clarendon, *Life*, I, pp. 58–62). His irenic and tolerant attitude was centuries ahead of his time. Yet he was no free-thinker, not even a basically secular-minded man like Sir Thomas Browne, but of a deeply Christian spirit. Hales was known as 'the ever memorable' for the quality of his mind and conversation, not for anything memorable or dramatic in the outward circumstances of his life. His career was indeed uneventful, yet bore the scars of the troubled age in which he lived. A fellow of Merton College, Oxford, he taught Greek in the university and assisted the Warden, Sir Henry Savile, in his munificent edition of the works of St. Chrysostom. According to Clarendon (ib. p. 58), he bore 'the greatest part of the labour'. In 1613 he became a fellow of Eton College where he continued his collaboration with Savile who was also Provost. Hales attended the Synod of Dort as an observer in 1618 and his experience there confirmed him in his incipiently liberal views. Significantly for our picture of the interaction of different theological emphases in the Church of England at this time, after criticising Hales' tract on schism (1536), archbishop Laud made him his chaplain and canon of Windsor.

During the troubles Hales was deprived of his canonry and his Eton fellowship and spent his last years in considerable poverty, being forced to sell much of his library. In his will Hales insisted on a private, almost secret funeral, on the grounds that as he in his life had done nothing for the Church of England, so in his death he did not wish the church to do anything for him. This was a cruelly severe self-assessment: through the wit and wisdom of his conversation Hales had made a significant contribution to the thinking of the Tew circle and through his limited publications he had injected an element of reasonableness, humanity and truly evangelical insight into the making of Anglican theology. His influence was indirect, through the assistance and criticism that he offered to others, notably Savile and Chillingworth. He tackled Laud in private, but here, it would appear, his counsel was less warmly received.

Hales' stress on the vocation of reason in theology was based on his own pilgrimage in the truth. 'For the pursuit of truth,' he explains to Laud in defence of his tract on schism, 'hath been my only care, ever since I first understood the meaning of the word. For this I have forsaken all hopes, all friends, all desires, which might bias me from driving right at what I aimed. For this I have spent my money, my means, my youth, my age, and all I have.' The light of reason is 'so goodly a piece of the Lord's

pasture . . . which he hath endued us with in the day of our creation'
(c. Jordan, p. 405). The appropriate method in theology for rational
beings, therefore, was not the accumulation and citation of self-evident
authorities but rather 'soundly discovering and laying down the truth of
things' (c. McAdoo, p. 15). If this undermines uniformity of opinion and
creates a conflict of ideas, so be it: the 'uproar of searching minds' is
healthy (c. Jordan, p. 405). Opinions were not the substance of religion:
we might differ profoundly in our views on non-fundamental doctrines
yet remain in communion with one another. This conviction underlies
Hales' view of the Reformation and his concept of the sin of schism.

What are the fundamentals for Hales? He never tells us. It is clear,
however, that for him as for Chillingworth, only what is plain and
generally understood in the message of scripture can be fundamental. In
Hales the reluctance of the genuine liberal to make divisive definitions of
doctrine is uppermost. He refuses to take the demand for a list of
fundamental articles entirely seriously:

> Now concerning the merriment newly started, I mean the requiring of a
> catalogue of fundamentals, I need to answer no more, but what Abraham
> tells the rich man in hell, 'they have Moses and the prophets,' the apostles
> and the evangelists, let them seek them there ('A Tract on the Sacrament of
> the Lord's Supper and Concerning the Church's mistaking itself about
> Fundamentals': I, p. 72).

When pressed Hales makes the apparently flippant, but actually
profoundly Hookerian reply that the fundamentals are those points
wherein we agree with Rome and non-fundamentals are those points on
which we differ (ib.). The dogmatic, disciplinary and liturgical differences
between Christians of different confessions are therefore in themselves no
bar to intercommunion. God does not require 'identity of conceit'
[i.e. opinion] but unity of the Spirit in the bond of peace.

> It is not the variety of opinions but our own perverse wills, who think it
> meet that all should be conceited as ourselves are, which hath so
> inconvenienced the church. Were we not so ready to anathematise each
> other, where we concur not in opinion, we might in hearts be united,
> though in our tongues we were divided (c. Tulloch, pp. 224f).

Hales insisted that he could not remain an Anglican if it required him to
believe any man to be damned. His rule and advice is: 'You may safely
communicate with all parties, as occasion shall call you' without being
implicated in inter-confessional or internecine conflicts (*Schism*, p. 15).

In an age when theological polemic on both the Roman and Anglican
sides centred on the charge and counter-charge of the damnable sin of
schism, Hales was unimpressed by this rhetoric. Accusations of heresy
and schism are 'two theological scarecrows' to intimidate the consciences
of the faithful (*Schism*, p. 3). Hales indicates his view of the Reformation
when he distinguishes between wilful schism and necessary separation.

Schism is separation that proceeds from passion, ambition, avarice 'or such other ends as human folly is apt to pursue', while justifiable separation arises from 'well weighed and necessary reasons' – when all other means have been tried and there remains no other course of action 'to save us from guilt of conscience'. We must be willing to put up with many things that are less than perfect and separation is only justified when we are compelled to participate in them ourselves against our conscience (ib., pp. 4, 6, 9).

Disagreements can be contained, and perhaps resolved by discussion so long as communion is not broken. Hales recalls the clash between predestinarians and arminians at Dort nearly twenty years before: 'As long as the disagreeing parties went no farther than disputes and pen-combats, the schism was all that while unhatch'd; but as soon as one party swept an old cloister, and by a pretty art made it a church, by putting a new pulpit in it, for the separating party there to meet, now what before was a controversy became a formal schism' (ib., p. 5).

Hales lays it down that 'to err in fundamentals is either to be ignorant of, or deny something to be fundamental that is, or to entertain something for fundamental which is not'. The latter is where Rome goes wrong (but it is not clear which point or points of Roman Catholic dogma Hales has in mind). Rome had 'adulterated the truth of God, by mixing with it sundry inventions of her own'. It was therefore to escape complicity in those so-called fundamentals that Rome required as necessary to salvation, and on grounds of conscience that the separation at the Reformation took place. For 'where the truth of God doth once suffer, their union is conspiracy, authority is but tyranny and churches are but routs'. The characteristically Halesian footnote comes when he insists that the Reformation, even if mistaken, was yet no schism for it was done in good faith (I, p. 72, 74). The nub of Hales' objections to Rome was not her errors in themselves, for in his view propositions were not of the essence of Christianity, but the imposition of these errors, as dogma, on the conscience of individuals. As Clarendon put it: Hales 'exceedingly detested the tyranny of the church of Rome, more for their imposing uncharitably upon the consciences of other men, than for the errors in their own opinions'.

But Hales was implacably opposed to all forms of uncharitable exclusivism and authoritarianism, as much in their protestant as their Roman Catholic dress. As an observer at Dort in 1618, disillusioned by the politics of the synod and 'hard pressed' by the universalism of John 3.16, as the remonstrants deployed it, Hales finally turned against that 'extreme and rigid tenet', double predestination, 'which Beza and Perkins first acquainted the world with' and resolved to 'bid John Calvin goodnight' (c.f. Peters). However, as Tulloch points out, if he bade Calvin goodnight, he did not bid Arminius good morning, 'because he saw from a higher field of vision how little dogmatic precision has to do with spiritual truth'

(p. 191). Such speculations beyond what is revealed were themselves a cause of division. The synod of Dort had taught Hales a lasting lesson. As he put it in his tract on schism nearly twenty years later:

> It hath been the common disease of Christians from the beginning, not to content themselves with that measure of faith which God and scriptures have expressly afforded us, but out of a vain desire to know more than is revealed, they have attempted to devise things, of which we have no light, neither from reason nor revelation; neither have they rested here, but upon pretence of church-authority (which is none) or tradition (which for the most part is but feigned) they have peremptorily concluded, and confidently imposed upon others, a necessity of entertaining conclusions of that nature, and to strengthen themselves, have broken out into divisions and factions, opposing man to man, synod to synod, till the peace of the church vanished, without all possibility of recall (pp. 10f).

Hales' disparaging comments on church authority and tradition in this passage require further comment. Hales was deeply sceptical about all forms of ecclesiastical authority on the grounds that they were invariably invoked to impose dogma, to instil obedience and to stifle liberty and diversity. Hales' view of the church did not require dogmas, beyond the fundamentals, and granted the greatest latitude of opinion within the unity of the Spirit. With Falkland, Chillingworth and the early Clarendon (Edward Hyde), Hales took a critical view of the authority of the fathers, Christian *antiquity*. Whereas the more mainstream and high church Anglicans, following Jewel's *Apology*, would set store by the *consent* of the fathers, Hales and the other members of the Tew circle subjected the appeal to antiquity to a rational critique (cf. Wormald, pp. 240–276). Pointing to the unedifying arguments in the early church over the date of Easter and the legalistic Judaising on which it was based, Hales condemns the leaders of the church for ignorance and the faithful for apathy and credulity – 'because through sloth and blind obedience men examined not the things which they were taught, but like beasts of burthen, patiently couch'd down and indifferently underwent whatsoever their superiors laid upon them'. And Hales points the moral for our concept of authority: if the leaders of the church failed to show wisdom and discretion in a point so plain and so trivial, it would ill become us to look to such 'poor-spirited persons' as arbiters of the points now at issue between the churches (*Schism*, pp. 7f). In his sermon, 'Of Enquiry and Private Judgement in Religion', Hales passes in review the various claimed authorities in theology. In his remarks on antiquity he anticipates Locke, asking, 'What is it else . . . but man's authority born some ages before us?'

> Now for the truth of things, time makes no alteration; things are still the same they are, let the time be past, present or to come. Those things which we reverence for antiquity, what were they at their first birth? Were they false? Time cannot make them true. Were they true? Time cannot make them more true (c. Tulloch, p. 249).

Time is irrelevant to the question of truth. Reason is the judge of opinions, whether ancient or modern.

Councils are, equally with antiquity in general, 'human authority after another fashion'. Hales is happy for church councils to make their contribution and for their decisions to be bought to the bar of reason. It is when infallibility is claimed for them that he protests. Infallibility is not the prerogative of 'any created power whatsoever' (*Remains*, p. 25). All agree that individuals may err, but 'can Christians err by whole shoals, by armies meeting for defence of the truth in synods and councils, especially general, which are countenanced by the great fable of all the world, the bishop of Rome?' In answering this question Hales takes no account of claims that promises are given to the whole church that are not the prerogative of any individual except the pope. His reply is purely *ad hominem*: 'To say that councils may not err, though private persons may, at first sight is a merry speech; as if a man should say, That every single soldier indeed may run away, but a whole army cannot.' He remains totally unimpressed by the calibre of most members of church councils:

> Considering the means how they are managed, it were a great marvel if they did not err: for what men are they of whom these great meetings do consist? Are they the best, the most learned, the most virtuous, the most likely to walk uprightly? No, the most ambitious, and many times men neither of judgement nor learning (I, p. 65).

Ecclesiastical history is largely the record of the 'factioning and tumultuating of great and potent bishops' (*Schism*, p. 12).

The note of *universality* is no safer guide; indeed it is the weakest of all: 'universality is such a proof of truth, as truth itself is ashamed of; for universality is nothing but a quainter and trimmer name to signify the multitude.' To say that truth lies with the multitude, or even the majority, contradicts the lonely voices of the Old Testament prophets and the notion of the faithful remnant. Such grounds may perhaps serve to excuse an error but never to warrant a truth (Tulloch, pp. 250f).

Anglicans of all complexions in this period accepted the holy *scriptures* as the paramount authority in the church, and Hales is no exception. He refers us to Moses and the prophets, the apostles and evangelists, for the fundamentals of Christianity. But his prescription contains an implicit restriction: it is indeed the function of the scriptures to show the way of salvation and the fundamentals of the faith, but not to legislate for every area of life. Like Hooker, Hales restricts the authority of scripture to the redemptive purpose for which it was given, while he sees others, on all sides, 'torturing them [the scriptures] to extract that out of them which God and nature never put in them' (*Remains*, p. 3).

Finally, in his concept of the *church* Hales marries a Lutheran doctrine of the spiritual nature of the true church to a humanist and rationalist idea of comprehension that began from Hooker's ideal of a church coextensive with the nation but infused it with a spirit of liberality by lowering the terms of subscription. By the church catholic Hales understood 'all factions in Christianity, all that entitle themselves to Christ, wheresoever dispersed all the world over' (I, p. 63). Like Luther, Hales insists that outward show of places and persons is no mark of a true church:

> For where, or amongst whom, or how many the church shall be, or is, is a thing indifferent; it may be in any number, more or less, it may be in any place, country or nation, it may be in all, and, for ought I know, it may be in none, without the prejudice to the definition of a church, or the truth of the gospel, north or south, many or few, dispersed in many places or confined to one: none of these do either prove or disprove a church (*Schism*, pp. 8f).

Hales was utterly unimpressed by all the energy and learning that for a hundred years had been devoted to specifying the marks of the true church. Discoursing on the text 'My kingdom is not of this world,' he insists: 'Mark and essence with her are all one, and she hath no other note but to be.' The doctrines of the notes of a true church are merely 'learned impertinencies' for scholars 'to busy their wits withall.'

> For the church is not a thing that can be pointed out . . . it is the glory of it not to be seen and the note of it to be invisible; and when we call any visible company of professors a church, it is but a word of courtesy: out of charity we hope men to be that which they do profess . . . the Lord only knoweth who are his (*Remains*, p. 201).

Hales' best advice to seekers for the true church (here he is enlarging on the text 'The kingdom of heaven is within you') is:

> Let every man therefore retire into himself and see if he can find this kingdom in his heart; for if he find it not there, in vain shall he find it in all the world besides (*Remains*, p. 202).

Hales follows a definitely Lutheran line on the universal priesthood. In his 'Tract concerning the Power of the Keys and Auricular Confession' he makes it clear that the power of the keys is not a sacerdotal prerogative but simply the privilege that belongs to all Christians of sharing the gospel with one another. The keys of the kingdom of heaven are the doctrines of the gospels (*Claves regni coelorum sunt doctrina evangelii*). In a direct echo of Luther, Hales proclaims:

> Every one, of what state or condition soever, that hath any occasion offered him to serve another in the ways of life, clergy or lay, male or female, whatever he be, hath these keys, not only for himself, but for the benefit of others . . . to save a soul, every man is a priest (I, pp. 83ff).

Hales' view of comprehension in the church was not, as Jordan points out, the mere toleration of dissent, but the enlargement of the church to include all Christians (p. 410). He believed that 'men of different opinions in Christian religion may . . . hold communion *in sacris,* and both go to one church' (*Schism*, p. 11). Against the prevailing trend of Laudian rigour on the one hand and puritan rigidity on the other, Hales set out to make Christianity 'rather an inn to receive all than a private house to receive some few' (c. McAdoo, p. 17).

John Locke

John Locke (1632–1704) was no theologian, but a man of affairs of wide reading and formidable intelligence who brought his experience of the world and a robust common sense to bear on a wide variety of problems, including those that had exercised the Anglican divines of the seventeenth century. Locke should not be seen as a rationalist and deist; unlike Toland, he did not suggest that Christianity (or anything else) was not mysterious. Though he appeals to reason, he is strongly impressed with a sense of its limitations, of the 'darkness' and 'blindness' of our condition. What Locke did claim was that the essentials of Christianity are few and simple. In this minimising interpretation of the fundamentals, and in the notions of comprehension and the scope of communion that go hand in hand with it, Locke is an exponent of that liberal tradition of early Anglicanism that finds its inspiration in Hooker and emerges as a distinct strand within the Anglican synthesis in Hales and Chillingworth. Locke and Falkland are the two great liberal lay thinkers of seventeenth-century Anglicanism.

(1) The Terms of Communion

Locke's first *Letter Concerning Toleration* (1689) is, like Hales' tract on schism, one of the classic treatments of the question of the comprehensiveness of the Church of England. Locke is dealing primarily with the toleration of dissenters, but he has much of value to say about the terms of communion within a church. He begins with a side-swipe at the controversies of the past two centuries as to the marks of the true church. For him 'the chief characteristic mark of the true church' is toleration (VI, p. 5). Toleration is possible where a clear line of demarcation is established between the state and the church. The state or commonwealth is a society of individuals constituted purely for the 'procuring, preserving and advancing of their own civil interests' – life, liberty, health and possessions. A church on the other hand is a voluntary society of individuals who join together of their own accord for the public worship of God 'in such a manner as they judge acceptable to him and effectual to the salvation of their souls' (pp. 10, 13). Since the church poses no threat to the state (atheists and Roman Catholics are excluded from the toleration; they cannot be trusted to be loyal subjects), the state has no need to interfere in the affairs of the church, to compel uniformity of belief or practice.

Locke has abandoned Hooker's vision of a church coextensive with the commonwealth as rendered invalid by the growth of dissent. He does not indulge in fantasies of reconstructing a national church on a bare minimum of conformity, as Arnold and Coleridge would do more than a century later. However, Locke's views on the terms of communion do have a potential for the reunion of the churches. He asks 'if it be not more agreeble to the church of Christ to make the conditions of her communion consist in such things only as the Holy Spirit has in the holy scriptures declared, in express words, to be necessary to salvation?' The conditions of communion are the conditions of salvation. Where two or three are gathered together in Christ's name, there is the church. Whether they have bishops or not, 'certain I am that nothing can be there wanting unto the salvation of souls, which is sufficient for our purpose' (p. 14). Locke rebukes those who require 'those things in order to ecclesiastical communion which Christ does not require in order to life eternal' and exclude such persons from their communion whom Christ will one day receive into the kingdom of heaven (p. 15).

Locke's discussion of the meaning of heresy and schism at the conclusion of his first letter on toleration is also relevant to the question of communion. He begins by laying down that a religion is distinguished by its rule of faith and worship. Those who share the same rule of faith and worship are members of the same religion. Since, for example, Roman Catholics and protestants do not have the same rule – the former being guided by tradition and the teaching office of the pope, the latter deferring to the paramount authority of scripture – there are different religions (by Locke's definition of religion) within Christianity. *Heresy*, therefore, is a separation between members of the same religion over opinions not explicitly contained in the acknowledged rule of faith. Protestant heretics are those who insist on certain propositions as fundamental, though not clearly found in scripture, and in consequence withdraw from the communion or expel others from it. *Schism* similarly is a separation effected on account of some point of worship or discipline that cannot be justified by the rule of faith and worship. In defence of his broad terms of communion, Locke maintains that 'he that denies not any thing that the holy scriptures teach in express words, nor makes a separation upon occasion of anything that is not manifestly contained in the sacred text . . . cannot be either a heretic or a schismatic' (pp. 55ff).

(2) *The Fundamentals of Christianity*

What then are these fundamentals which heretics and schismatics either deny or add to and in so doing force a break in church communion? Locke answered this question in his *The Reasonableness of Christianity* (1695). Appealing to the four gospels (of which he displays an impressive knowledge) and repudiating the deployment of proof-texts taken out of context, Locke reduces the fundamentals, belief of which is required for salvation (and on the premises of the letter on toleration, for church communion), to (a) belief in God as creator (which, for practical purposes, can be taken for granted) (b) Jesus as the messiah (c) repentance and a moral life. 'These two, faith and repentance, i.e. believing Jesus to be the messiah, and a good life, are the indispensable conditions of the new covenant, to be performed by all those who would obtain eternal life' (VII, p.105). 'Those are fundamentals, which it is not enough to disbelieve: every one is required actually to assent to them' (p.156). The fundamentals are plain and simple because Christianity was first preached to plain and simple people (pp.157f).

In theological argument, Locke has no place for tradition. Truth is truth in the light of reason, not because it is hallowed by centuries of history. Tradition casts no mantle of respectability over error and superstition. Locke is scornful of those who expect opinions 'to gain force by growing older'.

> What a thousand years since would not . . . have appeared at all probable, is now urged as certain beyond all question, only because several have since . . . said it one after another. Upon this ground propositions, evidently false or doubtful enough in their first beginning, come by an inverted rule of probability, to pass for authentic truths; and those which found or deserved little credit from the mouths of their first authors are thought to grow venerable by age and are urged as undeniable (*Essay*, II, p.258; c.f. Avis, *FMHT*, pp.110–120).

Locke's place in the formation of Anglican theological method is indicated by his twofold appeal to scripture and reason (not a hubristic, speculative reason, however, but one that is guided by probability and a sense of the limitations of our condition: c.f. Avis, *Ecum. Theol.*, p.55). In his sceptical attitude to tradition and antiquity Locke looks back to Hales, Falkland and Hyde; in his appeal to reason he looks to Hooker and Chillingworth; in his stress on probability and the moral conditions of the search for truth he points ahead to Butler and the Tractarians. Though no cleric and no divine, Locke has an influential place in Anglican theology that deserves to be recognised.

Gilbert Burnet

Burnet (1643–1715) was a phenomenon even in an age of prodigies like the seventeenth century. A man of immense learning, indefatigably acquired, and a prolific writer, he was also an effective man of affairs, if notoriously tactless and imprudent. His faults were blatant and made him many enemies. But, as Macaulay says, his outstanding gifts and virtues made him even more. (Macaulay's pen-portraits of Burnet's character are gems and not be be missed: *Hist.*, I, pp.640ff; II, pp.271ff, III, pp.188ff). Burnet was at the centre of events at the Revolution in 1688 and subsequently an oustanding diocesan bishop in an age of pastoral laxity and inertia (he also initiated the fund for augmenting low clerical stipends, 'Queen Anne's Bounty': Best, pp.30f). He was a liberal in an illiberal age and an ecumenist both at home and abroad. On his travels he was an acceptable emissary to Lutherans, Swiss, Dutch and French Reformed, and even cardinals in Rome. As bishop of Salisbury after 1689 he was committed to attempts to reconcile the presbyterians and, within his own diocese, he was tolerant to the presbyterians at one extreme and the nonjurors at the other. Burnet was a major historian of the Reformation and an expositor of the Thirty-nine Articles.

Gilbert Burnet was born in Scotland to a father of independent religious views (he condemned the Scottish bishops but refused to take the covenant) and a mother who was the strictest presbyterian. At the age of fifteen Burnet began an arduous, systematic and broadly based course of study in theology and by the age of eighteen he was said to have become 'imbued with the principles of Hooker's *Ecclesiastical Polity*' (*DNB*). At the age of twenty-three he was a parish minister in Scotland but got into trouble with the bishops for a memorandum in which he had attacked them for abuses, ensuring that they got the message by sending signed copies to them all. In 1669 Burnett worked with archbishop Leighton of Glasgow in his celebrated scheme of moderated episcopacy, intended to draw in the presbyterians. In the same year, at the age of twenty-six, Burnet was appointed professor of divinity in the university of Glasgow. He refused a choice of Scottish bishoprics; at the age of twenty-nine he was untempted by the offer of the next vacant archbishopric (*DNB*).

Moving into the swim of events south of the border Burnet settled for the chaplaincy of the Rolls Chapel in 1675, being dismissed ten years later by Charles II (who in the following year was to make his death-bed profession of Roman Catholicism) for preaching against popery. Burnet had not endeared himself to Charles by rebuking him for his dissolute life and the 'sinful pleasures' which had brought down on him 'the indignation of heaven'! In 1686, after the failure of attempts to exclude the Duke of York (James II) from the succession, Burnet made himself scarce travelling on the continent (he claims that James was plotting against his life). His fortunes were now tied up with those of William of Orange, with whom he sailed in 1688. Burnet's support and advice was rewarded with the see of Salisbury in the following year.

The status of foreign protestants and English dissenters was one of the issues at stake in the attempted censure of Burnet's *Exposition of the Thirty-nine Articles* (1699) by the Lower House of convocation in 1701. The *Exposition* carries an adulatory dedication to William. To reconcile the divided Christians of his new kingdom is the only task that remains outstanding 'to finish the brightest and perfectest character that will be in history'. Burnet did not believe that points of dogma should divide Christians from one another. He strove for the reconciliation of dissenters to the Church of England and for the strengthening of ties both with and between Lutherans and Reformed in Europe. His aim, in his exposition of such controverted and, to his mind, speculative doctrines as predestination was to bring 'men to a better understanding of one another, and to a mutual forbearance in these matters' (preface). Full agreement is more than can be hoped for yet much can be done through mutual understanding 'towards the healing of those wounds in which the church lies bleeding.' In the sacrament of the eucharist, given that Lutherans and Calvinists agree in the modes of worship and devotion, 'a mere point of speculation concerning the manner in which Christ is present' ought not to be divisive. Everyone may be left to the freedom of his own thoughts; private opinion does not affect practice and ought not to prevent fellowship.

Burnet concludes his preface with a telling anecdote. In 1686 he had studied at close quarters the Lutheran and Reformed churches and had conferred with their leaders. He had been saddened by the sorry state of Huguenot refugees and appalled by the fact that the external dangers to the protestant religion, which might have been expected to compel the protestants to make common cause, seemed rather to fan the flames of controversy and bigotry. The zeal of the reformed ministers impressed Burnet but he detected a lack of spiritual vitality. The 'inward state of the reformation' concerned him more than all its outward dangers (HOT, p. 437). Burnet recounted that 'a very eminent divine' among the German Lutherans, being urged by Burnet to seek to be reconciled with the Calvinists, retorted that 'he wondered much to see a divine of the Church of England, press that so much on him, when we, notwithstanding the dangers we were then in, . . . could not agree our differences.' Lutherans and Calvinists differed over matters of moment, the attributes of God and the doctrine of providence, but Anglicans were divided over things indifferent, forms of government and worship. 'Let the Church of England heal her own breaches, and then all the rest of the reformed churches will with great respect admit of her mediation to heal theirs' (Exposition, preface).

Burnet had achieved distinction for his writings against Rome and his life's work was his documentary history of the English Reformation, which was intended to refute the Roman Catholic claim that the English Reformation 'was begun by the lusts and passions of King Henry the Eighth, carried on by the ravenousness of the Duke of Somerset under Edward the Sixth and confirmed by the policy of Queen Elizabeth and her council to secure her title' (preface). When the first volume appeared in 1679 Burnet was accorded the thanks of both houses of parliament and urged to complete the task. The second volume appeared two years later: he had written his narrative in six weeks. The third volume came out in 1714, shortly before his death.

Burnet envisaged his exposition of the Thirty-nine Articles as complementary to his history 'to explain and prove the doctrine which was then established.' (*HOT*, pp. 264, 658). He had been persuaded to undertake this, the first major exposition of the Articles since that of Rogers, in 1586, by archbishop Tillotson, 'that great prelate, who then sat at the helm'. But just as he had held back the first volume of his Reformation history for a year to submit it to friendly assessors, he withheld his *Exposition* for five years, his friends intimating that it could provoke opposition. During this time, Burnet tells us in his preface, it was read with approval not only by the moderate and latitudinarian archbishop of Canterbury (Tillotson) and the bishop of Worcester (Stillingfleet), but also by the moderate but impeccably high church archbishop of York (Sharp).

Though Burnet's exposition of the Articles was thought to be doctrinally lax throughout – Robert South said that the author had served the Church of England as the Jews served St. Paul, giving it forty stripes save one – it was Burnet's comments on Article 23 'Of Ministering in the Congregation' that gave particular offence. The article lays down that no-one may preach or take upon himself the ministry of the sacraments without being called and sent by duly constituted authority; but any mention of episcopal ordination or apostolic succession is conspicuous by its absence. Burnet points out the general terms in which the article is phrased, 'far from that magisterial stiffness in which some have taken upon them to dictate in this matter.' The compilers of the Articles 'had the state of the several churches before their eyes, that had been differently reformed; and although their own had been less forced to go out of the beaten path than any other, yet they knew that all things among themselves had not gone according to those rules that ought to be sacred in regular times: necessity has no law, and is a law to itself.' 'Lawful authority' in Burnet's view is not synonymous with the episcopal office but is 'that rule which the body of the pastors, or bishops and clergy of a church, shall settle, being met in a body under the due respect to the powers that God shall set over them.' Like Hooker, Burnet envisages situations when the episcopate or other governing body of a church has become so corrupt that a fresh start has to be made, under the supervision of the Christian magistrate, the godly prince. There is nothing in the article to exclude Christians, in extreme necessity, making ministers from among themselves. Burnet knows that this is what Luther approved and he believes that the article intentionally makes room for such eventualities. 'We are very sure that not only those who penned the articles, but the body of this church for above half an age after, did, notwithstanding those irregularities, acknowledge the foreign churches so constituted to be true churches as to all the essentials of a church, though they had been at first irregularly formed, and continued still to be in an imperfect state.' If the choice facing Christians is either being without the church's ministrations, or joining in 'unlawful and defiled worship', they have the third option of 'breaking through rules and methods in order to the being united in worship and government'. Of the three, this is the least evil (pp. 286ff).

In his commentary on Article 19 'Of the Church', Burnet followed the Caroline divines in distinguishing between the essence and the perfection of a church. There are two senses in which a church may be described as a 'true' church. In the first sense a true church is one that preserves the essentials and fundamentals of Christianity. In the second sense a true church is one 'all whose doctrines are true, that has corrupted no part of this religion, nor mixed any errors with it.' Burnet clearly implies that both the non-episcopal churches of the Reformation and the Roman Catholic church are 'true' churches in the first sense, in that they preserve the essence of Christianity, the essence of Christianity being, as with Hooker, the baptismal faith: baptism is our guide in this question, as it brings us into the covenant of grace. It is implied that there can be inter-communion with the protestant churches; it is explicit that there can be no communicating with Rome while she withholds the cup from laity, for where part of the dominically instituted sacrament is cut off, the sacrament is damaged and to communicate in the damaged sacrament would condone it. But Burnet, the friend of protestants, the historian of the Reformation, is emphatic: we do not deny Roman baptism, orders and sacraments nor do we exclude our forefathers from the covenant of grace (pp. 209f).

It is interesting that when Burnet was in Rome in 1685 he was questioned by Cardinal d'Estrées about Anglican orders. With the Roman Catholic James II now on the throne of England, the cardinal appreciated that the reconciliation of the Church of England would be made a good deal easier if her orders could be held to be valid, though given in heresy and schism. Burnet was well briefed: he had composed a *Vindication of the Ordinations of the Church of England* in 1676. He assured the cardinal that 'as for the matter of fact, nothing was more certain than that the ordinations in the beginning of queen Elizabeth's reign were canonical and regular.' There is an ironical contemporary ring about the cardinal's response: 'He seemed to be persuaded of the truth of this, but lamented that it was impossible to bring the Romans to think so' (*HOT*, p. 423).

In the convocation of 1701, the vociferous high church element in the lower house was flexing its muscles under the dashing leadership of Francis Atterbury egged on behind the scenes by Trelawny in the upper house. To the consternation of most of the bishops, who saw it as part of their office to make judgements in matters of doctrine, the lower house began to embark on the censorship of publications, the first to come under their scrutiny being John Toland's infamous *Christianity not Mysterious*. The response of the upper house, when required to endorse the censures of the lower, was to point out that every bishop might proceed through his own diocesan court against the authors or retailers of 'ill books', and that the convocation itself did not have the power to summon individuals to appear before it and it would not be equitable to condemn an author unheard.

The lower house then turned its inquisitorial attention to Burnet's *Exposition* – no doubt a way of striking back at the bishops. They accused the book, in general terms, of introducing 'such a latitude and diversity of opinions as the articles were fram'd to avoid,' of distorting the true meaning of several articles and 'other receiv'd doctrines of our church', and of undermining the established religion and 'derogating from the honour of its Reformation' (*HOT*, pp.690ff; Every, pp.101f). It is significant that at this time, even for high churchmen, sound doctrine and the canonical government of the established Church of England were synonymous with the English Reformation. The bishops would not countenance the censure unless the lower house would give chapter and verse for their vague charges, and this they refused to do. One of the minority in the lower house hit the nail firmly on the head when he asked 'whether if the Lord Bishop of Sarum had drawn up the Articles instead of the exposition of 'em, they would not have found fault with those as much as with this' (Every, pp.101f).

Every points out that Burnet had 'offended the high church party by emphasising the impossibility of making a hard and fast distinction between the case of the foreign churches and that of English and Scottish presbyterians. He drove them on to develop their own arguments against the nonconformists in a way that made it increasingly difficult to recognise the validity of Lutheran ministrations' (p.103).

'From the fire raised thus in convocation,' concludes Burnet in his memoirs, 'a great heat was spread through the whole clergy of the kingdom: it alienated them from their bishops, and raised factions among them everywhere' (*HOT*, p.692). The arrogance of the inferior clergy, the resentment they felt against what they regarded as the feebleness of the bishops, and the acrimony generated between the two gives a foretaste of the situation that developed between clergy and bishops in the Oxford movement. 'Magnify your office,' urged Newman in the first of the *Tracts For The Times*: but when the bishops failed to do so along the lines required, their judgement was challenged and their authority undermined. As Burnet remarked of 1700–1, it seemed strange to see men who had so long asserted the divine right of episcopacy, challenging the authority of their fathers in God (*HOT*, p.691).

8

The Anglican Liberal
Catholics

John Bramhall

John Bramhall (1594–1663), the redoubtable Yorkshireman who became bishop of Derry in 1634 and ended his career as archbishop of Armagh at the Restoration, defended episcopacy against the presbyterians and the integrity of the Church of England against Roman Catholics. Bramhall was a man of remarkable courage and ability, a scholar, administrator and man of action. In his funeral oration for Bramhall, Jeremy Taylor praised him as combining the judiciousness of Hooker, the learning of Jewel, and the acuteness of Andrewes. The Anglican 'catholicity' of Bramhall's outlook is attested by his particular use of two writers as apparently diverse as Richard Field (d. 1616) whose treatise *Of the Church* mediated between the approach of the protestant Reformers and the approach of his friend Richard Hooker, on the one hand, and Thomas Aquinas, on whom Bramhall is explicitly dependent, on the other. As McAdoo has significantly observed: 'No picture of the development of theological method in the seventeenth century which hopes to achieve a degree of verisimilitude can fail to take account of the influence of the *Summa Theologica*' (p.383). These Anglican divines were not conscious of any inconsistency in drawing on both scholasticism and reformed theology, reason and faith, as they forged their characteristic synthesis.

(1) *The Church of England and the Reformation*
Bramhall's view of the Reformation is of course positive, though not unqualified. In *A Just Vindication of the Church of England from the unjust aspersion of criminal schism* (1654), he stresses the continuity of the English church through the Reformation: 'the Church of England before the Reformation and the Church of England after the Reformation are as much the same church, as a garden, before it is weeded and after it is weeded, is the same garden' (I, p.113). Our separation, he insists, is not

from the catholic church but from Rome (if we were to become more Roman we would thereby become less catholic) and not so much even from Rome as from her errors (pp. 257, 199).

The English Reformation was a vindication of ancient English liberties. This realm of England is an empire (as the Henrican legislation to annul Roman jurisdiction had insisted). English kings before the Conquest did not acknowledge papal jurisdiction. Furthermore, the English church goes back further than the Roman, having been founded by St. Joseph of Arimathea (archbishop Parker had made the same claim in Elizabeth's reign; Stillingfleet would hold that it was planted by St. Paul in AD60). Bramhall makes great play of the fact that it was the catholic bishops, abbots and universities who, though far from favourable to protestantism, supported the break with Rome and the instatement of Henry as supreme head. He particularly insists as do all the Anglican controversialists of this period, on the right of a national church to reform itself (I, pp. 115ff, 129ff, 150, 160; II, pp. 177ff).

But Bramhall nevertheless adopts a position that is independent of the continental Reformers and critical of the excesses of the English Reformation. As for Calvin, Bramhall remarks, 'We honour Calvin for his excellent parts, but we do not pin our religion either in doctrine or discipline or liturgy to Calvin's sleeve' (II, p. 62; cf. I, p. 38). He observes that 'three things are necessary to make a public reformation lawful: just grounds, due moderation and sufficient authority' (I, p. 168). As we have seen, Bramhall has no doubts about the 'just grounds' or the 'sufficient authority' on which the English Reformation was conducted. But he is highly critical of what he regards as the lack of 'due moderation', especially where the dissolution of the monasteries was concerned, and in this he believes he shares 'the judgement of moderate English protestants'. Religious foundations, which were good in their original foundation, ought not to have been destroyed because of 'accessory abuses' or for the faults of individuals. Reform of the religious houses was needed, for the clergy had grown to 'that excessive grandeur, that they quite overbalanced the laity'. 'But eradication, to pluck up good institutions root and branch, is not reformation, which we profess, but destruction' (I, pp. 118). Bramhall suggests that 'covetousness had a great oar in the boat' and that those responsible were more interested in the *goods* than the *good* of the church (I, pp. 118f).

(2) *The Roman Catholic Church*

Bramhall had been awarded his D.D. in 1630 for a strongly anti-papal thesis (*DNB*) but his view of Rome as a church is substantially that of Hooker. His motive is a pastoral one, for the salvation of 'our fathers'. Since it is Bramhall's contention that 'our religion is the same as it was, our church the same as it was, our holy orders the same they were, in substance,' it follows that English catholics before the Reformation were not lost, but saved by a 'general repentance'. 'We do not believe that they were guilty of any heretical pravity, but held always the truth implicitly in the preparation of their minds, and were always ready to receive it when God should be pleased to reveal it' (I, pp. 199, 269). Bramhall holds, as Field broadly did, that by rejecting the Reformation and by hardening this rejection canonically at the council of Trent, Rome herself was now guilty of schism (I, pp. 246ff). The universal office that Rome claims for the pope is a purely human institution. Princes therefore have the right to alter it within their territories. Like some of the Reformers, Bramhall will contemplate a moderate, reformed papacy, provided it is understood as a convenient human arrangement. But what we might be prepared to grant as of human right, he says, they insist is of divine right (I, p. 165; II, p. 282). But is Rome then 'a true church'? This was the form in which the dominant ecclesiological questions of the Reformation had been cast (cf. Avis, *CTR*, pt 1) and the Caroline divines inherited it. Bramhall's answer is equivocal. Rome is a true church 'metaphysically' because she holds the fundamentals of the faith, but she is no true church 'morally' because she errs in the superstructure she has built on to the foundation (II, p. 38; cf. p. 55).

Another way of putting this distinction between the metaphysical and the moral true church, was to speak of the essence or nature of the church and the integrity or perfection of the church. The marks of a true church are 'an entire profession of saving truth, a right use of the word and sacrament, and an union under lawful pastors'. The notes of the church claimed by Roman controversialists such as Bellarmine – antiquity, universality, splendour, etc. – are merely accidental. In adducing word, sacraments and ministry as the marks of the church, Bramhall is following Field rather than Hooker (who has a different emphasis) and is in line with the magisterial Reformers of the previous century. These marks are the key to both the 'essence' and the 'perfection' of a church. 'Being perfect they consummate the integrity of a church; being imperfect they do yet contribute a being to a church' (II, pp. 24f).

(3) The Non-Episcopal Reformed Churches

The distinction between the essence and the perfection of a church had been employed by bishop Joseph Hall who, in speaking of the foreign reformed churches, had professed 'we love and honour those sister churches as the dear spouse of Christ.' In their lack of episcopacy they 'lose nothing of the true essence of a church, though they miss something of their glory and perfection, whereof they are barred by the necessity of their condition' (X, p. 282). Bramhall too uses this distinction to assess the foreign reformed churches.

He rebuts Richard Baxter's claim that the 'new episcopal divines' unchurch those reformed churches which were accepted by the 'old episcopal divines'. 'Tell us no more,' Bramhall protests, 'of "old episcopal divines" and "new episcopal divines"; we are old episcopal divines one and all' (III, p. 523). He stoutly denies that 'either all or any considerable part of the episcopal divines in England do unchurch either all or the most part of the protestant churches . . . They unchurch none at all, but leave them to stand or fall to their own master.' While the Swedish, Danish and Bohemian churches, as well as other churches in Poland, Hungary, etc., possess 'an ordinary, uninterrupted succession of pastors, some by the name of bishops, others under the name of seniors, to this day,' the Lutheran churches not only 'assert episcopacy in their confessions,' and have superintendents in practice, but 'would have bishops name and thing if it were in their power.' This is admittedly a rosy picture of Lutheran aspirations, but even if Bramhall has not understood Lutheranism correctly, as McAdoo suggests (p. 370) it is clear enough evidence of his own views on the pastoral restraints to be observed in contending for 'bishops name and thing'. It is vital to distinguish, Bramhall concludes, between 'the true nature and essence of a church, which we do readily grant them, and the integrity or perfection of a church, which we cannot grant them without swerving from the judgement of the catholic church' (III, pp. 517f).

Bramhall suggests that the civil war in England has interrupted the progress of all the reformed churches towards mutual accord. 'Before these unhappy troubles in England, all protestants, both Lutherans and Calvinists, did give unto the English church the right hand of fellowship.' But the presbyterians were putting pressure on continental protestants to adopt a harder line towards Anglican episcopacy. 'If it were not for this disciplinarian humour which will admit no latitude in religion . . . I doubt not but the reformed churches might easily be reconciled' (III, p. 243).

As archbishop of Armagh, Bramhall adopted a conciliatory and charitable attitude towards clergy who lacked episcopal ordination. Without impugning their present orders, he gently but firmly insisted on the Anglican church's house rule of episcopal ordination. As his contemporary biographer relates:

> When he desired to see their letters of orders, some had no other but their certificates of ordination by some presbyterian classes, which, he told them, did not qualify them for any preferment in the church. Upon this, the question arose, 'Are we not ministers of the gospel?' To which his grace answered, 'that was not the question'; at least, he desired for peace sake, that might not be the question for that time. 'I dispute not,' he said, 'the value of your ordination, nor those acts you have exercised by virtue of it; what you are or might be, here when there was no law, or in other churches abroad. But we are now to consider ourselves as a national church limited by law . . . and I am desirous she may have your labours, and you such portions of her revenue as shall be allotted to you, in a legal and assured way' (c. Stranks, pp. 309ff).

Bramhall would presumably regard with equanimity the conclusion entailed in his assessment of Rome and the foreign reformed churches, namely that only the Church of England enjoys both the essence and perfection of a Christian church!

Jeremy Taylor

Jeremy Taylor (1613–1667) has always proved difficult to categorise: he is neither a straight high churchman nor a straight liberal. In his classical works of piety and devotion he rivals the nonjurors themselves in his aspirations after 'primitive holiness'. He was the protegé of archbishop Laud and at the beginning of his career was regarded as 'the highest of high churchmen' (Stranks, p. 52). He wrote in defence of a high view of episcopacy. But Taylor was also the author of the *Liberty of Prophesying* which undermined the authority of scripture and tradition and appealed to reason as the arbiter of religious controversies. It deployed the arguments earlier rehearsed by Chillingworth and Hales (Taylor had known Chillingworth at Oxford) and it was regarded as sufficiently unsound to provoke a reply from Hammond. Taylor also achieved some notoriety for his published views on original sin where he rejected the notion of inherited guilt and asserted that no one would be damned on Adam's account.

Taylor's breadth of reading, both sacred and profane, is astonishing. He seems to have drawn on Calvin for his eucharistic theology and on the adversaries of Calvinism, Episcopius and Grotius, for his doctrines of grace. Like Hales, he was impressed by Episcopius, claiming that his 'whole works are excellent and contain the whole body of orthodox religion' (c. Stranks, p. 161n). His liberalism had its limits, however, and it was said that he refused the sacrament to the dying Lord Herbert of Cherbury, the so-called father of English deism, unless he would recant (ib., p. 95).

Jeremy Taylor was not an innately radical spirit like Hales or Chillingworth, though he could be radical with established dogma when conviction demanded. Neither was he a pure high churchman like Hammond and Thorndike who reverenced authority and tradition too much to ever advocate a liberty of prophesying. It seems that Taylor belongs in a mediating position, that of liberal catholicism, as we find it in the early Charles Gore and the other contributors to *Lux Mundi* two hundred years later. Liberal catholicism embraces the catholic structure of the sacramental life, the threefold ministry and orthodoxy of doctrine in the fundamentals of the faith, that goes back behind the Reformation and the ecclesiological superstructures of medieval Christianity, to find its inspiration in the primitive church. But at the same time it adopts a principle of continual criticism of inherited dogma, and that principle is not simply the protest of the Reformation against unbiblical accretions and corruptions (as in what I have called 'reformed catholicism') but an appeal to reason and learning as competent to modify the interpretation of scripture and tradition. Let us now turn to illustrate this thesis from specific points of Taylor's teaching.

(1) Episcopacy and the Reformed Churches

Jeremy Taylor's first major work marks him as a genuine high churchman: *Of the Sacred Order and Offices of Episcopacy by Divine Institution, Apostolical Tradition and Catholic Practice* (for convenience, *Episcopacy Asserted*). He argues that episcopacy was indirectly but intentionally instituted by Christ in appointing the apostles as a distinct order from presbyters, with the power of confirmation and ordination and a mandate to appoint successors. He claims: 'Although we had not proved the immediate divine institution of episcopal power over presbyters and the whole flock, yet episcopacy is not less than an apostolical ordinance, and delivered to us by the same authority that the observation of the Lord's day is' (VII, p.74). The comparison between the episcopate and the Lord's day would of course weaken his argument in a less sabbatarian age.

Taylor goes on to raise the inevitable question: 'But then are all ordinations invalid, which are done by mere presbyters, without a bishop? What think we of the Reformed churches?' He is aware that earlier Anglican divines had taken a generous view of the non-episcopal orders of the reformed churches, but comments wryly: 'it is come to that issue that our own episcopacy is thought not necessary [he was writing in 1642, the year of the attack on the Laudian episcopate in parliament] because we did not condemn the orders of their presbytery.' It is not a question of comparing ourselves with the best reformed churches but with primitive antiquity: 'Why is not the question rather, what we think of the primitive church, than what we think of the reformed churches?' He then goes on to consider the well rehearsed matter of 'necessity': 'will not necessity excuse them who could not have orders from orthodox bishops?' But he seems to feel that this particular card has been somewhat overplayed: 'I consider that necessity may excuse a personal delinquency; but I never heard that necessity did build a church.' Further than this Taylor will not be drawn: he reiterates the Anglican position that states a principle but leaves others to apply its implications to themselves: 'But shall we condemn those few of the reformed churches whose ordinations always have been without bishops? No indeed: that must not be: they stand or fall to their own Master' (pp. 138ff).

When the *Liberty of Prophesying* appeared in 1647, readers noted a discrepancy of tone and chided Taylor for it. In the general dedication to Sir Christopher Hatton of the polemical discourses Taylor remarks: 'I have been told that my discourse of episcopacy, relying so much upon the authority of the fathers and councils, whose authority I so much diminish in my *Liberty of Prophesying*, I seem to pull down with one hand what I build with the other.' In his reply to this objection, Taylor defines his ground more carefully in line with the Anglican appeal to scripture and the consent of antiquity. Fathers and councils defend and support episcopacy, but in themselves they are not a sufficient authority. 'Episcopacy relies, not upon the authority of fathers and councils, but upon scripture, upon the institution of Christ, or the institution of the apostles, upon a universal tradition and a universal practice' (pp. xvif).

(2) *Liberty of Prophesying*

Taylor's great manifesto of Christian liberty and toleration appeared in 1647. Laud was dead, the Anglican church suppressed, the king on the run. Presbyterians and independents called the tune. Taylor was genuinely weary of conflict and mutual destruction. He found in the writings of Chillingworth and Hales a way of salvation for the nation (Chillingworth's book had been out for ten years; Hales' tract on schism had been published for five). Perhaps he believed that the rise of the independents, with their views on toleration, would provide a providential opportunity to implement these liberal principles. Taylor's dedicatory epistle to Hatton explains that his aim was to persuade 'the rough and hard-handed soldiers to have disbanded presently' and to turn their swords into ploughshares and their spears into pruning hooks. For if Christ's doctrine were followed, men would not make war on one another. Taylor was appalled by the rampant bigotry and intolerance – 'very much displeased that so many opinions and new doctrines are commenced among us, but more troubled that every man that hath an opinion thinks his own and other men's salvation is concerned in its maintenance; but most of all, that men should be persecuted and afflicted for disagreeing in such opinions' – for none of them are infallible. 'Why should I hate such persons whom God loves and who love God?' he asks. Our opinions are highly relative: we differ because of different upbringings, different teachers, reading different books, keeping different company, following different interests. Our mere opinions are not the substance of Christianity: they should not be 'obtruded as axioms', nor should disputed questions in the massive systems of divinity be made into terms of communion ('adopted into the family of faith'). Taylor urges that 'men would not call all opinions by the name of religion, and superstructures by the name of fundamental articles, and all fancies by the glorious appellative of faith.' Not every erring opinion is heretical, and even when it is, that is no excuse for beating the erring brother like a dog, convincing him with a gibbet or brainwashing him out of his convictions. Taylor foresees retribution for Christendom, perhaps at the hand of the Turk, for its 'pertinacious disputing about things unnecessary, undeterminable and unprofitable', for the mutual hatred and persecution of Christians.

All churches err. Rome denies that she errs, but the other churches reply that she errs most of all. The churches of the Reformation are no exception: the Lutherans maintain consubstantiation, the Zwinglians are sacramentaries (regarding the eucharist as a mere memorial), the Calvinists are fierce about predestination – and all of these reject episcopacy, and that the early church would have deemed heretical. Here are combined the liberal insistence on the fallibility of the pilgrim church and the characteristic reserve of the reformed Church of England towards other Reformation churches.

What is Taylor's solution (as summarised in this dedicatory epistle)? It is to seek the ground of our unity where it really belongs, in the central affirmations of the Christian faith, the essence of Christianity, that is, in the Apostles' Creed. Like Erasmus and the earlier liberal Anglicans, Falkland, Hales and Chillingworth, Taylor believes that 'there are but few doctrines of Christianity' that the Lord ordered to be preached to all the world and to be required as necessary articles of the belief of every Christian. The New Testament excommunicates no one for his opinions, except those who deny that Christ has come in the flesh and flagrant fornicators. There is an essential Christian truth which constitutes the church in being: it is comprised in the Apostles' Creed.

Beyond this 'common term', we are free to seek the truth as best we may, with 'a charitable and mutual permission' to others to disagree. But this franchise for Christian convictions has limits. Taylor will not tolerate attacks on the foundation of the faith or on fundamental articles, nor views that undermine morality and the social order. 'Permissions should be in questions speculative, indeterminable, curious and unnecessary.'

In the introduction to the treatise proper, Taylor underlines these general points:

> It is not the differing opinions that is the cause of the present ruptures, but want of charity; it is not the variety of understandings, but the disunion of wills and affections; it is not the several principles, but the several ends, that cause our miseries . . . we, by this time, are come to that pass, we think we love not God except we hate our brother, and we have not the virtue of religion, unless we persecute all religions but our own.

(3) The Terms of Communion

In the first and second chapters of his treatise ('Of Faith' and 'Of Heresy') Taylor lays down a principle that is common to the liberal Anglicans and liberal catholics (as I have called them) and is one of the most important contributions of the Anglican tradition to ecumenical theology. It is the principle that the terms of salvation and the terms of communion are identical. Whatever requirements are sufficient to make a person a Christian and save their soul, are also sufficient for membership of the church.

Taylor's premise is that the duty of faith is fulfilled in believing the articles of the Apostles' Creed. This is essential Christian belief. Following Hooker, Taylor is happy to sum it all up in the words 'Jesus Christ crucified' and 'Christ our Redeemer' (VII, pp. 443ff). This basic faith in Christ as our Saviour is sufficient for salvation. The church has no power (as the Thirty-nine Articles had insisted) to go beyond scripture in its requirement of doctrines necessary for salvation. The role of the church is to intensify and deepen our faith, not to multiply the terms of salvation: 'The church hath power to intend our faith but not to extend it; to make our belief more evident but not more large and comprehensive' (p. 452). This foundation, laid in scripture, is like its object 'the same yesterday, today and for ever' (p. 454).

Where individuals hold to this foundation, even if they go astray in their more speculative opinions, they are not to be treated as heretics. In the New Testament heresy is never predicated of sincere Christians, for it is not an error of the understanding but a fault of the will. The charge of heresy is to be employed with the utmost restraint, and only against those who deny the fundamental Christological dogma (pp. 461, 470, 494).

The terms of salvation are therefore the terms of communion. 'If the apostles admitted all to their communion that believed this creed, why should we exclude any that preserve the same entire?' 'For I demand: Can any man say or justify that the apostles did deny communion to any man that believed the Apostles' Creed and lived a good life?' (pp. 449, 494). With regard to the question of intercommunion or occasional communion that so exercised Anglicans then, as now, the conclusions are clear. We may communicate with those other churches that permit us, and particular churches 'are bound to allow communion to all those that profess the same faith upon which the apostles did give communion.' Charity is the rule to be followed.

> To make the way to heaven straiter than God made it, or to deny to communicate with those with whom God will vouchsafe to be united, or to refuse our charity to those who have the same faith, because they have not all our opinions, and believe not everything necessary which we overvalue, is impious and schismatical (VIII, p. 227ff).

(4) Reason and Authority

In the main part of his work Taylor exposes the inadequacy of the various authorities advanced within the churches to settle controversies. Tradition, councils, fathers, popes – none are infallible. Even scripture unaided is not a clear guide, except in 'things plain, necessary and fundamental', for it is often obscure and gives rise to different interpretations. Taylor has more than a dash of the sceptic in him: 'men do not learn their doctrines from scripture, but come to the understanding of scripture with preconceptions and ideas of doctrines of their own.' The scriptures are like those portraits that seem to look at you wherever you stand (VIII, pp. 1, 7). It comes to this: no individual or church is free from error on the one hand, or 'malice, interest and design' on the other; nothing is certain except the divine authority of scripture, 'in which all that is necessary is plain' and much that is not necessary to salvation is 'very obscure, intricate and involved'. Therefore we must either rest satisfied with the fundamental articles of faith grounded on the plain statements of scripture, or we must find some other guide. Reason is our best guide and judge (pp. 91ff). Needless to say, Taylor is not advocating letting our reason run riot to speculate about mysteries beyond our ken or to construct docrines *de novo*. The function of reason is to adjudicate in disputed questions of theology where scripture itself is unclear. He is substantially echoing Chillingworth, but though his tone is just as bold, Taylor operates in a context of received catholicism that preserves him from the brash rationalism of the author of *The Religion of Protestants*. It is worth pointing out, however, that both these writers were free of that secular rationalism that belongs to the Enlightenment. As Tulloch points out, 'It never occurred to them to doubt the reality of revelation, and its supremacy over the conscience and reason' (p. 404).

Towards the end of his life, as bishop of Down and Connor, Taylor had to combat the inroads that Roman Catholicism was making in Ireland as a result of the troubles of the previous twenty years in particular. If his *Liberty of Prophesying* had stressed the uncertainty of biblical interpretation in matters not necessary for salvation, his *Dissuasive from Popery* (1664) emphasised the sufficiency and certainty of the scriptures in all matters that are necessary for salvation. This principle of the sufficiency of scripture to salvation is 'the great foundation and ground of the protestant religion' (X, p. 383). All the doctrines of faith and the good life are found in the plain places of scripture 'and beside it there are and there can be no articles of faith' (p. 453). Here Jeremy Taylor the practical theologian rises above Jeremy Taylor the polemicist against Rome: 'Nothing is a necessary article of faith but that which ministers, necessarily, to the great designs of the gospel, that is, a life conformable to God, a Godlike life, and an imitation of the holy Jesus.' Beyond this, many things may be true without being required to be believed. They are 'not the Christian faith in the strict and proper sense . . . not the foundation of our religion' (pp. 457f). The Apostles' Creed constitutes 'a full and perfect digest of all the necessary and fundamental articles of Christian religion' and fundamentals are not to be extended beyond it, as Rome has done (in chapters one and two Taylor gives a detailed catalogue). With his last major work and almost, we might say, his last breath, Taylor enjoined the two precepts that he had uttered against the catastrophe of the civil war: follow simplicity; follow charity (pp. 458f).

I have called Jeremy Taylor a liberal catholic. The term is not important. He was a catholic, he was reformed, he was liberal. Though he seems to fit into this category rather than that of the high churchmen like Hammond or Thorndike, or that of the liberal protestants like Hales and Chillingworth, the boundaries are blurred. An Anglican consensus existed at this time and divisions of churchmanship were latent, not manifest. Stranks has pointed out the paradoxical aspect of Taylor's high churchmanship: in his doctrine of the eucharistic sacrifice and the Christian priesthood 'he was above most Laudians'; in his view of the real presence he was below them. His liberalism with regard to toleration, the office of reason and the doctrine of original sin was radical and courageous. In questioning aspects of the substance of the catholicism to which he was undoubtedly committed he followed the leading of his conscience and his own compassionate nature. But Taylor was neither inconsistent nor confused. In the mid-seventeenth century it was still possible to hold these things together. As Stranks puts it:

> Chillingworth and Laud both wished the Church of England to be truly catholic and at the same time to be unhampered both in thought and in learning. Suspicion and a lost cause had not yet made the high churchmen obscurantist, and the spiritual depth and fervour of the Latitudinarians had not yet been rationalised away. Chillingworth, More and their friends lived austere lives and pursued a high aim. They were engaged in the search for truth rather than in the pursuit of happiness, which seemed such a satisfying occupation to their spiritual descendants (p. 286).

The spirit of liberal catholicism in the Church of England would revive with Charles Gore and the 'Holy Party' (preceded to some extent by R. W. Church) but they would not find it easy to walk the tightrope between a more corrosive and scholarly criticism on the one hand, and a more inflexible catholic dogmatism on the other.

Edward Stillingfleet

If Stillingfleet (1635–99) had stuck to his early views he would probably have to be categorised as a liberal Anglican – a product of Cambridge Platonism and a follower of Hales and Chillingworth in his writings, an ornament of latitudinarianism. But the *Irenicum* which he published at the age of twenty-four drew down criticism for going too far towards dissenters. As Burnet cryptically says: 'The writing of his *Irenicum* was a great snare to him: for, to avoid the imputations which that brought upon him, he not only retracted the book, but he went into the humours of a high [i.e. extreme] sort of people, beyond what became him, perhaps beyond his own sense of things' (*HOT*, p. 129). If Burnet is implying that Stillingfleet was not quite true to his own convictions, that did not stop him (Burnet) from recommending him to William III in due course as 'the learnedst man of the age in all respects' (*DNB*). In his *Rational Account of the Grounds of the Protestant Religion*, published in 1665, Stillingfleet follows the consensus of liberal and high church divines on the questions of fundamentals, heresy and schism. If he had backed off from some of the more radical positions of his first brilliant work, he had retained a basically liberal standpoint. It seems appropriate to classify the mature Stillingfleet as a liberal catholic, along with Jeremy Taylor.

Stillingfleet was endowed with grace of body and mind – he was nicknamed 'the beauty of holiness'. He owed his advancement in the church to the outstanding merits of his publications. His *Irenicum*, says Burnet, 'was managed with so much learning and skill that none on either side ever undertook to answer it' (*HOT*, p. 129). He followed it in 1662 with an apologetic work on the divine authority of scripture, *Origines sacrae*, which met with general astonishment at the youth of its author. This impression was reinforced two years later when the *Rational Account* appeared, a vindication of Laud's position in his celebrated conference with Fisher. At this time, Pepys commented, the archbishop of Canterbury and the bishop of London believed Stillingfleet to be the ablest young man to preach the gospel since the apostles (*DNB*). In 1677 he became archdeacon of London and the following year dean of St. Pauls. In 1685 he published his work on British church history *Origines Britannicae*, and in 1689 William III appointed him bishop of Worcester (subsequently he was considered for the primacy). Earlier Stillingfleet had been on good terms with the nonconformists. He had not only written the *Irenicum* to reconcile them, but he had housed ejected ministers in 1662 and been a friend of Matthew Henry. Now he was put on the commission for Prayer Book revision and comprehension.

Let us turn now to the questions of 'ecumenical theology', if I may be allowed that anachronism, that Stillingfleet deals with in his *Irenicum* and his *Rational Account*. The *Irenicum* is sub-titled 'A Weapon-Salve for the Church's Wounds' and Stillingfleet offers it to an 'age wherein men talked of religion most and loved it least' (preface).

(1) *Church Government*
His purpose in this book is to show that no one form of church government – not even episcopacy – is of divine right and binding on all future ages. He presents an interesting survey (part 2, ch.8) of the judgement of various reformed divines on this question. They fall into three categories. First there are those who held that the form of church government was mutable and should be whatever was ordained by the

prince as suitable to the times. This was the view, according to Stillingfleet, of 'most divines of the Church of England since the Reformation' including Cranmer, Whitgift, Hooker, Hales and Chillingworth, as well as the first generation of German and Swiss Reformers. For these, church polity belonged to the sphere of *adiaphora*, things indifferent. Second, there are those foreign reformed divines who held equality of presbyters to be the primitive form, but did not condemn episcopacy. Third, there are those who judged episcopacy to be the primitive form of church government, yet did not regard it as necessary to the being of a church. Here Stillingfleet cites Jewel, Field, Bancroft, Andrewes, and Saravia among others.

One or two comments on this categorisation are desirable. First it is remarkable that Hooker can be grouped with Hales on this question. Hooker's position was a reformed catholicism, Hales' a liberal Anglicanism. But it would appear that Stillingfleet is correct in his assessment of Hooker (see Avis, *CTR*, pp. 115ff). But, second, it is even more remarkable that Stillingfleet is unable to cite a single Anglican divine who held that episcopacy is necessary to the church's being and without it a church is no true church.

Stillingfleet himself advocates one of the several schemes of modified episcopacy that were canvassed in the seventeenth century. He would like to see the end of grand prelates and the office of bishop becoming a more pastoral one in smaller dioceses where they would be assisted by synods of presbyters with the involvement of a consenting and enfranchised laity.

(2) *The Terms of Communion*

Stillingfleet's remedy for the separation of the churches involves a reduction of the terms of church communion to the terms of Christian discipleship. He sees the main cause of the 'distractions, confusions and divisions of the Christian world' as due to the churches' propensity to multiply conditions of communion beyond what were required by our Lord himself. The terms on which he accepted individuals for discipleship should suffice for church communion. 'What possible reason can be assigned or given why such things should not be sufficient for communion with a church which are sufficient for eternal salvation?' Again he asks: 'What charter hath Christ given the church to bind men up to more than himself hath done? or to exclude those from her society who may be admitted into heaven?' Stillingfleet's premise is the liberal one that 'the unity of the church is an unity of love and affection, and not a bare uniformity of practice or opinion' (preface).

(3) *Heresy and Schism*

The view that the unity of the church does not require unanimity of belief among its members (though we ought to seek agreement, he points out, unanimity of belief is unattainable), has two implications for Stillingfleet. First, it means that the church authorities have no need to molest Christians for their opinions, provided they pose no threat to her fellowship. Second, it also follows that there is no need for an infallible judge on matters that are not fundamental or necessary to salvation (pp. 106f). If here Stillingfleet is echoing Chillingworth, in what he has to say about schism he echoes – indeed quotes – Hales. Christians should remain in their church until it becomes sin to do so. When does it become sin to remain? When are we compelled to participate, against our conscience, in fundamental errors that are being implemented in practice. Errors of doctrine are not in themselves adequate cause of separation: they must be errors of fundamental doctrines. But errors of fundamental doctrines are not a sufficient ground either: they must be put into practice in such a way that we cannot avoid becoming implicated ourselves, or the church requires 'the owning of them' as a necessary condition of communion. These strict conditions applied to the Reformation but they do not justify departures from the Church of England now. Separation from Rome was necessary because of 'the sin of communicating with that church in her idolatry and superstition, and the impossibility of communicating with her and not partaking of her sins, because she required a profession of her errors and the practice of her idolatry as the necessary condition of her communion' (pp. 112–117). In all this Stillingfleet allows himself to be guided by Chillingworth and Hales, calling the latter 'as learned and judicious a divine as most our nation hath bred' (p. 120).

(4) The Fundamentals of the Faith

In *A Rational Account of the Grounds of the Protestant Religion*, Stillingfleet returned to the question of what was necessary to church communion and whether there was any valid distinction between this and what was necessary for salvation. His work is intended as a vindication of Laud in his conference with the Jesuit Fisher. Stillingfleet takes his cue from the claim of the council of Trent that the definitions of the church are to be held as necessary to salvation on the same basis as the creed and that explicit belief of these definitions is necessary for communion with the Roman Catholic church (p. 49).

Stillingfleet's position is set out in three points. First, nothing is necessary to salvation beyond what is necessary to the being of the catholic church. Whatever constitutes the church is sufficient for salvation. If the church then wants to promulgate domestic articles of agreement to preserve peace and unity, these will be 'inferior truths' and acceptance of them is not necessary for salvation. This is precisely the status of the Thirty-nine Articles, for, following the earlier Anglican divines, Stillingfleet insists that the Church of England makes no new articles of faith. Second, nothing may be required by the church as an article of faith, except what has been revealed as incumbent upon all irrespective of circumstances and the condition and capacities of individuals. Third, any such articles of faith must meet the test of the Vincentian canon, that is, they must have been believed by the catholic church of all ages. In practice this means that they must be included in the creeds, ordained by Christ and the apostles, and their denial universally condemned as heresy (pp. 54ff). Needless to say, this reduces the fundamentals to very manageable proportions!

Stillingfleet lays down this principle for the reconciliation of the churches: 'The union of the catholic church' depends upon it agreeing to make 'the foundation of its being to be the grounds of its communion' (p. 53). It is a principle that merits reflection in contemporary ecumenical theology, and will contribute to our conclusions in the final chapter.

William Wake

In the early eighteenth century the bold, courageous and charitable mind of archbishop William Wake (1657–1737) sought to heal some of the wounds of Christendom by working for unity with both the reformed and Gallican churches. His broad vision looked both ways – not to Rome itself, but to the Roman Catholic Gallican church in France and to the Lutheran and Reformed churches of the continent. Wake's churchmanship was orthodox high church Anglican combined with great breadth of charity and liberality, a Christian sympathy that embraced Swiss Calvinists and Gallican reformists. Norman Sykes comments that 'Wake stood in the authentic tradition of Caroline high churchmanship' (*Wake*, I, p. 32). For example, he commends sacramental confession as 'a practice which our church very much recommends, and which whosoever shall wisely and piously perform, will find neither popery nor any heresy in it.' He wishes penance was more fully used in the Church of England (N. Sykes, ib., p. 13; Wake, *Exposition*, pp. 40f). He rejects extreme Lutheran and extreme Calvinist tenets, namely salvation by faith alone without works and double predestination (N. Sykes, ib., p. 51). Like the high churchman John Sharp (and unlike the latitudinarian John Tillotson) he refused preferment to offices vacated by the non-jurors: turning down the deanship of Worcester and the bishoprics of Bath and Wells and of Norwich, Wake was preferred from dean of Exeter to bishop of Lincoln (1705) and thence to Canterbury (1716). Wake combined a high church insistence on episcopacy as of apostolic institution and the only basis for the union of protestants with a refusal to unchurch non-episcopal ministries for lack of it. For him, as for Tillotson (who coined the phrase) charity was above rubrics. Indeed Wake clashed violently with the champion of resurgent and extreme high church views, Francis Atterbury, over the powers of convocation. In his *The State of the Church and*

Clergy of England (1703) Wake asserted the subservience of convocation to the monarch and parliament. He was defending a view of the unity or perhaps interdependence of church and commonwealth that was rapidly becoming an anachronism (see N. Sykes, *Wake*, I, ch.2; Bennett, *Tory Crisis*, pp.48ff). It is Wake's unfailing liberality and his willingness to tolerate differences over non-fundamentals that sets him in the liberal catholic tradition, along with Taylor, Stillingfleet and Burnet.

Wake's liberality was not just temperamental: as an undergraduate he had been profoundly influenced by Descartes' treatise on method. The effect was, as Wake recalled, 'that I was thereby determined, though not to doubt of everything, yet to examine all things without prejudice or partiality; to lay aside all affection, as much as possible, for my own former notions; to give all arguments their proper weight; and particularly in matters of religion, to incline to nothing but the truth and to embrace it on what side soever I should find it to lie' (N. Sykes, *Wake*, I, p. 10).

At the age of twenty-five Wake went as chaplain to England's envoy extraordinary at the court of Louis XIV. There he attended Jesuit and Huguenot services and sermons impartially. He communicated the French protestants but did not receive communion from them. His friendship with Gallicans, Lutherans and Calvinists at this time profoundly influenced the ecumenical direction of his thinking:

> The consideration of the learning, the good lives and friendly conversation of all these moved me very seriously to consider the differences of our several sentiments in matters of religion; and made me almost ready, with Descartes, to suspect, or rather suspend, my judgement of all my principles, and with the utmost impartiality begin to examine anew what were the grounds upon which I received them, and how far I ought to continue in them (N. Sykes, *Wake*, I, p. 252).

(1) *Rome and Anglican Doctrine*

At the age of twenty-nine Wake published (anonymously) his *Exposition of the Doctrine of the Church of England* (which was followed by a defence and a second defence), in which he boldly challenged the illustrious bishop Bossuet, accusing him of concealing the unacceptable face of Roman Catholicism in his recent account of catholic doctrine. Here Wake announced the direction of his life's work for the unity of the church. He will not regard Bossuet as an enemy, but with all respect for his learning and character, he will set out objectively what our differences are and why we cannot subscribe, in the Church of England, to his system. Wake's intention is that Anglicans and Gallicans might live together in harmony as Christians and brothers:

> We do confess the Church of Rome to be a part of the true church, tho [sic] indeed we think one of the worst . . . we do with all our hearts desire a union with her; and in effect do show it as far as we are able, by retaining whatever we can of the same doctrines and practices with her (*Exposition*, pp.xviii, xxxiv).

To Bossuet's protest that the Church of England regards Rome unfavourably on account of transubstantiation, while welcoming the Lutherans who hold the same 'error' of a corporeal presence in the sacrament, Wake replies that it is not the mere doctrine of transubstantiation that is the cause of our separation from Rome, while not from the Lutherans, but the superstructure of adoration, sacrifice, satisfaction, etc, that Rome erects upon it (*Exposition*, p.71). Transubstantiation is not in itself a cause for separation, provided that 'the belief of it had not been pressed upon us neither as a necessary article of communion, nor any anathema pronounced against us for not receiving it' (c. N. Sykes, *Wake*, I, p.36). Wake will point out later in his career that the Lutherans are welcome to communion in the Church of England, consubstantiation being no barrier, 'so long as their outward actions are the same as our own and they give no offence to any with their opinions' (N. Sykes, ib., p.292). Let Rome reform these abuses and we will receive them with the same charity as we do the Lutherans. 'Let them at least do what the Lutherans have done; let them embrace our communion' (*Exposition*, p.72).

In this early work Wake set out a view of the primacy of the pope that he would later defend in discussions with the Gallicans. He admits a primacy of St. Peter among the apostles, but fails to see how that justifies the present pretensions to exorbitant papal power. 'Yet when other differences shall be agreed, and the true bounds set to his pretences, we shall be content to yield him' whatever authority the primitive councils and early fathers acknowledged (*Exposition*, p.81). In his correspondence with the Gallicans, Wake made it clear that he was prepared to allow that pre-eminence granted by general councils to Rome as the see of the imperial city (though it was not clear to him how that could survive the destruction of the empire), nor would he refuse a simple primacy of honour: 'we may all agree . . . to allow him a primacy of order in the episcopal college' (N. Sykes, *Wake*, I, pp.271, 285).

Preaching before William and Mary at Hampton Court (in 1689, aged thirty-two) Wake distinguished between those errors on account of which the Church of England had separated from Rome and the points of difference which arose between protestant churches who were in agreement in fundamentals. 'The former are in matters of the greatest consequence, such as tend directly to overthrow the integrity of the faith and the purity of our worship; and therefore such as are in their own nature destructive of the very essentials of Christianity' ('An Exhortation', p.190). Appealing for charity between Roman Catholics and protestants, Wake warned that there were serious obstacles in the way of intercommunion. 'We must not destroy the principles of Christianity out of a zeal to enlarge the communion of Christians.' Prayer to the Virgin Mary and the saints, veneration of images and adoration of the Host, and communion in one kind only were too high a price to pay. 'When all is done, the truths of Christianity must not be sacrificed to the peace of Christians' (ib., pp.194f).

(2) *Anglican – Gallican Dialogue*

From 1717 to 1720 Wake was engaged in exploring a scheme of unity with the Gallican Church which he had come to know early in his career as chaplain to the British ambassador in Paris. Wake's correspondents were two theologians of the Sorbonne, Du Pin and Girardin, who were particularly disaffected from Rome by the recent suppression of the Jansenist movement in the bull *Unigenitus* of 1713. They had the somewhat uncertain support of the cardinal archbishop of Paris. Wake's aim was to detach the Gallican church from the jurisdiction of the papacy in order to facilitate the creation of 'a true catholic unity and communion with one another' on the basis of fundamental articles (Wake believed that the creeds of the first four general councils of the undivided church would substantially comprise these articles), while agreeing to differ in non-essentials. 'To frame a common confession of faith, or liturgy, or discipline for both churches is a project never to be accomplished.' But mutual recognition as sound parts of the church catholic with inter-communion – this Wake believed was within the realms of possibility (N. Sykes, *Wake*, I, p.260; c.f. ib., *OPNP*, pp.197f). Alas, both here and in his project for protestant unity Wake was far too optimistic.

What is particularly impressive in Wake's foreign correspondence is his self-confident Anglicanism. He treats the other parties as equals, without condescending to the protestants and without being intimidated by Rome. Unlike we modern Anglicans he is not for ever looking over his shoulder. He never doubts that 'the Church of England, as a national church, has all the power within herself over her own members, which is necessary to enable her to settle her doctrines, government and discipline' (N. Sykes, *Wake*, I, p.260). With his liberal, almost latitudinarian view of the sufficiency of a modicum of fundamental articles, Wake was irritated by Du Pin's detailed analysis of the Thirty-nine Articles and requests for doctrinal reassurances. Wake wrote to the English chaplain in Paris, who had the delicate task of mediating his outspoken and informal comments to the doctors of the Sorbonne:

> If he [du Pin] thinks we are to take their direction what to retain and what to give up, he is utterly mistaken. I am a friend to peace, but more to truth; and they may depend upon it, I shall always account our church to stand upon an equal foot with theirs; and that we are no more to receive laws from them than we desire to impose any upon them. In short, the Church of England is free, is orthodox; she has a plenary authority within herself. She has no need to recur to other churches to direct her what to believe or what to do; nor will we otherwise than in a brotherly way and

with full equality of right and power, ever consent to have any treaty with that of France. And therefore if they mean to deal with us, they must lay down this for the foundation, that we are to deal with one another upon equal terms.

It is not because the Church of England lacks anything in herself that he is making these overtures. It is for the benefit of the Gallican as well as the Anglican church – 'or rather neither for theirs nor ours, but in order to the promotion of a catholic communion as far as is possible among all the true churches of Christ' (c. ib., pp. 266f; c.f. ib., *OPNP*, pp. 205f).

(3) *Protestant Unity*

Wake had announced his ambitions for the unity of protestants as early as 1689 in a sermon before William and Mary entitled 'An Exhortation to Mutual Charity and Union among Protestants', in which he pleaded for charity towards catholics and unity of worship between protestants, to be attained by the Church of England making concessions to the scruples of weaker consciences ('An Exhortation', pp. 196ff). When, as archbishop of Canterbury, he had the authority to translate his vision into action, Wake pursued a scheme for union between the Church of England and the foreign protestants based on the existing agreement on all fundamental matters of faith, on the one hand, and a *de facto* recognition of the validity of protestant non-episcopal ministries, upon which episcopal orders, derived from the Church of England, would be superimposed, on the other. Agreement in doctrine was not the obstacle, to a large extent it already existed: the obstacle lay in ecclesiastical polity.

Wake took steps to overcome this obstacle. Following the illustrious example of their monarch George I, a Hanoverian Lutheran, Lutherans (and Reformed) already communicated in the Church of England. In addition to this *de facto* limited intercommunion, Wake took the bold step of formally permitting visiting Zurichers to communicate at Anglican altars and Anglicans to reciprocate. Wake was conscious of standing in the mediating tradition of Hooker and Andrewes in his view of episcopacy. In his correspondence with Le Courayer, a French Roman Catholic priest inclined to reformed views, Wake definitively established the validity of Anglican orders, apparently convincing his correspondent, who in 1721 completed a vindication of those orders, as a result of which he was excommunicated and fled to England. Though of divine institution and the only conceivable basis of eventual unity between Anglicans and protestants, episcopacy, for Wake, was not the *sine qua non* of a true church. When confronted by the allegedly embarrassing fact that Elizabeth's archbishop Grindal had licensed John Morrison, who had presbyterian orders from the Scottish synod of Lothian, to preach and administer the sacraments in the province of Canterbury in 1582 (apparently Morrison was one of many such cases), Wake's response reveals his moderate, balanced and discriminating position. He could not approve but dared not condemn.

> I bless God that I was born and have been bred in an episcopal church; which I am convinced has been the government established in the Christian church from the very time of the apostles. But I should be unwilling to affirm that where the ministry is not episcopal there is no church nor any true administration of the sacraments.

By the Act of Uniformity of 1662, the Church of England had tightened its own house rules: no one could now be licensed to the ministry who had not received episcopal ordination, but in itself that implied no judgement on the validity of the ministries of non-episcopal churches (N. Sykes, *OPNP*, pp. 94ff).

> Though our constitution suffers no man to minister the sacrament of the Lord's Supper who is not in priest's orders, nor otherwise to officiate in the church who has not the order of deacon by episcopal ordination; yet no one when he receives these orders renounces his own which he had before taken, either in the foreign church abroad, or even by our own dissenting ministrations at home (N. Sykes, *Wake*, II, p. 19).

A letter of 1716 to Jean le Clerc of Amsterdam might be cited as typical of the line Wake took in his extensive and energetic correspondence with the leaders of the reformed churches abroad:

> I freely embrace the Reformed churches, though differing from our Church of England in some things. I could wish indeed that the episcopal polity, duly moderated and divorced from all unjust domination, as it stands amongst us and (if I know anything of these matters), as it has been received in the church since the times of the apostles, had been retained by all of them; nor do I despair that posterity will see it in due time restored, even if I do not see it myself. Meantime, far be it from me to be so iron-hearted that because of a defect of this kind (if I may be allowed so to call it without offence), I should hold that any of them ought to be cut off from our communion; or that (with some vehement writers amongst us) I should declare them to have no true and valid sacraments and therefore to be scarcely Christians.

Wake's aim is the ultimate full organic unity of the protestant churches, grounded in the widening of existing arrangements for intercommunion, and achieved through ever closer doctrinal agreement and the sharing of the historic episcopate.

> At all costs I desire to procure a closer union amongst all the reformed. If this could be secured in ecclesiastical government and in the public services of the churches, it would lead, unless I am greatly mistaken, in a short time to the fostering of an union of minds amongst them and would pave the way to the establishment of a full agreement in all doctrines of major importance (c. N. Sykes, *Wake*, II, pp. 3f).

It is interesting that Wake sees doctrinal accord as the fruit rather than the precondition of intercommunion.

In his monumental biography of Wake, Norman Sykes sums up Wake's position on this matter:

> On the one hand he defended episcopacy as the form of government universal in the church from the apostolic age to the Reformation, and as the indispensable foundation therefore of organic union amongst the protestant churches; and to this end he was ready to offer such practical help as the Church of England could proffer towards the restoration of episcopacy in the continental churches. On the other hand he recognised the validity of the presbyterian ministry and sacraments of the foreign Reformed churches; and as an interim measure authorised inter-communion in regard to members of the Lutheran and Reformed churches sojourning in England and Anglican churchmen abroad.

In so doing, Norman Sykes concludes, Wake was 'convinced of his adherence to the main stream of Anglican tradition, as moulded by leading representatives of Caroline high-churchmanship; though going further in some respects and prepared to make greater temporary concessions in face of the urgent necessity of unity amongst protestants' (*Wake*, II, p. 88).

(4) Agreement in Fundamentals the Key to Unity

As Wake looked back in 1719, in a letter to Turretini of Geneva, on that formative sense of spiritual affinity with Gallicans, Danish Lutherans and Dutch Calvinists that he had enjoyed in Paris as a young man, he commented: 'It was no difficult matter upon this foundation, as I went on, to come at last to this opinion: that the peace of Christendom can no way be restored but by separating the fundamental articles of our religion (in which almost all churches do agree) from others,' and to persuade churchmen to see that where the former were secured 'communion should not be broken for the rest, but a prudent liberty be granted to Christians to enjoy their own opinions, without censuring or condemning any that differ from them' (c. N. Sykes, *Wake*, I, p. 253). Wake believed that agreement on fundamentals already existed between protestants. In reply to Bossuet's *Histoire des Variations des Églises Protestantes*, Wake claimed that protestants, 'amid all our other divisions, are on all sides agreed in whatsoever is fundamental in the faith or necessary to be believed and professed by us in order to our salvation' ('An Exhortation', p. 186).

With Roman Catholics, there was plenty of work still to be done to establish agreement on the fundamentals which would enable both sides to recognise each other 'as truly catholic brethren'. As Wake wrote in connection with his Gallican correspondence:

> In treating of articles of evangelical doctrine, fundamentals should be carefully distinguished from non-essentials, and matters of greater moment from things of lesser weight . . . It is indeed a work of greater difficulty, not to say danger, to distinguish the essential articles of religion from the rest, in

> such wise that nothing in them is either superfluous or lacking; that nothing essential to salvation is omitted, nor anything non-essential included in the number of essentials (c. N. Sykes, *Wake*, I, p. 262).

Elsewhere Wake defined more clearly the distinction between fundamentals and secondary points that should not be allowed to become the cause of separation. 'When I say that Christians may, without any danger to themselves, or disparagement to the truth of their religion, differ with one another,' he stated in his sermon of 1689 on charity and union between protestants, 'I mean only . . . in lesser matters, such as do not concern the fundamentals of faith, nor destroy the worship of God, nor are otherwise so clearly revealed, but that wise and good men, after all their enquiries, may still continue to differ in their opinions concerning them' ('An Exhortation', p. 189).

For the Church of England, the fundamental articles were to be found clearly revealed in the scriptures and attested by the consent of antiquity. The latter was a point well worth stressing to Wake's Roman Catholic correspondents: 'You will see how much we on our part ascribe to ecclesiastical antiquity and how far removed we are from those to whom the innovations of the last two centuries count for more than the venerable authority of the preceding fifteen hundred years. Certainly I would make bold to claim that, whatever other churches firmly adhere to the Vincentian rule, the Church of England is pre-eminent amongst them; nor will ever repudiate anything which has been believed everywhere, always and by everyone' (c. N. Sykes, *Wake*, I, p. 282).

But the Church of England is not only an example of faithfulness to the teaching of the primitive church, but also of moderation and liberty of subscription in non-essentials. As Wake wrote to the Swiss cantons who were bitterly divided over the question of doctrinal uniformity:

> The moderation of the Church of England has been very exemplary in this respect; and we have felt the good effect of it in that peace we enjoy among our ministers, notwithstanding their known difference of opinion in many considerable articles of Christian doctrine. The Thirty-nine Articles have been subscribed more than once in our public synods, indifferently, by bishops and clergy of different persuasions. We have left every one to interpret them in his own sense; and they are indeed so generally framed that they may, without any equivocation, have more senses than one fairly put upon them (c. N. Sykes, *Wake*, II, pp. 32f).

To Jean le Clerc, Wake asserted that 'liberty of prophesying (*libertatem prophetandi*), provided it be pious and sober, joined to charity and courtesy, nor contrary to the analogy of that faith once for all delivered to the saints, I consider not to be denounced but rather to be approved' (c. ib., p. 262). Wake's churchmanship was indeed a truly liberal catholicism.

9

Origins of the
High Church Tradition

William Laud

Archbishop Laud's draconian reputation as an administrator and disciplinarian belies the balance and moderation of his theological writings. Laud
(1573–1645) regards the Church of England as the church of the *via
media,* and as such the 'nearest of any church now in being to the
primitive church' (II, p. 245). She finds herself in the early seventeenth
century poised precariously between two extremes, Rome and the
puritans. 'She professes the ancient catholic faith, and yet the Romanist
condemns her of novelty in doctrine; she practices church government as
it hath been in use in all ages and all places where the church of Christ
hath taken any rooting, both in and ever since the apostles' times, and yet
the separatist condemns her for antichristianism in her discipline.' Laud
appeals to Charles I to save her from being 'ground to powder' between
these two millstones (p. xiii).

(1) *Rome and Reformation*

At his trial Laud had to protest that he was no papist: 'Never any bishop
was so hated by the Church of Rome as I am. I have stayed more going to
Rome, and reduced more that were already gone, than I believe any
bishop or divine in the kingdom hath done.' However, he had defended
the Roman Catholic Church as a true church within which salvation was
to be obtained. In terminology this was going further than the Reformers
themselves, but then their assessment of the status of Rome had been a
contorted one, and their attitude ambivalent. Essentially Laud was saying
nothing new, and claimed that 'so much very learned protestants' had
acknowledged as much. 'For that church which receives the scriptures as
a rule of faith, though but as a partial and imperfect rule, and both the
sacraments as instrumental causes and seals of grace, though they add
more and misuse these, yet cannot but be a true church in essence'

(pp. 143f). Rome herself was to blame for the division of the church at the Reformation, for she refused to reform errors and abuses. In this the Church of England stands with all protestants (pp. 150f, 156). But if Rome were ever to reform itself according to the pattern of the primitive church, he would echo the words of Irenaeus 'that it will then be necessary for every church, and for the faithful everywhere, to agree with it' (p. 205).

On the question of the right and duty of a particular church to reform itself, Laud and the Caroline divines speak with one voice (pp. 166ff). But a reformed church is still one and the same church.

> There is no greater absurdity stirring this day in Christendom than that the reformation of an old corrupted church, will we, nill we, must be taken for the building of a new. And were this not so, we should never be troubled with that idle and impertinent question of theirs: 'Where was your church before Luther?' for it was just there, where theirs is now. One and the same church still, no doubt of that; one in substance, but not one in condition of state and purity; their part of the same church remaining in corruption, and our part of the same church under reformation (p. xiii).

But Laud is not prepared to endorse all that the Reformers did: in a way that is typically Anglican, he keeps a critical detachment. The Reformers were not above criticism: 'some among them were peevish and some ignorantly zealous' (II, p. 151). Reformation is so great and delicate a work, he says, that it was inevitable that the Reformers should either go too far or fall short in secondary matters, 'which in regard of the far greater benefit coming by the reformation itself, may well be passed over and borne withal.' But if there have been wilful and gross errors, not so much in opinion as in action, where the reform of superstition has passed over into sacrilege, 'that is the crime of the reformers, not of the reformation; and they are long since gone to God to answer it, to whom I now leave them' (pp. 173f).

(2) Episcopacy and the Reformed Churches

The Laud who had argued in his BD dissertation of 1604 that there could be no true church without bishops (*DNB*) was certain to be dissatisfied with Joseph Hall's *Episcopacy by Divine Right Asserted*. Hall had sent him the first draft for comment and Laud wrote to the author, 'Episcopacy is not so to be asserted to apostolical institution, as to bar it from looking higher, and from fetching it materially and originally, in the ground and intention of it, from Christ himself' (VI, p. 573).

With regard to the ministries of the non-episcopal reformed churches, while Laud – unlike some of his predecessors – would not have countenanced ministers operating within the Church of England without episcopal ordination, and was not as generous as Hooker was in his view of the Scottish presbyterians who could have the episcopate if they wanted it, Laud is satisfied, as were the Carolines generally, of the validity of Lutheran orders, since in their superintendents they have preserved the thing if not the name of episcopacy. 'Luther, since he would change the name, yet did very wisely that he would leave the thing, and make choice of such a name as was not altogether unknown to the ancient church' (III, p. 386; N. Sykes, *OPNP*, p. 78; c.f. Hooker III, xi, 16).

(3) *Scripture and Tradition*

Laud's high churchmanship is seen in his view of the authority of councils, particularly when we compare his view with that of a more 'protestant' theologian such as Richard Field. Whereas Field denies that ecumenical councils enjoy special divine assistance to direct them to the truth, Laud holds that they cannot err in matters of salvation. This is an apparent contradiction of article 21 of the Thirty-nine Articles which insist that councils 'may err, and sometimes have erred, even in things pertaining unto God' (the Latin text of 1563 says *ad normam pietatis pertinent*, pertaining to the rule of faith). But Laud's is a highly qualified and sophisticated position. General councils are preserved from error in matters of salvation only when they are fully representative of the whole church (thus Trent and indeed all councils since the separation of East and West are excluded), and when they submit themselves to the guidance of the Holy Spirit 'in the scripture' (this excludes tradition as a separate source of doctrine). Laud's view of councils is in fact an aspect of the doctrine, held by the Reformers as much as the later high churchmen, of the indefectibility of the church – it cannot lose the truth of salvation (*MC*, pp. 155f; Avis, *Ecum. Theol.*, pp. 101f).

The fundamentals are those truths accepted by all Christians and they remain unchanged, comprising the articles of the creed and the belief in scripture as the word of God. Deductions from fundamentals are not themselves fundamental. The Thirty-nine Articles are not a statement of fundamentals (II, pp. 32ff, 49ff, 60).

Laud's view of the relation of scripture to the teaching office of the church is that 'the scripture, where it is plain, should guide the church; and the church, where there is doubt or difficulty, should expound the scripture; yet so as neither the scripture should be forced, nor the church so bound up as that upon just and further evidence she may not revise that which in any case hath slipped by her' (II, p. xv). This is clearly not the same as the rule so beloved by the Tractarians 'The church to teach, the Bible to prove.' And Laud's view is interesting in that it clearly rules out the accumulation of unreformable tradition. He emphasises that the scriptures contain all that is necessary for salvation (pp. 61f). Laud's position on this matter is underlined in his personal confession of faith:

I have lived, and shall, God willing, die, in the faith of Christ as it was professed in the ancient primitive church, and as it is professed in the present Church of England. And for the rule that governs me herein, if I cannot be confident in my soul upon the scripture, and upon the primitive church expounding it, I will be confident upon no other.

(4) *Historical Postscript*

The case of Captain Henry Bell, painstakingly pieced together by Gordon Rupp, is significant not only for the way in which it suddenly illuminates, out of the obscurity of history, a single link in the chain of witnesses to the living power of the faith of Luther, as for what it tells us of archbishop Laud's own attitude to the Reformer. Captain Henry Bell, disgraced and imprisoned, consoled himself with translating Luther's *Table Talk*. In 1650 he published a prospectus recounting his own story and hailing Luther as stirred up by God to expose the corruptions of popery, to preach Christ and to set forth the *simplicitie* of the gospel. Bell had earlier conveyed his manuscript from his prison cell to the archbishop by the hand of Laud's chaplain Dr. Bray.

> After hee had kept it in his custodie two months, and had daily read therein, hee sent the said Dr. unto mee, to tell mee that I had performed *a work worthie of eternal memorie*. And that he had *never read a more excellent divine work* . . . the *more hee did read therein, the more desire hee had to go on therewith.*

It seems naïve of Bell to have appealed to the name of Laud in his prospectus, five years after Laud's execution. It is equally remarkable that the House of Commons was prepared to sponsor publication in 1652 of a work that had Laud's tacit imprimatur. But by this time Bell was almost certainly dead.

The resemblance between Melanchthonian Lutheranism and certain aspects of Laudian theology has been pointed out by Basil Hall. The Laudians have a pronounced affinity to Melanchthon's "synergism", his eirenic attitude to Roman Catholic liturgical ceremonial and things indifferent (*adiaphora*), his emphasis on patristic study and appeal to the *consensus patrum*. Certainly the seventeenth century divines took Melanchthon as a paradigm of the moderate, conciliatory approach to which they aspired themselves. 'Who is there,' asks Forbes the first bishop of Edinburgh, 'who is not acquainted with the singular learning and moderation of Philip Melanchthon?' (p. 305). 'Nevertheless,' Basil Hall adds, 'these matters are not sufficient to suggest the direct though delayed influence of Melanchthon: the Laudians could well arrive at similar conclusions by an independent though parallel route.' In any case, he concludes, 'by Laud's time Lutheranism was a dead issue' – though, if Bell's testimony is to be trusted this cannot be taken to mean that Laud himself was indifferent to the spell of Martin Luther (see also Wallace).

Henry Hammond
Though he did not live to see it (dying on the day that parliament was convened to welcome back king Charles II), Henry Hammond (1605–1660) is acknowledged as the principal architect of the reconstruction of the Anglican church. 'There is no doubt that to his "high church" contemporaries as well as to the nineteenth-century Tractarians, Hammond was regarded as the embodiment of Anglicanism in the seventeenth century' (Packer, p. 15). This being so, it is significant that Hammond was a member of Falkland's theological houseparty at Great Tew. Though inflexible in his high church principles Hammond's greatness and goodness were acknowledged on all sides, including those who did not share his views. Richard Baxter, while deploring Hammond's rigid conception of episcopacy, thought that things might have turned out better for the nation after 1660 if Hammond had lived to guide affairs. The liberal Gilbert Burnet echoed these sentiments. Hammond's death, he wrote, before he could take up the bishopric of Worcester for which Charles II intended him, was 'an unspeakable loss to the church: for, as he was a man of great learning and of most eminent merit, he having been the person that during the bad times had maintained the cause of the church in a very singular manner, so he was a very moderate man in his temper, though with a high principle, and probably he would have fallen into healing counsels' (*HOT*, p. 121). Isaac Barrow, who had been an early beneficiary of Hammond's generosity, composed an epitaph which hailed him as the 'chief of the theologians of his day'.

Hammond progressed from Eton to Magdalen College Oxford. As a young graduate his thinking was permanently marked by reading an edition of the epistles of Ignatius, our earliest evidence of the monarchical episcopate in the primitive church. The fact that the Reformed scholar Vedelius, publishing at Geneva (1623), could not deny seven of the fifteen claimed epistles to be genuine made a permanent impression on Hammond and was to bear fruit years later in his four Latin dissertations (1651) in defence of primitive episcopacy and the vindication in English which followed (1654). Though Hammond was an accomplished New Testament scholar, as his *Paraphrase and Annotations on the New Testament* (1653) shows, his argument that *episcopoi* and *presbuteroi* in the New Testament always mean bishops was not found convincing.

For ten years Hammond was the incumbent of Penshurst, Sussex and in 1643 he was made archdeacon of Chichester. In the same year, however, he was ejected from his living and retired to his college. In 1645, the year of Laud's execution, Hammond was appointed to a canonry at Christ Church by Charles I, but lost this three years later and withdrew into private life. During the Civil War he attended Charles and during the Commonwealth he remained in England: by writing, correspondence and organisation defending the Anglican faith and preparing for its restoration. He would make no concessions to conformity and disputed the judgement of Robert Sanderson, the deprived Regius professor of divinity at Oxford, an eminent moral theologian and casuist who was willing to paraphrase the liturgy, that some modification of the authorised liturgy was permissible in order to have some form of Anglican service. It is significant, however, that though they disagreed strongly on this question of conscience and also held different views on the doctrines of grace (Sanderson being more sympathetic to a Calvinist position), they remained friends and companions – Izaac Walton tells of Hammond's visits to Sanderson in Lincolnshire during the troubles. When the Anglican exiles returned after Hammond's death, moderation and charity towards those who had almost succeeded in rooting out the Anglican church from the life of England were not uppermost in their minds. And as Packer remarks, 'The sad conclusion to Hammond's contribution was, that the new Anglicanism was founded on the basis of Laudian doctrine without the moderating spirit of Henry Hammond to guide it' (p. 199).

Hammond's writing during these years included several short treatises that are still of value today, notable *Of Schism*, *Of Heresy* and *Of Fundamentals*. Like all the Caroline divines, Hammond was fighting on two fronts: first, against Rome, in defence of the English Reformation, and to steady Anglicans tempted by impressive Roman claims of catholicity and infallibility in times of uncertainty and confusion; second, against puritans and presbyterians, in defence of episcopacy and the liturgy. He justifies separation only where errors are proposed as a condition of communion (II, pp. 208f). Otherwise 'there is no crime as grave as schism' (citing Augustine: ib., p. 198). This principle justifies the Reformation but not the separation of presbyterians and independents from the Church of England. But was not the English Reformation a rebellion against due subordination in the catholic church, where pastoral rule deserves to meet with filial obedience? Hammond's reply is that of the English Reformers, civil lawyers and parliamentarians in the 1530s: the bishop of Rome has no jurisdiction in this realm of England. The English church's Reformation could not have been schismatical for the simple reason that 'all was done by those to whom, and to whom only, the rightful power legally pertained, viz., the king and bishops of this nation' (ib., p. 277).

But in company with Bramhall and others, Hammond feels no compulsion to defend every act of the English Reformation. Henry VIII cannot be cleared of the charge of 'acts of sacrilege and like impieties' – which 'are by us as freely charged upon the actors as by any Romanist they can be; but yet sacrilege is no more schism than it is adultery, and the church on which one sin hath been committed, cannot be from thence proved to be guilty of every other' (ib., p. 277f). It was and remains the intention and aspiration of the English Reformation 'to preserve the unity of the apostolical faith and primitive practices as entire as we would have done Christ's body or garment' (ib., p. 282).

Hammond deplores the breaking of communion within Christendom. It can only be justified where erroneous doctrines are made terms of communion. The Church of England herself sets up no such barriers:

> As we exclude no Christian from our communion that will either filially or fraternally embrace it with us, being ready to admit any to our assemblies that acknowledge the foundation laid by Christ and his apostles, so we as earnestly desire to be admitted to the like freedom of external communion with all the members of all other Christian churches

even Christians of the Roman obedience (ib., p. 282).

That foundation, to which Hammond refers, is explored in his treatise *Of Fundamentals*. As a high churchman he naturally has a maximising rather than a minimising interpretation of the fundamentals of Christianity, and in part what interests him about the concept of fundamentals is that it forms the basis for the 'superstructure' of Christian life and devotion – 'all the offices of piety'. But Hammond's treatment of this matter is markedly Hookerian in that he insists that Jesus Christ, crucified and risen, is 'the foundation of the foundation' and that the foundation itself consists of the church's baptismal faith with its trinitarian formula (ib., pp. 116ff, 82, 88).

Together with Laud, Hammond holds the highest view of general councils to be found within mainstream Anglicanism in this period. But Hammond acknowledges his view to be a pious opinion, neither grounded in revelation nor maintained by the catholic church.

> Though I make it no matter of faith, because delivered neither by scripture nor apostolic tradition, yet I shall number it among the *pie credibilia* that no general council, truly such, 1. duly assembled, 2. freely celebrated, and 3. universally received, either hath erred or ever shall err in matters of faith (II, p. 350).

The 'inerrability' of general councils thus constituted, is 'nowhere either affirmed by the word of God written or unwritten, or regularly deduced from thence' and is not therefore part of the catholic faith. But it may yet be believed on grounds of reason as a probability, for God would surely not permit councils to mislead the faithful over the essentials of the faith (pp. 271f, 275).

When Hammond defends episcopacy, he reminds the puritans that the bishops were the authors of the English Reformation: 'that ministry of ours, the very same that planted the protestant religion among us' and 'watered it with their blood' (c. Packer, p. 23). Hammond's first publication in defence of episcopacy was provoked by the bill abolishing the hierarchy which was passed in both houses of parliament though it naturally failed to gain the royal assent. In 1644, at the age of 39,

Hammond replied with a claim for episcopacy as of divine right. If not instituted by Christ's direct command, episcopacy was nevertheless of apostolical institution. Christ, the apostles and the other disciples were the pattern of bishops, presbyters and deacons respectively. 'In this kingdom' (the restriction may be significant: he is not judging the churches of the continental Reformation) ordination by a bishop is the appointed way to receive the divine commission (Packer, p. 105).

Hammond's view represented a hardening of Anglican doctrine of the ministry that would be put into effect with divisive results in 1662 with the ejection of many parochial clergy of the Church of England who had received presbyterian ordination. In the circumstances of the fight for the survival of Anglicanism it is explicable. In the hands of individuals less moderate and charitable than Hammond himself its results were disastrous for the unity of the church in England. Hammond's uncompromising doctrine would be kept alive by the nonjurors, revived in the high church movement at the turn of the eighteenth century and thence made an instrument of propaganda and polemic against the Reformation and all its works by the extreme Tractarians.

Richard Baxter distinguished the 'new episcopal divines' – Montagu, Laud, Heylin, Bramhall and Hammond – from the 'old episcopal divines' – Jewel, Pilkington, Abbot, Ussher, Hall and Davenant – claiming that the former 'denied the very being of the reformed churches and ministry'. They 'unchurch those churches that are not prelatical' and regard 'ordination by presbyters without prelates . . . to be no ordination, nor those so ordained to be any ministers but laymen.' They 'separate from their communion and teach the people to do so' and hold the non-episcopal foreign churches to be 'no true churches, though they acknowledge the church of Rome to be a true church, and their ordination valid' (Packer, pp. 48, 197f).

In the year of Hammond's death (1660) Henry Hickman brought out his attack on the high churchmen for departing from the reformed character of the Church of England. In *Laudensium Apostasia* Hickman observes, "Tis notorious that they have unchurched all the transmarine churches for want of such an officer' as they are not convinced Christ ever instituted (c. Packer, p. 127). Now both this judgement and that of Baxter are too absolute. Whatever may be the ultimate logic of their views, Thorndike, Bramhall and Jeremy Taylor, for instance, do not unchurch non-episcopal churches. The trend was clearly in that direction, but it had not yet reached its term. Even Hammond, the most unbending of high churchmen, belongs to the evident consensus within Anglicanism: that the Church of England was a reformed church, that there was one foundation of the Christian church and it was not bishops, that there could be co-operation, fellowship and mutual regard between Anglican churchmen who did not see eye to eye about where the emphasis should lie in the future direction of Anglicanism.

Herbert Thorndike

The great high church divine Herbert Thorndike (1598–1672) is one of the few truly systematic theologians that Anglicanism can boast. Together with Henry Hammond he deserves to share the title 'judicious' with Richard Hooker. But Thorndike is not a truly representative divine. Some of his views were challenged by members of his own school, as well as by those of a more liberal outlook.

(1) Episcopacy and the Reformed Churches

While asserting episcopacy as of divine right, Thorndike nevertheless draws the line at impugning the reformed churches of the Continent for their lack of it, let alone unchurching them. He is gratified by 'the honour and esteem which the learned of the reformed churches abroad have professed of the state of our churches', which is matched by 'our charity in excusing the necessities of theirs and acknowledging the efficacy of the ministry which they use.' This mutual goodwill and regard is sufficient to secure the continued fellowship that we desire with them (I, i, pp. 92ff).

Thorndike's attitude to the continental protestants is determined by his positive assessment of the Reformation. It is agreed by all who profess the Reformation, he says, that many matters of belief or practice, ordained by Christ and the apostles, 'were so abolished by injury of time, that it was requisite that they should be restored', though opposed by those (the Roman hierarchy) who bore the apostolic commission at the time. Where the succession was lost in the course of the Reformation, it was because other 'laws' of dominical institution 'of more moment' were given priority (I, ii, pp. 591f). Having now raised the question of the Reformation on the Continent, Thorndike must make himself clear; to dodge the question might give the impression that he has either a better or a worse opinion of it than he actually has.

His starting point, once again, is that 'it is agreed among us' that the pattern of apostolic belief and practice needed to be restored. His minor premise is that church order, with its divinely ordained episcopal succession, is a means, not an end – a means to the edification of Christians living together in the church. It would be sacrilege not to seek the end without the means where both cannot be had. It is clear that edification in the church can be attained by means other than episcopal government. There is a hierarchy of truths ('rank of precepts') to be observed here, the chief of which is 'living in the society of a church'. So where episcopacy is lacking, 'Christian people' may appoint from their number to the three orders of bishops, presbyters and deacons, and these orders then ought to be recognised by the rest of the church, without further ordination. Whether the Reformers were under this kind of necessity when they established ministries without the episcopal succession, Thorndike declines to judge (I, ii, pp. 603ff). He notes, however, that most of the bishops opposed the Reformation, their hostility creating a smoke screen that concealed the true nature of episcopacy from the Reformers (I, i, p. 93). Furthermore, the Reformers, while they did not enjoy plenary authority to establish ministries, did not lack all authority, since they were in presbyters' orders. Where they went wrong was in not creating their own threefold ministry, to which there was no barrier except that of 'false persuasion'. Thorndike is convinced, however, that God will overlook this failure since the threefold ministry is not part of what he has revealed as being necessary to salvation. The reformed churches 'profess all that is necessary to the salvation of all Christians,' both in faith and life. They are still Christian churches (though the Anglo-Catholic editor of the LACT edition would have us believe that Thorndike only called them churches in the popular sense: I, i, p. 92n) where salvation is to be found. If we are going to keep looking for the perfect church we will find ourselves living and dying out of communion with the Christian church altogether (I, ii, pp. 603–607).

Thorndike is not so charitably disposed, however, to presbyterians at home who had been ordained 'against bishops'. He regarded their orders as flagrantly schismatical: they are 'no more ministers of the church that are made by assemblies of divines and presbyteries, than those that are made by Commission of Triers [the ecclesiastical appointments commission during the Commonwealth] . . . They can no more be acknowledged by those that pretend to adhere to the Church of England, then Belial by Christ, or darkness by light . . . And therefore their priesthood [sic] is no priesthood, their eucharist is no eucharist, but sacrilege against God's ordinance' (c. Bosher, p. 35).

(2) Fundamentals of Christianity

Thorndike maintains in line with reformed and liberal thinkers alike, that the truths necessary for salvation are also the foundation of the church and are professed at baptism:

> The profession of that Christianity, which our Lord Christ delivered to his apostles to preach when he gave them authority to found his church, being the condition, without undergoing whereof no man was to be admitted a member of the church by being baptised a Christian; as it is [pre-] supposed to the being of a church, so must it of necessity contain whatsoever the salvation of all Christians requireth (IV, ii, p. 889).

Thorndike clearly regards the words of the 'great commission' in Matthew 28.19f as the key to the fundamentals of Christianity. 'I for my part believe,' he says, 'that the substance of Christianity necessary to salvation' is indicated there. But even these words about baptism in the name of the holy Trinity need to be interpreted (II, i, p. 83). For Thorndike does not believe that all truths necessary to salvation are clear to everyone on the surface of the scriptural text and in this he departs from the Anglican consensus – a reformed consensus – of the period (ib., pp. 76ff). Neither does he hold, therefore, that one of the primary truths, or fundamentals, of Christianity is that all things necessary to salvation are clearly apparent in the scriptures. This leads Thorndike to qualify the reformed teaching of his predecessors in several respects.

First, he only accepts the Reformation teaching that word and sacrament are the marks of the true church with the caveat that the word must be taught and the sacraments administered in line with the teaching of the whole church (IV, ii, pp. 894f).

Second, he only approves the claim that Christ alone is the foundation provided that this is understood as entailing the teaching of the church: 'he that admits our Lord to be the Christ, cannot refuse any part of his doctrine.' Whoever believes in Christ will be baptised; whoever is baptised will undertake to live as Christ taught, and believe in the Father, the Son and the Holy Spirit; and whoever commits himself to these things needs the instruction of the church concerning them (II, i, p. 85).

Third, it follows that Thorndike's view of the role of the apostles' creed in delivering the fundamentals of Christianity will be qualified by an insistence on the further instruction of the church:

> It is not my intent to insist that the words of the creed were delivered by the apostles themselves, or that the rule of baptism delivered by our Lord in the name of the Father, Son and Holy Ghost, is not a sufficient symbol or cognizance for a Christian; for what is there necessary for the salvation of all Christians that is not contained in the profession of him that desires to be baptised into this faith? But it is enough for my present purpose that it was always requisite that whosoever is baptised should be instructed upon what terms he is to expect to be saved by Christ.

And that instruction was according to the church's rule of faith (II, i, p. 119).

Fourth, Thorndike's summary of the fundamentals of Christianity which 'it is necessary for the salvation of all Christians to believe' is accordingly quite extensive, though it follows the narrative structure of the drama of creation, fall, the giving of the law, the incarnation, atonement, founding of the church and its means of grace, second coming, resurrection, judgement and eternal destiny. This is more than the mere gospel of the first Reformers, and a good deal more than many churchgoers could intelligibly profess today. But after all Thorndike's huffing and puffing about the teaching office of the church and the guidance of catholic antiquity, it is a comparatively slender product. He regards it as the bare minimum and echoes the Reformers when he exclaims: 'This is that precious pearl, and that hid treasure; this is that grain of mustard seed, that leaven; which being purchased at the price of all we have, and sowed in the heart, and laid up in the past of our thoughts, makes all our actions fruitful to the riches of everlasting happiness.' This, he concludes, is 'that little spot of truth' that religious conflicts, purportedly in its defence, have actually obscured and prejudiced (IV, ii, pp. 890f). In the final analysis, perhaps Thorndike, for all the catholic hedging around of Christian truths, is not so far from that evangelical and christological centre that the Reformers saw as constituting the church.

Daniel Waterland

It is said of Waterland (1683–1740) that he did more than any other theologian of his generation to check the advance of unorthodox doctrines in the Church of England. Edmund Gibson, the powerful bishop of London, who valued Waterland's theological orthodoxy and sanity promoted him: the master of Magdalene College, Cambridge, also became canon of Windsor and archdeacon of Middlesex. Waterland was disappointed not to obtain the Lady Margaret chair of divinity at Cambridge, but he actually declined the bishopric of Llandaff in 1738.

(1) Aspects of Protestantism

Waterland was a high church protestant theologian in the days when such a combination was still possible, indeed the norm, and an orthodox Whig (like Gibson himself) when the high theological ground was assumed to lie with the Tories. He rejoiced to defend central truth against the deviations of Latitudinarians and nonjurors alike. Waterland's principal works were written in defence of the doctrines of the Trinity and the deity of Christ, and of Old Testament revelation against the deists.

Waterland upheld the English Reformation, but held no brief for less regular developments on the continent:

> When our pious Reformers, about two hundred years ago, went about restoring religion to its ancient purity, they did it in a regular and orderly way, under the direction and countenance of the ruling powers and with due regard to such a regular ministry as Christ had appointed in his church (c. Holtby, p. 207).

Waterland defended what he called the 'protestant', 'evangelical' doctrine of forensic justification, citing such 'protestant' divines as Andrewes and Bull as well as Cranmer's homily 'Of Salvation' (IX, pp. 429, 456f). In his teaching on the eucharist, he asserts that the eucharist is a real, true, but at the same time spiritual and immaterial sacrifice, a sacrifice of worship. Against Johnson of Cranbrook in his *Unbloody Sacrifice*, Waterland rejects any expiatory connotations:

To imagine any expiatory sacrifice now to stand between us and the great sacrifice of Christ is to keep us still at a distance when we are allowed to draw near: it is dishonouring the grace of the gospel; and, in short, is a flat contradiction to both Testaments (VIII, p. 178).

Waterland entered into controversy privately over the question of lay baptism where he followed the views of some nonjurors that lay baptism was invalid. He distinguished between 'authorised' lay baptism as in the Roman Catholic Church or the Church of England before the canons of 1604, where lay persons seemed to exercise a delegated canonical authority, and 'unauthorised' lay baptism, such as by midwives. 'The true and only baptism,' he asserted, is 'episcopal baptism' (c. Holtby, p. 120). Waterland denied that his view of baptism unchurched foreign reformed churches who lacked bishops, provided – he added – 'their want of episcopal ordination does not [unchurch them], which is a distinct question' (ib., p. 207). On the point of lay baptism, Waterland was forced to admit that he had Whitgift, Hooker and other patriarchs of Anglican theology against him, and it is ironical to observe that his theory leads him to side with Calvin, who opposed lay baptism, against the Roman Catholic Church, which permitted it. (See further Barnard.)

(2) *Authority: Scripture, Antiquity and Reason*

Waterland is a typical exponent of the Anglican synthesis in the matter of doctrinal authority. His appeal is to 'scripture, antiquity and reason' (c. Holtby, p. 210) and he holds it to be the protestant position that authority in the church gives us 'a proper certainty in matters of faith, doctrine and discipline, without infallibility' (ib., p. 40). As a reformed Anglican, Waterland upholds the paramount authority of scripture and looks to the guidance of the early church where scripture itself is unclear. It is interesting that Waterland has little time for catholic consent as a criterion, except when it is the consent of antiquity. Mere consensus among Christians, he asserts, is 'a rule as uncertain in its application and use as it is false in its main ground' (VIII, pp. 117f).

In his dissertation on 'The Use and Value of Ecclesiastical Antiquity with Respect to Controversies of Faith' (V, pp. 253–), Waterland defends the role of antiquity in clarifying, endorsing and illuminating the teaching of scripture. While scripture is 'plain in necessaries' (p. 284) and perfect according to its intended purpose, 'to be a rule of life and manners', it remains words in a dead language (p. 283). And while no one would suggest that anything other than scripture is a sufficient basis for an article of faith (certainly not oral tradition: p. 261), 'the subordinate proof from antiquity may be a good mark of direction for the interpretation of scripture in the prime doctrines' (p. 271). Thus 'there is no occasion for magnifying antiquity at the expence [sic] of scripture,' but 'antiquity ought to attend as a handmaid to scripture, to wait upon her as her mistress, and to observe her; to keep off intruders from making too bold with her, and to discourage strangers from misrepresenting her' (p. 257).

Waterland deployed the sanction of antiquity against both liberal Anglicans and Roman Catholics. Against the charge of latitudinarian liberals that a deference to antiquity derogates from the authority of Christ, Waterland replies:

> We think that Christ never sits more secure or easy on his throne than when he has his most faithful guards about him, and that none are so likely to strike at his authority or aim at dethroning him as they that would displace his old servants only to make way for new ones (p. 282).

Waterland's response to those who set the appeal to reason above the appeal to antiquity is that to use such help is entirely rational:

> In a strict and proper sense, I do not know that the fathers have any authority over us; they are all dead men; therefore we urge not their authority but their testimony, their suffrage, their judgement, as carrying great force of reason. Taking them in here as lights or helps is doing what is reasonable and using our own understandings in the best way.

'I follow the fathers,' Waterland concludes, 'as far as reason requires and no further; therefore this is following our own reason' (pp. 330). While liberal Anglicans, echoing Chillingworth, claimed that there were fathers against fathers, councils against councils, etc., Waterland counters that such oppositions were not on the substance of the faith (p. 315).

Against Rome, Waterland argues that antiquity has 'a negative voice' and acts as a check on innovations of doctrine, for example against 'the novel and supernumerary articles of the Trent creed or creed of pope Pius IV, imposed upon the consciences of men as necessary to salvation' (p. 277). Like Jewel before him, Waterland believes that antiquity is as effective as scripture against the accretions of Roman doctrine and practice and that the Church of England has reformed itself in accordance with the primitive pattern:

> If there be any church now in the world which truly reverences antiquity and pays a proper regard to it, it is this church. The Romanists talk of antiquity, while we observe and follow it. For with them, both scripture and fathers are, as to the sense, under the correction and control of the present church: with us, the present church says nothing but under the direction of scripture and antiquity taken together, one as the rule, and the other as the pattern or interpreter. Among them the present church speaks by scripture and fathers: with us, the scripture and fathers speak by the church (p. 319).

While the fathers were neither inspired nor infallible, they were preserved from falling into fundamental error. So whatever they held as true and important – provided scripture in its natural sense concurred – ought to be regarded as scriptural doctrines (pp. 293, 278f). All in all, 'scripture and antiquity (under the conduct of right reason)' are the criteria of correct doctrine (p. 322).

(3) *Fundamentals of Christianity*

In two successive archidiaconal charges (1734–1735), Waterland expounded the notion of fundamentals and did so in a way that developed the high church views of such as Hammond and Thorndike and criticised the latitudinarian approach of Hales, Chillingworth, Jeremy Taylor, Stilling-fleet and Locke. His treatment is relevant to the questions of the essence of Christianity, the terms of communion in the Church of England, and the grounds of Christian reunion, questions that exercise the contemporary church as much as they did the church of the early eighteenth century.

Waterland begins his *Discourse of Fundamentals* (VIII, pp. 85–125) with a definition. A fundamental truth is 'something essential to religion or Christianity; so necessary to its being, or at least to its well-being, that it could not subsist, or not maintain itself tolerably without it' (p. 88). He quotes a writer who he takes to be Sherlock, but who was probably Thomas Long, prebendary of Exeter: 'A fundamental doctrine is such a doctrine as is in strict sense of the essence of Christianity, without which the whole building and superstructure must fall; the belief of which is necessary to the very being of Christianity, like the first principles of any art or science' (p. 95).

What is the relation of these fundamentals that are of the essence of Christianity to those truths that are required to be believed for salvation? Abstractly they coincide, replies Waterland, but relative to the varying capacities of individuals they diverge. The fundamentals are fixed, things necessary for salvation depend on the individual. Waterland observes that, in practice, all parties make their terms of communion stricter than the conditions of salvation, because we cannot make allowances as can God who looks upon the heart (p. 92).

Waterland takes issue with Locke's argument that belief in God as creator and Jesus as messiah (together with his resurrection and coming judgement) are sufficient for both salvation and church communion. Waterland agrees that the whole of Christianity is doubtless implied in that one article of Jesus as the messiah, and that a denial of any aspect of the Christian faith is an implied rejection of that article. But he wants to make some of those implications explicit (pp. 115f). He does this by construing the fundamentals on the model of the *covenant* of salvation. The covenant concept includes belief in God and his attributes, man as a free moral creature, the scriptures as divine revelation, the office of Christ as mediator between God and man, the future state, judgement to come, heaven and hell (pp. 95ff). Waterland summarises: 'Whatever verities are found to be plainly and directly essential to the doctrine of the gospel covenant, they are fundamental verities: and whatever errors are plainly and directly subversive of it, they are fundamental errors' (p. 123).

Two corollaries follow from this focus on the centrality of the gospel covenant, that would be unwelcome to more rigidly scholastic theologians, both protestant and catholic. The fundamentals are not synonymous with either the scriptures or the creeds. Those who equate the teachings of scripture as such with the fundamentals are confusing the truth or usefulness of a doctrine with its importance and necessity. The importance of a doctrine is determined by the content of that doctrine, its connection with the rest of the Christian scheme, and the consequences of denying it (pp. 106, 111). On the other hand, the fundamentals are not simply synonymous with the creed – and here Waterland acknowledges that he parts company with such Anglican divines as Ussher, Davenant, Chillingworth, Stillingfleet and Tillotson. The creed does not contain all necessary articles of simple belief, and it contains some articles that are clearly not fundamental, for example the mention of Pontius Pilate and the descent into hell, 'whatever it means'. The creed does not mention the fundamental article (here Waterland differs from Thorndike) of the divine authority and inspiration of scripture. Furthermore, the creed is unsuited to the question of church communion which involves fundamentals of Christian worship and morals as well as of belief (pp. 111f).

Where a non-fundamental point is rigorously insisted on, so that we are compelled to deny a certain truth, separation is called for (p. 103). But Waterland's great concern is for the unity of the church and his examination of the concept of fundamentals is intended to be relevant to this. 'A comprehension or coalition of religious parties is a thing very desirable in itself; and so far as it can be effected by throwing out circumstantials and retaining only essentials, it is well worthy of every good man's thoughts and care' (p. 118). While it is morally certain that a perfect union of Christians is an unattainable as world peace, we called to do all we can to promote it, by 'instruction, counsel and endeavour', leaving the outcome to God (p. 91). When Waterland's older contemporary archbishop William Wake attempted to translate this vision of peace, concord and unity into action, in his approaches to the Gallican and Reformed churches, he regarded precisely this distinction between fundamentals and non-fundamentals as the key.

Part Three

THE NINETEENTH AND EARLY TWENTIETH CENTURIES

Resurgence of the
Apostolic Paradigm and the
Making of Modern Anglicanism

10

The Church in Danger

Renewal and Conflict

In the middle decades of the nineteenth century Anglicanism in the Church of England underwent a sea change that profoundly affected its ecclesiological identity. These developments comprised the twin phenomena of *renewal* and *conflict*. The conflict was a condition of the renewal; the renewal was at the price of conflict. These twin manifestations of the nineteenth-century Church of England have contributed significantly to making contemporary Anglicanism what it is. When, in 1868 Gladstone looked back, in an autobiographical fragment, to the circumstances in which he had written his treatise *The State in its Relations with the Church* in 1838, he noted that renewal and conflict had proceeded hand in hand. 'Since that time,' he observed, 'the Church of England may be said to have bled at every pore; and at this hour it seems occasionally to quiver to its very base.' 'And yet,' he added, 'all the while the religious life throbs more and more powerfully within her' (*Autobiography*, p. 55).

Before the renewal movement of the 1830s, Gladstone recalled, 'the Church of England had been passing through a long period of deep and chronic religious lethargy.' No other period or land could show a clergy 'so secular and lax, or congregations so cold, irreverent and indevout'. 'Our churches and our worship bore in general too conclusive testimony to a frozen indifference.' 'With all our Romanising and all our rationalising,' Gladstone asked, 'what man of sense would wish to go back upon those dreary times?' (pp. 48f). The movement of renewal which centred on Oxford (though Gladstone singles out Blomfield and Hook as pioneers) was like a Russian spring, 'when, after long months of rigid cold, almost in a day, the snow dissolves, the ice breaks up and is borne away, and the whole earth is covered with a rush of verdure' (p. 52). At the time, however, Gladstone had not anticipated the pain and conflict that renewal would generate (pp. 54f).

The doctrinal consensus of earlier Anglicanism was challenged. Its coherence was stretched to the limits. Its integrity was impugned. The Church of England seemed to dissolve into its constituents and ecclesiastical parties began to take their identity more from the particular insight or emphasis that they had hitherto contributed to the common vision, than from that comprehensive vision itself. Each tended to absolutise aspects of the total inheritance that had until now formed the ingredients of a synthesis. Thus evangelicals began to sit loose to structures and sacraments, emphasising the Bible and individual conversion. The old high churchmen, ridiculed by the radical spirits within their tradition, the extreme Tractarians, as 'mere Anglicans' for clinging to an anachronistic concept of the relation of church and state, were doomed to extinction. The best of the broad church, liberal tradition, sickened by bigotry and obscurantism, allowed itself to be pushed to the margins of Anglican life.

Only with Charles Gore and the *Lux Mundi* school did the high church movement, now purged of establishmentarian fantasies, and renewed by contact with the advanced learning and critical methods that had seemed the preserve of liberals, come back into the centre. In Gore and Scott Holland high churchmanship even adopted views of the authority of scripture and of justification that might have seemed the prerogative of evangelicals, though not in detachment from the tradition of the primitive church in the one case and the sacramental system in the other.

A Crisis of Church and State

The catalyst for this disruption of Anglican identity was a revolution in the relation of church and state. The dynamics of the church-state nexus are the key to understanding three centuries of Anglicanism and particularly those momentous events of the 1830s and 40s that have had such an impact on the subsequent history of the Anglican church.

Hooker had provided a theoretical justification of the Elizabethan settlement of religion. Church and state were two inseparable aspects of one commonwealth. The sovereign was head in both, supreme governor in the external, mundane affairs of the church. The first duty of a Christian commonwealth was to provide for true religion. For the first one hundred years of the reformed Church of England's existence, the sovereign was regarded as the divinely appointed protector and guardian of the church against all dangers both at home and abroad. Anglicanism was a state religious monopoly and its symbol was sacred kingship.

Since the mid-seventeenth century, however, Anglican self-understanding had been engaged in a long and reluctant retreat from this normative position. Charles I had failed effectively to defend the church; its two great sacred symbols, the king himself and the archbishop (Laud) had been destroyed, and the episcopate abolished. The 'No bishop, no king' of James I had become 'No king, no bishop.' The Anglican commonwealth was replaced by a radical protestant state which anticipated the pluralistic society of a later period. Both Charles II and James II – though the Anglican system had been reimposed with a vengeance – failed to defend the church's privileges and monopolies. Their crypto-Romanism led to concessions to all dissenters from which Roman Catholics were intended to benefit. Their successors, William III and George I naturally looked with favour on Calvinists and Lutherans. The Whig ministries of the early eighteenth century saw high churchmen as a threat, for their brand of Anglicanism was still identified with passive obedience to a hereditary monarchy by divine right. The Anglican consensus was as much threatened by heterodox bishops like Hoadly, who was advanced for political reasons by the Whig government, as it was by the high churchmen who could not accept the new regime of 1688 and went out into the wilderness, where extreme views always flourish.

In the early nineteenth century the legatees of the old 'passive, peaceable protestantism' as Izaak Walton defined Anglicanism, were the old high churchmen (the Hutchinsonians, the 'Hackney Phalanx' and others). They still held to the notion of a sacral monarchy and the divine origin of all power and authority, not only in the church, where it was invested in the bishops in the apostolic succession, but in the state. Kings were still to be the nursing fathers of the church, defending its rightful privileges against the usurpations of erastian reformers and utilitarians. Against all the evidence, the old high churchmen still clung to the belief that the time-honoured relationship of interdependence could be made to work again. Joshua Watson summed up their position in 1834: 'We believe that the consecration of the state by the public maintenance of the Christian religion is the first and paramount duty of a Christian people.' His words were embraced and endorsed by the younger traditional high churchmen such as William Palmer of Worcester College. But the position was becoming more and more difficult to sustain.

The spiritual authority of the church was emasculated: convocation had not met since 1717. Now its political authority was decisively undermined. The monopoly of the established church had been preserved on paper by a series of anomalies. For eighty-five years dissenters had been able to sit in parliament, and to hold municipal and other public offices, by the passing of annual acts of indemnity exempting them from the statutory penalties formally imposed upon those who took office without first receiving Holy Communion in the Church of England (Norman, p. 77). 1828 finally saw the repeal of the Test and Corporation Acts that had made these anomalous arrangements necessary. In the following year Catholic Emancipation 'made the bishops realise that they were no longer living in the sort of friendly political climate where they could afford to compromise principles and tolerate the creation of constitutional anomalies, as those can who occupy positions of unassailable strength' (ib., p. 79). For the Oxford men, the suppression of ten Irish bishoprics in 1833 on purely secular, progressive, utilitarian grounds by parliament was the last straw. It provoked Keble's Assize Sermon which was the symbolic inauguration of the Oxford Movement. High churchmen, old and young, looked in vain for king William IV to honour his coronation oath to 'preserve unto the bishops and clergy of this realm, and to the churches committed to their charge, all such rights and privileges as by law do or shall appertain unto them' and to defend the established church against a hostile legislature. The ancient Anglican ideology of kings as the nursing fathers of the church was a dead letter (see also Best, chs 4 and 6).

Gladstone's *The State in its Relation to the Church* was the swansong of the old doctrine. Gladstone was more concerned for the spiritual witness of the church to the whole nation than for the theological purity and integrity of the church. The aim of the church was 'the greatest holiness of the greatest number'.

> The interest of the church ... is the production, not of the greatest possible excitement connected with religion, nor of the greatest possible enjoyment connected with religion, nor of the greatest possible appearance of religion; nay, not even the greatest possible quantity of actual religion at any time or place; but the greatest possible permanent and substantial amount of religion within that sphere over which its means of operation extend.

'By religion,' Gladstone added significantly, 'I would be understood to mean conformity to the will of God' (*State ... Church*, I, pp. 258f). Gladstone's conception of national religion was, then, primarily moral, not sacramental as it was for Keble. It was thus consistent with what today we call 'folk religion', as Keble's was not. Gladstone's established church embraced 'those who are too timid to make religious profession; those who hesitate between this world and the next; those who give a limited and insufficient scope to the action of Christian principle; those who attend Christian ordinances only in compliance with human opinion; and those who see nothing in Christianity but a system of outward forms, in an establishment nothing but a method of preserving social order and of repressing religious extravagance' (I, p. 259).

As Perry Butler has commented, for the more extreme Oxford men who looked to Froude, only the spiritual integrity of the church mattered. 'Fearful though they were of "national apostacy", they were more concerned that the church should be free than that the nation should be Christian.' But this cut at the root of Gladstone's political vocation (I, p. 89). Not only so, but it was not compatible with his conception of the Christian church. She did not dwell on her own rights, privileges and dignities, but reached out compassionately to embrace the humblest stirrings of spiritual quickening:

> Her principle is, to gather up the very crumbs of devotional offerings; to feed the babes with milk, not to break the bruised reed, nor to quench the smoking flax . . . a small obedience is better than none. To think of God seldom is better than not to think of him at all. To love him faintly is better than . . . indifference or aversion (*State . . . Church*, I, p. 261).

It is significant that Gladstone believed that the very Keblean qualities that are enshrined in say *The Christian Year* were fostered by establishment. An established religion, he suggested, was likely to be 'more calm, more catholic, less alloyed by the contagion of spiritual pride and selfishness' (I, p. 263).

However, Gladstone was giving up the old high church position that he had defended with such precocious learning and eloquence, even as the book went into successive editions. 'Scarcely had my work issued from the press,' he later wrote, 'when I became aware that there was no party, no section of a party, no individual person probably in the House of Commons, who was prepared to act upon it. I found myself the last man on the sinking ship' (*Autobiography*, p. 25). But it is also highly probable that Gladstone's confidence in his theory was already being eroded by Macaulay's critique in the *Edinburgh Review*: quite apart from his 'redundant opulence' of illustration and a logic even more remorseless than Gladstone's own, Macaulay's appeal to natural justice, and a sense of what was proportionate and appropriate to the untidy circumstances of history could hardly have failed to make a deep impression on a mind that was imbued with Hooker, Butler and Burke (Macaulay, 'Gladstone'; c.f. Lathbury in Gladstone, *Correspondence*, I, p. 16).

In departing from the old high church camp over this issue, Gladstone took with him Hook and Churton. Christopher Wordsworth condemned the *volte face* as a betrayal motivated by romantic dreams of a pure church and abstract ideals of catholicity. Gladstone and his fellows underestimated, he claimed, the extent of the anomalies that had existed prior to 1828. But in Gladstone's case at least the criticism was misplaced – a misguided attempt to tar him with the same brush as Froude and Newman. Gladstone's move was a pragmatic adjustment to changing circumstances. He did not renounce the principle of establishment as such, provided it fitted the facts of the situation (as in Ireland he came to believe it did not), nor retract his early insistence, derived from Hooker and Burke, on the spiritual and moral ends of the state. In the thirty years since he had written *The State in its Relation with the Church*, he observed in 1868, 'the dogmatic allegiance of the state to religion has been greatly relaxed, but its consciousness of moral duty has been not less notably quickened and enhanced.' It is by a practical rather than a theoretical test that establishments of religion should be tried. An establishment 'that has a broad and living way open to it, into the hearts of the people,' that does not seek to intimidate its opponents, or maintain itself with the aid of state sanctions, is worth keeping (*Autobiography*, pp. 61ff).

On the other hand, Froude, followed by Newman, gave up the high church hankering for the restoration of the old relationship. They retained for a time the high church royalism and the cult of Charles King and Martyr, but married it to a theocratic ideal in which the church would continue to enjoy the protection of the state without its spiritual independence being compromised. Newman looked for 'the continuation and development' of the principles of archbishop Laud: 'The so-called union of church and state as it then existed had been a wonderful and most gracious phenomenon in church history . . . a realisation of the gospel in its highest perfection when both Caesar and St. Peter [Charles I and Laud] knew and fulfilled their office' (c. Rowlands, diss., pp. 135f). A significant factor in creating this one-sided theory of the church-state relation was the Tractarians' aversion to admitting the laity to the government of the church. Alongside Charles I and the nonjurors, Froude and Newman began to invoke the ghosts of Hildebrand and Becket. 'Let us tell the truth and shame the devil; let us give up a national church and have a real one,' urged Froude (III, p. 274). State protection had been minimal; state interference had been intolerable (*Tract 59*).

Meanwhile erastian control of the church was being extended through the progressive absorption of disciplinary machinery by the Judicial Committee of the Privy Council. In the Gorham Judgement of 1850 this committee appeared to be defining doctrine when it refused to endorse baptismal regeneration as the only permissible interpretation of the Church of England's baptism service. As Norman has commented: 'The Gorham case appeared to symbolise all the theoretical anomalies which the reforms of the previous twenty years had stacked up' (p. 121). It triggered Manning's secession to Rome, but Keble and Pusey stood firm.

Keble had passive obedience in his blood. His attitude to these tribulations was summed up in the title of his sermon of 1837 'Patience and Confidence the Strength of the Church'. Pusey had learned the old high church doctrine from Keble. His response to the Gorham judgement ('We have seen a doctrine, to us as plain as the sun itself, called in question in a court from which there is no ordinary appeal.') was not to deny the royal supremacy or to call for the dissolution of the bonds between church and state, but to recall both to a juster appreciation of the conditions that it imposed. In *The Royal Supremacy, not an arbitrary authority but limited by the laws of the Church, of which Kings are Members* (1850), Pusey argued that the judgement reflected adversely not on the church but on the civil power: 'No authority less than that of the church can decide in her name, that she does not receive the creeds which she uses in the sense in which the church has ever read them. If any authority, not coextensive with herself, decided wrongly, he condemns himself, not her' (p.6; c.f. p.10; see also Nockles in Butler, ed.). Nevertheless Keble and Pusey did more than almost anyone to replace the national paradigm of Anglicanism, centred on the royal supremacy, by the catholic paradigm, centred on the apostolic succession.

Ecclesiastical Patterns and Parties

Within the Oxford Movement then three strands emerged: first the old high church tradition represented by Hugh James Rose and William Palmer of Worcester College, Hook and Gladstone; second, the high church tradition radicalised by a rejection of the Reformation and of the protestant character of the Church of England, seen in Keble, Newman, Manning and Pusey, following the lead of Hurrell Froude; thirdly, the extreme left wing, Frederick Oakeley and W. G. Ward who, also provoked by Froude, set the pace for radical measures and preceded Newman into the Roman fold. Of these three groups, only the first, the faithful high churchmen like Rose and Palmer, respected the reformed nature of the English church and dissociated themselves from the Tractarian platform of *unprotestantising* the Church of England. In the second group, Keble (a hereditary high-churchman – though Griffin disputes this: pp.6f) and Pusey (a convert) set out from the same position but moved steadily towards a negative attitude to the Reformation and a determination to change the face of the church. Together with the third group, the extremists, the avowed Romanisers, they presented a deliberate challenge to a consensus within Anglicanism. Such a consensus clearly existed prior to the Oxford movement. In general terms, it comprised an acceptance of the protestant character of the Church of England in its articles, liturgy and polity. Specifically, it meant the central Reformation principles of justification by faith, the supreme authority of scripture and the role of the sovereign – a lay person – in the government of the church. It was a consensus of all living traditions in the church, evangelicals, high churchmen and latitudinarians.

The evangelicals saw themselves as custodians of the reformed character of Anglicanism. Tractarianism provoked a vigorous reaffirmation of protestant principles by the evangelicals. They responded to Tractarian editions of the Fathers and the Caroline divines with new editions of the English Reformers. The Parker Society published fifty-three volumes for 7000 subscribers between 1841 and 1853. Foxe's *Acts and Monuments* appeared in a new edition in 1837 and the Calvin Translation Society commenced publication in 1843. Notable evangelical divines like William Goode and E. A. Litton adorned Anglican theology and were a match for the heavy guns of the Tractarians like Pusey. Litton's major treatise *The Church of Christ* (1851) took up its ground on the principles of 'evangelical protestantism, the protestantism of Luther, Calvin and our own Reformers.' But at that time, the evangelicals also had fraternal links with both the high church and the latitudinarian tradition (Toon, pp. 36f, 60f, 174; c.f. Conybeare). Through such mediators as C. P. Golightly, prime instigator of the Oxford Martyrs' Memorial (1839–40), the evangelicals joined forces with the high-churchmen – a tradition within Anglicanism that like the evangelicals, though perhaps less fervently, accepted the heritage of the Reformation. Golightly himself, a staunch Hookerian, is difficult to place, being a high-churchman in all his instincts yet implacably hostile to Tractarianism and its most indefatigable Oxford opponent (Greaves). As Peter Toon has commented: 'To distinguish an evangelical high-churchman from an evangelical with a high doctrine of the visible, episcopally governed, national church is not easy and between about 1838 and 1848 perhaps impossible in some cases' (p. 5).

The developed Tractarian position, however, which had no hesitation in claiming that protestant sacraments were no sacraments, their ministers mere laymen and their churches no churches, was no republication of a temporarily obscured high church consensus, claiming unbroken con-tinuity with Laud, but a harking back to the unrepresentative nonjurors. To Hurrell Froude authentic Anglicanism meant 'Charles the First and the Non-jurors' (I, p. 308). The researches of Peter Nockles have demonstrated 'the essentially party, extraneous and sectarian character of the Oxford Movement' (diss., Abstract).

In response to Tractarianism, the term 'evangelical high-churchman' was coined, to designate the traditional, sound high churchmanship that stemmed from the Caroline divines. These high churchmen were appalled by the language used by the extreme Tractarians about the Reformers. Edward Churton wrote, 'If Froude is right, Clarendon and Pearson, Bull and Waterland, and all our divines "whose footsteps I adore", down to good Bishop Jebb and Alexander Knox, are wrong. Who ever held such language about Ridley and Cranmer before . . .?' (c. Nockles, diss., p. 313). For the older high churchmen, there was an unbroken and living tradition of Anglican theology:

> Anglicanism [wrote E. Churton to W. Gresley in 1846] as it is now called, is not a new party, but has come down to us in regular descent from the Reformation, from Hooker to Andrewes, Andrewes to Laud, Bramhall to Hammond, thence to Pearson and Jeremy Taylor, thence to bishop Bull, thence to Hickes and Robert Nelson, Leslie and other names . . . After the succession of George III these principles were again enquired for, and [bishop] Horne and Jones [of Nayland] answered to the call. Horne and Jones have their disciples still living. Tell the world this . . . (c. Nockles, diss., p. 609).

For these high churchmen, Anglicanism was still a middle way and they looked on the advanced Tractarians as extreme, innovative and irresponsible. 'The distinguishing title of a member of the Church of England,' wrote H. H. Norris, 'is a reformed catholic . . . a central situation from which the papist and the larger portion of that mixed multitude known by the name of protestant diverge in opposite directions indeed but to equal distances' (c. ib., p. 174).

It was the Gorham case (1847 onwards) that drove a wedge between the evangelicals and the high-churchmen who had been united in their opposition to the Romanising tendencies of the Tractarians. While the evangelicals took refuge in the secular courts, thus bringing the old charge against the Reformers – erastianism – out into the open again, the high-churchmen lined up behind Henry Phillpotts, bishop of Exeter, on sacramental doctrine – though Phillpotts was never anything but his own man (c.f. Thurmer). In *Tract 81*, ten years before Gorham, Pusey cites him as the last witness in his *catena* of fathers of the English church who held to a sound doctrine of the eucharistic sacrifice.

Evangelicals in this period were firm in their confidence that they had the Reformers on their side. They were their true heirs and authorised interpreters. On the questions of justification and the authority of scripture their confidence was well founded. But on the priesthood of all believers and the right of private judgement – as well as in the problematical area of sacramental theology where the Reformers themselves were not agreed – evangelicalism had diverged from Reformation theology. As Peter Toon has pointed out, even the scholarly William Goode, 'was so influenced by what we now know to be latitudinarian interpretations of the Reformation that he believed that the doctrine of private judgement was an essential principle of the Reformers, and this claim became a standard evangelical presupposition' (pp. 204f).

As this point reminds us, there was another influential tradition of interpreting the Reformation, the latitudinarian or broad church one. Just as the high church tradition should not be identified exclusively with the nonjurors, so too the liberal Anglicans in our period should not be placed with the shallow rationalism of the likes of Benjamin Hoadly (1676–1761). Coleridge, Arnold, Maurice, Hare and the others have their antecedents in the Tew Circle of the early seventeenth century which interpenetrated with high church circles. They perpetuate the authentic Anglican ethos of cultured liberality, balance and breadth of view that we find in the moderate latitudinarian position from the Tew Circle and the Cambridge Platonists in the seventeenth century to Hensley Henson and William Temple in the twentieth. It was a liberality and sense of proportion conspicuously lacking in extremes of churchmanship, whether high or low. That is not to say, however, that it lacked passionate conviction where questions of principle were concerned.

In Anglicanism before the Oxford movement there was no sense of exclusive adherence to, say 'catholicism' at the expense of the Reformation, or protestant principles to the exclusion of a high view of the church's tradition and sacraments. Coleridge, a close student of the seventeenth-century divines as well as a passionate advocate of Luther, symbolises this integrated position. In this Coleridge was doing no more than Hooker or even Laud.

In the mid-nineteenth century, elements within evangelicalism could make common cause with broad church liberals in defence of Reformation principles and in opposition to Romanist tendencies. On the question of justification they could stand together against notions of salvation by infused sacramental grace (though the latitudinarians would tend to favour a more moralistic position than the evangelicals for whom moral striving was confined to the sphere of santification). On authority they could unite in defence of scripture against tradition (though latitudinarians would give a larger role to reason). On private judgement they were at one in taking the Reformation to be an assertion of the principle of conscience and the first dawn of religious toleration. The evangelical predilection for a simple gospel, comprising those doctrines on the surface of Pauline Christianity, linked up with the undogmatic, minimising approach of the liberals for whom faith was expressed in a 'personalist' way in the practice of the Christian life.

The liberal Anglicans or broad-churchmen are to be clearly distinguished from the low-churchmen who were, as Peter Toon points out, none other than right-wing evangelical churchmen who worked with dissenters and who set little store by the historic episcopate (pp. 208f). The limited and pragmatic partnership between evangelicals and liberals came to an end in mid-century as the debate between religion and science began to claim more of the limelight from the protestant-versus-catholic controversy. The parting of the ways was the question of the inspiration of the Bible and matters came to a head with the publication of *Essays and Reviews* in 1860.

However, on the eve of the Oxford movement, the party-structure of the Church of England could be likened to a series of mutually overlapping circles; high church, broad church and evangelical. What united them was an unquestioned, tacit consensus with regard to the protestant character of the Anglican church – a character that was evidenced above all in the doctrines of justification by faith and the paramount authority of scripture, in a fraternal regard for the continental churches of the Reformation, in esteem of the Reformers both English and foreign, and in loyalty to the standards of the Church of England – the Thirty-nine Articles and the Book of Common Prayer, as well as unofficial secondary standards among which Richard Hooker's *Ecclesiastical Polity* stands pre-eminent.

The Tractarians set out to challenge the consensus on each of these points. In opposition stood conservative high-churchmen, led by William

Palmer of Worcester College who had felt betrayed by the trend of the movement, bowed out and turned against his former colleagues; evangelicals, with William Goode spearheading their counterattack; and liberal Anglicans, including professed Coleridgeans, who reinterpreted Reformation principles and held up the Reformers as men to affectionate admiration. But together they did not succeed in preventing the break up of the Anglican consensus or the partial unprotestantising of the Church of England.

The Apostolic Paradigm

The Oxford Movement was born in a crisis of authority. If the government of the day could act unilaterally to suppress a number of Irish bishoprics, what did this imply for the nature and power of episcopacy? If the powers that be could set in hand a root and branch reform of 'abuses' with the church powerless to restrain its hand, what did this suggest about the doctrine of a visible divine society? The 'erastian' paradigm, under which Anglicanism had been formed and had flourished, had failed. But the essentially medieval, hierarchical conception of the universe remained. The Tractarians were not Tories for nothing: order, 'degree', delegated authority remained the presupposition of their thought. A new paradigm was needed which would preserve those values while detaching them from their national, establishment, basis. Such a model was available in the old high church doctrine of apostolic succession. Detached indeed from its context in an ideology derived from the Reformation, the 'apostolic' paradigm would be absolutised by the Tractarians as their *articulus stantis vel candentis ecclesiae* – the sole channel of salvific sacramental grace and the *sine qua non* of a true church. Above all, the apostolic model provided fertile soil for the growth of sacerdotal notions of the ministry.

Much heart-searching took place at the pastoral level. 'The first question that rose in my mind,' wrote Manning looking back in the 1870s, 'was, What right have you to be teaching, admonishing, reforming, rebuking others? By what authority do you lift the latch of a poor man's door and enter and sit down and begin to instruct or to correct him?' (c. Newsome, p. 203). And in the first of the *Tracts for the Times* Newman put a similar question to his 'fellow presbyters': if their ministerial commission was not from the government, Whig or Tory, whence did it come?

> Should the government and country so far forget their God as to cast off the church, to deprive it of its temporal honours and substance, *on what* will you rest the claim of respect and attention which you make upon your flocks? Hitherto you have been upheld by your birth, your education, your wealth, your connections; should these secular advantages cease, on what must Christ's ministers depend? . . . There are some who rest their divine

mission on their own unsupported assertion; others, who rest it upon their popularity; others, on their success; and others, who rest it upon their temporal distinctions. This last case has, perhaps, been too much our own; I fear we have neglected the real ground on which our authority is built . . .

That ground was of course, 'our apostolical descent'. Newman has no qualms about using a 'pipeline' theory of grace: 'The Lord Jesus Christ gave his Spirit to his apostles; they in turn laid their hands on those who should succeed them; and these again on others; and so the sacred gift has been handed down to our present bishops, who have appointed us as their assistants, and in some sense representatives.' 'We must necessarily consider *none* to be ordained,' Newman concluded, 'who have not been *thus* ordained.'

Manning had come to the same conclusion. No culture or reading or knowledge of dead languages could qualify a man for the sacred office. 'If I was not a messenger sent from God, I was an intruder and impertinent.' In a sermon preached in Chichester cathedral in 1835, Manning, like Newman, called upon the clergy to magnify their office, for it is great, almost too great for any man to bear. Through the apostolic succession it is raised high above any 'other office of moral teacher or labourer in God's service.' Against this, 'the indestructible essence' of the church, no reforming Whigs and radicals, no not the gates of hell themselves would prevail. 'The invisible spiritualities of our apostolical descent, and our ministerial power in the word and sacraments, no prince, no potentate, no apostate nation can sully with a breath of harm' (c. Newsome, p. 204).

Like Karl Barth's own theological revolution, this was thrown up by a crisis of pastoral duty. Barth wrestled with the question, 'What should I preach to them?'; the Tractarians with the question, 'How dare I preach at all? And who am I to give the body and blood of Christ to the faithful?' 'No ordinance of an earthly legislature,' wrote J. W. Bowden in *Tract 5*, 'could invest us with power over the gifts of the Holy Ghost.' The power to offer sacrifice to God in the eucharist had not yet been explicitly raised. The doctrine of eucharistic sacrifice could easily be grafted on to the stock of apostolic succession, and has usually been associated with it, although as certain varieties of Lutheranism and Methodism prove, it is capable of a life of its own. But the strict doctrine of apostolic succession, in the rather crude form in which Newman put it in the first of the Tracts was clearly of decisive and shaping significance in Tractarian theology. It was the foundation upon which the other distinctive doctrines would rest their weight. It determined the whole direction of the catholic movement in England. If a man's office was validated not by the word that he preached, or by the body that he represented, but by a mystical power imparted to him by the latest in a line of potent prelates whose mandate referred back to remote Christian antiquity, it was natural that a shift should take place in authority in doctrine and practice towards the bishops in their writings and conciliar decisions, i.e. towards tradition. If a man's call to the ministry bore little relation to a local or national church but depended on an episcopate which in its catholicity transcended space and time, it was to be expected that he should begin to take more interest in the Roman and eastern churches who also had the episcopate. So while drawing the Church of England closer in spirit to the Roman and eastern churches, and so preparing for the ecumenical movement, the Tractarians called into question the unity of their own church, Anglo-Catholicism tending like all revivals to become an *ecclesiola in ecclesia*, and widened the gulf between the established and the dissenting churches in England, and between the Anglican churches and the other reformed churches.

The Tractarian emphasis provoked two important developments in the Anglican doctrine of ministry in the nineteenth century: Maurice's attempt to achieve a meeting of opposites and Lightfoot's influential counter-attack against sacerdotalism.

(a) Reviving an insight which is basic to Calvin's theology that Christ's offices of prophet, priest and king are given to him for the benefit of his people and in a sense shared with and bestowed upon them, Maurice exploded what we might call 'the protestant fallacy' (though it certainly does not belong to the Reformers themselves) that whatever is predicated of Christ cannot be predicated also of the church and its members. According to the protestant fallacy, if Christ is priest, there cannot be any human priesthood. Maurice argues that the reverse of this is actually the case: only Christ's priesthood makes human priesthood possible. He points out that the protestant fallacy also rules out the priesthood of all believers! His own doctrine, however, is: if the Incarnation means anything, if the church is not a dream, 'all offices exercised by her on behalf of humanity must be offices first exercised by Christ.' And again: 'The language which makes Christ known to us is the only language which can fitly make the church known to us' (*Kingdom*, II pp. 125f). This position enables Maurice to defend episcopacy and priesthood at the highest level. He was substituting a Christological model for the apostolic one of the Tractarians. Maurice believed that on this basis he had established a doctrine of representative priesthood which was catholic and reformed. He opposed to it the Romish doctrine, as he understood it, of vicarious priesthood – the priest ministering in place of an absent Christ to those otherwise cut off from him, instead of the priest ministering on behalf of a present Christ to those already by baptism in relation to him did they but recollect it (ib., p. 149). He had developed a doctrine of representative priesthood in which the priest represents God to the people and the people to their God.

(b) In his highly influential dissertation on *The Christian Ministry*, appended to his commentary on Philippians (1865), J. B. Lightfoot attacked the sacerdotalism which was being imported into the Anglican church by the legatees of the Oxford movement. The dissertation became the charter of those broad churchmen who joined battle with 'priestcraft' in all its forms. Hensley Henson, no evangelical himself but the patron of dissenting aspirations to be taken seriously and the defender of the reformed nature of the English church, swore by Lightfoot's book and quoted it frequently.

Lightfoot attempts to uncover the origins of sacerdotal language about the priesthood before pronouncing on the propriety of it. It was 'a new principle, which is no where enunciated in the New Testament, but which notwithstanding has worked its way into general recognition and seriously modified the character of later Christianity.' It was Cyprian who deflected the course of Christian tradition by his use of Old Testament typology to bolster the authority of the clergy in a time of crisis. 'As Cyprian crowned the edifice of episcopal power, so also was he the first to put forward without relief or disguise these sacerdotal assumptions' (p. 259: Lightfoot perhaps overlooks the significance of Ignatius of Antioch in these developments). Gentile influences, the misinterpreting of New Testament metaphors about sacrifice, and the appeal to the correspondence between the threefold orders of the Old Testament and those of the church, were responsible, according to Lightfoot, for introducing the doctrine of an exclusive priesthood into the Christian church.

How far can this sacerdotal conception, now bearing the warrant of centuries of use, be justified?, asks Lightfoot. The answer is clear. What is itself absent from the teaching of the New Testament cannot be decisive for our understanding of the nature of the church. In the strict sense, the word 'priest' has no place in the Christian vocabulary. But at this point, Lightfoot embraces Maurice's doctrine, referring his readers to the relevant passage in *The Kingdom of Christ*. If 'the word be taken in a wider and looser acceptation, it cannot well be withheld from the ministry of the church of Christ'. While prepared to allow this, Lightfoot thinks that the word priest is still liable to misunderstanding: 'it might have been better if the later Christian vocabulary had conformed to the silence of the apostolic writers'. But 'according to this broader meaning, the priest may be defined as one who represents God to man and man to God'. The threefold ministry is the safeguard of good order and offers the clearest divine sanction that we can hope for. Probability is the guide of life for Lightfoot too. 'If the facts do not allow us to unchurch other Christian communities differently organised, they may at least justify our jealous adhesion to a polity derived from this source' (pp. 259, 266f).

The minister first of all represents God to men:

> The Christian minister is God's ambassador to men: he is charged with the
> ministry of reconciliation; he unfolds the will of heaven; he declares in
> God's name the terms on which pardon is offered; and he pronounces in

God's name the absolution of the penitent . . . As empowered to declare the
conditions of God's grace, he is empowered also to proclaim the
consequences of their acceptance. But throughout his office is representative and not vicarial. He does not interpose between God and man in such a
way that direct communion with God is superseded on the one hand, or
that his own mediation becomes indispensable on the other.

He is also the people's representative before God. 'He is a priest, as the
mouthpiece, the delegate of a priestly race. His acts are not his own but
the acts of the congregation.' He is not therefore indispensable (pp. 267f).

The conception of representative ministerial priesthood that Lightfoot
had developed from Maurice's insights received definitive statement in
Moberly's *Ministerial Priesthood* of 1897. The ministry is 'the representative and organ of the whole body, in the exercise of prerogatives and
powers which belong to the body as a whole. It is ministerially
empowered to wield, as the body's organic representative, the powers
which belong *to the body*, but which the body cannot wield except
through its own organs duly fitted for the purpose.' The whole body acts
by and through its ordained ministers (pp. 241f). Moberly is indebted to
Gore and Lightfoot (though critical of him), but does not mention
Maurice.

The difficulty – impossibility rather – of combining an essentially
reformed doctrine of the Christian ministry as representative priesthood
with an inflexible insistence on the apostolic succession as the necessary
condition of a valid ministry offering sacramental grace, is conveyed by
the tensions in Charles Gore's ecclesiology. Gore, who died in 1932, was
a third generation Tractarian, a catholic Christian in all his instincts. He
inherited the Tractarians' insistence on the apostolic succession. He
fanatically defended it against all compromise in convocation and at
Lambeth Conferences. Gore rejected Lightfoot's account of the evolution
of the episcopate from below: he believed that the evidence supported the
high view of the apostolic institution of episcopacy. And yet Gore was no
friend to sacerdotal conceptions of the priesthood. His doctrine of the
ministry echoes Maurice and Lightfoot. Though he defends the use of the
term 'priesthood' he safeguards and qualifies it. 'If the church is a high
priestly race,' he writes in *The Church and the Ministry* (1886), 'and if in
the church there is a ministry of divine authority both in the
communication of God's gifts to man and in the offering of man's gifts to
God, that ministry can quite legitimately be called a priesthood' (p. 200).
The church is the priestly body because 'it lives in the full enjoyment of
[Christ's] reconciliation and is the instrument through which the whole
world is to be reconciled to God.' Those who are ordained to devote
themselves to the ministry of reconciliation have a representative, not a
vicarious role. Theirs is a difference of function not of kind (p. 84).

Gore's emphasis on the universal priesthood – the whole priestly body
of the church that celebrates the eucharist and preaches the gospel

through its commissioned representatives – led him perforce to modify the inflexible line of the Tractarians towards non-episcopal churches. He did not deny them grace or impugn their sacraments and ministries, but ascribed their evident enjoyment of divine blessing to 'uncovenanted mercies'. It did not permit Gore to condone any *communio in sacris* with the free churches in England.

The apostolic paradigm remains intact though not unmitigated in the remarkable essay of the young Michael Ramsey *The Gospel and the Catholic Church* (1936). Ramsey acknowledged Gore as his teacher and the same tensions as we have seen in Gore persist in Ramsey's work. It is bold and reformative of the Anglo-Catholic tradition in its vindication of the Reformation and reveals a remarkable insight into the Reformers' quest for the 'true treasure of the church', the holy gospel. But Ramsey's appeal to the gospel is not, as it was for the Reformers, to word and sacrament alone within the community of believers, but to 'the gospel of God uttered in the one body by its whole structure' (p. 66). Michael Ramsey's aim is to vindicate episcopacy as the *sine qua non* of the church and the God-given ground of unity. The gospel has an integral corporate dimension: 'in telling of this one visible society the church's outward order tells indeed of the gospel' (p. 50). For Ramsey the converse is also true: 'the structure of catholicism is an utterance of the gospel' (p. 54); the episcopate is part of the utterance of redemptive love and of the *esse* of the church; the orders of non-episcopal bodies are 'gravely deficient' (pp. 67, 84, 219). In other words, without the apostolic succession, we cannot have the gospel in its wholeness.

The doctrines of ministerial priesthood and apostolic succession do not sit happily together. In the former the emphasis and centre of gravity lies in the universal priesthood; the rationale of the ordained ministry is derived from that. The sacrament of baptism is primary and the key to the understanding of communion and ministry in the body of Christ. But there has been a shift of ideological apparatus also. The medieval, hierarchical, monarchial model of society, that operates through delegated authority and finds expression in transcendental symbolism, has given way to an egalitarian, democratic model of society that operates through mutual participation and comes to expression in the immanental symbolism of body and spirit.

The flaw in the Tractarian conception of the church lay not in its stress on sacramental grace but in its absolutising of a socially conditioned idea of the hierarchical structure through which grace is mediated to the faithful in the church. This ideological legitimation of historically conditioned channels of grace was the baneful legacy of the Oxford movement. F. D. Maurice astutely judged that the Tractarians were opposing to the profane spirit of the age, not the Spirit that blows where it wills, but the spirit of a past age.

11

The High Church Heritage

The more radical Tractarians challenged a tacit consensus in the Church of England as to the protestant character of the Anglican church. The old high church school was as much a party to this consensus as were the evangelicals or the latitudinarians. The Oxford movement, as its aim to *unprotestantise* the church became apparent, caused a split in the ranks of the high churchmen between those, like Hugh James Rose and Palmer, who stood firm on the old principles, including a belief in the necessity of the Reformation, and those, like Keble, who shifted their ground under pressure from more extreme spirits such as Froude.

Hugh James Rose: 'Restorer of the Old Paths'
'If to any one man,' wrote J. W. Burgon at the end of the century, 'is to be assigned the honour of having originated the great catholic revival of our times, that man was Hugh James Rose' (pp. 83ff). To Rose, Burgon gives the title *Restorer of the Old Paths*. Rose was the convenor of the Hadleigh conference in 1833, which acted as a catalyst to the publication of the *Tracts for the Times*. He founded and edited the *British Magazine*, a principal Tractarian organ, and edited the *Theological Library*. He directed Newman's first theological efforts and sponsored the research which became *The Arians of the Fourth Century*. Yet Rose was deeply distressed by the direction later taken by the Oxford men. He remained on terms of great personal regard with Newman. Yet he was of Cambridge and the new seats of learning, Durham and King's College, London, and remained outside the magic circle of the Oxford divines.

A continental journey in 1824 was the occasion for an attack on protestantism *The State of Protestantism in Germany Described* which helped to alert the instigators of the Oxford movement to present dangers – though it provoked a riposte (soon disowned) from the young Pusey. For the last half-century and more, Rose reported, the protestant churches of Germany had presented the 'very singular spectacle' of a large majority of theologians who rejected 'all belief in the divine origin of Christianity'. This was attributable to their lack of adequate confessional standards (Melanchthon's *Apology for the Augsburg Confession* was 'long, tedious and inaccurate'), the deficiencies of their liturgy and their lack of episcopal government. The Reformation principle *sola scriptura* 'bestows on the ministry the most perfect liberty of believing and teaching whatever their own fancy may suggest.' Following Mosheim, Rose claimed that, by the seventeenth century, the Lutherans had 'degenerated into a state of unbridled licentiousness which held nothing sacred, but with audacious insolence threw down and trod on the most sacred truths of religion.' While the Reformers themselves had reverenced the fathers and referred to them, their later descendants discarded all authority except that of reason (*State*, pp. 1, 15f, 35). For Rose, all were tarred with the same brush; even those most in revolt against the age of reason – Herder, Jacobi, Schleiermacher – were condemned as rationalist. And on Rose's premises they were.

As far as he is concerned, the only sanctioned method in theology is deductive. He once commented that Froude was 'not afraid of inferences'. Rose was not afraid of them himself.

> This then is the state of things, on the hypothesis of a divine revelation; truth was as clearly revealed at the outset of Christianity as it was ever intended to be known; its record is in scripture; and if doubt as to the meaning of scripture with respect to doctrine occurs, we can appeal to witnesses competent from the time they lived or the knowledge they must have enjoyed, to remove those doubts entirely.

There is no scope for 'earthly philosophy' here, 'for its discoveries or inventions, no room for its theories, no arena for its genius.' 'There is nothing to discover in revelation.' The rightful province of human reason with respect to revelation is, 'when its truth is acknowledged, to believe and to obey it' (ib., pp. 34, 219f).

When Pusey appeared as the champion of German scholarship, Rose denounced him to the bishop of London as a liberal and an 'ultra-protestant', observing that Pusey did not depore the Lutherans' lack of episcopacy. He saw Pusey's attack on the arid orthodoxy of seventeenth-century Lutheran scholasticism as implying a threat to any orthodoxy (*Letter*, pp. 99, 104).

Rose tried to warn Newman against the more innovative and reckless of the Tractarian views. He was worried about the effects of turning readers of the *Tracts* 'out to grass in the spacious pastures of antiquity without very strict tether', adding the admonition, '*All* that is in antiquity is not good; and much that was good for antiquity would not be good for us.' Rose early on saw the danger of a 'sort of quackery of *affecting* antiquity'. Perceptively, he points out that the readers of the *Tracts* will conclude:

> The *hearts* and *affections* of these writers are not with us. Their *judgement*, arising from deep learning, thought and piety, is *against* Rome decidely; while they still think that she has much which we want. In this unhappy state, they feel that in the Church of England – there alone – is *safety;* but they feel that there is nothing more. A good deal to tolerate – a good deal to *deplore;* something no doubt to be *thankful* for . . . but little or nothing to *love.*

They use the Church of England, he concluded, as 'any port in a storm' (c. Burgon, pp. 110ff).

Rose, who had never held any other position than the high church one, counselled Newman, the convert to high church views, against enthusiasm. They should hold their ground and resist the temptation to change – though merely defending a safe, solid position might seem 'tedious' to Neman. For Rose, it is the faith once delivered to the saints. For Newman, the catholic faith had the excitement of discovery. While Rose held the apostolic succession as 'a regular, undoubted doctrine, held undoubtingly by all true churchmen, and only a little neglected,' Newman presents it as 'a thing to which we were to recur as a sort of ancient novelty – a truth now first recovered.' Newman should not imply that the church lacks a true doctrine of the sacraments and ministry: 'Too much *neglected,* undoubtedly, they have yet always been held and taught by a very large body of churchmen as being, what they really are – the true doctrine of the church'. Rose accuses the more extreme Tractarians of attempting the 'vain course of reproducing the past, *which can never be'.* When Froude's *Remains* were published, Rose commented on the Tractarians' 'disposition to find fault with our church for not satisfying the wants and demands – not of the human heart – but of the imagination of enthusiastic and ascetic and morbid-minded men' (c. Burgon, pp. 110ff, 136).

He will comply with Newman's inhibition against speaking of 'the glorious Reformation', protesting however, that 'deliverance is deliverance'. He deplored an innovating spirit, whether in the Whig reformism that would meddle with the divine constitution of the church, or in Tractarian fancies for the Roman breviary and exorcism at baptism. 'It is only novel ignorance which has deserted or abandoned the grounds which the Reformed church always meant to hold' (c. Burgon, pp. 110ff).

Rose's last years were darkened by disagreements with the movement that he had done much to bring to birth. Newman especially smarted under Rose's rebukes. But that did not stop him from dedicating the fourth volume of his sermons to the man 'who, when hearts were failing, bade us stir up the gift that was in us, and betake ourselves to our true Mother.'

William Palmer: A Case of Alienation
William Palmer of Worcester College (1803–1885) stands out as the Oxford movement's foremost theologian. Like Rose, a pure high-

churchman, he stood firm against the innovative tendencies of the more radical Tractarians in the 1840s and was not tempted by the lure of Rome. Palmer defended the Church of England as a true branch of Christ's church, upholding the validity of the Reformation and the reformed character of Anglicanism. He was not impressed by theories of development, such as Newman's. His greatest work, the *Treatise on the Church*, was described by W. F. Hook, the high church vicar of Leeds, as 'a complete vindication of the English Reformation on catholic principles'. Gladstone was profoundly influenced by it, describing it more than half a century after its publication as 'perhaps the most powerful and least assailable defence of the position of the Anglican church from the sixteenth century ... onwards' (*Later Gleanings*, p. 294) – though Gladstone was disturbed by Palmer's harsh rejection of non-episcopal bodies from the communion of the true church (p. 295).

Palmer had come into contact with Newman and Froude – and through them with Keble – as a result of his liturgical studies. In 1832 he published *Origines Liturgicae* which traced the roots in Christian antiquity of the Book of Common Prayer. Palmer intended it as a steadying influence on those unstable elements in the church who were inclined to be critical of their own tradition and to regard the Reformation as innovatory. He aimed to show that 'the dogma and worship comprised in the Prayer Book are those which the church has in all ages professed and taught.' The doctrine and polity of the Church of England were apostolic and the liturgy 'embodied, in the language of ancient piety, the orthodox and primitive faith' (*Narrative*, pp. 25ff, 117).

Palmer soon became uneasy about Froude, chiding him for expressing views on church and state and the Reformation that seemed 'extremely unjust' to the Reformers and 'injurious' to the church (ib., p. 123). He also had early reservations about Newman's leadership. Because the *Tracts* were the personal responsibility of Newman and his chosen collaborators, they evinced a strong strain of 'private judgement'. Palmer pointed out that a movement professing to restore authority, to elevate the episcopate and to lead to unity, based on adherence to the received standards of the Church of England, was evolving into its opposite, 'introducing as an essential principle the most unbounded freedom of speculation.' When Newman suffered rebuff over *Tract 90*, Palmer wrote him a letter of support out of personal loyalty, though in his *Narrative* he attributed to Newman 'a spirit of resistance and even of hostility, arising from personal feelings and indignation at the censure of the great body of the church.' Newman would not submit 'and would permit the church to be injured in return for his condemnation.' (The later secessions, including Newman's – a 'moral earthquake' – Palmer attributed to 'enthusiastic and irrational movements of self-will': ib., pp. 56f, 77f, 238f). After the loss of Newman, Palmer observed with 'very great uneasiness'

Pusey's activities as the 'self-constituted leader' of the Tractarian party – though in the end he became satisfied that the position held by Pusey was 'for the good of the church' (ib., p. 240).

In 1843 Palmer published his *Narrative of Events* in which he vindicated the initial Tractarian impulse from the charge of incipient Romanism and traced his progressive disenchantment with the trend of the Oxford movement. He deplored the rise of party spirit and the cult of personality that developed around Newman. He condemned the lust for innovation whereby every peculiarity and novelty, however startling, became for the moment a sort of *articulus stantis cadentisve ecclesiae* (!). There could be no doubt that originally the tracts and their principal authors were 'opposed to the Romish system' and that 'they concurred in this with protestants and with the Reformers themselves,' looking with repugnance on Roman corruptions and with favour on the Reformation (ib., p. 148). But a new school had reared its head in the church: 'a spirit of dissatisfaction with her principles, of enmity to her Reformers, of recklessness for her interests' – together with an attitude of 'servility and adulation' towards Rome. The Anglican Reformers are 'denounced in the most vehement terms'. 'Every unjust insinuation, every hostile construction of their conduct is indulged', no allowance being made for their difficulties or the weight of error they had to oppose (ib., pp. 149f).

Palmer singled out the articles by Ward, Oakeley *et al.* in *The British Critic* which were consistently subversive of the Reformation and laudatory of Rome. Palmer was particularly scathing about their pipedreams of restoring medieval catholicism. These propagandists for Rome knew nothing of what the middle ages were really like. They were peddlars of mere 'theory' characterised by 'unreality'. When the *British Critic* ceased publication in 1843, 'the relief of the church at the termination of this unceasing sore was indescribable' (ib., pp. 195, 243).

(1) *The Concept of the Christian Church*

In the first volume of his monumental *Treatise on the Church of Christ* (1838) Palmer sets out his conception of the Christian church as a perpetual visible divine society. 'External visible communion between all Christians in matters of religion was instituted and commanded by God' (I, p. 46). The sixteenth-century Reformers, Lutheran, Reformed and Anglican, affirmed both the perpetuity and the visibility of the church (pp. 10, 33). No sin could therefore be more heinous than schism or 'voluntary separation': it is 'a sin against our brethren, against ourselves, against God; a sin which, unless repented of, is eternally destructive to the soul' (p. 54). Separation can never be justified except where the church has become totally apostate, the synagogue of Satan (p. 64). However, there is no guarantee that the external communion of the universal church can never be interrupted – it evidently has been and still is. But not all doctrinal differences are proper causes of separation:

> There may be doctrinal differences in the catholic church generally, or between particular churches; . . . doctrines of faith actually revealed may sometimes be controverted in the catholic church; and . . . erroneous doctrines may sometimes be received as matters of faith; in either case without heresy or separation from the unity of faith (p. 111).

Palmer departs from the mainstream of Anglican ecclesiology in not availing himself of the concept of fundamentals as the basis of unity. The term fundamentals, he claims, is so ambiguous and has been employed in so many different senses as to make it useless for this purpose. If the notion of fundamentals is to be used, it needs careful definition and prior agreement on the method by which the fundamentals are to be ascertained. But altogether it seems to Palmer 'exceedingly dangerous to attempt by human reasoning to weigh the importance of truths, certainly revealed by Christ, relatively to each other' (I, pp. 122ff, 130). The Anglican Newman thought Palmer too dismissive of this concept (*Essays Crit. and Hist.*, I, p. 175).

The Christian ministry is essential to the church and is an aspect of its catholicity. 'As the church can never have failed, so the ministry can never have failed' (I, pp. 161, 165). But the continuance of the ministry depends on the succession of ordinations: if that had been broken, 'the catholic church must have entirely failed – a position which is directly and formally heretical' (I, pp. 171, 174). Episcopacy was 'universally established by the apostles, either personally or by injunction' and is therefore always binding on the church' (II, p. 389). Though Palmer here hardens the Anglican insistence on episcopacy compared with the position of the sixteenth-century divines, and takes no cognisance of the extreme situation envisaged by Hooker in which episcopacy, instituted by divine positive law, might be abrogated by the inherent power of the church, nevertheless he continues the Anglican tradition of indulgence and understanding to the reformed non-episcopal foreign churches. The Lutherans are 'not to be blamed for not instituting bishops among themselves at first, because they were appellants to a general council, and looked forward to reunion with the bishops of Germany. Calvin himself acted as a bishop at Geneva; and both he and some of his principal disciples approved of episcopacy' (II, p. 390).

On the other hand, it is not essential for the integrity of a Christian church to be in communion with the bishop of Rome. The churches in communion with Rome before the Reformation were true Christian churches and, in Palmer's view, continued so afterwards – here he knows he speaks for the consensus of Anglican divines, while noting Jewel and Field as dissenting (I, pp. 275ff; c.f. *Tract 15*, p. 10). But the claims of the papacy are vigorously refuted. Peter did not enjoy a formal primacy since all the apostles were equal and shared the supremacy over the church. Such an office of primacy could not therefore have been transmitted to any putative successors in Peter's see of Rome. 'The pre-eminence of the Roman church may be sufficiently accounted for without any divine institution' (II, pp. 492, 497). The pope has no universal jurisdiction *jure divino*, is not infallible, and is not the divinely ordained centre of unity for the church (II, pp. 506, 525ff, 528ff). Nevertheless, Palmer does not wish to detract from the privileges of primacy accorded to the papacy in the primitive church, honours founded not on divine right but on 'reason and Christian charity', though in a divided church Rome has ceased to be the centre of unity (II, p. 537).

(2) *The Anglican Church*
Palmer maintains the so called 'branch theory' of the church. The Roman church, the eastern churches and the Anglican church are the authentic 'portions' of the catholic church. Palmer vigorously defends the integrity and catholicity of the Anglican church. In England, the Church of England is continuous with the pre-Reformation church. At the Reformation she threw off the *jurisdiction* of the pope, but did not separate from his *communion* (I, p. 223). The British churches have existed continuously as visible societies in unbroken succession from the earliest period of Christianity (p. 218). The Church of England 'does not imagine for a moment that she has ever separated from the catholic church, or been separated by its authority.' Of course she does not accept that to be out of communion with the pope (and that against her will) is equivalent to being out of communion with the catholic church (I, pp. 221f). The Church of England was not created at the Reformation:

> If indeed, as is alleged, the Church of England was founded at the Reformation by separation from the catholic church; if its faith was then invented or changed by Henry VIII ... if the Reformation was the introduction of a new gospel ... and if the Church of England was responsible for all the views, motives, acts of Henry, Edward, Elizabeth and their courtiers ... we need not pretend to form any part of the church.

But, Palmer insists, 'we altogether deny these positions' (I, p. 426).

Palmer is admittedly defensive about the royal supremacy. Some Anglican theologians have 'spoken unadvisedly' on this – though they have not gone further than some Roman theologians (I, p. 258). The Anglican teaching on the royal supremacy cannot be derived merely from the preambles to acts of parliament. And the church does not admit all that monarchs have claimed for themselves (I, pp. 254ff, 261ff). Palmer maintains the classical Anglican position – which was also that of Keble and the early Gladstone – that it is the duty of the Christian magistrate to protect the church and maintain its work. Though the state should not persecute dissenters – Palmer approves the repeal of penal legislation against nonconformists and papists – it should never show them favour or encouragement (II, pp. 317ff, 365f). However, Palmer appears not to share Hooker's interpretation of the royal supremacy as admitting in principle the role of the laity in the church's legislative procedures. For Palmer, as for the Tractarians in general, 'the right of making public and formal decrees in controversies of religion is vested in the ministers of Jesus Christ' (II, p. 103).

Against Roman controversialists and Anglican waverers, Palmer declared:

> Since then it is certain that our churches have been perpetually visible even from the earliest ages; since they preserve the unity of communion both in themselves and as respects the catholic church; since they equally preserve the unity of faith; since they have never been in any way separated from the unity of the catholic church; since they have all the characteristics of Christian holiness which can belong to a branch of the true church; and since their ministry is derived in regular and valid succession from the apostles; there can be no reasonable doubt that they are indeed churches of Christ (I, p. 242; c.f. *Tract 15*, 'On the Apostolic Succession in the English Church').

3. Palmer's Defence of the Reformation

In his *Treatise on the Church of Christ* Palmer provided a systematic account of the principles on which his opposition to Tractarian trends was based. He insisted, as the Anglican Reformers and seventeenth-century divines had done, on the duty of provincial or national churches to reform themselves (I, p. 492). He defended the Reformers against the accusation of schism and heresy, pointing out that they were unwilling parties to separation. Luther himself was the 'involuntary instrument' of reformation. The Reformers were not to be held responsible for the irregular nature of their ministries (though it was doubtful whether their orders were valid and their 'societies' could not be regarded as properly constituted churches) (pp. 362ff, 382ff; c.f. *History*, p. 236).

The Reformation, he pointed out, was not aimed at any doctrines defined by the church catholic (he did not identify catholic teaching with the promulgations of the Council of Trent, as Ward and Oakeley did). The Reformation was consistent with the Vincentian Canon: *semper, ubique et ab omnibus*, what had been held always, everywhere and by all. The Reformation did not depart from the mainstream of Christian tradition. The English Reformers, like their continental counterparts, acknowledged the authority of universal tradition (I, pp. 494ff).

Newman had directed the weight of his attack on the Reformation against the doctrines of justification by faith and the right of private judgement. Palmer thought Luther's teaching on justification 'of very little weight' and did not regard this as the main issue. He agreed with Newman that Luther had disparaged good works (I, p. 384).

But Palmer strongly defended the Reformers against criticisms based on the supposed right of private judgement. This was not an authentic Reformation principle. The Reformers gave no countenance to the notion that it was 'the absolute right of every individual to deduce his own religion from the Bible only, to the exclusion of creeds, articles, catholic tradition and the authority of the church, and to maintain with unlimited freedom whatever doctrines appear, to his own private judgement, most consistent with scripture.' This was a view 'falsely' and 'impudently' attributed to the Reformers. The public statements of all the Reformers are 'diametrically opposed' to it. The Reformers revered the doctrine of the primitive church and constantly appealed to the ecumenical councils and the writings of the fathers. As far as the English Reformation is concerned, 'the authority of catholic tradition and of the universal church, as opposed to the unlimited freedom of private inventions' was consistently upheld (I, pp. 374ff. 382, 499).

Palmer's tone changes, however, when he comes to speak of contemporary protestantism. Here he is dependent on Rose and they both anticipate the sort of language later used by Newman. The continental Reformation is 'a thing that has passed away'. Lutheranism and Calvinism are now little more than matters of history. The 'feeble and lifeless relics' which they have left behind, and which still bear their name, are merely 'painful memorials' of 'systems whose imperfections and faults, whatever they might be, were dignified by a holy ardour and zeal for God and God's revelation.' The churches of the Reformation present a very different picture today. Overrun by the 'audacious impiety' of rationalism, or sunk into the 'deadly slumber' of Unitarianism, Lutheranism and Calvinism, as religious sytems, have 'nearly perished' in their countries of origin (pp. 388ff. German rationalism is a manifestation of the spirit of unbelief: it subjects divine revelation to human reason, evacuates the faith of mystery, strips away all that is distinctive about the Christian gospel and imputes 'falsehood and folly' to the scriptures themselves (*History*, p. 330).

But this does not detract from the glory of the Reformers' witness. Palmer is kind even to Cranmer: though his opinions changed, his sincerity and honesty should not be doubted. His recantations 'are only proofs that his natural firmness did not exceed that of the great majority of men;' 'his last hours shed a splendour on his name' (*Treatise*, I, pp. 544ff). However, amongst the 'noble army of martyrs' who 'contended even to death for Christian truth against Roman errors and superstitions', the name of Nicholas Ridley stands supreme and here Palmer's language reveals a different spirit to that of the Newmanite Tractarians:

> Never, since the days of the apostles, was there a nobler manifestation of Christian faith and heroism. It was worthy of the brightest days of the primitive church; and not even Polycarp, in the amphitheatre of Smyrna, exceeded the glory of Nicholas Ridley (*History*, p. 276).

When, two years before his death, the First Vatican Council and the definition of papal infallibility having intervened, Palmer reissued his *Narrative*, he added an introduction in which the anti-Roman stance of the *Narrative* itself is, if anything, intensified. The papacy with its 'monstrous pretensions' was 'the mother of superstitions and errors', a 'usurpation' in the Christian church that blasphemously identifies itself with the first article of the creed, claiming the faith in itself that belongs only to God. It was the 'centre of worldliness and idolatry'. The Reformation, on the other hand, was 'the work of Jesus Christ' and the English Reformers, though not remarkable for genius or fame, enjoyed the 'surpassing glory' of martyrdom 'in vindication of the truths of the gospel' (*Narrative*, pp. 4–8).

W. F. Hook: An Evangelical High Churchman

W. F. Hook (1798–1875), successively vicar of Leeds and dean of Chichester, initially welcomed the *Tracts for the Times*, but was repelled by the emergence of Romanising tendencies and became an implacable opponent of the movement in the name of the old high churchmanship. Hook can be described as an evangelical high churchman – evangelical because he held to the forensic interpretation of justification, with the imputation of the righteousness of Christ; high churchman because he held that justification was received through the sacrament of baptism, not through personal conversion as the evangelicals maintained.

Hook's *Church Dictionary* of 1842 (from which his views on justification, just cited, are derived) offers useful summaries of his opinions on controverted matters. The Reformation, for example, was 'the rescue of our church from the usurped dominion of the pope and its restoration from the corruptions of popery to a nearer approach to primitive purity.' In his preface to the sixth edition, however, Hook commented on sinister developments within the Tractarian movement. When the dictionary was first published, 'the protestantism of the Church of England was universally recognised, and the fear was lest her pretensions to catholicity should be ignored.' But now, he complained, 'an affectation of repudiating our protestantism is prevalent, while by ignorant or designing men protestantism is misrepresented as the antithesis, not as is the case, to Romanism, but to catholicism.' At the same time, 'catholicism is confounded with Romanism, primitive truth with medieval error, and the theology of the schools with that of the fathers.' (As Hook later stated the same point: catholicism is opposed, not to protestantism, but to popery, because catholicism is opposed to heresy: *Three Reformations*, p. 79.)

Hook was here identifying the influence that Hurrell Froude had exerted on Oakeley, Ward and Newman. Hook wrote to Pusey in 1844 with fears for Newman: 'May he be preserved from the fangs of Satan.'

While Newman and others were turning to Rome as the only safe home of salvific sacramental grace, Hook was persuaded that by doing so they were actually jeopardising their salvation: 'Any person going from light to darkness would endanger his salvation. I should fear that it would be scarcely possible for anyone who should apostatise from the only true church of God in this country to the popish sect to escape perdition' (c. Greenfield in P. Butler, ed., p. 169).

Hook was profoundly assured of the catholicity of the Church of England. It was 'pure and reformed'; 'that pure and apostolical branch of the church which is the bulwark not of the Reformation only, but of catholicism itself.' It takes its stand on scripture and the primitive church (*Three Reformations*, pp. 9, 41). Hook believed that the principles of the English Reformation could form the basis for the reunion of Christendom. Writing in support of the Jerusalem Bishopric, he claimed:

> Our view of the Reformation – the view of the good old Church of England divinity – leads us to look upon our church as a model – not perfect indeed, but still a pure model of a reformed catholic church . . . We will not tolerate an attempt at union until the principle of our Reformation is recognised, especially that principle which asserts the right of each particular church to reform itself in perfect independence of the see of Rome (c. Nockles, diss., p. 238).

By a high churchman Hook meant 'one who, having ascertained that the Church of England was reformed on the right principle, cordially accepted the Reformers . . . one who, thinking the church wiser than himself, observed her regulations and obeyed her laws' (c. Fuller in Rowell, ed., p. 54). Hook deplored the party spirit, the personality cult and conspiratorial mentality of the more extreme Tractarians. 'I love Pusey, Newman and Keble with all my heart,' he wrote to Samuel Wilberforce, 'but I call no man my master. Christian is my name, catholic my surname: when my Oxford friends are acting as catholic Christians then I agree with them; when they act otherwise, their great names have no influence upon me' (c. ib., p. 53). But relations deteriorated between Hook and the Oxford leaders: Newman embraced darkness; Pusey promoted 'Romish Methodism', morbid, superstitious fanaticism. Hook formally severed relations with Pusey after bitter disagreements over Romish practices at St. Saviour's Leeds, the church that Pusey had endowed as a witness to all he was fighting for in the Church of England.

Gladstone: A Lay Theologian
At the end of his life Gladstone wrote *The Impregnable Rock of Holy Scripture* in which he upheld the inspiration and authority of the Bible against what many regarded as the assault of biblical criticism (the legitimacy of which, in its responsible forms, he did not deny). Gladstone's faith in the Church of England and the vocation of

Anglicanism was itself an impregnable rock, buffetted but unmoved by Tractarian extremism, defections to Rome, advanced ritualism and state interference. Gladstone was a bastion of Anglicanism and a remarkable example of lay leadership exercised for the greater well being of the church. He devoted his gigantic intellect and superhuman energies – ample portions of which remained after all the exertions of political life, classical scholarship, tree-felling and the rescue of prostitutes – to theological and ecclesiastical questions. Gladstone's views on these matters would not perhaps merit our attention if they were those of a regius professor of divinity or a diocesan bishop. But as the part-time contributions of a layman, professionally engaged in other spheres, they are worth noting. Gladstone had given some thought to the role of laymen in the church and was an advocate of lay representation in synodical government (*Gleanings*, VI, ch. 1).

Gladstone had a fervent evangelical upbringing and hoped to take holy orders. He never renounced the evangelical preoccupation with personal salvation, but added catholic ecclesiology to an evangelical soteriology (P. Butler, p. 56). A deep study of the church fathers and the Anglican divines, especially Hooker, led Gladstone to accept the doctrine of baptismal regeneration, and with it the sacramental principle, before his twentieth year. The agitation surrounding the Reform Bill (1830–1832) turned Gladstone into a doctrinaire high Tory in the Keble mould – 'the rising hope of those stern and unbending Tories', as Macaulay introduced the youthful author of *The State in its Relations with the Church* in his famous review of 1839. In 1832 Gladstone added a sense of catholicity to his sacramental theology: spending Holy Week in Rome he was fired with a vision of the reunion of Christendom. Both his evangelicalism and his Anglo-catholicism were fed from a common source in Augustine, one of Gladstone's so called 'four doctors' – the others being Aristotle, Dante and Butler (P. Butler, p. 43). At this time Gladstone might well have added a fifth, Edmund Burke, from whom he learned of the corporate, organic nature of society and (following Hooker) the spiritual ends of government. But as during the 1830s he enriched and completed his synthesis of catholic and evangelical elements by adding the principle of liberty, he came to feel that Burke's reactionary principles had misled him (ib., p. 40). Abandoning his Hookerian theory of church establishment, he henceforth advocated a liberal catholicism, a catholicism without the dogmatic principle which Newman despaired of in the Church of England.

Gladstone renounced party to follow principle, both in politics and theology. He was critical of the extreme Tractarians, but defended them when they were persecuted. He gave a balanced assessment of *Ecce Homo* (1865) which drew down such vituperation on its anonymous author (Seeley) on account of its presentation of the figure of Jesus of Nazareth in its human aspect exclusively (*Gleanings*, III, ch. 2). Gladstone accepted the assured results of biblical criticism. Even in his work on church and state, he had refused to unchurch non-episcopal communions and had been disturbed by the harsh verdict that his guide and mentor in catholic principles, William Palmer of Worcester College, had pronounced on them (*Later Gleanings*, p. 295).

As Perry Butler has pointed out, Gladstone's liberalism should not be confused with the liberalism against which the Tractarians set their faces in the 1830s. 'That liberalism was secular, utilitarian, committed to the "march of mind", hostile to dogmatic faith. It wanted the church subordinate to the civil power' (p. 151). Gladstone's liberalism, however, looked back to Hooker and Butler: it stood for moderation, natural justice, a sense of what was appropriate in various circumstances, and followed probability as the guide of life.

Gladstone became a critic of both evangelicalism and the Oxford movement. He was aware that their roots were entwined together. In embracing a sacramental theology, he did not need to surrender much in the evangelical tradition because 'so many of its tenets were part of the common stock of an older religious tradition to which he was always committed' (P. Butler, p. 52). Gladstone was a continuator of the old high church Anglicanism – he was an evangelical high churchman who combined 'church principles' (the sacramental life and the apostolic succession) with an evangelical (ie. forensic) doctrine of justification. The study of the Prayer Book and Palmer's *Treatise on the Church* led Gladstone to his settled position. Palmer's book, he recalled, 'took hold upon me, and gave me at once the clear, definite and strong conception of the church which through all the storm and strain of a most critical period has proved for me entirely adequate to every emergency and saved me from all vacillation' (c. P. Butler, p. 58).

Gladstone worked out his catholic Anglicanism in the uninspiring *Church Principles* of 1840, which followed hard on the heels of his work on church and state. Is is a stout defence of the claims and principles of the Church of England and one that he would stand by all his life. That church, he wrote:

> gives credibility to her doctrine, and clear authority to her ministrations, by the fact that she teaches no articles of faith but such as have been drawn out of scripture by the universal consent of the church from the beginning, and that she is at this day historically the same institution through which the gospel was originally preached to the English nation; preached then, as it is preached now, by the ascertained commission of the apostles of Christ, and through them by the will of Christ himself (p. 313).

In numerous publications Gladstone defended the English Reformation: it had preserved the apostolic faith and order; it had legality and regularity on its side. Before Cranmer and the other Reformers came on the scene, and before the rupture with Rome over Henry VIII's divorce, the Anglican bishops and clergy, believing themselves entitled to deal with the ordinary jurisdiction of the pope, had set in train the liberation of the national church from Rome. These reforms were thus 'not acts of the state forced upon the church, but acts of the church herself' (*Later Gleanings*, pp. 165, 179, 220; c.f. *State ... Church*, II, pp. 95ff). Reviewing W. G. Ward's *Ideal of a Christian Church* with its bitter invective against the Reformers, Gladstone rebuked Ward for advancing 'grotesque and fanciful' interpretations of the Reformation, totally unsubstantiated by research; Ward's were 'wild and wanton opinions' (*Gleanings*, V, pp. 90ff). Gladstone's own knowledge of the political, constitutional and ecclesiastical (if not the theological) history of the Reformation is impressive.

Gladstone was sympathetic towards the Lutheran Reformation also. 'When men were most unjustly anathematized and excommunicated, as Luther; and when they had no choice but to forego Christian ordinances altogether, or to affirm as truths the grossest and most destructive abuses, against which their soul and conscience revolted' they cannot be accused of schism or regarded as severed from the church (*Church Principles*, p. 421; c.f. *State ... Church*, II, pp. 79ff). Quoting Bramhall, Andrewes and Laud, Gladstone insists – and here he shows his independence from the harsher Oxford school – that non-episcopal churches are not deprived of sacramental grace. 'When the fact of holiness is established, the inference of grace is certain' (*Church Principles*, pp. 415, 210f). Here Gladstone anticipates the view of later liberal catholics such as Gore who, while holding inflexibly to apostolic succession, somewhat inconsistently allowed 'uncovenanted mercies' to those bodies who lacked it.

In a very late (1894) essay on heresy and schism, Gladstone argued that a rigid application of these concepts was undermined by any reading of church history. How do you apply them to the separation of east and west in the eleventh century? How to the rival popes of Avignon and Rome in the fourteenth? 'If either party be excluded,' he comments astutely, 'then the light of half western Christendom had been extinct for half a century. If on the other hand it be attempted to include them all by the doctrine of an upright intention, that doctrine, when once admitted with respect to church communion, may be found to render all sharp application of the argument against schismatics ... in truth against all non-Roman Christians, nearly impracticable' (*Later Gleanings*, p. 286). In his old age Gladstone came to place great emphasis on the fundamentals or essence of Christianity, the Incarnation and the Trinity, embodied in our common baptismal faith, as the ground of hope for the future unity of Christians (ib., pp. 298ff, 384ff).

Without renouncing his evangelical birthright, Gladstone was critical of evangelicalism: he believed that it must share the blame, with

Tractarian excesses, for secessions to Rome. Both evangelicalism and Tractarianism, he wrote in 'The Evangelical Movement' (1879), 'created instincts and stimulated longings which they could not satisfy.' The evangelical thirst for holiness, precision and separation from the world, led some of its most ardent spirits to embrace catholic principles in the absolute form represented by the more extreme Tractarians; this led them to long for a more complete system, an efficient machine for the promulgation of dogma and the exercise of discipline. Anglican catholicism was not to blame – 'It was not Hooks or Kebles or Williamses, but Newmans, Mannings and Wilberforces', the ertswhile evangelicals, 'who organised and led the host, so considerable alike in numbers, learning and devotion.' The ultimate flaw lay in the nature of evangelicalism: beneficial though it was as a religious impulse and moral example, it was 'incomplete' and 'abnormal' as a system. It did not represent the whole of Anglicanism. 'It dislodged the centre of gravity.' It lacked a theology (*Gleanings*, VII, pp. 232ff).

Gladstone missed the first phase of the Oxford movement. He did not read the early *Tracts* and only became acquainted with its platform and personalities from 1836 (*Correspondence*, I, pp. 226, 262). 'I was not under any important theological influence at any time, from the authors of the Tracts,' he insisted (ib., p. 264). In *Church Principles* (1840) he protested: 'It is the greatest possible error to suppose that the teaching of these doctrines in the present day is peculiar to certain pious and learned individuals in the university of Oxford' (p. 230). (This claim is substantiated by the researches of Dr Peter Nockles, notably, which have enabled us to see the Oxford movement in a proper historical perspective – prejudiced hitherto both by the extravagant claims of the Tractarians themselves, who disparaged the old high churchmen because of their anachronistic views on church and state, and by the subsequent hagiography of the Anglo-catholic movement.)

Gladstone certainly misjudged the early Oxford movement. As Perry Butler has written, he took it for 'the revival of historic Anglicanism, emerging after a century of latitudinarianism and worldliness, a revival complementing and correcting the evangelical revival.' It would renew the national church; Hooker's great ideal would become a reality (p. 102; c.f., *Autobiography*, pp. 54ff). Gladstone did not appreciate at first the essentially sectarian, party nature of the movement, nor did he realise how far its leading theorists had departed from Tory principles – not of course in the direction of a pluralistic society as Gladstone was to do after 1840, but in the direction of a free but sectarian church subsisting in a hostile environment. He wrote to James Hope [-Scott], who had originally introduced Gladstone to the movement, in 1840: 'True church principle utterly rejects the notion of party or combination standing between the individual and the church, and binds men, inwardly at least, to disclaim every such spurious association . . .' 'If there be such a party,' Gladstone went on, 'I am no member of it, not only for the reason that I cannot allege concurrence in its distinctive opinions, but also because the whole basis of party seems to me to be uprooted and abolished by the first principles of catholicity in religion' (*Correspondence*, I, pp. 232f).

Like so many other Englishmen of the nineteenth century, Christian or agnostic – Maurice, Kingsley, Acton and Tait; Jowett, Huxley, Leslie and Fitzjames Stephen, and Mark Pattison – Gladstone profoundly distrusted Newman. In Gladstone's view, Newman had never been 'an instructed English churchman' and had never grasped Palmer's conception of the historic church. His ignoring of the eastern churches in coming to conclusions about the catholicity of the Church of England, was 'one of the boldest pieces of tactic in the history of controversy.' Newman's lectures on justification caused Gladstone 'the greatest apprehension': he saw in them the spectre of human merit. He wrote to Manning in 1843, when Newman's destiny was all but apparent, 'I am persuaded that this powerful man has suffered and is suffering much in the healthful tone of his judgement from exclusiveness of mental habit and from affections partly wounded through cruelty, partly overwrought into morbid action from gloating as it were continually and immediately upon the most absorbing and exciting subjects.' Newman had over-reacted to the condemnation of *Tract 90*, for in Gladstone's view, 'there never was an uproar, and there never were censures, which were more ascribable to the manner and language of a publication as contrasted with its substance.' In the eyes of the world Newman was already 'a disgraced man'. Gladstone's verdict in 1845 was that Newman had lost 'that sort of authority which depends upon judgement as apart from argument' (*Correspondence*, I, pp. 281, 285; P. Butler, pp. 58, 167, 173ff, 229, 196).

12

The Reformation Under Attack

Hurrell Froude and a Subversive Document
Richard Hurrell Froude, more than any other individual, was responsible
for transforming a movement of moral and pastoral renewal – Tractarianism in its first phase – into a crusade for catholic truth. Newman regarded
Froude as the 'author' of the Oxford movement (*Cert. Diffs*, p. 36).
Symbolic and instrumental of this decisive change of direction was his
attack on the protestant Reformers and avowed intent to unprotestantise
the Church of England. Froude's directness of manner, force of
personality and love of the shocking paradox, while they earned him the
rebukes of Keble, sharpened the issues and forced the Tractarian leaders
to face the logical conclusions of their principles.

Froude comes across in his journals as an unattractive figure –
immature, irresponsible and egotistic – but the impression he made on his
close circle of contemporaries was strikingly different. John Keble
thought sufficiently highly of him to invite him to Southrop, together
with Robert Wilberforce and Isaac Williams, for guided reading and
training in character. Williams remarked that Froude 'was considered a
very odd fellow at College, but clever and original; Keble alone was able
to appreciate and value him' – adding, 'If he had not at this time fallen
into such hands, his speculations might have taken a very dangerous turn'
(a suggestion that Froude might have been tempted by scepticism).
Williams compared Froude to Hamlet, adding, 'Froude was a person
most natural, but so original as to be unlike anyone else, hiding depth of
delicate thought in apparent extravagances . . .' (pp. 83f). Two days after
Froude's death from consumption in 1836, Newman wrote to J. W.
Bowden: 'I can never have a greater loss . . . In variety and perfection of
gifts I think he far excelled even Keble. For myself, I cannot describe
what I owe to him as regards the intellectual principles of religion and
morals.'

The idea of publishing Froude's *Remains* apparently originated with a remark of Isaac Williams that, if only people could see Froude as he really was, they would begin to understand what his remarks – on the face of it so shocking that 'one constantly trembled for him' in company – were really driving at (Williams, p. 84). Alas! readers of the *Remains* found them doubly scandalous. Keble had once advised Froude to burn his confessions, but now, with Newman, he shared in preparing them for publication. Friends such as W. F. Hook and Samuel Wilberforce were afraid that the revelation of Froude's morbid introspection would harm the Tractarian cause. Sir James Stephen referred to 'this suicidal portraiture' that affection would have committed to the flames, but party spirit had given to the press – adding, with pardonable exaggeration: 'the most unscrupulous publisher of diaries and private correspondence never offered for sale a self-analysis more frank or less prepossessing' (p. 450).

It was, however, Froude's remarks about the protestant Reformers, rather than his indiscreet private revelations, that aroused the greatest indignation. Gladstone, himself a patron of Tractarianism, deplored these 'rash, intemperate censures'. Thomas Arnold condemned the 'extra-ordinary impudence' of Froude's comments on the Reformers, for 'the way in which he, a young man and a clergyman of the Church of England, reviles all those persons whom the accordant voice of that church, without distinction of party, has agreed to honour, even perhaps with excess of admiration.' (On reading Newman's *Tract 90* in 1841, Arnold was moved to exclaim, 'They hate the Reformation; they hate the Reformers.') The publication of the *Remains* led directly to the building of the Martyrs' Memorial in Oxford and the founding of the Parker Society for the publication of the works of the English Reformers (Stanley, pp. 336, 455).

Sir James Stephen wittily brought together the twofold scandal of the *Remains* when, in his essay 'The Evangelical Succession', he compared Froude's dilettantist asceticism with the consuming purposefulness of George Whitefield:

> When Whitefield would mortify his body, he set about it like a man. The paroxysm was short indeed, but terrible. While it lasted, his diseased imagination brought soul and body into deadly conflict, his fierce spirit spurning, trampling and well-nigh destroying the peccant carcase. Not so the fastidious and refined 'witness to the views of' the restorers of the catholic church. The strife between his spiritual and animal nature is recorded in his journal in such terms as these: 'Looked with greediness to see if there was goose on the table for dinner'; 'Meant to have kept a fast and did abstain from dinner, but at tea eat [sic] buttered toast.'

Stephen spares us Froude's scruples about 'a bit of cold endings of a dab at breakfast, and a scrap of mackerel at dinner'.

He does not mean to mock; these revelations, he says, will provoke a contemptuous smile from no one who knows much of his own heart. But he thinks that it would be taking Froude altogether too seriously to regard him as a threat to the reformed character of the Church of England.

> Luther and Zwingle, Cranmer and Latimer, may still rest in their honoured graves. 'Take courage, brother Ridley, we shall light up such a flame in England as shall not soon be put out' is a prophecy which will not be defeated by the successors of the Oxonian divines who listened to it, so long as they shall be vacant to record and to publish contrite reminiscences of a desire for roasted goose and of an undue indulgence in buttered toast.

But here Sir James Stephen was being altogether too sanguine (Stephen, p. 455).

Froude's comments on the Reformers occur largely in the letters of volume I of the *Remains*. By the time the third volume appeared, the editors had to reply to the chorus of indignation. In the preface to volume III, Newman and Keble claimed in extenuation of Froude (in my view, justly) that he had 'entered on the study of the Reformers' theology with the general and natural impression that he should find on the whole a treasure of sound Anglican doctrine and a tone of thought in unison with the ancient church,' but 'found himself greatly disappointed . . .' He speaks in these confessions with 'the fervour of an earnest enquirer and the indignation of one who had met, or thought he met, with irreverence where he expected primitive piety.' That this is not special pleading is borne out by the first long passage, dated 1832, about the Reformation (Froude, III, p. xxi).

Froude had set himself a reading programme in the documents of the English Reformation, but the more he read, the less impressed he became. 'One must not speak lightly of a martyr, so I do not allow my opinions to pass the verge of scepticism. But I really do feel sceptical whether Latimer was not something in the Bulteel line' (Bulteel being an Oxford evangelical whose licence to preach was revoked by the bishop of Oxford; he left the Church of England in 1831, becoming an Irvingite and then a Plymouth Brother: to the Tractarians, Bulteel was symbolic of the most egregious form of protestantism). Froude also doubts 'whether the catholicism of their formulae was not a concession to the feelings of the nation with whom protestantism had not yet become popular and who could scarcely bear the alterations which were made; and whether the progress of things in Edward VI's minority may not be considered the jobbing of a faction.' But he still has an open mind: 'I will do myself the justice to say that those doubts give me pain and that I hope more reading will in some degree dispel them . . . Certainly the *ethos* of the Reformation is to me a *terra incognita* and I do not think it has been explored by anyone that I have heard talk about it' (I, p. 251).

Froude continued his studies and shortly afterwards reported: 'I have been looking into Strype's *Memorials* and Burnet a good deal, without finding much to like in the Reformers.' His problem was to understand what motivated the opposing parties. 'The sincerity of the leading men on both sides seems so equivocal that I can hardly see what attracted them to their respective positions.' Froude was further disillusioned when he discovered that the English Reformers and even the divines of Elizabeth's reign did not claim divine right (*jus divinum*) for episcopacy, compounding their error by claiming that the queen herself was the source of ecclesiastical power. Froude regarded this as a cynical lack of principle, failing to realise that the reformed doctrine of the godly prince was founded on biblical precedents and the theological principle of the role of the laity in the church. He also failed to make the distinction, so important to Hooker, for example, between two sorts of ecclesiastical power – the power of order (*potestas ordinis*) or sacramental power, on the one hand, and the power of jurisdiction (*potestas jurisdictionis*) or the authority to carry out acts of ecclesiastical government in the realm, on the other. The queen was held to be the source of ecclesiastical power in the second sense only and Henry VIII was the only monarch to hint that he held the *potestas ordinis* and even he did not dare to claim it outright (I, p. 253; cf. Avis, *CTR*, ch. 10).

It is interesting that Froude preferred the puritans to the Reformers because they at least believed that church government (ie. presbyterianism) was *jus divinum*; at least they fought for divine right, 'though not the true one'. Taught to despise history and tradition, they turned in their ignorance to the Bible in isolation for the divine pattern of church government. Froude thinks that this superfluous biblicism is a pardonable error and considers writing an apology for the early puritans (I, pp. 325ff).

The tone of Froude's remarks gradually changes from that of sincere enquiry to that of outright rejection of the Reformation and all its (real or imagined) works. In 1834 he confesses in a letter to Keble: 'I am every day becoming a less and less loyal son of the Reformation. It appears to me plain that in all matters that seem to us indifferent or even doubtful, we should conform our practices to those of the church which has preserved its traditionary practices unbroken. We cannot know about any seemingly indifferent practice of the Church of Rome that it is not a development of the apostolic *ethos*.' And in the following year he declares: 'Really I hate the Reformation and the Reformers more and more and have almost made up my mind that the rationalist spirit they set afloat is the *pseudoprophetes* of the Revelations.' The Reformation has become synonymous with error and heresy. Froude's working hypothesis is that, on any disputed point, the Reformers are to be rejected and the Church of Rome accepted – a presumption of guilt in the case of the Reformers, of innocence in the case of Rome. 'Why do you praise Ridley?' he asks, 'Do you know sufficient good about him to counter-balance the fact that he was the associate of Cranmer, Peter Martyr and Bucer?' (I, pp. 336, 389, 393f).

Froude singles out the great apologist of the Anglican settlement, John Jewel, for special denunciation. With characteristic anachronism he labels Jewel an 'irreverent dissenter' and – in a passage that Newman and Keble tactfully omitted from the published version of the *Remains* – asserted that Jewel's doctrine 'ought to be denied under pain of damnation.' Froude is offended by Jewel's polemical style (though one might have thought that he would recognise a kindred spirit!) and interprets Jewel's reformed teaching in a minimising sense.

> He calls the mass 'your cursed paltrie service', laughs at the apostolic succession both in principle and as a fact, and says that the only succession worth having is the succession of doctrine. He most distinctly denies the sacrament of the Lord's Supper to be a means of grace as distinguished from a pledge . . . He says the only keys of the kingdom of heaven are instruction and correction and the only way they open the kingdom is by touching men's consciences . . . Jewel justifies Calvin for saying that the sacrament of the Lord's Supper 'were superfluous' if we remembered Christ's death enough without it, ridicules the consecration of the elements and indirectly explains that the way the Body and Blood are verily received is that they are received into our remembrance.

In a note published among the fragments in volume III, Froude remarks: 'I am weary of Jewel. He puffs Calvin and the Church of Geneva as saints, especially their way of receiving the sacrament, in such terms as make one think he wished for it in England.' On the other hand, Froude was captivated by Cardinal Pole, Mary's archbishop. He was 'the person I like best of all I have read about'. 'He seems a hero of an ideal world,' added Froude, 'a combination of chivalrous and catholic feeling' (I, pp. 339, 254; III, p. 407).

Froude's rejection of the English Reformers was instinctive. The whole ethos of the Reformation repelled him. But it was not a reaction supported by sound historical judgement. Froude's comments are anachronistic, impressionistic and subjective. He is comparing the beliefs and lives of the Reformers of the sixteenth century with those of the Tractarians of the nineteenth, as though nothing else had changed. As Piers Brendon has rightly remarked, the parallel between the Erastian Reformers of the sixteenth century and the apostate Whigs of 1832 was too obvious for someone as analogically-minded as Froude to miss (p. 112). But, from the historiographical point of view, this was precisely Froude's mistake. In his imagination he envisaged Keble amid the political intrigue of the magisterial Reformation and set Jewel down in an Oxford common room full of Tractarian dons. What would Keble have made of it? Why does Jewel come off so badly? This not parody: it is, as we have seen, precisely Froude's method.

To him, the Reformers were 'the very kind of fellows' Keble 'would most have hated and despised if he had known them.' Latimer was 'something in the Bulteel line'. If Hooker had lived now he would have rejected the royal supremacy. If the puritans had not been prejudiced against tradition they might have grasped the true *jus divinum*. Froude is scandalised by the English Reformers' involvement in politics: little does he realise how much in the early church was equally attributable to 'the jobbing of a faction'. He is willing to assume for the sake of argument that Rome has preserved apostolic practice uninterruptedly – a problem to which Newman devoted a decade of research and a book of the calibre of the essay on development.

Froude's influence on Keble and Newman (and posthumously, through the *Remains*, on W. G. Ward) with respect to the Reformation was decisive. He attempted to sting Newman into more extreme courses by charging him with 'Tract protestantism'. As Newman recalled in the *Apologia*, 'He taught me to look with admiration towards the church of Rome and in the same degree to dislike the Reformation' (p. 114).

Froude's most recent biographer, Piers Brendon, has written:

> It is not too much to say that the electric suggestiveness of the *Remains* charged the extreme high church movement with its initial life. Froude's personal example of holiness, his romantic vision of the medieval church, his corresponding denigration of the Reformation, his ambitions to 'unprotestantise' the church – all these things inspired the secessionist wing of the Tractarian movement.

'Ward and others of his ilk,' Brendon concludes, 'were willing to rack Froude's principles to their logical breaking point' (pp. 185f).

Radical Voices: Oakeley and Ward

(1) Frederick Oakeley

Froude's anti-protestant polemic found a fertile reception in the minds of Frederick Oakeley and William George Ward. Though Oakeley took the direction of his views from Ward, he can be mentioned first as by far the lesser of the two men, both fellows of Balliol. 'Mr Oakeley,' recalled R. W. Church, 'without much learning, was a master of a facile and elegant pen. He was a man who followed a trusted leader with chivalrous boldness and was not afraid of strengthening his statements' (*Oxford Movement*, pp. 321f). Isaac Williams' judgement corroborates this: 'His abilities were rather showy, from an elegant and pleasing style, than either acute or deep' (p. 86). On Williams' advice, Oakeley left Oxford to become minister of (what later became) All Saints, Margaret Street, London, where he pioneered the ritualistic developments of second-generation Tractarianism. As Church remarks, he was 'perhaps the first to realise the capacities of the Anglican ritual for impressive devotional use, and his services . . . are still remembered by some as having realised for them, in a way never since surpassed, the secrets and consolations of the worship of the church' – no slight praise coming from Church.

Oakeley claimed that 'the hardest trial to which my faith was ever exposed was that of being asked to see in the Anglican bishops the successors of the apostles' (c. Nockles, diss., p. 321). Lacking the force and originality of Ward, his articles in the *British Critic*, by then a Tractarian organ, were nevertheless, as Church remarks, more attractive reading than Ward's. His article on John Jewel, the great apologist of the Anglican settlement, was 'a landmark in the progress of Roman ideas'. Oakeley began by attacking – in brilliant polemic! – the polemical thrust of Jewel's writings. Whatever he touched turned to controversy, Oakeley complained. 'His works are like nouns, defective in all cases but the accusative.' He went on to brand the Reformation 'that deplorable schism' and called for the 'unprotestantising' of the Church of England. In a subsequent article, Oakeley was forced to defend his bold assertions and qualified his position by stating that the English Reformers had not, in his opinion, actually maintained an 'uncatholic system of theology' but had shown a 'too uncatholic tone of mind'. On the great project of the Parker Society to publish the works of the English Reformers, Oakeley commented that, far from harming the catholic cause, it would only serve to further it. 'It is only because the writings of that period are so imperfectly known that they are so generally admired.'

(2) *W. G. Ward*

Williams recalled (p. 85) the effect of Froude's *Remains* on one significant individual who was to become the most forceful, singleminded and formidable advocate of extreme Tractarian views:

> On the day of the book coming out, I went into Parker the bookseller's with Copeland and there we were startled at seeing one who was then the chief opponent of church principles of Newman and ourselves. It was Ward of Balliol, author of the *Ideal*. He sat down with the book in his hands, evidently much affected; and then we afterwards heard, to our astonishment, that he had been very much taken by the book, had bought a copy for himself and another to give away and was, in fact, quite converted.

Ward himself later confessed that Froude's *Remains* 'delighted me more than any other book of the kind I ever read: from that time began my inclination to see the truth where I trust it is. The especial charm in it to me was, combined on the other hand with his great strictness, his hatred of our present system and of the Reformers and his sympathy with the rest of Christendom.' Ward was in fact to exaggerate to an extreme these two dominant principles of Froude's writings – moral rigorism and repugnance for the Reformation. Moreover, it was precisely on moral grounds that Ward rejected the Reformation (Wilfred Ward, p. 180).

The Lutheran doctrine of justification by faith without works, Ward asserted, 'formally denies the truth, which seems to me the key to all moral and religious knowledge . . . namely, that careful moral discipline is the necessary foundation whereon alone Christian faith can be reared.' 'The very essence of Lutheranism in the abstract' is, according to Ward, 'disregard of moral principle' in as much as it makes conscience, instead of the guide to salvation, the only impediment to it. 'The essence then of Luther's gospel is this, that a person . . . has only one great struggle to go through' and that struggle is, not against sin, but against his own conscience 'which would fain impede his full assurance of immediate pardon.' Lutheran theology thus undermines the fundamentals of natural religion:

> That obedience to the will of God, with whatever sacrifice of self, is the one thing needful; that sin is the one only danger to be dreaded, the one only evil to be avoided; these great truths are the very foundation of natural religion: and, inasmuch as this modern system denies those to be essential and necessary truths, yea, counts it the chief glory of the gospel that under it they are no longer truths, we must plainly express our conviction that a religious heathen, were he really to accept the doctrine that Lutheran language expresses, so far from making any advance, would sustain a heavy loss, in exchanging fundamental truth for fundamental error (pp. 185, 171n, 304, pref. to 1st edn).

Ward admitted to a 'deep and burning hatred' of the English Reformers; no movement in the history of the church, with the possible exception of Arianism, is 'so wholly destitute of all claims to our sympathy and regard as the English Reformation;' it was a 'miserable sin'. Justification by faith is 'radically and fundamentally monstrous, immoral, heretical and antichristian.' It is doubtful whether 'any heresy has ever infested the church so hateful and unchristian as this doctrine' which makes Lutheranism the 'hateful and fearful type of antichrist'. With 'almost incredible boldness', Luther devised his theory, 'from his own invention, against the plainest testimonies of scripture, against the unceasing and continuous voice of the church.' To Ward, the distinguishing characteristics of the continental or English Reformations were justification by faith and the principle of private judgement: these – 'in their abstract nature and necessary tendency' – 'sink below atheism itself' (*Ideal*, p. 587; 'Arnold's Sermons', p. 309n).

In a review of Arnold's sermons in the Tractarian organ *The British Critic* in 1841, Ward repaid with interest Arnold's scathing denunciations of the movement in his article 'The Oxford Malignants' of five years earlier. Ward finds Arnold's muscular Christianity wanting. It may appeal to 'that large class who are blessed with unfailing health and unflagging spirits, who take with pleasure to a life of active employment, who have warm and kindly but not deep affections.' But it has little to offer those who travail and are heavy laden, 'whom sorrow or long sickness have disgusted with the world and with active life' and those who repine at their lot. He accuses Arnold of the very same 'Judaizing tendency' as Arnold detected in the Tractarians. To Arnold it was implied in their obsession with apostolic succession, 'episcopolatry'. To Ward, it was contained in Arnold's stress on outward works and neglect of the transforming power of inward grace (pp. 306, 313).

In power of polemic, Arnold had now met his match. Ward dismisses him for his 'unreal' and 'delusive' grasp of Christian truth, his 'imperfect' view of even the 'surface' of the sacred volume that he professes to venerate, his 'scanty' knowledge of the deeper feelings of the human heart, his 'inadequate' representation of the practical Christian life – 'so superficial intellectually, so deficient in depth and reality morally'. In taking mere reason and his own conscience as his guide, Arnold reveals his usual imperfect knowledge of human nature 'which his historical studies have done but little to improve.' While other modern heretics invoke the authority of Luther, Calvin or Zwingli, Arnold has the effrontery to set his own private interpretation against a system, the catholic one, that satisfied Origen, Basil, Gregory, Augustine, Anselm, Aquinas, Bernard, Borromeo, Xavier, Andrewes and Ken – a cloud of witnesses representative of the Tractarian's pantheon of fathers, schoolmen, Counter-Reformation missionaries, Caroline divines and nonjurors (pp. 320, 360, 315).

Ward's research into Reformation theology was confessedly minimal. He admitted that he had read nothing of Calvin 'except a few pages of his *Institutes* on the subject of faith' and the sum total of his work on Luther was to read, as he claimed, 'great part of' his commentary on Galatians. He was not, however, impressed. 'Never was my conscience so shocked and revolted by any work not openly professing immorality . . . I can see nothing in it shewing any spirituality of mind whatever or any deep and true insight even into human corruption, much less into the marvels of grace; while there is very much of a most contrary character.' Luther's commentary, Ward concludes, 'considered intellectually as a theological effort, is perhaps one of the feeblest and most worthless productions ever written' (*Ideal*, pp. 169n, 172n). Forced by the outcry against his book *The Ideal of a Christian Church* to look again at the evidence, Ward was constrained to add: 'I now perceive in one place (and very likely the same may be found in other passages) that he distinctly admits that Christians after justification continually advance in conquest over sin.' But this admission contradicted Ward's whole thesis. In a desperate attempt to save the sinking ship, he claimed that Luther's teaching about the progressive conquest of sin was inconsistent with his fundamental principle (*Ideal*, p. 169n).

The *Ideal* may have been, as R. W. Church remarked (*Oxford Movement*, p. 323), 'a ponderous and unattractive volume, ill arranged and rambling, which its style and other circumstances have caused to be almost forgotten'; it may have been, as far as Reformation theology was concerned, derisorily ill-informed: but it constitutes the most violent attack on the Reformation and the reformed character of the English church to have emerged from within the Anglican fold in the nineteenth, or possibly any other century. Technically, it was an Anglican production, but in reality it signalled its author's seccession to Rome.

Ward's book, with its claim to subscribe to the Thirty-nine Articles of the Church of England without renouncing one syllable of Roman dogma, was formally condemned by the Convocation of Oxford university on 13th February, 1845. Though Ward's right to hold his views was defended, for their own peculiar reasons, by Keble, Maurice and Gladstone, Ward himself was deprived of his degree – degraded to the rank of undergraduate. A third motion, to censure Newman's *Tract 90* of 1841, in which he had attempted, in a less extreme way, to interpret the Articles in a sense favourable to Roman teaching, was dramatically defeated by the veto of the proctors, one of them being R. W. Church. These events triggered 'the catastrophe' (as Church entitled the final chapter of his history of the Oxford Movement) when Ward and Oakeley preceded Newman into the Church of Rome. Sir James Stephen's witty dismissal of Froude's attack on the Reformers had been a serious miscalculation.

J. B. Mozley: Critique of Luther and Arnold

Though the author of solid theological works on predestination, baptismal regeneration and miracles, J. B. Mozley (1813–78) put his most polemical and brilliant writing into his essays. These include devastating criticisms of Luther, the consequences of Luther, rationalism and romanticism alike, and the present champions of Luther, Thomas Arnold and Carlyle.

The essay on Luther (1848) presents the Reformer as the embodiment of pagan vitality. Though for Mozley the antithesis of catholic truth, for us this has an undeniable appeal! Luther was a luxuriant and a glowing character. 'Wholly without the airs of a great man, free as air, easy and welcome as home, he radiated social heartiness and comfort; and men were happy round him as they are happy round a fire.' At his best, among his family, he radiates 'affection, warmth and tenderness'. As a human being, Luther is a standing contradiction of his own doctrine of total depravity. It is precisely in his view of man that Mozley detects Luther's most serious departure from the true faith. The catholic church, according to Mozley, takes 'a practical, common sense' view of man. Not insisting on some impossible perfection, she has always been 'moderate, gentle and discreet, making allowances and admitting approximations.' Catholic faith, Mozley continues, 'is emphatically a natural kind of faith.

It is not violent or forced, it has only to believe in the future expansion and perfection of that which it now sees.' Mozley is certainly right to acknowledge that this is precisely the sort of humanistic understanding of man that Luther treated with scorn and contempt. But it must be admitted that, in a twentieth-century perspective, Luther's existential, eschatological concept of *fiducia* stands up better than the broken reed of human perfection.

Mozley brings the issue right into the open when he relates his 'catholic' view of man to the central Reformation contention – the doctrine of justification. With regard to justification, the church has maintained a position consistent with 'all the teaching of natural religion and the whole language of reason'. Here it is apparent that Mozley is flirting with Pelagianism – the only heresy, as William Temple used to say, that is inherently damnable. On justification, Mozley follows bishop Bull and his rejection of Luther's doctrine is as violent as W. G. Ward's. 'Formally and literally stated,' he asserts, 'the Lutheran dogma of justification by faith is so inconsistent with the first principles of common sense and natural religion, that in this shape, no human being can possibly believe it.'

Luther arrives at this impossible position not only by flying in the face of reason, but by ruthlessly and consistently distorting the text of scripture, explaining away wholesale the abundant ethical instructions of the New Testament. 'There was no liberty . . . which he was not prepared to take with the sacred text. He found the New Testament in every page appealing to a law which he declared the New Testament had abolished.'

> In this way the whole system of law and precept which confronts us on the very surface of scripture was reduced, by a method of esoteric interpreta-tion, into a mere husk and outside, the external fabric of the deeper truth that there was no law. The surface was for the natural man, the truth was for the believer.

According to Luther's logic, the language of the gospels was merely a 'pious fraud', a 'piece of legerdemain'.

But was it not Luther's celebrated method to take the words of scripture literally? Think of the scrupulous literalness of his approach to the dominical words of institution, *Hoc est corpus meum*. The discrep-ancy is easily resolved: 'Luther's modes of proceeding seldom require very nice criticism to explain. He was very scrupulous with respect to scripture when it interposed against another man's dogma; very unscrupulous with respect to it when it interfered with his own.' Do not be deceived by Luther's reverence for the body of Christ. His sense of mystery in the presence of the sacrament was all one with his love of the supernatural, 'his ghost and fairy lore, the very grotesquenesses into which his supernaturalism ran.'

Luther's battles with temptation, his torments of conscience, did not impress Mozley. The *Anfetchungen* were 'loose and degrading prostrations' that revealed a lack of discipline and a dominant streak of superstition. Luther's melancholy 'revelled in a coarse supernaturalism and summoned grotesque phantoms from the lower world'. A more 'absurd and debasing view' of human suffering could hardly be conceived than Luther's conviction that he was the object of the personal attentions of the devil himself. Luther's belief in an imminent end of the world in which the pope, the Turk and the fanatics would meet their just deserts elicits this gem: 'He embraced it in the spirit of a person who felt an actual private interest, and private pique gratified by its accomplishment.'

Luther narrowed the broad social scope of Christian faith into a vicious individualism:

> Withdrawing from the wide ground of reason and nature, the unsupported faith of mere will – choosing to believe because it wished to do so – as it derived all its strength from the individual, interested itself about the individual only; and faith became, in its whole scope and direction, personal.

Mozley takes Julius Hare to task for his *Vindication* of the Reformer which had appeared in its first form, two years earlier (1846). No apology can or should be offered for the language Luther uses of the epistle of James: 'a right strawy epistle'. Hare also overreached himself in coming to the defence of Luther's involvement in the bigamy of Philip of Hesse. 'An apologist,' Mozley pronounces (implying that Hare's apology could reflect on his own moral probity), 'however enthusiastic, should never defend his author beyond the point where the defence does justice to himself.' Luther is denounced for throwing open the forbidden degrees of marriage, and his treatise on marriage of 1522 for giving licence 'from which the natural conscience of a heathen and a savage would recoil'. After his own marriage, Luther felt continually a 'deep blow to his self-respect'.

Luther is the prototype of German romanticism, with its nature-mysticism, irrationalism and demonic destructive power which, in theology, has 'explained away inspiration, reduced the Bible to legend, distorted the Christian creed and left a void for the human mind to fill up at its will.' The same immanental religion of German naturalism is the thrust of Mozley's critique of Thomas Arnold.

The essay on Arnold gives Mozley a further opportunity to illustrate his thesis of two opposed systems contending for mastery over the minds of men: the true, catholic system, divine in origin, disciplined, ascetic, logical; and the false Lutheran system, a counterfeit of the divine, naturalistic, carnal, irrational. Unfortunately for Mozley's argument, it is the false creed that is presented in the more attractive light.

> The catholic system, as it advanced from the worlds beyond the grave [sic], came with some of the colour and circumstance of its origin. It contrasted strangely with the light, hearty and glowing form of earth that came from

wood and mountain, sunshine and green fields to meet them. And the unearthly, supernatural, dogmatic church opposed a ghostly dignity to the church of nature and the religion of the heart.

Arnold, with his profound classical culture, broad-minded liberalism, and robust rational approach to mystery-mongering and dogmatism, his vital, muscular, fell-walking Christianity, is the archetype of the false faith that Mozley labels 'Lutheran'.

> Arnold's character is too luscious, too joyous, too luxuriant, too brimful. The colour is good, but the composition is too rich. Head full, heart full, eyes beaming, affections met, sunshine in the breast, all nature embracing him – here is too much glow of earthly mellowness, too much actual liquid in the light.

Lytton Strachey's exercise in denigration in his chapter on Arnold in *Eminent Victorians* evidently had a precedent and perhaps a model.

Arnold's native good spirits were transmuted into religious feelings. The 'deep, solid, glowing and constant pleasure of life' became incorporated into the spiritual substance of his religion. And Mozley deduces that a religious theory – the Lutheran one – 'lurks beneath the outward symptoms'. Arnold was a German intellectually – 'the representative of high, joyous Lutheranism'. His ethos was that of 'genuine religious Germanism'. His was 'the genuine Lutheran instinct', and his scheme of church reform represents the 'utopia of Lutheranism'.

Mozley justly remarks that Arnold was 'a most ardent, affectionate, loyal, devoted, enthusiastic and genuine disciple, admirer and son' of the Reformation, who saw in it 'the first dawn of a new order of things, the first blow struck to priestcraft' and – he adds tendentiously – 'the first breath in the total absorption of the church into the state'. Though he was critical of some of its methods, the reform movement in principle enjoyed Arnold's 'unfeigned admiration and adhesion'. Its fundamental principle – that is, as Mozley sees it – the subordination of the church to the state, 'appealed to his very deepest religious sympathies and heartfelt aspirations'. Whereas the evangelicals idolise the Reformers, Arnold himself meant to emulate and outdo them. Mozley points to the irony of Arnold's accusing Froude of 'impudence'. While Froude had wanted to 'unprotestantise' the church of England, Arnold had 'unchristianised' the church in the whole course of its development from the apostles on, by making 'the very disciples, friends and successors of the apostles teachers of corruption' and the emergence of the priesthood a manifestation of antichrist; then, to cap it all, shocking the whole church by promulgating a theory of church reform, 'repugnant to the feelings and ideas of almost all her members to a man'.

13

Keble and Pusey: Retreat from the Reformation

John Keble: A Hardening of Positions

Keble (1792–1866) had attempted to hold Froude's extreme views in check. 'He used sometimes to give me such snubs for speaking disrespectfully' of the Reformers, Froude recounted with an air of barely-concealed satisfaction. 'He was a long time in giving up Cranmer.' But in fact it was Keble himself who had helped to set Froude's mind moving in this direction, getting him, for example, to give up the popular notion that the pope was antichrist. (Keble espoused the 'branch' theory of the church; Rome was 'another vineyard'.) But now Keble found himself under pressure from Froude who accused him of being 'cramped with protestantism'.

Like others in the old high church tradition, Keble had begun by honouring the (English) Reformation. In 1830 he rebuked Perceval for not paying sufficient attention to the Reformers, 'to whose authority we are pledged in our formularies' (Nockles, diss., p. 120). As a movement, the Reformation had 'claims to our sympathy and regard'. Under the influence of Froude, Keble moved to a position hostile to the Reformation, gradually losing all his respect for the Reformers as men. In 1836 he wrote of them: 'I certainly do think that as a set they belonged to the same class with the puritans and radicals.' If he had lived in those times, he went on, he would have wanted nothing to do with them. Here, of course, Keble is indulging the same anachronistic fantasies as Froude: 'If we had lived in those times' (c. Brendon, p. 149). Two years later, Keble was writing to Pusey that 'anything which separates the present church from the Reformers I should hail as a great good' (Liddon, II, p. 71). In the ostensibly apologetic preface to the third volume of Froude's *Remains*, Keble announced agreement with Froude that the Reformers 'were not, as a party, to be trusted on ecclesiastical and theological questions' nor to be imitated in the way they handled the 'unspeakably awful' matters in which they were engaged.

Keble's view of the continental Reformers was inevitably harsher still. In his preface to his edition of the works of Richard Hooker he remarks *à propos* Hooker's view of Calvin (but wildly astray as a representation of either Hooker or Calvin):

> He saw in the writings of . . . Calvin a disposition to treat irreverently, not only the creeds, the sacred guards provided by the church for Christian truth, but also that holiest truth itself, in some of its articles. He knew who had called the Nicene creed *frigida cantilena*, had treated the doctrine expressed in the words "God of God, Light of Light" as a mere dream of Platonising Greeks (Hooker, I, p. lxxxi).

Keble had begun to take up his work on Hooker at about the same time as he had come under the influence of Froude with respect to the Reformation.

His critical edition of the works of Hooker was one of Keble's greatest gifts to Anglicanism. But Keble openly deplored Hooker's accommodations on the doctrine of the apostolic succession. Keble noted with disapproval that Hooker did not draw the inference that the apostolic succession was the sole divinely appointed channel of sacramental grace and therefore of 'our mystical communion with Christ' (Hooker, I, p. lxxvii). Keble spoke truly when he said, 'Hooker is not my master . . . I have dared to differ widely from him' (c. Nockles, diss. p. 104).

In *Tract 4* 'Adherence to the Apostolical Succession the Safest Course' (1833), Keble made it clear that the ministries of the protestant churches were no valid ministries at all. He warned English dissenters that separation from the Church of England was not only separation from a 'decent, orderly, useful society' (which was all that the broad churchmen would claim) but from 'the only church in this realm which has a right to be quite sure that she has the Lord's Body to give to his people'. (In keeping with the intention of the early tracts to be short propaganda broadsheets, Keble's admonition is printed in capitals.) This did not mean, he hastened to add, that presbyterians and Roman Catholics (we are still a far cry from the Romanophilia of some Tractarians in the early 1840s) were excluded from salvation since 'necessary to salvation' and 'necessary to church communion' are not convertible terms. (However, Keble seems to be intentionally reserved on whether his crumbs of comfort ought to be offered to Methodists, Baptists, independents and other chapel folk.) He adds, perhaps with continental protestants in mind: 'It is one thing to slight and disparage this holy succession where it may be had, and another thing to aquiesce in the want of it where it is (if it be anywhere) really unattainable' (pp. 4f).

The spirit of rationalism in contemporary German theology he traced right back to its incipient forms in the Reformation itself. 'During the struggle of the Reformation,' he writes in *Tract 89* ('On the Mysticism Attributed to the Early Fathers of the Church'), 'men had felt instinctively, if they did not clearly see, that the Fathers were against them, so far as they had begun to *rationalise*, whether in ecclesiastical practice or in theological inquiry.' But only when their later disciples had wearied themselves in the fruitless task of attempting to reconcile the first three centuries of the church with Calvin and Zwingli, did they dare to openly admit this intention to themselves (p. 1).

Keble was the heir of the old high church tradition of passive, peaceable obedience that was synonymous with Anglicanism itself in the seventeenth century. He never lost his faith in the royal supremacy (Rowlands, diss., p. 113): his quarrel was with parliament. Hooker's one nation Anglicanism, in which parliament functioned as the synod of the church with the laity in the Commons and the bishops in the Lords, was now defunct. In his preface to Hooker, commenting on that divine's 'large concessions to the civil power', Keble points out that 'Hooker always implies, not only that those who exercise it are Christians, but also that they are sound and orthodox churchmen, in complete communion with the church which they claim to govern.' (Against such perfectionist views, the old high churchmen asked whether the Tractarians supposed that there were no papists in the Elizabethan parliament: Nockles, diss., p. 76). Where that condition ceases to apply, continues Keble, on Hooker's own principles 'the identity or union of church and state is at an end; and the church as a distinct body is free, without breach of loyalty, to elect officers, make laws, and decide causes for herself, no reference at all being had to the civil power' (Hooker, I, p. lxxix). At one point of extreme exasperation, Keble talked of excommunicating parliament.

His reply to Gladstone's treatise on state and church, is Keble's most revealing account of his views on this question ('The State in its Relations with the Church', 1839). In the vein of old high churchmanship Keble designates kings and queens as the church's nursing fathers and mothers, whose God-given vocation is 'to execute the laws of Christ's church, not impose laws upon her' (pp. 374). With Hooker, Keble condemns 'the notion that the civil magistrate as such has nothing to do with religion'; this is 'practical atheism' (p. 360). 'The nursing fathers in God's household cannot in faithfulness either neglect the laws which he has set for the correction of his erring children, or take into their own hands the regulation of the whole family, or separate at their will between the portions of it.' In all these ways, Keble pronounces, 'the state in England is clearly in sin' and 'it is at least doubtful how far the church has made herself a party to that sin' (p. 393).

Keble then considers the question of separation from the communion of the Church of England. Patristic theology remains his guide in this as in other matters. The whole church had settled the question in the controversy with the Donatists: 'no amount of faultiness in church governors can make separation cease to be schism.' If the Church of

England exacted 'unlawful terms of communion' he would 'bear her censures patiently': there was always the possibility of lay communion. But her terms of communion remain sound: none of her members is required to assent to any of the regrettable recent developments. 'She is still the church, the true mystical body of Jesus Christ, having his commission, his word and his sacraments, from whom it is unlawful to separate' (pp. 393f).

Edward Bouverie Pusey

(1) The Enigma of Pusey

Though not the most appealing personally of all the churchmen and thinkers here under review, Edward Bouverie Pusey (1800–82) is certainly one of the most intriguing. Pusey's *volte-face* from ardent liberal protestantism to reactionary Anglo-catholicism remains an enigma. The contrast is so clear-cut that the early Pusey could appropriately be treated as one of the liberal Anglicans. On the Reformation, modern protestantism, the authority and interpretation of the Bible, even the doctrine of eternal punishment, Pusey moved from one end of the theological spectrum to the other.

In later life, rationalising his progress, Pusey liked to think of himself as an hereditary high churchman, like Keble or Palmer, who had suffered a temporary aberration, lured from the path of truth by the specious attractions of German pietism allied to rationalistic biblical criticism. It is true that his home environment was of extreme conservatism and its churchmanship of the high and dry school. His father, a reactionary and a martinet, had a powerful hold over Pusey. The father's grip was intensified after his death by the pathological guilt feelings it induced in his son. But it will not do to present Pusey as a 'doctrinally orthodox scriptural protestant', seeking assistance from German biblical science in his defence of the faith (Frappell in P. Butler, ed., p. 3).

The liberalism of the young Pusey was real enough. The influence of Schleiermacher and Tholuck went deep. Pusey drank at the fountain of romanticism. He read Byron and identified with the tragic wayward hero. He was acquainted with the families of Scott, Coleridge and Southey. He assimilated the notions of symbolism and self-expression disseminated by Coleridge and sanctified by Keble in the *Christian Year* and his lectures on poetry. In Pusey's case it was a romanticism wedded to radicalism – not, as with Keble, conservatism.

It has been argued (by Frappell) that there is a fundamental continuity between this and the later Pusey, the author of *Daniel the Prophet* and *What is of Faith as to Everlasting Punishment?* This is special pleading. In the personality at least there is nothing less than a decisive *caesura* between the young romantic, enraptured and intoxicated by his life-loving sweetheart Maria Barker, allying himself with the progressive movement in nineteenth-century theology, and the guilt-mongering penitent who made Maria as obsessive as himself and scarred his children's minds with the wrath of God and the rod of chastisement in their father's hand (see Forrester, diss.).

The stages on the way of penitence were the successive deaths of his father, his mentor and 'second father' bishop Lloyd, his infant daughter Katherine and his wife. Each one made him reproach himself more severely; each was a judgement and a warning; each one tightened the spiral of guilt, penitence and punishment, with the corollaries of Counter-Reformation piety, discipline and doctrine.

(2) *Pusey and Protestant Scholarship*

Pusey went to Germany, at the suggestion of professor (later bishop) Lloyd, hoping to find 'assistance from the German literature in all the critical and scientific parts of divinity' (Liddon, I, p.71). In other words Pusey was already converted to critical scholarship before he set foot on the continent. He returned from his second, longer visit, not only a learned orientalist and semitic scholar, but a friend, colleague and correspondent of many of the leading critical scholars. And he knew that they were looking to him to answer Hugh James Rose's recent attack, *The State of Protestantism in Germany Described*. Pusey's reply came in 1828. Patently the work of a young man, it is vigorous, passionate and partisan. It was a remarkable overture to half a century of scholarly and polemical publications.

Pusey begins by accusing Rose, a respected pillar of the high church – astute, learned, intellectual – of perpetrating a work lacking in arrangement, analysis and judgement. But Pusey's indictment is of its thesis, an attack on the integrity of modern protestantism and by implication on the Reformers – a thesis that reveals that its author has abandoned the 'fundamental principles of protestantism' and the absolute authority of 'the word of God' (*Enquiry*, I, p.x).

Pusey admires Luther for his correct understanding of scripture and his 'intuitive insight into the nature of Christianity' – a special gift or charisma that elevated him above the 'assumed authority' of the church, the weight of tradition, the pressure of scholastic opinion (p.8). In the sequel, after Rose's reply, Pusey unrepentantly praised the Reformers as 'the immortal heroes, the mighty agents of the Reformation', and Luther as 'this great instrument of God', raised up in response to a 'deep longing' in Christendom for a 'renewal of the pure gospel'. The Augsburg Confession (1530) is 'venerable', the first protestant confession, and a 'monument of unshaken faith', dear to Anglicans as the source of much in their own articles. The Reformation was a glorious bursting forth of the light. Elsewhere, Pusey pronounced Luther the greatest Christian since St. Paul, and Calvin a saint (II, pp. 363, 367, 19, 412).

But tolerance and enforced uniformity (here speaks the liberal in the tones of Arnold) sowed the seeds of later negative developments. Gospel truth was taken as a subject for speculation instead of as a motive for practice (echoes of Arnold again). The Formula of Concord of 1577 which was intended to settle differences between rival schools of Lutheran orthodoxy, set up mere scholastic opinions as articles of faith, and substituted human technicalities for the free spirit of the gospel, a logical formalism for the scriptural and living expression of revealed truth (it could be Maurice speaking) (I, pp. 15, 21f).

The scholastic doctrine of mechanical inspiration of scripture belongs in this context. Pusey explicitly rejects the notion that 'the whole of scripture was immediately dictated by the Holy Spirit' and accepts a theological pluralism in the biblical books, which are not all of equal value. He gives full weight to the human element in revelation: the biblical writers' minds were adapted to receive certain truths and they conveyed them to the extent that they were capable of doing so (I, p. 30).

Pusey espouses an advanced hermeneutic of indwelling in the tradition of idealist philosophy of history that stretches from Schleiermacher to Collingwood. The interpreter seeks to stand 'at the centre of the same circle' of understanding as that of his author. The lack of historical critical study in the ages of scholasticism meant that the past was a sealed book to those unable to shed modern presuppositions and to transport themselves back in time (I, pp. 26, 39f).

Though a convinced liberal at this stage, Pusey carries no brief for rationalism. He links it with medieval and seventeenth-century scholasticism. Just as the Reformation was the bursting forth of new life in the arid desert of scholasticism, so the new romantic-idealist philosophy, enunciated by Herder and Schelling, will bring a new creative era in protestant theology.

Though Herder's views were rather 'dim and distant conceptions' which 'flashed across' his mind, by his imaginative hermeneutical power of indwelling he showed up the pretensions of rationalism and brought the Bible to life.

> The natural simplicity and deep feeling of his mind enabled him, partially at least, to understand much of the deeper contents of the Christian doctrines, which the satisfied self-sufficiency of his contemporaries had pronounced åo be the mere temporary disguise of the eternal truths of reason: through his genuine oriental spirit he was enabled to penetrate and to show the fuller meaning of much in the Old Testament which their partial and unhistorical rationalism had neglected or despised as mythos or unmeaning exaggeration.

But Herder lacked a comprehensive insight into Christian truth and in his later writings 'everything seems to float in a dim mist' (I, pp. 157ff). Schelling continued the good work of putting rationalism to flight and substituting a more spiritual conception of reality. His thought 'excited a vivid consciousness of the universal presence and agency of a living and infinite being', substituted contemplation for abstract thought and allowed for mystery beyond 'the compass of intellectual speculation' (I, p. 169).

Critical study, informed by this spiritual perception, had dug deep, not to undermine the faith but to reveal its unshakable foundations (I, pp. 175f). The prospect now was of a new alliance of science and theology comparable to the alliance of humanism and the Bible in the work of the Reformers. Pusey was full of hope that what they were witnessing was a new dawn of protestantism.

> The time is not far distant when the religious energy, now widely visible in Germany, shall produce its fruits, and the Evangelical church, strengthened by the increasing internal unanimity, fortified against error by past experience, and founded on a scriptural faith, shall again, in religious as well as scientific depth, be at least one amongst the fairest portions of the universal church of the Redeemer (I, pp. 178f).

Doctrine was not unaffected – contrary to those who see the liberal episode as a passing flirtation that made no difference to Pusey's essential Anglican orthodoxy. The notion of eternal punishment is rejected as an unscriptural doctrine 'repugnant to the nature of God' (I, p. 51). The idea of orthodoxy of doctrine itself is rendered suspect. Recent developments in Germany had had the beneficial effect of banishing 'reliance upon the mere letter of a received system, of a mere intellectual conception of Christianity, of a deadening formularism, of the undervaluing of scripture in behalf of an over-refined human system, of an uncharitable polemic' (I, pp. 175f). Rose and others were right to see in this a challenge to all orthodoxies, high church or evangelical.

In his reply (the open letter to the bishop of London), Rose took exception most of all to Pusey's radical views on the inspiration of scripture – 'the method in which Mr. Pusey expresses his conviction of the absurdity of believing in the inspiration of the historical parts of scripture'. Pusey was prepared, in his second volume, to tone down his remarks, but they are still a far cry from *Daniel the Prophet* (Liddon, I, pp. 163f).

Rose also singled out Pusey's failure to identify the Lutheran system of church government as a prime cause of the decline into heresy. Bishops were defenders of the faith. Pusey had not felt this worth mentioning: what did this imply about his own doctrinal soundness?

On this point, Pusey's response was utterly unrepentant. He accused Rose in turn of violating a central principle of protestant ecclesiology by making human authority of the *esse* of the church. Pusey confessed that he had no reason to think that a different form of ecclesiastical polity would have changed the destiny of the Lutheran church. In England bishops had indeed attacked unbelief, but in their private capacity, as divines, not by decree. Human authority can merely repress the outward manifestations of unbelief. The 'melancholy state' of the Italian and Spanish clergy shows that the outward imposition of uniformity cannot prevent inward 'corruption and rottenness' (II, pp. 1ff, 15f).

In the *Historical Enquiry* Pusey appears as a true broad-churchman. Like other liberal Anglicans he evinces a protestantism that is tempered by the Enlightenment and tinged with romanticism. As R. H. Greenfield has pointed out, in teaching that 'Scripture is the only authoritative source of Christian knowledge' and that 'Scripture is its own interpreter', Pusey decisively set himself apart from the high church tradition (in P. Butler, ed., p. 163).

(3) Retreat from the Reformation

Throughout the entire period of the publication of the tracts, Pusey took the line of the moderate mainstream high-churchmen like Palmer: the fundamental principles of the Reformation conformed to the pattern of the primitive church.

In 1839 he wrote to Newman of the English Reformers: 'Whatever faults there were, we should never have been "apostolical" without them. We owe our peculiar position as adherents of primitive antiquity to them.' Here of course Pusey is comparing the Church of England favourably with English dissent and German Lutheranism, rather than – as Newman tended to do – making invidious comparisons with Rome (Liddon, II, p. 76).

In *Tract 81* (1837) on eucharistic sacrifice, Pusey approximated to the developmental, providential approach of the liberal Anglicans. 'The divines of the sixteenth and seventeenth centuries had different offices': in the sixteenth to lay down 'strong broad statements of truths' obscured by popery, but to do so without refinement and balance; in the seventeenth to attain the 'calmer, deeper statements of men to whom God had given peace from the first conflict'. We disparage the Reformers only if we expect to find in them 'that which was not their office' – 'a well-proportioned and equable exhibition of the several parts of the catholic faith' – an achievement that was, 'in the appointed order of things', reserved for the Jacobean and Caroline divines (p. 25).

In this tract Ridley is praised as 'the great upholder of catholic truth' and as the Reformer 'most imbued with the doctrines of the early church' because of his association with the fuller sacramental doctrine of the prayer book of 1549. While the first stage of Reformation was a necessary opposition to the church as it was, the second was an opposition to scripture itself, whose results we see in modern Lutheranism. It is the privilege of the Church of England to be separate from foreign protestants 'with whom and whose theology we have never had any large commerce without injuring our own' (pp. 22, 33). This of course is an implicit self-judgement on his own theological awakening and his first work of scholarship.

As the Oxford movement took a lurch to the left at the instigation of Oakeley and Ward, Pusey, like Palmer, deplored the Romanising tendency and the abuse of the Reformers that accompanied it. When Oakeley's infamous article on bishop Jewel appeared in *The British Critic*, Pusey wrote to Newman, then editor of the journal, of his grief that Oakeley and Ward thought it necessary to act as 'public prosecutors' of the Reformers (Liddon, II, p. 218). The programme to unprotestantise the Church of England, pursued vociferously by Oakeley and Ward and tacitly by Newman, did not at this time have Pusey's support. It was better to think positively of the gains won by the movement so far, he wrote to Newman. Oakeley speaks 'as though it were nothing to have recovered the true doctrine of the two sacraments, of justification, the church, judgement to come, repentance, apostolic succession, charity, fasting, submission to the authority of the church, the *quod ubique*, etc. unless' – Pusey added – 'we take a certain view of the Reformation and "go forwards", he does not say whither' (ib.).

Why not give the English Reformers the benefit of the doubt and allow that their intention was a catholic one? Their 'perplexed views' on certain subjects were attributable to the detrimental influence of the foreign Reformers and should not obscure the primary fact that they submitted to the authority of the early church. Why not try to see them as implicitly catholic, even though their language is Zwinglian? Why should their appeal to Zurich be thought fatal to their catholicism, when model catholics like Cosin, Andrewes and Laud held that the foreign Reformers were equally catholic? (ib., pp. 218f).

The English Reformers, Pusey insists, 'wished to be catholic'. Their appeals to antiquity were sincere, but they were 'entangled' with the foreign Reformers with whom they were 'unhappily intimate'. He will interpret their Zwinglianism in the light of their catholicism, not *vice versa*, 'looking upon them as implicitly catholic and sympathising with their difficulties.' While Ward and company point to their fraternising with Calvin as proof of their inherent anti-catholicism, Pusey reminds Newman that Laud, Cosin and Hooker interpreted Calvin and the Reformed in a sound sense as to the sacraments at least (ib., p. 224).

At this point in his correspondence with Newman, however, Pusey introduces a qualification which shows that he has moved from his early position and points to a later hardening. Employing the very concept of development on which Newman was then working, Pusey suggests that protestantism appears in its true nature when seen in the light of its development into rationalism. Here the continental scene contrasts unfavourably with the Church of England:

Our Reformation has had, amid whatever reverses, a steady tendency to develop itself into catholicism and to throw out the impure elements which came into the church; the foreign Reformation has developed the contrary way into rationalism and pantheism.

We are entitled therefore, Pusey continues, to infer a difference of ethos – 'ours intrinsically catholic, though with something uncatholic clinging to the agents in it, theirs intrinsically uncatholic, though with some semblance of catholicism'. Even the English Reformation, Pusey is constrained to add, was not without its sinful aspects, in the suppression of the monasteries, acts of sacrilege, etc., but these are more properly attributable to the state than the church, to 'the indirect, not the direct instruments of the Reformation' (ib., pp. 225, 227).

Thus there emerges at this stage in Pusey's development a distinction between the English and the continental Reformers. In retrospect we see this as a progressive distancing from protestant principles: the foreign Reformers were the first to be discarded.

Though the incident of the Jerusalem bishopric in 1841 failed at first to provoke Pusey to such indignation as it did Newman and Keble, his letter to the archbishop of Canterbury reveals the principle of discrimination between Anglican and Lutheran that he was increasingly resorting to.

> The one holds 'One holy catholic church, throughout the world', knit together by its bishops . . . under its one head Christ, and joined on by unbroken succession to the apostles: the other, an indefinite number of churches, hanging together by an agreement in a scheme of doctrine framed by themselves and modified by the civil power . . .; the one holds confirmation to be the act of the bishop: the other deems such to be unnecessary but accepts it for its younger members; the one holds ordination to be derived from the apostles: the other that presbyters, uncommissioned, may confer it, and that those on whom it has been so conferred may consecrate the holy eucharist; the one recites the creed of Nicea: the other has laid it aside; in the one ancient prayer, the inspired psalms and hearing God's word are the chief part of their weekly service: in the other uninspired hymns and preaching with prayer extempore; the one kneel in prayer: the other not even at the holy eucharist; with the one the Lord's day is a holy day and the other a holyday; the one receives 'the faith' as 'once for all delivered to the saints': the other as susceptible to subsequent correction and development.

The Anglican church, Pusey continues remorselessly, derives from the ancient church, the Lutheran is confessedly modern; the former not of mere human origin, the latter patently founded by Martin Luther (ib., p. 283).

By the time that the bishopric came up for renewal in 1846 and it was the turn of the king of Prussia to nominate a Lutheran pastor for consecration by the archbishop of Canterbury, Pusey's attitude had hardened. He wrote to Gladstone: 'What a misery it would be if the ultimate object of the Prussian government were attained and they were to receive episcopacy from us and we were to become the authors of an heretical succession ... To give episcopacy to Prussia now ... is like arraying a corpse or whitening a sepulchre.' His words to the arch-bishop's chaplain, the erstwhile disciple Benjamin Harrison, will strike a chill into anyone familiar with Pusey's treatment of his own family: 'I feel as [if] I could bless God more fervently for the suspension of the Jerusalem bishopric than for the life of a dying child: by how much the church must be dearer to one than one's own life or one's child' (ib., III, pp. 71, 75).

But Pusey was being overtaken by events. In the mid 1840s he was still fighting the rearguard action in defence of the Anglican *via media*, against protestantism on the one hand and popery on the other, that Newman had begun to abandon after *The Prophetical Office of the Church* in 1837. In a letter to Samuel Wilberforce in 1845, the year of Newman's *Essay on Development* and secession to Rome, Pusey took his stand with 'unshaken faith' in the Church of England which, he affirmed, 'by declarations of the Reformers, by her canons, and by the combined teaching of approved divines' rested upon the church of antiquity (ib., pp. 43f).

In his university sermon of 1851, 'The Rule of Faith as maintained by the Fathers and the Church of England', he claimed that the English Reformers were not merely paying lip-service to the authority of the fathers: they were in earnest about emulating the apostolic church. The Anglican Homilies were based on primitive purity of doctrine and the leading English Reformers – Cranmer, Ridley and Jewel – were faithful to the Vincentian canon. The Church of England since the Reformation had 'held implicitly, in purpose of heart, all which the ancient church ever held' (pp. 46f). Pusey was right to see that the English Reformers would not have wished to claim more than this; he was sadly mistaken in failing to realise that the continental Reformers claimed nothing less.

1845 seems to have been a watershed in Pusey's attitude to the Reformation. Writing to Manning – then veering towards Rome – Pusey makes concessions and implies that Anglicanism has to make a choice. There was much that was merely human in the English Reformation; things were not done as they ought. He is disturbed by the 'temper' of those who took part. 'Our subsequent history makes me feel that we thus brought in a wrong element into our church, which has been struggling with catholicity ever since, and that one or the other must in time be ejected' (c. Greenfield in P. Butler, ed., p. 173).

By now Pusey had made his own choice. The passing of the years would only harden it. Anglicanism must be pushed as far as possible in the direction of catholicism without a quasi-infallible pope and without mariolatry. The Thirty-nine Articles were to be taken as comprehending the doctrinal decrees of the council of Trent; Roman devotional manuals, made available by his own editorial efforts, were to steer Anglican piety into new channels. The doctrine of eternal punishment was to be reaffirmed against hopeful liberals without wavering; critical enquiry into the biblical literature was to be 'superseded by divine authority' (*Daniel*, p. 6).

A. M. Allchin writes positively of Pusey as 'a man with a large, profound, independent, radical mind, a man of a powerful and volcanic spirit, who saw things in light and darkness, a man with a capacity for grief, self-reproach, self-condemnation which may frighten or repel us; a man marked at times in his life by a sadness, an austerity, a lack of flexibility, which we find it difficult to accept.' 'Above all,' Allchin concludes, we have in Pusey 'a witness to the reality of God, a man wounded by the divine love' (in P. Butler, ed., p. 366).

That may be so: it is a generous assessment. But another interpretation suggests itself. It is possible, without undue psychologising, to see Pusey as a man wounded not only, no doubt, by divine love but also – literally – in his father's house; who in turn wounded, in the throes of his own anguish, his wife and children. No doctoring of the evidence would be required to see Pusey's early radicalism as a rebellion against paternal tyranny and the flourishing of his critical scholarship as due to the truly fatherly protection and encouragement of his bishop. Pusey's later rejection of his own early views and scholarly achievements (particularly his revision of the Authorised Version Old Testament) and his return to the high church principles of his father would be attributable to the guilt feelings induced in him by the death of his father, followed by that of his father in God, bishop Lloyd.

Pusey's change of views did not come about through steadily deepening theological study: it was a *volte face* under psychological pressure, a disowning of his own past with which he never came to terms, a conversion in fact that involved the betrayal of the light he had enjoyed as a young scholar and acceptance of a life-rejecting spirituality and theological defensiveness (witness *Daniel* and *Eternal Punishment*) that savours of the very kind of dead orthodoxy that he had singled out in his first book as the cause of rationalism and heresy. Wounded indeed, psychologically afflicted, a casualty of human conflict: it was such a man, author both of good and of harm, who exerted an unparalleled influence on the course of the catholic movement in the Church of England.

(4) *Pusey and the Unity of the Church*

That interpretation of Pusey's extraordinary development is admittedly speculative – let others offer blander explanations if they can – and I would be unwilling to let it be my last word on Pusey. In the context of this present work it is appropriate that we should conclude our discussion of Pusey by seeing him as a man with a profound and heartfelt vision for the unity of the Christian church. To that statement of course there must be one proviso – by the unity of the church Pusey meant the reconciliation of east and west and particularly the healing of the breach between Rome and Canterbury: he did not include protestant ecclesial bodies, whether Lutheran, Reformed, Methodist or Baptist.

In 1865 Pusey published his *Eirenicon*, a rambling treatise addressed to Keble. Written in reply to an attack by Manning on the church of his baptism, it was subtitled, 'The Church of England a Portion of Christ's One, Holy, Catholic Church and a means of restoring Visible Unity'. It contains a vision of a profound, mystical, inward unity in the spirit between Christians who are divided over doctrine and even out of communion with one another. Such a spirit of unity was symbolised by the meeting at Hursley of Keble, Pusey and Newman shortly after publication. (In his subsequent reply to the *Eirenicon*, Newman accused Pusey of discharging his olive branch from a catapult.)

Pusey's aim in this work was twofold: first to revive the approach of Newman's *Tract* 90 of more than twenty years before, towards reconciling the Thirty-nine Articles with the council of Trent; second to invite the Roman Catholic Church to draw a clear line between doctrines that were *de fide* and beliefs and practices that had merely quasi-official status and, in Pusey's view, constituted the greatest obstacle to reunion (pp.98f). The details of Pusey's arguments against divine right papal supremacy and infallibility, and an unchecked Marian cultus, need not concern us here. What is of greater importance in the ecumenical perspective is the essential presupposition that undergirds Pusey's argument – the unity in Christ that is the indestructible possession of the whole church.

Contrary to Manning's accusations, Pusey affirmed, the Church of England holds to the indissoluble unity of the catholic church – but faith in the unity of the church 'is kept alive by prayer more than by definitions' (*Eirenicon*, p.45). Unity is the gift of God infused by the Holy Spirit, but it falls to the church to receive and nurture it. Objectively considered, unity is imparted primarily through the sacraments: 'By baptism we are ingrafted into the mystical body of Christ; by partaking of his body [in holy communion] we continue to be members of his body' (pp.54f). This sacramental grace of unity flows from its divine source through the apostolic ministry through which 'the whole body is held together in one and . . . spiritual nourishment is ministered to the growth of the whole' (p.55).

Pusey therefore claims of the branches of the catholic church, Anglican, Roman and Eastern:

> They are one in their one original, from which they continually and unchangeably derive their being. They adore God, the Father, Son and Holy Ghost, with the same new song of the gospel; they confess him in the

same words of apostolic faith; they offer to him the same incense of praise and the same holy offering . . . pleading on earth to the eternal Father the one sacrifice as presented in heaven; they receive the same 'bread which came down from heaven to give life to the world.'

Of course Manning, Newman and those who went with them to Rome no longer believed that the Church of England had the body and blood of Christ to offer or that salvation was to be found in her, but their doubts left Keble and Pusey unshaken. Pusey continued:

Unknown in face, in place separate, different in language, opposed, alas! in some things to one another, still before the throne of God they are one holy, catholic, apostolic church; each several portion praying for itself and for the rest, united in the prayers and obligations which it offers for all, by the one bread and the one Spirit which dwelleth in all (pp. 56f).

Subjectively considered, the duty of maintaining unity finds expression above all in intercommunion. But intercommunion between these branches of Christ's church has long since ceased. Pusey therefore asks, 'But is all unity forfeited, where the unity of intercommunion is suspended?' and replies, 'No one, in the face of church history, can or does maintain that all interruptions of intercommunion destroy unity' (pp. 58f). But Pusey longs for the restoration of communion between the branches of the catholic church. Citing the petition of the prayer for the church militant in the communion service of the Book of Common Prayer (1662) that God will 'inspire continually the universal church with the spirit of truth, unity and concord,' Pusey ends his *Eirenicon* with the words, 'For this I pray daily. For this I would gladly die. "O Lord tarry not"' (p. 335).

14

The Anglican Newman

Evangelical and Catholic Roots

Newman's mind has been justly described as one with a deep feeling for the life of the church through history. The literature of Romanticism (especially the novels of Sir Walter Scott) had awakened in Newman a profound sense of the past. But his gift of historical empathy had one major blind spot – the Reformation. He could identify with Athanasius or Ambrose, relive their struggles for the truth of the catholic faith and enter into the spirit of fourth century Christianity, but when it came to the Reformers, Newman confessed, 'I suppose in my heart I dislike the Reformers as much as anyone' (Liddon, II, p. 222). Newman's vast and intimate knowledge of patristic thought was not matched by a corresponding acquaintance with the teaching of the Reformers. Misrepresentation founded on ignorance set the trend for the habitual caricaturing of Luther and his teaching that, as Michael Ramsey has pointed out, has marred Anglican writing on the Reformation until comparatively recently (in Coulson and Allchin, ed., p. 7).

Newman once expressed the view that 'it requires no deep reading to judge the Reformation.' 'The *historical* characteristics of its agents,' he added, 'are such, that one need not go into their doctrines or their motives.' Elsewhere he admitted that he had not read Calvin. His comments on the Reformers should be appraised accordingly (Liddon, II, p. 226; Newman, *Present Position*, p. 343).

Though it was the fathers who made Newman a catholic and taught him 'a more excellent way' than that of the Reformers, it was the standard evangelical authors of the eighteenth century who made him a serious Christian and pointed him to the fathers. The writer who, Newman testified, 'made a deeper impression on my mind than any other and to whom (humanly speaking) I almost owe my soul' was Thomas Scott, the tireless seeker after the truth of holy scripture interpreted solely by itself and indefatigable commentator on the sacred text. Scott was born in 1747 and died in 1821, 'neglected,' as James Stephen remarked, 'if not despised, by the hierarchy of the Church of England, although in him she lost a teacher, weighed against whom these most reverend, right reverend, very reverend and venerable personages, if all thrown into the opposing scale, would at once have kicked the beam' (p. 416).

Scott provides a connection between Newman and Hooker – though not one to give Newman any pleasure. Dissatisfied with the thin diet of unitarianism and Arminianism that he had accepted when, as a wretched grazier determined to better his lot, he had first applied himself to serious study, Scott dedicated his enormous labours to finding out the truth of Christian claims, summoning to his aid the standard latitudinarian divines of the eighteenth century. Last of all, as James Stephen writes, 'there appeared in Scott's secret chamber one before whose majestic presence Locke and Burnet, Tillotson and Jortin, Jenyns, Clarke and Law retreated into obscurity and silence, like the interlocutors in the Platonic dialogue when the voice of Socrates is heard.'

> With his 'Sermon on Justification', the great and judicious Hooker put to flight once and for ever the more oppressive doubts which had over-shadowed the mind of the student, and enabled him to plant his foot immovably on Luther's rock, *stantis aut cadentis ecclesiae* ... the great adversary of the puritans, the illustrious champion of the polity of the Church of England, had announced that doctrine with as full an emphasis and with as fearless an unreserve as the German Reformer and as the founders of Methodism (p. 419).

Newman owed to Thomas Scott indelible impressions of evangelical Christianity, and though he came to reject their dogmatic content, he continued to acknowledge their spiritual power. Similarly, he revered Hooker as an exponent of the *via media* and forerunner of those Caroline divines whose authority the Tractarians delighted to invoke at length. But on the crucial question of justification, Newman was forced to concede that Hooker was against him.

The evangelical church history of Joseph and Isaac Milner provided Newman's introduction to the early church. Above all, he was enthralled by the long extracts from the fathers. 'I read them' he recalled, 'as being the religion of the primitive Christians' (*Apol.*, p. 100). Just as Rome had claimed an apostolic succession of order, the Milners set out to show that there was an evangelical succession of faith. Like the Reformers in the sixteenth century, they were out to prove that justification by faith was no mere invention of a renegade friar but a republication of the faith once for all delivered to the saints. The history attempts to deduce the 'theological genealogy' (J. Stephen) of the churches of Britain from the apostolic Church. Hugh James Rose aroused the wrath of evangelicals by accusing Milner in 1837 of being 'bigotedly attached to certain opinions and quite resolved to find or make them everywhere, and to give the history – not of Christianity, but – of those opinions which he deemed to be the whole of it' (*Church History*, p. 42).

The Milner brothers, as James Stephen pointed out, saw 'the finger of God in every step of the Reformation' and justification by faith as its 'most capital object' (p. 438). But they did not have access to Luther's works in the original or in translation, and Calvin was hardly mentioned. The history's importance to Newman, however, did not depend on its historical competence. It had opened up to him the world of patristic Christianity – the true church of the fathers and martyrs – and thus sown the seeds of the Tractarian vision (c.f. Walsh). As Newman recalled after his conversion to Rome: 'I have never lost, I have never suffered a suspension of the impression, deep and most pleasurable, which his [Milner's] sketches of St Ambrose and St Augustine left on my mind.' 'From that time,' he added, 'the vision of the fathers was always, to my imagination, I may say, a paradise of delight to the contemplation of which I directed my thoughts from time to time' (*Cert. Diffs.*, pp. 370).

Newman's first loyalty was to his mental vision of these, the first and best Christians, and he would pay any price to retain their fellowship.

> Sooner may my right hand forget her cunning, and wither outright, as his who once stretched it out against a prophet of God – perish sooner a whole tribe of Cranmers, Ridleys, Latimers and Jewels – perish the names of Ussher, Taylor, Stillingfleet and Barrow, from the face of the earth – ere I should do ought but fall at their feet in love and in worship, whose image was continually before my eyes, and whose musical words were ever in my ears and on my tongue! (ib., p. 388).

It was when he had reached the certainty that if Athanasius or Ambrose were to return to earth, they would instinctively make their way to a Roman chapel rather than an Anglican parish church, that Newman's destiny was sealed.

Newman had written in *The Prophetical Office* (1837): 'Tradition is uniform custom . . . It is latent but it lives. It is silent like the rapids of a river, before the rocks intercept it . . . it is the mode in which a society has felt or acted during a certain period' (pp. 39, 41; cf. *Pres. Pos.*, p. 328). It was 'the great, manifest, historical phenomenon which converted me,' Newman recalled (*Cert, Diffs.*, p. 368). Newman never attempted to deny the aesthetic appeal of catholicism. We cannot help it if catholicism is beautiful, he protested as an Anglican against the criticism made by both old high churchmen and broad churchmen that the Tractarians were being swayed by romantic dreams of returning to an idealised past (*Essays Crit. & Hist.* I, pp. 282ff). They found in catholicism, Newman explained to Jelf in defence of *Tract 90*, those sublime feelings that had been evoked by Sir Walter Scott, Wordsworth and Coleridge, 'feelings of awe, mystery, tenderness, reverence, devotedness.'

Newman: Exponent of Anglicanism

In 1834 Newman took over a correspondence with the Abbé Jager in which he defended Anglicanism as a true branch of the catholic church. Over the two year course of correspondence, during which he was also lecturing on the same themes, Newman developed his conception of fundamentals and outlined his celebrated distinction between episcopal and prophetical tradition. Much of his material he worked up into his *Lectures on the Prophetical Office of the Church viewed relatively to Romanism and Popular Protestantism* (1837). This remains a valuable exposition of the Anglican position.

In the first letter Newman uses the notion of fundamentals to distinguish the respective roles of scripture and tradition. 'Scripture is the ultimate basis of proof, the place of final appeal, in respect to all fundamental doctrine.' While ceremonies and practices may rest upon tradition, doctrines – or at least fundamental doctrines – may not. But patently not all the doctrines – even the central doctrines – of the Church of England are clearly taught by scripture. The threefold ministry is a case in point: but Newman (surprisingly) allows that this may be regarded as a point of *discipline* rather than doctrine. The doctrine of the Trinity is clearly fundamental, and this we receive '*immediately* from tradition, *ultimately* from scripture' (Allen, pp. 35f).

In the *Prophetical Office* Newman further clarifies the relation of scripture and tradition. 'Though we consider scripture a sufficient, we do not consider it our sole informant in divine truths . . . We rely on antiquity to strengthen such intimations of doctrine as are but faintly, though really, given in scripture' (pp. 36f). While scripture contains all things necessary to salvation – Newman is emphatic about this – that does not make it the only ground of faith, or the guide to faith, or the teacher of faith, or the source of all religious truth whatsoever. But it remains 'the document of ultimate appeal in controversy and the touchstone of all doctrine' (pp. 369f). As Newman wrote to the Abbé Jager, scripture is 'the rule of faith', 'the court of ultimate appeal, which has the right of definitely settling all questions of faith' (Allen, p. 117).

What then are the fundamentals of the faith, that are grounded on scripture, form the foundation of the church, and are necessary for salvation and church communion? As Newman asks in the *Prophetical Office*: is there 'some one object, some circle of sacred truths . . . doctrines independent and external, which may be emphatically called the gospel, which have been committed to the church from the first, which she is bound to *teach* as saving, and to *enforce* as the terms of communion' (p. 258)? Such truths are found in the Apostles' Creed, of which the Nicene Creed is merely an expansion and exposition. This is the 'common faith' which all branches of the church hold now as they always have done (p. 259). The Church of England does not teach and enforce the Thirty-nine Articles as fundamentals of the faith. They are merely articles of religion, not of 'faith'. They are not necessary for salvation, except in so far as they contain the truths of the creed (p. 278). The error of the council of Trent, however, lay in enforcing its articles of religion as necessary points of faith (p. 280).

But the ultimate foundation of the church is the radical and simple one of our confession of faith in Christ. With Richard Hooker, Newman reduces the foundation to its simplest expression in the gospel faith. 'In the first instance the doctrine of Christ is the foundation,' for 'other foundation can no man lay'. But the simple confession of Jesus as 'the Christ, the Son of the living God', needs to be seen in the context of the whole trinitarian baptismal formula (Allen, p. 38f, 83). Newman summarises his position to the Abbé thus: 'As then I may impose nothing to be believed as terms of communion, but the creed, so I may impose nothing to be believed in order to salvation but what is founded on scripture' (p. 122). In essence, Newman seems to be defending the classical Anglican position that the baptismal faith is the basis both of saving belief and of church communion.

The correspondence and the *Prophetical Office* advance the traditional high Anglican branch theory of the church: the Roman, Anglican and (though this is not an issue here) the Orthodox churches are sister communions of the one church catholic (*Proph. Off.*, pp. 313, 315). If this is so, Newman makes an objector ask, 'Where then, in the English church is that one eternal voice of truth; that one witness issuing from the apostles' times, and conversant with all doctrine, the expounder of the creed, the interpreter of scripture, and the instructer of the people of God?' (p. 311). Newman's answer is assured:

> Now in spite of differences within and without, our own branch may be considered among us as the voice of her who has been in the world ever one and the same since Christ came . . . She transmits the ancient catholic faith simply and intelligibly . . . She speaks in her formularies and services. The daily prayer, the occasional offices, the order of the sacraments, the ordination services, presents one and the same strong plain edifying language . . . and that not as the invention of this Reformer or that, but as the witness of all saints from the beginning (p. 313).

'The Spirit of Luther is Dead'

'Whatever be historical Christianity,' asserts Newman in the essay on development, 'it is not protestantism. If ever there were a safe truth it is this' (p. 72). Wrestling, in his private notebooks, with the problem of certainty, Newman finds one conviction that he cannot doubt – St Paul would have considered protestantism a great heresy! (*Faith and Certainty*, p. 5). But if we comb Newman's writings for the evidence on which this claim is based, we come up with a bizarre mixture of fact and fiction.

Newman unashamedly interprets the Reformation in the light of intellectual trends in the Germany of the *Aufklärung* and its aftermath. Kant and Strauss are principal witnesses. Luther is the source of that 'spurious Christianity' that combines subjective feeling with a rationalistic approach to the mystery of the faith. The modern Luther is Schleiermacher. 'Lutheranism, as is well known, has by this time become almost simple heresy or infidelity; it has terminated, if it has even yet reached its limit, in a denial both of the canon and the creed, nay of many principles of morals.' But what else could one expect when Luther himself rejected the book of Revelation, called the epistle of James *Straminea* (straw), condemned use of the word 'trinity', espoused an early heresy (Eutychianism) on the omnipresence of the manhood of Christ and in one case (Philip of Hesse) sanctioned bigamy? However, this was only the tip of the iceberg: at the root of Luther's 'doctrine and personal character' was naked pantheism (*Dev.*, pp. 136, 140; *Essays Crit. & Hist.* I, p. 96).

Calvin fares no better. Calvin 'seems' to have denied our Lord's eternal Sonship and ridiculed the Nicene creed. No wonder, then, that in a number of countries Calvinism has evolved into Socinianism. Newman identifies an unholy trinity as the source of protestant error: 'Luther did but a part of the work, Calvin another portion, Socinus finished it.' The history of protestantism supports Newman's theory of development – in this case, of course, spurious, counterfeit development:

> The equable and orderly march and natural succession of views by which the creed of Luther has been changed into the infidel or heretical philosophy of his present representatives is a proof that that change is no perversion or corruption but a faithful development of the original idea (*Dev.*, pp. 136, 184, 140).

On the Austrian emperor Joseph II's suppression of the Jesuits, the catholic Newman of 1850 comments: 'The mystery of protestantism is unravelled; the day of Luther is come' (*Cert. Diffs.*, p. 325).

In 'The Catholicity of the Anglican Church' (1840) Newman, who at this stage was still committed to defending the *via media*, contrasts salutary developments in Anglicanism with the heretical trends of the protestant churches. While Lutheranism has become rationalistic and Calvinism Socinian, the Church of England has become progressively more catholic since the 'miserable' low point of the reigns of Edward and Elizabeth (*Essays and Sketches*, II, pp. 90f).

Intrinsic to the Reformation was a runaway notion of private judgement born of spiritual pride. Wycliffe and Hus had first taken it upon themselves to kindle those 'miserable bonfires' which are still raging to the ruin of mankind's highest interests. The Reformers had despised the fathers of the church, and 'those who spoke as they did of all who went before them have no claim on the reverence of those who come after.' Luther's revolution was achieved 'not by appeals to the fathers, not by reasonings on the nature of the case, not by elaborate deductions from scripture, but by positions venturous, striking, stamped with originality and suited even to the ignorant.' The theological efforts of the Reformers have 'no internal consistency, no external proof, no part or lot in antiquity' (*Univ.Ed.*, pp. 147; *Essays Crit. & Hist.*, II, pp. 132f; *Justification*, p. 210).

Luther's mistake was in attempting to deal with the problem of late medieval catholicism with the carnal weapons of his own invention, with the result that the last state of Christendom was worse than the first.

> He found Christians in bondage to their works and observances; he released them by his doctrine of faith and he left them in bondage to their feelings . . . For outward signs of grace he substituted inward; for reverence towards the church, contemplation of self . . . whereas he professed to make the written word all in all, he sacrificed it in its length and breadth to the doctrine which he had wrested from a few texts.

And the rampant judgement that he unleashed remains as a cancer at the heart of modern protestantism (*Justification*, p. 386).

While all protestant sects agree as to the standard of faith, namely the Bible, no two of them agree on its interpretation. The result is a cynical relativism of belief, a doctrinal permissiveness that seems to imply that, for protestants, truth is merely a matter of opinion and 'that is truth to each which each thinks to be truth, provided he sincerely and really thinks it.' Protestantism today, judges Newman, 'considers it a hardship to have anything clearly and distinctly told it in elucidation of scripture doctrine, an infringement on its right of doubting and mistaking and labouring in vain.' And all this it dignifies as a crusade in defence of the sacred principle of private judgement, which, replacing the catholic dogmatic principle, renders protestantism not merely a debased and enfeebled version of the catholic faith but its actual antithesis (*Proph. Off.* 3rd edn, pp. 26f, 238, 41).

English protestantism is full of anomalies and inconsistencies which constitute the seeds of its own destruction. It is composed of miscellaneous fragments of other faiths, fortuitously thrown together: 'something of Lutheranism, and something of Calvinism, something of Erastianism and something of Zwinglianism, a little Judaism and a little dogmatism and not a little secularity.' Its present inchoate state will resolve itself in rationalism. Popular protestantism has taken 'tavern toasts' for the notes of the church (*Essays Crit. & Hist.*, I, pp. 295f, 159).

Incidentally, observe how Newman copes with the fact that he has departed from the position set out by Richard Hooker, interpreter *par excellence* of the Anglican middle way, in his lectures on justification. Newman was not in the least abashed to have Hooker against him: 'since we are not allowed to call any man our master on earth, Hooker, venerable as is his name, has no weight with any Christian, except as delivering what is agreeable to catholic doctrine' (*Justification*, 3rd edn, p. 403). The *Lectures* present a travesty of Luther's teaching.

The sacrifice of Hooker was one stage in the progressive disengagement from Anglicanism that began with the rejection of the Reformation. In 1839 Newman declared that protestantism was no longer a live option; it was out of tune with the needs and tendencies of the time. The spirit of the age pointed to popery perhaps – to dogmatism, mysticism and asceticism – or to pantheism or democracy, but not to Reformation principles. 'England cannot any longer be Calvinistic or Zwinglian or Lutheran; does it wish to be democratic or pantheistic or popish? . . . The spirit of Luther is dead; but Hildebrand and Loyola are still alive.' When this was written, Newman was still hopeful of restoring the Anglican *via media*. Before long he came to the conclusion that this had never existed except on paper. The choice was now between protestantism and popery. There could never really be any doubt that, in Newman's case, 'dogmatism, mysticism and asceticism' would prevail (*Essays Crit. & Hist.*, I, pp. 305f).

The Road to Rome

'How shall I name thee,' wrote Newman in Rome in 1833, 'light of the wide west or heinous error seat?' (c. Rowlands, diss., pp. 232f). Returning to England, Newman threw himself with astonishing energy and self-assurance into the movement to regenerate the Church of England by recalling her to her roots in Caroline theology and piety. The *Tracts for the Times* defended the claims of the Church of England and repudiated those of Rome and protestant dissent. They attempted to sting the Anglican church into disowning the worldly, profane, commercial and utilitarian Whig establishment, that she might not be condemned along with it. 'We are reformed,' asserted *Tract 31* (1834), 'we have come out of Babylon and have rebuilt our church; but it is Ichabod; "the glory is departed from Israel"'. In his two-part essay on the 'Via Media' (*Tracts 38* and *41*, 1934) Newman maintains his distance from Rome – he concludes with a catalogue of Romish errors, following bishop Joseph Hall, beginning with the doctrine of infused righteousness in justification – but he widens the gap between the Tractarians and the Reformation. 'The glory of the English church is that it has taken the *via media* . . . it lies between the (so called) Reformers and the Romanists.' Newman concludes with a call for a second reformation – a reformation of discipline to counteract the inroads of erastianism and latitudinarianism.

In the following year (1835) Newman wrote in *Tract 71* ('On the Controversy with the Romanists'): 'We find ourselves under the Anglican regimen; let every one of us, cleric and layman, remain in it, till our opponents have shown cause why we should change.' The memory of

our great teachers, champions and confessors of the seventeenth century –
Hammond, Hooker and Ken – 'bind us to the Anglican church by cords
of love.' If, however, we came to believe the English church to be
heretical and the Roman church to be pure and catholic, it would be our
duty to separate. Is this the cloud 'no bigger than a man's hand' that ten
years on would become The Deluge?

Soon Newman was wondering whether the *via media* could ever be
implemented. In his lectures on *The Prophetical Office of the Church*
(1837) Newman seems to look back on the flowering of Anglicanism in
the seventeenth century as tainted with erastianism. The Church of
England was not free to be herself even then, and the prospect for the
future is no brighter. 'Protestantism and popery are real religions; no one
can doubt about them; they have furnished the mould in which nations
have been cast: but the *via media* has never existed [*2nd edn*: viewed as an
integral system has scarcely had existence] except on paper, it has never
been reduced to practice.'

> It still remains to be tried whether what is called Anglicanism [*2nd edn*:
> Anglo-Catholicism], the religion of Andrews, Laud, Hammond, Butler and
> Wilson is capable of being professed, acted on and maintained on a large
> sphere of action and through a sufficient period, or whether it be a mere
> modification [*2nd edn*: or transition-state] either of Romanism or of
> popular protestantism, according as we view it (pp. 20ff).

The lectures on justification of 1938 were an attempt to work out the
middle way in a concrete, central area of doctrine (*Apol.*, p. 150). But in
them Newman parodies Luther's doctrine of *sola fide* and the notion of
imputed righteousness, as though the Reformers had not believed in a real
incorporation into Christ:

> That the scheme of salvation should be one of names and understandings;
> that we should be but said to be just, said to have a righteousness, said to
> please God, said to earn a reward, said to be saved by works; that the great
> disease of our nature should remain unstaunched . . . when merely
> propounded fifteen centuries after Christ came it has no claims upon us.

Newman savages his man of straw:

> Away then with this modern, this private, this arbitrary, this unscriptural
> system, which promising liberty conspires against it; which abolishes
> sacraments to introduce barren and dead ordinances: and for the real
> participation of Christ and justification through his Spirit, would at the
> very marriage feast feed us on shells and husks who hunger and thirst after
> righteousness.

Luther's is a 'new gospel', unheard till three hundred years before
(*Justification*, pp. 62f).

In 1837 Newman had discussed the common protestant view that
Rome was antichrist, but without espousing it (*Proph. Off.*, pp. 54f). In

the following year, defending Froude's opinions published in the *Remains*, Newman denies the pope to be antichrist.

In the *Apologia* Newman describes the Anglican *modus vivendi* that he had carved out for himself by 1839. It is an appeal to Anglican comprehensiveness and he rightly claims that he had as much right to his particular emphases as the evangelicals or liberals had to theirs:

> I held a large, bold system of religion, very unlike the protestantism of the day, but it was the concentration and adjustment of the statements of great Anglican authorities . . . I claimed that [one] might hold in the Anglican church a comprecation with the saints with Bramhall, and the mass all but transubstantiation with Andrewes, or with Hooker that transubstantiation itself is not a point for churches to part communion upon, or with Hammond that a general council, truly such, never did, never shall err in a matter of faith . . . or with Thorndike that penance is a propitiation for post-baptismal sin . . . (p. 166).

The reception and fate of *Tract 90* of 1841, in which Newman attempted to stretch the Thirty-nine Articles to accommodate these and other (Tridentine) doctrines, demonstrated that the Church of England was not – at that time at least – willing to extend its hospitality to such views. But before that dramatic episode, two other incidents had prepared Newman's mind for what was to follow ultimately.

Newman had enough historical knowledge and historical imagination to recreate and relive the remote past, but not enough scientific detachment to respect, with Vico, Herder and Niebuhr, the pastness, the finality and the separate integrity of other ages. In the summer of 1839, his over-heated historical imagination led him to draw disturbing conclusions. Studying the history of the fifth century heretical monophysites, Newman saw sixteenth and nineteenth century church history reflected. 'I saw my face in that mirror, and I was a monophysite' (*Apol.*, p. 182). The protestants were re-enacting the role of the heretics in that obscure controversy. The experience ('the shadow of a hand upon the wall'), though he suppressed it for a time, shattered his faith in 'the tenableness of the fundamental principle of Anglicanism' (*Cert. Diffs.*, p. 373). In the same year a second seed was planted in his mind – the phrase of Augustine against the Donatists, *Securus judicat orbis terrarum*, that a friend pointed out to Newman in an article by Wiseman. After prolonged reflection, it seemed to say to Newman: 'the deliberate judgement, in which the whole church at length rests and acquiesces, is an infallible prescription and a final sentence against such portions of it as protest and secede.' 'By these words of the ancient father,' said Newman later (exaggerating perhaps: Lash, p. 14), 'the theory of the *via media* was absolutely pulverised.' Subliminally, in the tacit dimension, where the gravitational pull of cumulative data is stronger than the collected judgements of conscious thought, Newman was being prepared to make his great decision. 'He who has seen a ghost cannot be as if he had never seen it. The heavens had opened and closed again. The thought for the moment had been, "The church of Rome will be found right after all;" and then it had vanished' (*Apol.*, pp. 184f).

The turning point came with the publication and subsequent rejection of *Tract 90* in 1841. This was Newman's final challenge to the Church of England. Admitting the imperfections of the church, Newman professed a willingness to work within her provided she was willing to allow an extreme latitude of interpretation of her articles of religion that would allow those more extreme than Newman himself to remain. He dressed the work up as a peace offering – a final attempt at reconciliation. Others saw it as a deliberate challenge and provocation; Newman seemed to be saying, 'Turn me down.'

Newman stated his aim as being 'merely to show that, while our prayer book is acknowledged on all hands to be of catholic origin, our articles also, the offspring of an uncatholic age are, through God's good providence, to say the least, not uncatholic and may be subscribed by those who aim at being catholic in heart and doctrine' (p. 4). For example, where the articles state that general councils may err, Newman attempts to uphold 'the consistency of this article with a belief in the infallibility of ecumenical councils.' Where the 'Romish doctrine' of purgatory, pardons, images, relics and invocation of saints is condemned as 'a fond thing vainly invented and grounded upon no warranty of scripture', Newman claims the right to deduce that the *primitive* doctrine of these matters is not affected (pp. 21, 23).

Newman supports his case from the variety of doctrinal views to be found in the Homilies, suggesting that the articles too were 'not framed on the principle of excluding those who prefer the theology of the early ages to that of the Reformation'. The articles, though admittedly a protestant confession, were drawn up with the aim of including catholics – 'and catholics now will not be excluded'. 'What was an economy in the Reformers is a protection to us. What would have been a perplexity to us then is a perplexity to protestants now. We could not then have found fault with their words; they cannot now repudiate our meaning' (pp. 81, 83).

Grant them this and they will submit to the Anglican yoke, until in the providence of God things improve. Meanwhile

> let the church, our Mother, sit still, let her children be content to be in bondage; let us work in chains; let us submit to our imperfections as a punishment; let us go on teaching through the medium of indeterminate statements, and inconsistent precedents and principles but partially developed. We are not better than our fathers; let us bear to be what Hammond was, or Andrews or Hooker (p. 3).

Newman's tract was a peace offering to the Church of England – delivered with a slap in the face.

The tract had appeared anonymously. Four Oxford tutors called upon the author to come forward, pointing out that in the offending tract it was being claimed that the articles condemned, not the doctrines authoritatively taught by the Church of Rome, but only 'certain absurd practices and opinions, which intelligent Romanists repudiate as much as we do.' The tutors concluded that it tended 'to mitigate, beyond what charity requires, and to the prejudice of the pure truth of the gospel,' the very serious differences which divide Rome and Canterbury. The Hebdomadal Board ruled that *Tract 90*, 'evading rather than explaining the sense of the Thirty-nine Articles, and reconciling subscription to them with the adoption of errors which they were designed to counteract,' contravened the statutes of the university. The next day, disowned and discredited in his university, Newman declared his authorship. It was a decisive step into the wilderness.

One disciple of Newman was not at all abashed. Ward came to Newman's defence in a pamphlet which praised *Tract 90* as offering 'a view of our formularies full of comfort'. At this juncture Ward was still committed to restoring the catholic face of the Church of England. That this enterprise was now doomed to failure – at least in the terms in which Ward saw it – was entailed in his uncompromising assertion that the tract '*did* imply that . . . the articles do not condemn the decrees of the council of Trent' ('A Few Words').

Developing Christianity

Newman's *Essay on the Development of Christian Doctrine* (1845) signalled his departure to Rome, but it was very much in the spirit of contemporary trends in Anglican theology, overlapping as it did in its central concept with the developmental theories being explored at the same time by liberal Anglican thinkers such as Arnold, Milman, Hare and Thirlwall, who had learned their philosophy of history from the Germans, especially Niebuhr.

(a) In the second edition (1878) of the essay, Newman considers the 'hypothesis' that 'Christianity has even changed from the first and ever accommodates itself to the circumstances of times and seasons', but rejects it on the grounds that it is incompatible with the idea of revealed (propositional) truth – adding (with considerable caution be it noted) that 'its advocates more or less abandon, or tend to abandon the supernatural claims of Christianity' (p. 7). Newman perhaps had in mind Henry Hart Milman's *History of Christianity* (1840) which he had already found wanting for its detached, phenomenological, naturalistic, reductionistic method (see *Essays and Sketches*, II, pp. 217ff). Milman defined his aim in this work as

> to trace all the modifications of Christianity, by which it accommodated itself to the spirit of successive ages; and by this apparently almost skilful, but in fact necessary condescension to the predominant state of moral culture, of

which itself formed a constituent element, maintained its uninterrupted dominion . . . to mark the origin and progress of all the subordinate diversities of belief; their origin in the circumstances of the place and time at which they appeared; their progress from their adaptation to the prevailing state of opinion or sentiment . . . in short, to exhibit the reciprocal influence of civilisation on Christianity and of Christianity on civilisation (c. Rowlands, diss., p. 221).

Arnold had spoken of his vision of a Christianity translated out of inferior, outdated Hebrew thought forms into the sublime concepts and idioms afforded by classical Greek culture.

Such views offended Newman's 'dogmatic principle'. For him there was one truth, revealed intact, not the product of human enquiry or discovery. Dogmas were 'supernatural truths irrevocably committed to human language, imperfect because it is human, but definitive and necessary because given from above' (c. Rowlands, diss., p. 225; *Dev.*, p. 356). But the idealist epistemology with which the liberal Anglicans worked enabled them to conceive of a persisting identity of Christianity from one historical period to another, embodied not in propositions but in ideas or symbols, and apprehended not by the mere understanding (*Verstand*) but by intuitive reason (*Verstehen*). Although Newman cannot be adequately explained in terms of an empiricist epistemology, in the tradition of Locke and Hume, and constantly strains to burst through it, it is clear that it hampered him in working out his notion of development, as it did in other areas. While the liberal Anglicans thought in terms of the development of *Christianity*, Newman was restricted, at least ostensibly and within his self-imposed bounds, to the development of *doctrine*. But the notion of development was in the air and Newman could not have been ignorant of it. With his immense sensitivity to the *Zeitgeist* he would have been in the forefront of response to these new directions in historical and philosophical ideas, even though he was largely ignorant of German scholarship.

(b) A second variation of the concept of development that Newman mentions only to discard is that of the *Disciplina Arcani*, or secret discipline – the theory that doctrines which emerged later in the church's history were known from the first but held back to save them from the ridicule of unbelievers, or so as not to overwhelm catechumens, or to preserve the church's deposit of faith from persecutors. The theory fails, Newman observes in the first edition of the essay on development, because the doctrinal 'variations' continue long after the time when it is conceivable that the discipline was still in force (p. 90). And Newman adds in the second edition (1878): 'and because they manifest themselves on a law, not abruptly, but by a growth which has persevered up to this time without any sign of its coming to an end' (p. 21).

The notion of 'reserve in communicating religious knowledge' (to quote the title of Isaac Williams' celebrated *Tract 80*) was central to the

Tractarian ethos. Newman had deployed the idea of *economy* in the dispensation of truth in his work on *The Arians of the Fourth Century* (1833), where he had described the church releasing piecemeal the contents of revelation as the occasion and the recipients required – the revealed truth that dwelt in plenitude in the heart of the church.

> As the mind is cultivated and expanded, it cannot refrain from the attempt to analyse the vision which influences the heart, and the object in which the vision centres; nor does it stop till it has, in some sort, succeeded in expressing in words what has all along been a principle both of its affections and of its obedience.

The apostolic writings had been addressed more directly to the heart; the full dogmatic system of Christianity had been 'kept in the background in the infancy of Christianity, when faith and obedience were vigorous, and brought forward at a time when, on being proportionately developed, and aiming at sovereignty in the province of religion, its presence became necessary to expel a usurping idol from the house of God' (c. Allen, p. 13).

(c) Here the notion of reserve and economy slides into the rather different version of development, that of all truth subsisting implicitly or tacitly in the bosom of the church, and coming to conscious expression as the need arose. This was a conception profoundly consistent with Newman's stress on the significance of subliminal thinking and what Polanyi has called 'the tacit dimension' of personal knowledge, as we find it in Newman's *University Sermons* and the *Grammar of Assent*.

Newman pondered this possibility in his 1840 essay on 'The Catholicity of the Anglican Church'. Roman apologists seemed to claim, he observed, 'that the whole faith was present in the minds of the apostles, nay of all saints at all times, but in great measure as a matter of mere temper, feeling and unconscious opinion, that is, implicitly, not in the way of exact statements and in an intellectual form' (*Essays and Sketches*, II, p. 53). In the essay on development itself, Newman suggests that 'the holy apostles would know without words all the truths concerning the high doctrines of theology, which controversialists after them have piously and charitably reduced to formulae and defended through argument' (*Dev.*, p. 138). Newman calls this note of true development 'logical sequence' but there is more of mysticism than of logic in it.

Later as a Roman Catholic, Newman wrote to Acton, 'What is meant by development? Is it a more intimate apprehension, and a more lucid enunciation of the original dogma?' For himself, he continued, he thought it something more. 'I think it is what an apostle would have said when on earth, what any of his disciples would have said, according as the occasion called for it.' For example, 'If St Clement or St Polycarp had been asked whether our Lady was immaculately conceived, I think he might have taken some time to understand the question, and perhaps (as St Bernard) he might have to the end misunderstood the question; but if he did ever understand it, I think he would have said, "Of course she was." ' It was Acton's considered view that Newman held that 'a divine of the second century, on seeing the Roman catechism, would have recognised his own belief in it, without surprise, as soon as he understood its meaning' (McDougall, pp. 162ff).

The test of 'logical sequence' (like the others: continuity of principles, power of assimilation, anticipation of the future, conservative effect and 'chronic vigour') is evidently only the first – 'preservation of type' – expanded into its collateral aspects. To ask whether there is a recognisable affinity between later and earlier manifestations of Christianity is a pretty central function of any critical theology but it obviously cannot be done like a litmus test. By 'preservation of type', his principal test of authentic development, and the one to which Newman devotes a substantial proportion of the work, Newman seems to mean a continuity of ethos, an intuitively recognisable similarity of style, in spite of all outward changes. Just as the apostolic fathers would have endorsed the Tridentine catechism, so Athanasius and Ambrose, could they return to earth, would instinctively embrace the Roman communion of, say, Pius IX (pope from 1846) as the closest of all existing churches to the undivided catholic church that they knew (*Dev.*, p. 185). Doctrines may have changed and practices altered but the ethos remains the same.

Again and again Newman holds up his imaginative construction of the ethos of the primitive church and asks whether we cannot see in it the original of contemporary Roman Catholicism:

> If there is a form of Christianity now in the world which is accused of gross superstition, of borrowing its rites and customs from the heathen, and of ascribing to forms and ceremonies an occult virtue; a religion which is considered to burden and enslave the mind by its requisitions, to address itself to the weak minded and ignorant, to be supported by sophistry and imposture, and to contradict reason and exalt mere irrational faith . . . a religion which men hate as proselytising, anti-social, revolutionary, as dividing families, separating chief friends, corrupting the maxims of government, making a mock at law, dissolving the empire, the enemy of human nature . . . if there be such a religion now in the world, it is not unlike Christianity as that same world viewed it, when first it came forth from its divine Author (pp. 270f; cf. 294, 334).

Here Newman is characteristically skating with exhilaration on the thinnest of thin ice: his soon-to-be Roman friends would not thank him for drawing attention to aspects of the catholic tradition that the more forward-thinking of them were already taking steps to disown or correct. And, soon after experiencing it all at first hand, Newman would throw his weight behind them.

(d) Newman described his argument in the *Essay* as 'an hypothesis to account for a difficulty' (p. 90). Newman's modest aim was mainly negative, to remove an objection. What was this difficulty? What was the objection?

The difficulty arose from the apparent conflict between two of the credal notes of the Christian church – catholicity and apostolicity. Newman's work had for many years been dominated by the pursuit of these ideals. The whole Tractarian theological programme can be regarded as a defence of the apostolicity of the Church of England against erastianism on the one hand and Romanism on the other. It meant 'taking antiquity, not the existing church, as the oracle of truth; and holding that the apostolic succession is a sufficient guarantee of sacramental grace, without union with the Christian church throughout the world' (*Apol.*, p. 216). Newman himself had given priority to apostolicity over catholicity. He recognised that Anglicans took their stand on antiquity or apostolicity, while Roman Catholics rested their case mainly on catholicity or ecumenicity. 'England and Rome had divided these notes or prerogatives between them; the cause lay thus: apostolicity versus catholicity' (ib., p. 176). Of course Newman's fellow Tractarians – unwavering upholders of the Anglican position such as Palmer, Keble and Pusey – would not for one moment concede that Anglicanism was neglectful of, or deficient in catholicity: their branch theory of the church held that the Roman, Eastern and Anglican churches were authentic sister communions of the one church catholic. Their historical perspective was perhaps broader, though not deeper, than Newman's: they were not so wrapped up in the controversies of the early centuries that they overlooked the ecclesiological significance of the separation of east and west; whereas Newman's disregard of the situation of the eastern churches was, as Gladstone put it, one of the boldest tactics in the history of controversy.

For Newman, however, apostolicity represented the authority of normative Christianity, the appeal of Christian perfection, the voice of the fathers. Catholicity, on the other hand, represented the historical unfolding of the Christian phenomenon, its universal claim and jurisdiction, its voices uplifted with one accord to proclaim the truth, denounce error and recall those who had gone astray to the one true fold. As Newman pressed on with his reading of the fathers of the undivided church, the compelling power of primitive catholicity became irresistible. Augustine's *securus judicat orbis terrarum* as deployed by Wiseman sealed Newman's destiny. Between 1841 and 1844 'a clear conviction of the substantial identity of Christianity and the Roman system' emerged. By 1844 Newman was saying that he 'saw more in the early church to convince me that separation from the see of Peter was the token of heresy and schism, than that the additions which that great body . . . has received upon the primitive faith were innovations' (c. Lash, p. 8).

But one great problem remained: this vision of catholicity was the bait that had led Newman to look to Rome, but the requirements of apostolicity had to be satisfied too. How was he to explain the fact that Rome had added to apostolic doctrine and altered apostolic practice? This was the 'difficulty' that the theory of development was intended to dispose of. Newman ingeniously stood the classical Anglican test of apostolicity on its head: an appeal to process, to teleology, to ultimate fruition, would take the place of the standard appeal to origins. This process was 'the development of an idea, being the germination, growth and perfection of some living, that is, influential truth, or apparent truth, in the minds of men during a sufficient period' (*Dev.*, p.99). To enjoy communion with Athanasius and Ambrose – the champions respectively of doctrinal orthodoxy and the spiritual independence of the church – it was not enough to rely on the tenuous link with antiquity: safer by far to seek communion with the church that they would instinctively recognise as continuous with their own were they to 'come suddenly to life' (p.185). For they would undoubtedly 'find themselves more at home . . . with the lonely priest in his lodgings, or the holy sisterhood of mercy, or the unlettered crowd before the altar' than with the members of any other communion. Furthermore, to follow the ghosts of Athanasius and Ambrose would mean not only turning one's back on the Church of England, forsaking the establishment – and who could doubt how the establishment would deal with an Athanasius? – but renouncing Oxford too, that 'fair city, seated among groves, green meadows and calm streams' – the city that had rejected Newman (p.185).

(e) Newman had not developed a philosophical theory of historical development – though he had let loose an idea with immense potency for good or ill in the church – but he had pursued a vision of wholeness that had haunted him from his youth. He had allowed himself to 'be guided not by controversy, but by *ethos* . . . the quiet growth of a feeling through many years,' as he had once written to Robert Wilberforce (c. Newsome, p.291). 'In spite of my ingrained fears of Rome,' he later recalled, 'I had a secret, longing love of' her (*Apol.*, p.222). The most powerful and most crucial parts of the essay on development are where Newman lovingly and longingly evokes the ethos of the early church. This is why the seven so-called tests of true development fail as tests: they argue in a circle because they are doing no more than describing the developments that have actually taken place.

Assessments

(a) In the present book we are interested in understanding Newman at this stage of his Anglican career, not in criticising him, but perhaps it is permissible to suggest that Newman's prolific illustrations of correspondences between the ancient undivided church and the Roman

Catholic church of his day actually seem to entail a negation of development, since he does not allow for the possibility (his purpose of course would not let him) that other forms of Christianity such as Anglicanism or the reformed churches, might have developed authentically (on Newman's assumptions) and that the Roman church was actually closer (if it was indeed closer) to patristic Christianity, not because it had developed, but because it had not developed enough.

A further objection to Newman's slippery and elusive notion of development was raised by the Roman Catholic 'modernist' George Tyrrell. Tyrrell was suspicious of the use Newman made – and others would make – of the potentiality for growth and development of what existed implicitly in the minds of the apostles (to use Newman's formulation).

> An implied potential belief is not the same as an implied actual belief. Under this ambiguity of the word 'implicit' a new conception of tradition has been quietly substituted for the old. If a man is said to believe and admit, in spite of his explicit denial, all that is objectively implied by his data, then every avowed atheist is a theist, and every heretic orthodox. If St Thomas was not a heretic for denying the Immaculate Conception, neither was Arius a heretic for denying the godhead of Christ (p. 22).

(b) It is ironical that Newman's *Apologia* was provoked by Kingsley's charges of lack of candour and sitting lightly to the truth: these were the very faults that Newman, writing in 1840, attributed to Rome. 'We Englishmen,' he wrote, in words that ten years later would have been laden with sarcasm, 'like manliness, openness, consistency, truth. Rome will never gain on us till she learns these virtues' ('Catholicity of the Anglican Church', p. 105). Newman's very gifts – his golden tongue and seraphic intellect – carried him away to the boundary of intellectual integrity and sometimes beyond it.

Kingsley was far from alone in bringing the charge of duplicity of word and thought. It is perhaps not surprising that liberals like Jowett and Huxley took a poor view of the way Newman had applied his gifts. 'In speculation,' said Jowett, 'he was habitually untruthful and not much better in practice.' Huxley called Newman 'the slipperiest sophist I have ever met with.' But Newman's correspondent Lord Acton – a severe judge to be sure, but at least a catholic, if not a typical one – supported Kingsley's charge. Newman's practice, he said, was 'not to say the truth if it injures religious interest' (see Livingston). Henry Sidgwick said of Newman: 'As a *reasoner* I have never been disposed to take him seriously . . . regarding him as a man whose conclusions have always been influenced primarily by his emotions, and only secondarily by the workings of his subtle and ingenious intellect' (c. Bantock, p. 660). F. D. Maurice reacted to Newman's essay on development: 'Of all the books I ever read it seems to me the most sceptical; much more calculated to make sceptics than Romanists' (*Life*, I, p. 422).

Newman was constantly arguing himself by the momentum of his remorseless logic – or possibly persuading himself by the power of his own eloquence – out of every position he had taken up.

> He is always skimming along the verge of a logical catastrophe, and always relying on his dialectic agility to save himself from falling: always exposing what seems to be an unguarded spot, and always revealing a new line of defence when the unwary assailant has reached it (G. M. Young, c. Vargish, p. 19).

Newman had learned his logical skills from Richard Whately and had polished them in the cut and thrust of the Oriel senior common room. But his characteristic method was borrowed from bishop Butler, who had triumphed over the deists in the eighteenth century by adopting their presuppositions for the sake of argument and, by superior dialectical skill, producing conclusions opposite to theirs. Pitt said of the *Analogy* that it raised as many questions and doubts as it solved and R. W. Church agreed (*Pascal*, p. 32). In the hands of Newman, Butler's method became an exemplification of the dogmatist's *either/or* dilemma. As Tyrrell put it, summarising Newman: 'If you come so far, you must either come further or go back. If you are a deist, you must become a Christian or a rationalist; if you are a Christian, you must become a catholic or atheist. In short, if you are not a Roman Catholic, you must become a sceptic' (p. 31; cf. Lash, p. 15). As Newman demonstrates in *Certain Difficulties* (1850): 'To imbibe into the intellect the ancient church as a fact, is either to be a catholic or an infidel' (p. 393).

It was the view of the redoubtable Connop Thirlwall, the liberal Anglican historian and bishop, that Newman had not been swayed, in taking the path to Rome, by aesthetic considerations but, sceptical and sophistical, he had sought solid grounds to which he could abandon himself (*Life*, pp. 207f). We know that when Newman went over to Rome, he was not intellectually convinced about the papacy, but accepted it as part of the package – almost perhaps as the price to be paid for communion with the true church (cf. Lash, pp. 16f). Examples of the *sacrificium intellectus* are thick on the ground at this time. W. G. Ward was one of the first: he wanted a papal edict, along with his daily paper, to greet him at the breakfast table each morning. Mark Pattison's friend Robert Ornsby announced in 1847 that the 'intellect as well as the will ought to be sacrificed' and was soon able to add: 'the long dreary struggle in me is over . . . I am at last in the catholic church' (c. Green, p. 21). Bernard Dalgairns, who also went over to Rome in 1845, confided 'I long for a visible authority, to which I can yield obedience,' adding, 'This authority must be divine' (c. Nockles, diss., p. 204). Newman later wrote that the essence of religion was 'the submission of the reason and heart to a positive system, the acquiescence in doctrines which cannot be proved or explained' (*Via Media*, I, p. 22). 'What a comfort it would be,' muses

Charles Reding in Newman's novel *Loss and Gain*, 'to know, beyond all doubt, what to believe about God, and how to worship and please him.' But if Rome should fail him, he would 'have no competent authority to tell [him] what to believe' (pp. 159).

(c) It is perhaps difficult for Christians, Anglican or Roman Catholic, in an ecumenical age to appreciate the urgency that impelled Newman. His quest for catholicity was not merely for aesthetic satisfaction: it was for salvation. Charles Reding in *Loss and Gain* reflects that 'nothing could justify so serious an act' as secession to Rome 'but the conviction that he could not be saved in the church to which he belonged' (p. 230; cf. 252, 264). Those, like Newman and Manning, who left the Church of England for Rome did so to save their souls. Those who remained, Keble, Pusey, *et al.*, believed on theological grounds that they could save their souls equally well in the church of their baptism. Newman and Manning had given up the branch theory of the church; for them (as for the sixteenth century Reformers and their Roman opponents) there was only one true church and only in that church was salvation to be had. As Newman had written to the Abbé Jager: 'You at once hurl at me darts which you deem to be lethal, namely that the Donatists were considered by the church as excluded from salvation . . . I answer, almost in your own words, that to maintain an opinion against the voice of the whole church stubbornly and publicly is of itself without any doubt a mortal sin' (c. Allen, p. 103). The Tractarian emphasis on the transmission of sacramental grace through the apostolic succession was responsible for their dilemma. If mere apostolicity was no guarantee of the safe conveyance of sacramental grace, without also being in communion with the descendants of the apostles in that church that claimed catholicity for itself alone, only one course of action was open. They were not breaking communion with the Anglican church because they had come to believe that it was no true communion. They had come to accept the claim of the Roman Catholic church – so fiercely contested by the Reformers with their insistence that nothing not plainly taught by holy scripture could be imposed as a condition of salvation – that for salvation it was necessary to be in communion with the pope.

Newman's quest was for 'a whole doctrine stated by a whole church' (*Dev.*, p. 78). But as R. P. C. Hanson has argued, his schematic view of development 'ignored all the discontinuities, the periods spent in blind alleys, the returns to earlier doctrine, the prunings of tradition, the revivals of neglected elements, the attempts to suppress such features of Christianity as eschatology or sacramental life, which later take their vengeance in a violent *revanche*.' These considerations, Hanson adds, 'make Newman's scheme of steady expansion and articulation of dogma after dogma appear artificial and unreal' (*Attractiveness*, p. 36).

It was all part and parcel of Newman's 'dogmatic principle' that there should be one truth, promulgated by one church, based on one unchanging deposit of revelation. 'As God is one, so the impression which he gives us of himself is one' (*Univ. Sermons*, p. 330). Development should be regular, linear and homogenous; catholicism imperial, political and dogmatic; the church's unity centralised, uniform, monarchical. The theory was blatantly *a priori*, but the motives that dictated it were understandably agonised, existential, and down to earth. Gladstone blamed the outcome on the impact on formative serious and sensitive minds of an evangelicalism that promised more than it could deliver.

The Anglican Manning

When Henry Manning came to Lavington in 1833, his theological views were still in the making. He already believed in baptismal regeneration – the doctrine at the centre of the controversy that prompted his decision to forsake the Church of England in 1851 – but Samuel Wilberforce sent him to Hooker to learn the Anglican doctrine of the Real Presence. 'As to the church,' he later recalled, 'I had no definite conception.'

> I had rejected the whole idea of the established church. Erastianism was hateful to me. The royal supremacy was, in my mind, an invasion of the headship of our Lord. In truth, I had thought and read myself out of content with every system known to me. Anglicanism was formal and dry, evangelicalism illogical and at variance with the New Testament, nonconformity was to me mere disorder. Of the Catholic church I knew nothing, I was completely isolated (c. Newsome, pp. 200f).

Like the Tractarians themselves, Manning saw immense potential for the catholicising (though not at this stage the unprotestantising) of the Church of England, writing to Gladstone in 1841:

> I abhor and tremble at Romish error . . . but I cannot refuse to sympathise with what is high and true and lovely in their system. And as for the hollow false soulless shapeless no-system of protestantism I can yield to it neither the homage of reason nor of affection. The English church is a real substantive catholic body capable of development and all perfection – able to lick up and absorb all that is true and beautiful in all Christendom unto itself – and this is our problem (ib., p. 267).

In 1839 Manning published his sermon *The Rule of Faith* in which he condemned the naked biblicism of popular protestantism and argued for the normative role of the apostolic tradition in the interpretation of scripture. The Reformation was defended as a necessary return to antiquity, though Calvinism was charged with being subversive of the authority and teaching of tradition (pp. 46, 114f). But the shape of things to come in Manning's life is intimated in his apotheosis of the church:

It pleased God, in the beginning, to store up in her the whole treasure of the gospel: her sacred books were as a stedfast memory ever correcting her conceptions of heavenly things; her living ministry, a thousand tongues; her rule of faith, an universal instinct; her councils, acts of deliberation; her decrees, utterances of judgement. She was, and is a living responsible being; witnessing, defining old truths, condemning false novelties. Her charge is to sustain, from age to age, the whole body of revealed wisdom; to imbue each successive generation of her children with the conclusions of the faith, openly tendering also the proofs of holy scripture; and thus going before us from our childhood, being ever herself of one ripe age, teaching us what things are necessary, probable or doubtful – both what we must and what we may believe (pp. 44f).

Until the mid 1840s Manning was optimistic about the Church of England. He could not remember, he wrote, any movement within the church, until now, that had caused it to 'put forth such tokens of life and power.' It was almost incredible, he added, that 'a body which 15 years ago was elated at being an establishment should now be conscious of being a church' (c. Newsome, p. 316). But by the end of the decade Manning was deploring the lack of Anglican theology. 'Our whole theology is without *order*; we have not one *Theologia* of any system, unity or completeness. And that which is true even of dogmatic theology is still more true of all moral, spiritual and ascetical theology.' 'There seems about the Church of England,' he later wrote, 'a want of antiquity, system, fulness, intelligence, order, strength, unity; we have dogmas on paper; a ritual almost universally abandoned; no discipline, a divided episcopate, priesthood and laity' (ib., pp. 275, 325).

Manning's great work of Anglican theology is *The Unity of the Church* (1845), which he published as archdeacon of Chichester. It was a defence of the branch theory of the church along the lines of Palmer's *Treatise*, to which Manning acknowledges his debt. The Reformation is defended and the claims of Rome refuted. Luther was not guilty of schism, as he was excommunicated before his case was heard, and 'many who were involved in the effects of the excommunication, though violently driven from the unity of the visible church, were not cut off from the unity of Christ's mystical body' (pp. 328f). As for non-episcopal Lutheran ministries, it is easier to justify the initial break in the succession than its perpetuation. 'In what sense they possess the present authority of Christ among them, by what commission they administer baptism, confession, absolution, orders, the holy eucharist, in Christ's stead and name, we know not.' But 'we may hopefully trust that many may belong to the soul of the one true church who have never been made partakers of its visible body' (pp. 344, 349).

The English Reformation was a justifiable protest against 'the extravagant and intolerable claim of the universal pontificate' and the last rejection of Roman jurisdiction was 'no more than a successful effort after many a failure'. At no point were or are the British churches guilty of heresy or schism. 'The Anglican church has rejected – what the Eastern churches rejected before – the pretensions of an universal pontificate rashly alleged to be of divine right, imposed in open breach of apostolical traditions, and the canons of many councils' (pp. 259–263).

As David Newsome has written, 'Both emotionally and intellectually Manning yearned for unity, discipline and system' (p. 325). At this stage, in the mid 1840s, the objective unity of the church is secured, for Manning, by the apostolic succession, not by the papacy (*Unity*, pp. 97ff, 280ff). Discounting Hooker's location of episcopacy in the category of mutable revealed law, Manning argues that episcopacy is immutable. By rejecting establishment and absolutising the episcopate Manning sealed his adhesion to what I have called 'the apostolic paradigm' of modern Anglicanism.

But in this work, the moral, spiritual or subjective unity of the church loom large for Manning. It was to be achieved by subordination to authority and by mutual charity. 'The moral unity of the church . . . consists in a communion of all churches in worship and practice, in friendly intercourse and correspondence, and in all judicial, deliberative and executive acts.' This moral unity may be breached without organic unity being destroyed and without either side incurring the sin of heresy or schism (pp. 156ff, 161, 274). Manning means that communion could be broken, but provided the apostolic succession was maintained, the unity of the church would be essentially undamaged.

Manning had hoped to enjoy the catholic faith within the church of England. 'The subjects I have pressed,' he later wrote to Samuel Wilberforce, 'are as you know, besides the great mysteries of faith, such points as repentance, obedience, and devotion, and as related to these the Christian priesthood, the power of absolution, the Real Presence, the Christian sacrifice, the authority of divine tradition and the unity of the church: points every one of which is either broadly and literally taught by the offices and ordinal of the Church of England or by its chief writers.' 'You know,' he added, 'that there does not exist in any of the seven or eight volumes I have published a doctrine which is not to be found in Andrewes' (c. Newsome, p. 364). By remaining within the Church of England, Keble, Pusey and others made it possible to hold these doctrines. Manning took the Gorham judgement as the decisive signal that they would not be tolerated. Baptismal regeneration had not been upheld; the prerogatives of the church of Christ had been compromised. Manning had already found himself unable to refute Newman's theory of development. The Gorham debacle gave him the release he was now longing for. In 1851 he was received into the Roman Catholic church 'after a terrible and prolonged struggle in which Manning had been compelled to make the final act of abjuration – the agonising admission of the invalidity of his Anglican orders' (Newsome, p. 366). The apostolic paradigm had proved a broken reed.

15

Challenge to the Apostolic Paradigm

Coleridge: Heroic Luther

(1) *What Luther Meant to Coleridge*

'He is of all men,' said Coleridge, placing his hand on an engraving of Luther, 'the one whom I especially love and admire.' The rediscovery of Luther and the Reformation in the early nineteenth century stemmed above all from the seminal influence of Samuel Taylor Coleridge. Like so many other movements of thought in that period – literary, philosophical and theological – the reawakening of the spirit of the Reformation has the scattered insights of Coleridge at its source. F. D. Maurice, Julius Hare and F. J. A. Hort seem to owe their interest in Luther to him. Again and again Coleridge invokes the spirit of Luther – the heroic Luther, the philosophical Luther, the delightfully mischievous and even impossibly wrong-headed Luther, the intriguing under-researched Luther.

Coleridge's knowledge of the Reformer was not confined to Luther's *Table Talk* (he had picked up an edition of Luther's works in Germany) but it was in the pages of that volume, borrowed from his friend Charles Lamb, that Coleridge came closest to the real Luther. Here he not only discovered a figure of flesh and blood, the all-too-human Luther, but also a being of transcendent spiritual power: he found words of life for his soul's sustenance. As F. J. A. Hort remarked in his essay 'Coleridge' (1856):

> The old thin folio of Martin Luther's *Table Talk*, translated by Captain Henry Bell with Laud's sanction and approval and, after an interruption by the civil wars, finally published under the auspices of Oliver Cromwell, seems to have lain nearer to Coleridge's heart than any book except the Bible . . . He found in Luther's strongest meat the very marrow of divinity: he believed that since St. Paul no man had been brought into such living contact with central truth (p. 345).

It was not for merely literary or antiquarian reasons that Coleridge read Luther: it was for salvation. 'No where else,' he says, 'the inspired volume of course excepted, have I found the doctrine of Christian faith so clearly and distinctly set forth, so vitally substantiated in scripture and in the very nature of a human soul.' And when Luther calls upon the reader to rest all upon Christ, Coleridge comments: 'Ay! this, this is indeed to the purpose. In this doctrine my soul can find rest: I hope to be saved by faith – not by my faith by the faith of Christ in me' (*Letters*, p. 845; *Notes*, p. 33).

In his marginalia to the *Table Talk*, Coleridge seems to open his heart. His marginal jottings are perhaps the most appealing of everything he wrote: but they are also true to the character of this 'archangel a little damaged', as Lamb described him. His comments not only endear but exasperate. As Gordon Rupp has remarked:

> To read Coleridge's marginal notes in his copy of that work is again and again to be halted by some earnest ejaculation, some prayer, some confession of a soul's struggle so intimate that the student almost desists, as though intruding into confessions too private and personal for academic survey. Then one remembers that this is simply the Coleridge manner, the least satisfactory trait of his romanticism, that in fact he was wont to treat the margins of all his books in this way, even books from circulating libraries, even books borrowed from his friends, not without half an eye to what they would make of it! (*Righteousness*, p. 49).

In this case, however, the comments were not destined for Lamb to see: the book was never returned, in spite the owner's protests.

(2) *Luther's Moral and Philosophical Significance*

Coleridge revels in Luther and glories in Hooker but he certainly does not take a triumphalist view of the Reformation, regarding it as a 'necessary evil' (*Table Talk*, p. 250). It was called for to combat a greater evil, the reign of antichrist, and only the conviction that the papacy was antichrist, Coleridge holds, could have justified the Reformation. What does he mean by this? Antichrist is defined by Coleridge as 'a power in the Christian church which in the name of Christ and at once pretending and usurping his authority, is systematically subversive of the essential and distinguishing characters and purposes of the Christian church.' In the case of Rome, this took the form of the 'erection of a temporal monarch under the pretence of a spiritual authority' – a transposition only possible in Christendom by 'the extinction or entrancement of the spirit of Christianity.' Nothing less than this supreme issue of principle could, in Coleridge's view, have justified the revolt of the sixteenth century. If the papacy is not antichrist, 'the guilt of schism in its most aggravated form lies on the authors of the Reformation. For nothing less than this could have justified so tremendous a rent in the catholic church, with all its foreseen most calamitous consequences ... Only in the conviction that Christianity itself was at stake, that the cause was that of Christ in conflict with antichrist, could or did even the lion-hearted

Luther with unquailed spirit, avow to himself: I bring not peace but a sword into the world' (*Church and State*, pp. 116f).

For precisely this reason, Luther's mission had to be a violent one; the moderation of an Erasmus would not have met the case.

> Think you that a man could have gone through what he did, have stood alone before assembled diets, dared sovereigns, continued with his pen scourging a pope here and a monarch there and treating both of them as his inferiors . . .? Think you that such a man could have done this with the cool rational language of what is now called philosophy . . .? No – Luther's mistakes might have been superfluous but the spirit which made them inevitable was not superfluous (*Phil. Lectures*, p. 309).

Luther needed to be an heroic figure and he more than matched his destiny.

When Coleridge is not addressing Luther as his 'dear Luther', it is as the 'heroic Luther', or sometimes both appelations together: 'this dear man of God, heroic Luther'. Above all, it is as an heroic figure that Coleridge sees the Reformer. Luther is 'this Christian Hercules, this heroic cleanser of the Augean Stable of apostacy'. He is 'the heroic Luther, a giant awakening in his strength . . . the German Son of Thunder' (*Notes*, pp. 9f, 42; *Friend*, I, pp. 75n, 132).

As an avowed Kantian, Coleridge saw every issue in moral terms and his own moral failings only served to sharpen his sense of the pervasive conflict of good and evil. Hort rightly refers to 'the universal supremacy which moral considerations held in his mind' (p. 338). Coleridge's view of the Reformation was no exception: Luther's was a moral struggle and no considerations of expediency or moderation could outweigh this over-riding claim. 'Luther felt and preached and wrote and acted as beseemed a Luther to feel and utter and act. The truths which had been outraged, he reproclaimed in the spirit of outraged truth at the behest of his conscience and in the service of the God of truth' (*Friend*, I, p. 64). And in 1818 Coleridge writes:

> O what a genuine son of Paul is he not! As in our Articles and Homilies the doctrine of our apostolic church appears in the meakness of wisdom, so in the writings of Luther does it *thunder* and *lighten* in it's [sic] sublimity – O how the painted mist of mock-rationality dissolves before him – the hollowness of self-procured gradual self-reformation by force of prudential reflections and enlightened self-interest . . . (*Letters*, p. 845).

The opium-eating Coleridge had tasted bitterly this kind of failure.

The same ideas and images constantly recur: Luther as the worthy successor of St. Paul ('The only fit commentator on Paul was Luther – not by any means such a gentleman as the apostle, but almost as great a genius'; 'Paul and Luther – names which I can never separate'); the doctrine of the Reformers flashing like lightning across the 'papal darkness'; and the living power of Luther's words: he was 'as great a poet as ever lived in any age or country, but his poetic images were so vivid that they mastered the poet's own mind! He was *possessed* with them, as with substance distinct from himself: Luther did not *write*, he *acted* poems. The Bible was a spiritual indeed but not a *figurative* armoury in his belief.' (This is how Coleridge reconstructs Luther's throwing the ink pot at the devil, in a marvellous passage too long to quote.) Coleridge saw Luther as the embodiment of the principle – central to his own philosophy and the tradition that takes its rise from him – that 'words are not *things*, they are *living powers*, by which the things of most importance to mankind are actuated, combined and humanised' (*Table Talk*, p. 212; *Notes*, p. 23; *Friend*, I, pp. 62, 140f; *Aids*, intro. aphorism 17).

Like his disciple, F. D. Maurice, Coleridge regarded Luther as a thinker of profound philosophical significance – not in the sense that Luther posessed a fully articulated epistemology or metaphysic that could be borrowed uncritically by his admirers in the nineteenth century, but in as much as he consistently reduced theological questions to first principles and pointed to the transcendent reality of God as man's essential and ultimate concern. Coleridge comments in passing that Luther's *Table Talk*, 'to a truly philosophic mind, will not be less interesting than Rousseau's confessions' (*Friend*, I, p. 137). Even Luther's extravagant mistakes could not conceal the fact that he had the root of the matter in him. 'Luther – a hero, one fettered indeed with prejudices; but with those very fetters he would knock out the brains of a modern Fort Esprit [ie. rationalist]' (*Anima Poetae*, p. 11).

Even when Luther is wildly astray, there is some flash of insight in what he says that makes us treasure his words: 'Even in Luther's lowest imbecilities what gleams of vigorous good sense!' On some Martinian absurdity about the fathers, Coleridge glosses: 'O Swan! thy critical cygnets are but goslings.' And on Luther's warning of devils lying in wait in desolate places to molest people: 'Yes! heroic Swan, I love thee even when thou gabblest like a goose; for thy geese helped to save the Capitol.' Coleridge makes a similar comment on Hooker's teaching about angels: 'Childish; but the childishness of the age, without which neither Hooker nor Luther could have acted on their contemporaries with the intense and beneficient energy with which they (God be praised!) did act' (*Notes*, pp. 36, 57, 47, 50; *Coleridge on 17th Cent.*, pp. 150f).

Coleridge possessed a rare insight into many issues of Reformation history and theology. He recognised the continuity of the Reformers with the great scholastic thinkers of the later middle ages: the Reformation was 'truly the egg of the schoolmen tho' they ostrich-like left it to be hatched by chance' (*Phil. Lectures*, p. 284n). He acknowledged the justice of Luther's claim that, while Wycliffe and Hus had attacked the morals of the papacy, he alone had struck at the root of corruption by attacking false doctrine: as Coleridge paraphrases, 'I take the goose by the neck and set the knife to the throat' (*Notes*, p.41). He also understands the obsession of the Reformers with trying to prove that they alone were the true church in continuity with the fathers and councils of the early church by their implacable opposition to heresy. What comes across to us as bigoted dogmatism in the Reformers is better explained as their bending over backwards to ward off the imputation of heterodoxy:

> At the Reformation, the first Reformers were beset with an almost morbid anxiety not to be considered heretical in point of doctrine. They knew that the Romanists were on the watch to fasten the brand of heresy upon them whenever a fair pretext could be found; and I have no doubt that it was the excess of this fear which at once led to the burning of Servetus and also to the thanks offered by all the protestant churches to Calvin and the church of Geneva for burning him (*Table Talk*, p.116).

Coleridge knows too that the violent language of the Reformers was characteristic of their age. He will not undertake, he says, to defend 'sundry harsh and inconvenient expressions' in Calvin's writings; and he adds with studied understatement: 'Phrases equally strong and assertions not less rash and startling are no rarities in the writings of Luther.' 'Catachresis' – misuse of words – 'was the favourite figure of speech in that age'! Coleridge perceives both the common ground shared by Luther and Calvin and the distance between Calvin and the Calvinist puritans. On the doctrine of the bondage of the will, for example, he comments: 'Now as to the difference of a captive and enslaved will, and no will at all, such is the difference between the Lutheranism of Calvin and the Calvinism of Jonathan Edwards.' He delightfully – and almost without exaggeration – captures the narrow bibliolatry of the puritans when he remarks: 'They would not put on a corn-plaster without scraping a text over it' (*Aids*, pp. 116f; *Table Talk*, p.96).

(3) Coleridge's Luther Projects

Coleridge's mind was always brimming with literary projects: when he had a good title and a number of ideas in his head he was likely to attempt to interest a publisher in the book that was 'nearing completion'! He had what might be called a 'proleptic' concept of the writer's task in that his imagination leapt straight from promise to fulfilment!

Whether or not Coleridge ever contemplated preparing an edition of Luther himself, he certainly tried to interest others in such a scheme. An adequate life of Luther in English was the first requirement and Coleridge wrote to William Hart Coleridge in 1818 that he should 'even now look forward to some important work' and proceeded to outline what form that work might take: 'We have no life of Luther, no English work that could bear the title otherwise than ironically.' But William Hart did not know German. Samuel Taylor characteristically plays down the difficulties: 'In less than three months, could you spare but one hour a day, you might make yourself sufficient master of the German to read Luther's German tracts with few dictionary interruptions – and these decreasing with every page you read . . .' (*Letters*, p. 845).

Coleridge was fascinated by the under-researched Luther and remarks in *The Friend* that a life of Luther – an account both of the man and his thought – is 'a desideratum in English literature, though perhaps there is no subject for which so many unused materials are extant, both printed and manuscript'. Alongside the life might go an English edition of the letters: 'I can scarcely conceive a more delightful volume than might be made from Luther's letters . . . if they were translated in the simple, sinewy, idomatic, hearty mother-tongue of the original' (*Friend*, I, pp. 134, 139n). To achieve this, Coleridge remarks in the *Table Talk*, the translator 'should be a man deeply imbued with his Bible, with the English writers from Henry VII to Edward VI, the Scotch divines of the sixteenth century and with the old racy German' (p. 156).

To attempt to collect Coleridge's references to Luther is to be impressed above all with his love for the man. Luther frankly delighted Coleridge. He is the 'dear honoured Luther', 'the dear man Luther', 'dearest Luther', 'thou rare black Swan!', whom Coleridge confessed to like and love all the better because he spoke as the mood took him. Luther is 'the man of life, the man of power' (*Notes*, pp. 9ff). Coleridge loves to picture him – a romantic figure for a new romantic age – in the Wartburg with a price on his head, bringing all his scholarly and intuitive powers to bear on his study of the sacred text and proving that words were not things but living powers. Luther's evangelical message was born out of arduous critical study of the text of scripture. As A. G. Dickens has pointedly remarked: 'Luther's interpretation of Christianity depended on how one translated certain Greek words.' This is precisely where Coleridge lays the emphasis himself and the point at which we may take our leave of Coleridge and Luther. 'Methinks I see him sitting, the heroic student, in his chamber in the Wartburg, with his midnight lamp before him . . . Below it lies the Hebrew Bible open, on which he gazes, his brow pressing on his palm, brooding over some obscure text' (*Friend*, I, p. 140).

Arnold: Reformation and the Age of Reason

(1) Arnold on Church and State
Thomas Arnold (1795–1842), a pillar of the broad church and one of the greatest of the liberal Anglicans, nevertheless stands apart from the disciples of Coleridge – labelled by him 'German-Coleridgeans'. Though he felt a deep spiritual affinity with Coleridge and planned his house in the Lake District to be a neighbour to Wordsworth, Arnold was critical of romanticism and drew strength from the critical, rational legacy of the eighteenth century.

Truth was to be discovered in history, not in introspection; fulfilment in social action, not in personal cultivation. Profoundly conservative in his view of church and state and working in the tradition that runs from Hooker through Burke to Coleridge, Arnold was at the same time committed to radical change in social conditions as well as in educational methods. He felt revulsion for the reactionary conservatism of the Tractarians, regarding their programme as a reversion to the dark ages of sacerdotalism and superstition. Against their concerted campaign of opposition to the protestant character of the Church of England, Arnold was a decided, though far from uncritical, defender of the Reformation.

Arnold's theory of a Christian society in which the state accepted moral and spiritual functions and dissenters would be accommodated within a broadened concept of the national church, were fully formed before the Oxford movement, with its platform of autonomous apostolic power, provoked a polemical restatement of his position. The *Principles of Church Reform* appeared in 1833.

As Arnold put it in 1835: 'The "*Idea*" of my life, to which I think every thought of my mind more or less tends, is the perfecting the "idea" of the Edward the Sixth Reformers – the constructing a truly national and Christian church, and a truly national and Christian system of education' (*Life*, p. 261).

But Arnold, who had learned from the philosophies of history of Vico and Niebuhr, had renounced the uniformitarian assumptions that still hampered the Tractarians. His vision of a national church was based on a perceived unity of common tradition, symbolised by the parish church in every community, not on an enforced uniformity of belief and practice. He regarded the Acts of Uniformity as unmitigated disasters. The true bond of unity was in a way of life and a shared moral purpose. In this he was adhering closely to Burke's conception of a tacit compact between the various groups that make up society – a compact, Burke stressed, not of trade and commerce, but of all that makes life worth while, of all that we owe to one another. Arnold was under no illusion that this vision was easily attainable. The Reformation ideal of a church coextensive with the nation, he observed, had been abandoned in the seventeenth century with the calculated alienation of the dissenters. Its accomplishment, he concluded, 'must be reserved for happier and better times' (*Lectures*, p. 248).

Meanwhile, however, Arnold preached the moral responsibilities of the state: its duty to uphold and nurture the moral and spiritual values of its people. Against Macaulay and the Utilitarians, who seemed to see the state as merely a political device for the protection of persons and property and without positive collective aims, Arnold claimed that the state ought to have the moral and spiritual welfare of its people at heart – like a good tutor who not only imparts technical skills but has regard to the overall well-being of his pupil (*Lectures*, p. 38).

It is significant that the establishment of the Jerusalem Bishopric in 1841, a localised scheme of unity without uniformity between Anglicans and Lutherans (which for the Tractarians signalled a further stage in the slide towards national apostasy) was hailed by Arnold as a fulfilment of his plans for a reform of the church that would bring dissenters within the fold while respecting differences of belief and practice. 'Thus the idea of my church reform pamphlet, which was so ridiculed and condemned, is now carried into practice by the archbishop of Canterbury himself ... Yet it was thought ridiculous in me to conceive that a national church might include persons using a different ritual and subscribing different articles' (*Life*, p. 431).

(2) 'The Oxford Malignants'

The state of the church in the first quarter of the nineteenth century stirred Arnold just as much as it did the Tractarians to scathing denunciation of the *status quo* and spurred him, like them, to dream of and work for renewal. Instead of 'striving to grow up into a true branch of Christ's glorious church, perfect even after the infinite perfection of its head,' the church had allowed itself to become subservient to a state that was increasingly shedding its spiritual obligations. Arnold complained of 'idle language about the doctrines of the Reformers and the excellence of the British constitution'. Torpor and complacency reigned (*Fragment*, p. 137). Here Arnold speaks with the same voice as the Tractarians. But his prescription to remedy these ills was very different from theirs.

The two enemies most implacably opposed by Arnold – a secular state and a sacerdotal church – he perceived went hand in hand. A hieratic and hierarchical church, with spiritual sovereignty invested in bishops or pope, inevitably asserts its autonomy of the state that is then provoked into further secularisation. But where the state acknowledges its spiritual responsibilities and the church renounces hierarchical, sacerdotal pretensions, a fruitful partnership like that of Reformation England, can come into being (*Lectures*, p. 50).

Arnold believed, together with Hare and Maurice, that the programme of the Tractarians was fundamentally anachronistic. Before his death, Arnold complained that they were attempting to put the clock back 'to ages which we had known only in history' – as though England were suffering again after hundreds of years a visitation of the plague (*Christian Life*, p. 394). Arnold was no romantic of the pageant-of-the-past Walter Scott variety. For him the middle ages were not the golden age of chivalry and the flower of Christian civilisation. They were the 'second infancy of society', a 'noisesome cavern of dirt and darkness' (on Niebuhr, p. 78; *Life*, p. 431).

Even the Reformation and the century that followed were contaminated with medieval crudities – 'as if the sixteenth century and seventeenth centuries, scarcely waking as they were from the accumulated moral ignorance and insensibility of thirty generations, could offer anything to satisfy our aspirations after Christian excellence; as if the consummated work of the Spirit of God were to be found in the dregs of the papal and feudal institutions!' (*Fragment*, p. 137).

Though as devoted as the Tractarians to pastoral renewal in the parishes of England and to personal consecration to moral purity, Arnold rejected a central plank in the Tractarian platform: *the dogmatic principle.* Newman believed the dogmatic principle (his term) to be of the essence of authentic, apostolic Christianity; and the liberal, relativising, accommodating, minimalist approach of the broad churchmen – Whately, Hampden and Arnold – to be heretical. He wrote in the essay on development:

> That there is truth then; that there is one truth; that religious error is in itself of an immoral nature; that its maintainers, unless involuntarily such, are guilty in maintaining it; that it is to be dreaded ... that truth and falsehood are set before us for the trial of our hearts; that our choice is an awful giving forth of lots on which salvation or rejection is inscribed; that 'before all things it is necessary to hold the Catholic faith;' that 'he that would be saved must thus think,' and not otherwise ... this is the dogmatical principle (*Dev.*, pp. 356f).

Pusey and Liddon held that abandonment of the Athanasian creed in the liturgy was sufficient ground for resignation of one's orders and withdrawal from the ministry of the Church of England.

Arnold, on the other hand, regarded the cognitive component in faith as secondary and action, not belief, as the bond of Christian – as of any other – society. 'All societies of men, whether we call them states or churches, should have made their bond to consist in a common object and a common practice, rather than in a common belief; in other words, their end should be good rather than truth' (*Lectures*, pp. 39f).

It was an axiom of the Oxford movement, however, that goodness was a precondition of truth, that 'without holiness no man shall see the Lord,' that 'the fear of the Lord is the beginning of wisdom'. The Tractarians laid great stress on the antecedent moral conditions of faith. For them and their later disciples such as Liddon, it was inconceivable that a good man should reject the deity of Christ. In this sense, the agonising of the Victorian crisis of faith over the moral difficulties of Christian doctrine had passed them by. Arnold perceives that belief is not within our power to give or withhold. 'We may consent to act together, but we cannot consent to believe together ... action being a thing in our own power. But no motives can persuade us to believe together; we may wish a statement to be true, we may admire those who believe it, we may find it very inconvenient not to believe it; all this helps us nothing; unless our own mind is freely convinced that the statement or doctrine be true, we cannot . . . believe it.' He draws the consequences for the question of subscription to the church's formularies and the nature and extent of Anglican comprehensiveness:

> The social bond cannot directly require for its perfectness more than union of action. It cannot properly require more than it is in the power of men to give; and men can submit their actions to a common law at their own choice, but their internal convictions they cannot (*Lectures*, pp. 39f).

The unity and perfection of the church are, according to Arnold, independent of 'theological articles of opinion' (as he disparagingly calls them). If individuals are prepared to participate in the liturgy, it is neither prudent nor charitable to question their intentions (*Misc. Works*, pp. 285, 325). The well-being of the church consists rather in its 'moral state' and the 'religious affections' of its members. These have 'existed in good Christians of all ages and all communions, along with an infinitely varying proportion of truth and error' (*Life*, p. 232).

Far from recreating the primitive church, as they would claim, the Tractarians are merely re-establishing medieval scholasticism based on a propositional idea of truth. While it is true, as Arnold admits, that all concerted action implies a common belief, since men who agree to do a certain thing must believe that it is worthwhile, there is a vast difference between 'belief in the desirableness of an act' and 'belief in the truth of a proposition' (*Lectures*, pp. 39ff).

Arnold's attack on the Tractarians reached its climax in an intemperate and rather paranoid article defending R. D. Hampden against the *Oxford Malignants* (not Arnold's phrase but his editor's) who had unsuccessfully opposed his appointment to the regius chair of divinity in 1836. To Liddon, looking back as Pusey's biographer, the article exhibited 'bigotted ferocity and insolence' (Liddon, I, p. 282).

'The attack on Dr. Hampden,' Arnold avers, 'bears upon it the character not of error, but of *moral wickedness.*' The Tractarians, with their dogmatic principle and narrow intolerance belong with the circumcision party that persecuted St. Paul. They are the sort of 'formalist Judaizing fanatics . . . who have ever been the peculiar disgrace of the Church of England.' The Tractarian's insistence on episcopacy is the same as the Judaizer's insistence on circumcision. It is 'schismatical, profane and unchristian' ('Oxford Malignants', pp. 238, 235; cf. *Life*, p. 219).

As Arnold's disciple and biographer A. P. Stanley comments:

> The one doctrine which was then put forward as the cure for the moral and social evils of the country, which he felt so keenly, was the one point in their system which he always regarded as morally powerless and intellectually indefensible, as incompatible with all sound notions of law and government, and as tending above all things to substitute a ceremonial for a spiritual Christianity (*Life*, p. 256).

When in December 1833, Pusey signalled his adherence to the movement with *Tract 18* on fasting, Arnold wrote chastising him for lending support 'to a party second to none in the tendency of their principles to overthrow the truth of the gospel' (Liddon, I, p. 282).

Froude's *Remains* made an impression of 'extraordinary impudence' on Arnold. Froude had the temerity to revile the English Reformers whom 'the accordant voice' of the church, 'without distinction of party, has agreed to honour' (*Life*, p. 336).

(3) *'Daybreak' of Reformation*

Arnold's appreciation of the Reformers and all that they stood for was not merely the fellow-feeling of a latter day would-be reformer for his predecessors. It belonged to a coherent interpretation of history that he had learned from Vico and Niebuhr. It entailed a philosophical rather than a merely chronological periodisation of history. History was the biography of a nation (*Lectures*, p. 21). All nations developed from infancy to manhood, from the age of feeling to the age of reflection. Wordsworth's lines:

> The child is father to the man,
> And I would wish my days to be
> Bound each to each by natural piety

apply as much to nations as to individuals (ib., p. 254).

The Reformation was western Europe's coming of age: dogmatic authority and blind assent began to give way to critical enquiry and rational reflection.

> The period of the Reformation, when compared with the ages preceding it, was undoubtedly one of inquiry and reflection. But still it was an age of strong feeling and of intense belief; the human mind cleared a space for itself vigorously within a certain circle ('Thucydides', p. 397).

Arnold was no uncritical defender of the Reformation. He was the first to point to its deficiencies and to deplore that so much of the heritage of catholicism, including the practice of confession, had been lost to Anglicanism. The error of the Reformation was to destroy the good along with the bad; its 'evils' were superstition, profaneness and violence – on both sides (*Life*, pp. 213ff). He appears to make a distinction of principle between the religious renewal of the early Reformation and the political contrivance of the Elizabethan settlement. (This marks a break between Arnold and the later Coleridgean F. D. Maurice for whom the settlement of 1559 represents a perfect union of opposites.) The imposition of unity by force of law under Elizabeth concealed the fact that the problem of authority raised by the action of the Reformers had not been settled. Those who enforced subscription to articles and liturgies by threats of legal penalties 'forgot that while requiring this agreement, they had themselves disclaimed, what alone could justify them in enforcing it – the possession of infallibility' (*Misc. Works*, p. 237).

Arnold deplored uncritical deference to the views of the Reformers among the evangelicals just as much as he did blind submission to the authority of the fathers among the Tractarians with their vast catenae of patristic texts – 'looking at the scripture through the unworthy medium of the fathers and the Reformers, instead of applying the added experience of each successive age to develop its riches in their full perfection' (*Fragment*, p. 140). Apart from the primary witness of scripture, Arnold reserved the right to treat the witness of history with critical freedom. He wrote to Julius Hare: 'You appear to me to look upon the past with feelings of reverence, in which I cannot participate' (*Life*, p. 140).

The lessons of the Reformation were interpreted and applied to current questions by Arnold in a non-polemical way – for example in his sketch of the development of religious parties in the *Introductory Lectures on Modern History* (pp. 200–214) and in his presentation of justification by faith in the sermons on *The Christian Life*.

Arnold wanted to combat ignorance and prejudice about the Reformation. He described Cobbett's *History of the Protestant Reformation* as 'a queer compound of wickedness and ignorance with strong sense and the mention of divers truths' that ought to be better known. 'Its object' he added, 'is to represent the Reformation in England as a great national evil, accomplished by all kinds of robbery and cruelty, and tending to the impoverishment and misery of the poor, and to the introduction of a careless clergy and a spirit of ignorance and covetousness amongst everybody. It made me groan, while reading it, to think that the real history and effects of the Reformation are so little known, and the evils of the worldly policy of Somerset's and Elizabeth's government so little appreciated.' 'As it is,' Arnold concluded, 'Cobbett's book can do nothing but harm, so bad is its spirit, and so evident its unfairness' (*Life*, pp. 43f).

In striking contrast to F. D. Maurice, Arnold carried no brief for the Thirty-nine Articles. While, for Maurice, the articles represented a definitive model of theological method in that they began with the nature of God and moved on to treat of man's relationship with him in the states of nature and of grace, Arnold saw the articles only as arid statements of controversial points expressed in a purely theoretical and abstract way. Arnold contradicts Maurice in asserting that the articles should never be made an object of study for undergraduates. 'There can be no more fatal error than to acquaint the mind with the truths of religion in a theoretical form.' The scriptures and the Catechism of the Prayer Book approach Christian teaching in the practical context of the soul's relation to God. Article 1 on the being of God is the prime offender: 'Everything in the article is abstract, it contains a series of propositions precisely of the sort which the devils may believe . . . the assent given to them need not have anything of the character of Christian faith' (*Fragment*, pp. 162f).

But for all his reservations, Arnold ranges himself decisively with the Coleridgeans or liberal Anglicans in upholding the legacy of the Reformation against Tractarian attempts to unprotestantise the Church of England. For Arnold, the Reformation meant 'daybreak' after centuries of darkness (*Life*, p. 431).

Connop Thirlwall: Heavyweight Scholarship and Independent Opinions
One of the most massively learned of the broad churchmen – author of an eight-volume history of Greece, translator, with Julius Hare of two volumes of B. G. Niebuhr's history of Rome, articulator of a post-Vichean philosophy of history – Connop Thirlwall (1797–1875), for thirty-five years bishop of St. David's, takes his place alongside Thomas Arnold as an up-holder of the protestant character of the Anglican church against Tractarian subversion – but from a liberal, not an evangelical point of view (c.f. *Life*).

Thirlwall believed that as a reformed church, the Church of England took a middle way between two extremes. He regarded her character of moderation as 'her most honourable attribute, as the very stamp of prudence and charity combined, and the safest criterion of truth' (*Remains*, I, p. 28). Like Maurice, he was indignant at the suggestion that protestantism was a mere negation of positive truths, deploring the 'arbitrary misuse' of the word to mean 'a mere negation of everything that men on both sides profess to revere' (ib., p. 48).

Thirlwall had no time for what he regarded as Tractarian dilettantism. He thought, however, that the distinct principles of the Tractarians had had much less effect on the mind of the public than the language that some of them used of the church of Rome, on the one hand, and the English Reformers, on the other. This naturally 'raised a suspicion, that where so much was said in spite of public opinion, and against the spirit of the times, still more might be meant, and only reserved for a more favourable juncture' (ib., p. 46).

But Thirlwall defended the Tractarians' right to be critical of the Reformation. He knew, he said, of no authority entitled to prescribe how we should interpret church history or what lessons we should deduce from it. And, after all, a critical attitude to the Reformation was not peculiar to the Tractarians. There was Thomas Arnold – 'an admirable person', whose premature death had deprived church and nation of 'one of the most strenuous as well as able opponents' of the Oxford movement (ib., p. 49). Like Arnold, Thirlwall deplored uncritical adulation of the Reformers and their work on the part of those who believed that 'the Reformation has nothing left to desire and that it has taken away nothing that we ought to regret' (ib.).

In the dispute over Newman's lectures on justification, Thirlwall took a liberal adiaphorist view. It was a matter of semantics 'involving no real difference of opinion', both Newman and his critics being equally orthodox. But Thirlwall, accomplished historian and philosopher of history as he was, was not so kind to Newman's theory of the development of doctrine, accusing him of 'confusion of terms', 'vague and indefinite propositions', 'fallacious reasoning', 'arbitrary constructions of historical data', and 'erroneous appeals to ancient testimonies'. It would produce an effect opposite to that intended (ib., pp. 102f).

Mark Pattison: The Whig Interpretation

Mark Pattison (1813–84), latterly Rector of Lincoln College, Oxford, could be said to represent liberal Anglicanism in decline. There is a world of difference between the ardour and aspiration of a Thomas Arnold and the disillusionment of Mark Pattison. But there is a link, not only in their common detestation of Tractarianism, but in the liberal or 'Whig' interpretation of history that saw the Reformation as the dawn of truth and enlightenment. Pattison sponsors an explicit liberal myth that the Reformation was a protest against dogmatism and fanaticism on behalf of liberty of conscience and the principle of toleration. Pattison had shaken off his 'inherited pietism of an evangelical type', become deeply implicated in the more extreme wing of the Oxford movement ('Tractarian Tories') and finally emerged into a sardonic critical agnosticism. No mean historian of ideas, he was, however, betrayed by the pervasive liberal progressivism of the age (*Memoirs*, pp. 208, 167; see Green).

Writing in 1859, he remarks that 'we are apt to regard the Reformation as a revolution in theology and church arrangements. It became so. And the importance of the afterbirth has thrown into the background the true issue as it was originally joined between the friends of progress and its enemies' ('Antecedents').

In his essay 'Calvin at Geneva', first published in 1858, Pattison accuses Calvin of doing more than any other man 'to deprive protestantism of its character as a protest in favour of freedom.' He adds: 'We shall hate him personally for his bigotry, inhumanity, vindictiveness; above all, as the author of the great crime of the age – the murder of the heroic Servetus.' His historical sense momentarily reasserting itself, Pattison admits that, though the Reformation had the effect of producing the right of free enquiry and liberty of conscience, the Reformers themselves did not recognise such principles.

Here he is almost anticipating Butterfield's withering comment on this anachronistic interpretation of the Reformation as a conscious assertion of liberal values and a stage on the road to the open society: 'It was anything but the religious fanaticism of the Renaissance popes that drove Luther to exasperation'! (p. 32).

Julius Hare's Vindication of Protestantism

(1) *Protestant Theology and German Culture*

'I have felt bound to do what I can,' writes Julius Hare in his *Vindication of Luther*, 'for him to whom I owe such a debt of gratitude and love as can never be paid' (p.75). Hare was, as Gordon Rupp remarks, the one Victorian Englishman who combined acute thelogical perception with accurate first-hand study of Luther (*Righteousness*, p.50). But his feeling for the Reformers was far more than merely academic or antiquarian – it was ardent devotion, passionate personal commitment. As the man 'of larger literary and artistic cultivation than any other English theologian of his time' (Vidler, p.222), Hare brought the not inconsiderable resources of a superbly informed mind and an outstandingly well stocked library to the defence of Luther's character and teaching and to the creative restatement of his principles in the face of the Tractarian challenge.

'If any foreigner landing in England in 1853 had asked where he should find the man best acquainted with all modern forms of thought here and on the continent,' wrote A. P. Stanley in a memoir, – 'where he should find the most complete collection of the philosophical, theological or historical literature of Germany – where he should find profound and exact scholarship combined with the most varied and extensive learning – what would have been the answer? Not in Oxford, not in Cambridge, not in London. He must have turned far away from academic towns or public libraries to a secluded parish in Sussex and in the minister of that parish . . . he would have found what he sought.' This was Julius Charles Hare (1795–1855), rector of Herstmonceaux and archdeacon of Lewes (Hare, *Victory*, p.xcii).

Hare's feeling for Luther was bound up with his sense of indebtedness to German literature in general – its theology, philosophy and philology. He confessed that he owed to German scholars his 'ability to believe in Christianity with a much more implicit and intelligent faith' (*Guesses*, p.xlv). His library contained three thousand volumes in German (a fraction of the total). At the end of his life Hare was awarded the Golden Medal of Science by the king of Prussia for his defence of Luther.

Hare was an individualist – not only in his character and whims (he devised a scheme of spelling reform and adhered to this distinctive orthography throughout his life), but also ecclesiastically. He stood aloof from church politics; like Maurice, he was against party and system. Truth was to be found in flashes of insight not in dogmatic formulations. It was not for nothing that Hare was a confessed follower of Coleridge and that his own philosophical outlook was expressed in the two volumes *Guesses at Truth*. Like Arnold, Hare deplored the recrudescence of dogmatism in the Oxford movement and observed that, in striking contrast to the Tractarians, the Reformers has allowed a wide latitude of belief: they had 'discerned that the business of a church is not to lay down a system of dogmatic theology but to bring her members to Christ'.

Hare's refusal to identify with a party left him free not only to criticise the Tractarians for their ill-informed and tendentious remarks on Luther, but also to condemn the partisan approach of the evangelicals whose individualistic and pietistic gospel had obscured, he believed, the cosmic dimension of the Christian gospel and who had failed to follow the sixteenth-century Reformers in their emphasis on the renewal of the catholic church of antiquity.

As fellow and college lecturer in classics at Trinity College, Cambridge, Hare had taught F. D. Maurice the dialogues of Plato and Greek tragedy. Hare and Maurice were related by marriage – Hare married one of Maurice's sisters and Maurice's second wife was half-sister to Hare. They shared a deep sympathy for Platonic thought and they both stood apart from ecclesiastical politics. But Maurice and Hare developed their own distinctive theologies and many of Maurice's most characteristic themes – the universal headship of Christ and the concept of the divine order, for example – are not reflected in the teaching of Hare. Hare was not a pure theologian, more a philosopher of history and – as archdeacon of Lewes – a churchman. The churchmanship was, in a sense, accidental: the philosophical bent was innate and it was here that he came closest to Coleridge.

Hare regarded Coleridge as 'the profoundest thinker whom England has produced for centuries' and revealed the depth of his indebtedness in dedicating *The Mission of the Comforter* (1846) 'to the honoured memory of Samuel Taylor Coleridge, the Christian philosopher, who through dark and winding paths of speculation was led to the light, in order that others by his guidance might reach that light without passing through the darkness' and who helped them 'discern the sacred concord and unity of human and divine truth.' Hare and Coleridge shared a love of German literature and with it a profound affection and admiration for Martin Luther.

(2) *The Vindication of Luther*

Hare had been taken to the Wartburg at the age of ten and shown the mark on the wall where Luther had thrown the ink pot at the devil. As Gordon Rupp remarks, Hare was to develop a considerable talent for throwing ink pots on his own account – rising up in defence of the unjustly condemned and ignorantly misrepresented – producing "Vindications" not only of Luther but of Coleridge, Niebuhr (whose Roman history Hare had translated with Thirlwall), Hampden, the broad church divine and bishop, and Baron Bunsen, the Lutheran ecclesiastical diplomatist and biblical critic (detestable therefore to the Tractarians on both counts!).

Hare's *Vindication of Luther*, which falls into the category of books that many have heard of but few have read, began as a footnote to *The Mission of the Comforter* and, as Plumtre remarked, 'it will probably remain for ever the longest treatise calling itself a note, in the English language' – 220 pages in the original edition, 300 pages when printed separately in 1855. In this work, Hare demolished the misrepresentations of Luther's character and teaching perpetrated by Newman, Ward, Sir William Hamilton and J. A. Möhler, the catholic dogmatician. Dean Stanley's enthusiastic assessment of the *Vindication* is no more than it deserves.

> The unparalleled knowledge displayed of the Reformer's writings is not only most valuable as a mine of reference, but is in itself a testimony to the greatness of the man who could inspire, at the distance of three centuries, such a vast, such an enthusiastic research. The numerous explanations of expressions long misunderstood and of falsehoods long believed, are amongst the most decisive triumphs of literary investigation that we have ever seen. And above all, the breadth and energy of Luther's genius, the depth and warmth of his heart and the grandeur of his position and character, amidst whatever inconsistencies or imperfections of expression, are brought out with a force and clearness which must often be as new to his admirers as to his detractors (intro. to Hare, *Victory*).

Consisting largely of academic documentation and laborious refutation, the *Vindication's* strong underlying thrust of argument and the frequent flashes of polemical power make it, in Gordon Rupp's phrase, 'one of the most interesting volumes on Luther in the English language'.

Hare begins by noting that 'perhaps there is no one in the whole history of the world against whom such a host of implacable prejudices and antipathies have been permanently arrayed, as against Luther. For the contest in which he engaged is the most momentous ever waged by a single man: it had been secretly preparing for centuries and its issue is still pending.' Luther's contemporaries, as well as later generations, felt (as G. M. Trevelyan once remarked to Lord Moran about Churchill) that everything about this man must be known. No one, until Rousseau produced his *Confessions*, had been so exposed to the public gaze as Luther.

> No man ever lived whose heart and soul and life have been laid bare as his have been to the eyes of mankind. Open as the sky, bold and fearless as the storm, he gave utterance to all his feelings, all his thoughts; he knew nothing of reserve and the impression he produced on his hearers and friends was such that they were anxious to treasure up every word that dropt from his pen or from his lips. No man therefore has ever been exposed to so severe a trial: perhaps no man was ever placed in such difficult circumstances or assailed by such manifold temptations (*Vindication*, pp. 2, 293).

Hare was thinking most of all of the way that the Tractarians, with their unhistorical, blinkered approach to the Reformation, were at that very moment making capital out of the ambiguities of Luther's life and thought.

(3) A Phantom Theology

Hare was roused to defend the Reformers whom he claimed, were being 'attackt with unscrupulous ignorance and virulence', while at the same time the whole course of Reformation history was being misrepresented and distorted by the Tractarians. It was not only Hare's theological convictions that were affronted by their handling of the Reformation: his historical sense was outraged too. The Luther about whom Newman has so much to say in the *Lectures on Justification* seems to come, suggests Hare, out of a story told by Wordsworth's idiot boy, for he dwells 'in the region where the cocks crow, towhoo! towhoo! and the sun shines so cold.' For all the resemblance that Newman's Luther bears to the real Luther – 'the Luther of Eisleben, of Wittenberg, of Worms' – 'you might as well call Hercules a milksop or Socrates a sentimental blockhead!' Newman's caricature bears about as much relation to the real Luther as to the man in the moon. But this, adds Hare, 'is no more than an instance of a practice which has been growing upon him, that of substituting the creations of his own mind for the realities of history.' When the Tractarians discuss Lutheranism, they are grappling with a phantom theology derived from impressions of English evangelicalism and the aunt sallys of Roman polemic – in other words, Hare concludes, 'from gossip pickt up no matter how or where, from everything except its one genuine source', the Lutheran confessional documents (*Mission*, p. x; *Vindication*, pp. 89, 96; *Contest*, p. 84).

As far as Hare was concerned, W. G. Ward, even more than Froude or Newman, was the prime culprit. As we have seen, Ward defended his denunciation of Luther and his theology by saying that his remarks referred to an abstract doctrine that could not be held even by devils. Hare's rejoinder is crushing:

> This is a novel kind of apology. Suppose a man were to keep on month after month publishing gross libellous attacks on the Duke of Wellington, calling him a robber and a murderer, with a garniture of suitable phrases, and then, on being prosecuted, were to plead that he had been inveighing against the abstract notion of a conqueror which, he verily believed, was too hateful and horrid for any human being ever to come up to it, what would such a plea avail him?

Ward was Newman's poodle and had looked at Luther through his master's eyes. Like him, he found the whole ethos of the Reformation repugnant. But 'where the master spoke on the whole intelligently and moderately, the disciple, merely following his master's whistle, without knowing the country, has dasht and floundered through all sorts of extravagances' (*Vindication*, pp. 104ff). While entirely appropriate to Ward, this is perhaps too kind to Newman.

Newman, who made no secret of the element of antiquarian appeal in the Oxford movement, had, according to Hare, fallen into the

'Romanising Fallacy' of postulating an age of perfection in the past and attempting to recreate it in the present as though nothing had changed. Hare accused the Tractarians of 'pampering their fancies with delusive visions of former ages and with fantastical wishes for their revival' (Forbes, p. 105). Hare's objection was not only on theological but on historiographical grounds. He held that Newman and company were being fundamentally and disastrously unhistorical. They glamourised the patristic age, shut their eyes to the true nature of the middle ages and approached the Reformation in a totally anachronistic way – as though its rough passions, earthy assumptions and turbulent struggles were about to be inflicted on the tranquil spires and sheltered quadrangles of the Oxford of the 1840s. With the pageant-of-the-past romantics like Walter Scott and Macaulay, they felt the fascination of other ages, but unlike the Germano-Coleridgeans, failed to understand them on their own terms and to realise that other ages were also in fact other worlds.

The Jerusalem Bishopric elicited a letter from Newman to the bishop of Oxford condemning the plan for union with the continental churches of the Reformation on the grounds that Lutheranism and Calvinism were 'heresies, repugnant to scripture'. Hare reacted vigorously, writing to Manning (at the time his fellow archdeacon in the Chichester diocese), that this was 'the hateful fruit' of 'episcopolatry'. He was astounded by Newman's 'audacity'in calling 'those doctrines heretical which almost all the great divines of our church' had regarded as 'among the best expositions of the truth.' So how does he, John Newman, dare to call them heresies? Hare conjectured that Newman was now well on the way to 'dooming his adhesion to the council of Trent' (Distad, p. 164).

But at least the Tractarians realised that Luther and the Reformation stood or fell together. Hare had no quarrel with their assumption that, in rejecting Luther, they were rejecting the Reformation and all its works. Luther, he remarks, unlike some of his contemporaries, cannot be envisaged apart from the great struggle whose issues called him forth from academic obscurity. Melanchthon we can imagine as an eminent divine living in another age, perhaps the friend of Augustine or even the companion of Fénelon. Calvin too could be set in other circumstances, among the schoolmen or in the counsels of the medieval popes, at the synod of Dort or among Cromwell's chaplains. 'Hence it is easier to form an independent candid judgement on their characters.' Not so with Luther.

> Luther, apart from the Reformation, would cease to be Luther. His work was not something external to him, like Saturn's ring, on which he shone and within he revolved: it was his own very self that grew out of him while he grew out of his work. Wherefore, they who do not rightly estimate and feel thankful for the Reformation, cannot rightly understand Luther or attain to that insight into his heart and spirit which is never granted except to love (*Vindication*, pp. 2f).

Hare deplored the revival of allegorical biblical interpretation by the Tractarians. For them it provided an avowedly essential buttress of their system, but for Hare it was a return to an unreformed irrationalism. 'We seem about to be inundated,' he complained, 'with all that is most fantastical and irrational in the exegetical mysticism of the fathers and are bid to see divine power in allegorical cobwebs and heavenly life in artificial flowers.' An effective antidote to the inventions of Tractarian exegesis are the commentaries of John Calvin with their 'exemplary union of a severe masculine understanding with a profound insight into the spiritual depths of the scriptures' (*Mission*, p. 243).

(4) *Sola Fide: The Cloud of Witnesses*

The sixteenth-century humanists had helped to recover the literal sense of scripture, but humanism alone could not have achieved a reformation. The writings of the humanists would have been about as effective in producing the Reformation as a dozen candlesticks would be to light up the night. 'A mightier spirit was needed for this work, one which drew its power from deeper sources of truth, human and divine.' In comparison with his predecessors, Luther's 'deep and living apprehension of the primary truths of the gospel' seems almost like 'the sunburst of a new revelation'. He takes his stand 'on the eternal rock, gazing steadfastly with unsealed eyes at the very sun of righteousness'. Luther sent forth his writings 'like flights of birds' and, taken as a whole, they constitute 'the first great utterance of the most momentous crisis the human mind has had to go through since the original reception of Christianity.' 'Day by day he rose up to wield the sword of the gospel almost single handed against all the force and fraud of a corrupt and lying church which had cast it fetters over the mind and breathed its rottenness into the heart of Christendom' (*Vindication*, pp. 67, 7, 12, 42; *Mission*, p. 361).

Hare singled out the *articulus stantis*, the doctrine of justification by faith, as the key to Luther's theology and his most valuable legacy to the Christian church. Luther had not invented this doctrine but rediscovered it. It was no 'shooting forth of a new star' but rather 'a star which for ages had been standing overhead and towards which the eyes of many generations had been turned'. Faith, for Luther, was 'an intense, vivid reality which governs the pulses of his heart and the motions of his will'. In his sermons *The Victory of Faith*, called forth by Newman's lectures on justification, Hare gave a powerful exposition of the protestant doctrine of faith, endorsing the Reformers' principle that faith signifies trust: *fides est fiducia, fides significat fiduciam* (*Vindication*, p. 89; *Victory*, pp. 75, 26).

The Victory of Faith reaches its climax in Hare's most powerful piece of prose – a roll call of the protestant heroes of faith in the style of Hebrews 11. The spirit of this remarkable passage is the direct antithesis of the Tractarian stereotype of the Reformation.

By faith Wycliff, the morning star of the Reformation, rose out of the darkness and heralded the coming daylight. By faith Luther proclaimed his theses against the doctrine of indulgence. By faith he burned the pope's bull and thereby for himself and for thousands of millions after him, threw off the crushing yoke of Rome. By faith he went on to the Diet at Worms though warned that the fate of Huss would await him, going in the strength of Christ, despite of the gates of hell and of the prince of the power of the air. By faith, a single friendless monk standing before the princes of the Empire, he witnessed a noble confession with meekness in behalf of the truth. By faith he translated the Bible and received the blessed reward of being the interpreter of the word of God to his countrymen for all generations.

The English Reformation too has its heroes of faith.

By faith Rogers, the protomartyr of our Reformation, when his wife and his eleven children met him on his way to the stake and an offer of life and pardon was brought to him in their sight, if so be he would recant, walked on with a stout heart and washed his hands in the flames while he was burning, rejoicing in the fiery baptism whereby he gave up his soul to God. By faith Ridley looked forward with joy to the fire that awaited him . . . By faith the aged Latimer, when stript to his shroud, . . . cheered his own heart and his companions by the prophetic assurance that on that day by God's grace they should light such a candle in England as should never be put out.

'And what shall I say more? For the time would fail me to tell of . . . Huss and Melanchthon and Zwingli and Calvin and Knox and Hooper . . .' (*Victory*, pp. 230f).

Holding apart from both the latitudinarian liberals, who praised the Reformation as a supposedly anti-dogmatic movement, and the evangelicals, who by this time invoked the Reformers' authority for views more typical of the anabaptists whom they had sent to the stake, Hare succeeded in vindicating not only the man Martin Luther but also the primary principles of Reformation theology.

16

F. D. Maurice:
The Shaking of the Seven Hills

Critical Reverence

As Michael Ramsey has pointed out, F. D. Maurice (1805–72) is one of the few exceptions to 'the almost constant failure of Anglican theologians to understand Luther' (*Maurice*, p. 28n). Maurice possessed a rare insight into the central concerns of Luther's thought. He probably did more than anyone to bring about the recovery of Reformation principles within Anglicanism. Maurice's most sustained treatment of Reformation theology is found in *The Kingdom of Christ*; it has recently been claimed that 'the book's most significant and lasting contribution was the rediscovery of the Reformation in an age when its evangelical heirs had distorted it and its Tractarian enemies pronounced it dead' (Brose, p. 138).

Maurice's sympathetic treatment of the Reformers was set against a background of denigration and misinterpretation on the part of the Tractarians who attempted to play off the Reformers against the fathers. Maurice argues that the principle is the same in both cases. The habit of sneering at the great, even if we cannot agree with them, is destructive of all spiritual insight: 'If I adopted the habit . . . fashionable in certain quarters, of disparaging and insulting [the Reformers],' Maurice says, 'instead of being able the better to reverence the early fathers of the church, I should lose the sense of reverence altogether.' He concludes: 'Having trampled upon the graves of those who are among us and whom we have been taught from childhood to honour, I am quite sure that no more large or catholic feelings would ever grow up within me' (*Three Letters*, p. 17).

But Maurice was not one to idolise the Reformers or attribute finality to their teaching. Criticising Cobbett's history of the Reformation (1824), which ascribed all England's social and political ills to the Reformation, Maurice made it clear that, while he did not subscribe to Cobbett's thesis, neither did he wish to be identified with a triumphalist protestant view of the Reformation. Those 'who maintain that all was wrong before the Reformation and that in protestant countries all has been right since – who assert . . . that the great object was then accomplished and secured . . . and that the world at that time received the stamp of those lineaments which it must always wear until they are destroyed by the great conflagration' – make as much of an idol of the Reformers as Roman Catholics do of the pope (*Sketches*, p. 26).

Maurice accused the Tractarians of opposing to the spirit of the age the spirit of a former age, rather than the Spirit of the living God (*Life*, I, p. 226). He did not intend to make the same mistake himself. So while he does, admittedly, tend to romanticise the Reformation, he cannot be accused of absolutising it.

Maurice and Luther

Maurice felt an instinctive kinship of spirit with Luther. In the first book to reveal Maurice's distinctive views *Subscription No Bondage* (1835), he echoes Coleridge when he speaks of 'the *man* of the Reformation, the brave, hearty, home-bred Luther' (pp. 5f). As a recent biographer has commented: 'All Maurice's instincts and sympathies went out to Luther and his treatment of the turbulent Reformer shows his own capacities at their best' (Brose, p. 141). It was above all his recognition of Luther's inner struggles that bound Maurice to him: it was a condition that he knew within himself. The same early work refers to the Luther 'who had fought the beast in the closest arena, who had felt every one of its claws at his heart'. Every page of Luther's writing and every hour of his life bear witness to a tremendous struggle.

> The sense of a struggle of two powers in the man himself, one of which requires to be vanquished, destroyed, sent to hell, that the other may attain the good which it needs and for which God has destined it, makes the thoughts of Luther breathe and his words burn . . . The experience of this conflict makes faith not a fine quality but a necessity of his inmost being. He must believe or be crushed and perish (*Kingdom*, I, p. 91; *MMP*, II, p. 117).

The 'great glory' of the Reformation was in liberating the human mind from indifference. It was this – the clash of ideas and the need to take sides – that made Maurice describe the Reformation as 'the greatest event (except the introduction of Christianity) the world has ever witnessed' (Brose, p. 22). Luther's achievement was to replace the dry, academic and impersonal theology of the schoolmen with a practical and personal faith that 'broke through the webs of scholasticism and claimed a personal affiance in the Son of God who had taken our nature' (*Revelation*, p. 225).

Against the claims of Tractarian extremists like W. G. Ward that Luther was an inherently profane person, Maurice showed him as a God-fearing, God-intoxicated man. 'A more *godly* man, one who more set

God before him in all his thoughts and acts ... I do not think ever existed' (*Thoughts*, p. 35).

Maurice has a flair for turning a protestant shibboleth on its head to get at the Reformers' original intention. He does this with the doctrine of justification by faith and he takes the same approach to 'the right of private judgement'. He notes that the Reformers' doctrine of the authority of scripture has become identified with the notion of private judgement, but points out that to the Reformers themselves, the question presented itself 'in the most dissimilar form imaginable'.

> They expressly proclaimed the Bible to be that book which puts down and humbles private judgements, which asserts its claim to be heard above them all and in opposition to them all and is able to make that claim good. They believed that its words were with power; that when it spoke men felt that power and either submitted to it or consciously rebelled against it.

Luther himself, Maurice asserts, 'distrusts, dislikes his own private judgement and that of every man. It is to God's judgement he appeals' (*Kingdom*, I, p. 100; *MMP*, II, p. 117).

Luther may have been reckless in some of his expressions of opinion, Maurice admits, but that does not detract from his essential message. Those who search Luther's writings for inconsistencies will no doubt be amply rewarded for their pains. But those, on the other hand, who look in Luther for 'a strong steady current of thought and meaning running through all his perplexities and contradictions, and often made more evident by them' will also find what they seek. Luther's extravagant language cannot always be excused, but he had a burning message to proclaim and he announced it in the direct, earthy, 'biblical' language of the common people. Luther believed that his words would be understood 'by those who were suffering from the power of evil, as he was, by those who were hungering and thirsting after righteousness, as he was'. He cared little who else misunderstood them (*Kingdom*, I, p.93, cf. 74f; *MMP*, II, pp. 117f).

Theological Method: God at the Centre

Maurice believed that his own teaching implied a radically different concept of God to that underlying much nineteenth-century religion. He felt, therefore, that Luther's significance lay in the way that he referred every question back to the most fundamental theological question of all: what is to be believed about the nature of God.

> It was the steadiness with which Luther kept his mind fixed upon this issue – it was his happy indifference to many points which the mere protestant of later days would put most prominently forward – that entitled Luther to our everlasting gratitude. It is this which makes his name more precious to moral and metaphysical students than the names of nearly all the formal writers on morals and metaphysics.

The God-centredness of Luther's theological enquiry raises the most profound metaphysical issues.

> Luther, who was so weary of teaching philosophy, so desirous to abandon philosophy for theology, gave rise to more philosophy, provoked more eager enquiry into the mysteries of man's own being, as well as into the mysteries of nature, than anyone who had sat longest in the philosophical chair and worn the cloak with the greatest admiration (*MMP*, II, pp. 116, 121).

Reformation theology, Maurice perceived, was characterised by a quest for objectivity. The Reformers were convinced that the theological centre of gravity had to undergo a radical shift from human states of soul to an unchanging divine object. 'The idea of an object to which a man might look and in which he might rest took precedence of all others in the heart and reason of Luther.' This concern for objectivity underlay the dominant principles of Reformation theology. The actuality of revelation, the believer's assurance of salvation and the finished state of Christ's work constitute 'Lutheranism according to Luther' and contain 'the germ' of all authentic Reformation theology. The explicit recognition of the fact of revelation, that God has freely chosen to make himself known 'gave the Reformation all its moral strength and grandeur and . . . imparted to the protestant doctrine respecting the Bible all its meaning' (*Kingdom*, I, pp. 74f, 100).

The same principle of objectivity was at the heart of Maurice's own thought. In moving from unitarianism to trinitarian orthodoxy, he had not lost his profound sense of the unity of God. Christian theology, according to Maurice, is radically and determinatively theocentric. The being, nature and name of the one God in trinity is the one foundation of Christian doctrine. Maurice professed his intention

> to ground all theology upon the name of God the Father, the Son and the Holy Ghost; not to begin from ourselves and our sins; not to measure the straight line by the crooked one. This is the method which I have learnt from the Bible. There everything proceeds from God; he is revealing himself; he is acting, speaking, ruling. Next my desire is to ground all human morality upon the relation in which man stands to God; to exhibit whatever is right and true in man as only the image and reflex or the original righteousness and truth (*Sacrifice*, p. xli).

This approach provided a link with Scottish Calvinism which Maurice appropriated through the influence of Edward Irving (1792–1834), founder of the Irvingite movement (later the Catholic Apostolic Church). Maurice did not subscribe to Irving's views on speaking with tongues or the millenium: Irving's influence on him was indirect yet profound. The creed of Scottish Calvinism Maurice had believed to be 'hard narrow and inhuman'; Irving taught him to respect it for its 'belief in God as a living being, as the ruler of the earth, as the standard of righteousness, as the orderer of men's acts in all the common relations of life'. This 'theocratic faith', as Maurice calls it, was part of Irving's 'covenanting, Calvinistical culture'. Maurice pays high tribute to this tradition: 'I . . . pay it the profoundest homage . . . I have found nothing to supersede this. I have found nothing . . . which is good without this. I reverence it as protestant theology in the highest, purest meaning of that word and as the very ground of all theology.' Olive Brose believes that Maurice's debt to Calvinism was much greater than the *Life* suggests. It was Calvinism that first generated the seriousness, warmth and emotion so lacking in the coolly rational unitarianism in which Maurice had grown up (*Sacrifice*, pp. xiiiff; Brose, p. 14). Though Maurice did not recognise the evangelicals as the true heirs of the Reformation, he pays tribute to 'the unspeakable worth of that evangelical movement in favour of conscious faith to which we owe what is most vital in our English Christianity' (*Revelation*, p. 296).

Theological Method: The Thirty-Nine Articles

Maurice's theological position was decisively shaped by 'the most unlikely document ever to ignite a religious radical': the Thirty-nine Articles of the Church of England. As Olive Brose remarks, 'No one in his right mind in any century would have thought of the Thirty-nine Articles in connection with religious conversion' (pp. 8, 77). Maurice himself admitted that the articles were usually associated with 'large wigs, afternoon slumber and hatred of all youthful eagerness and hope'. But to him they provided an authoritative model of correct theological method (*Subscription*, p. 79).

In his *Autobiography*, John Stuart Mill commented of Maurice that he had prostituted his paramount intellectual powers in an unworthy cause – the defence of the Church of England and, specifically, the Thirty-nine Articles. Maurice used them, claimed Mill, to prove to his own mind that the Church of England had been right all along, that she 'had known everything from the first and that all the truths on the ground of which the church and orthodoxy have been attacked . . . are not only consistent with the Thirty-nine Articles but are better understood and expressed in those articles than by anyone who rejects them' (p. 153).

But for Maurice the articles were no mere function of self-justificatory Anglican apologetics. They were a paradigm of the method of Christian theology in that they took their starting point, not from man and his sinful state, but from the eternal truth of God's being. Only having laid this foundation do they go on to incorporate the anthropology and soteriology of the Reformation. Maurice's discovery of the witness of the articles came with the force of revelation: 'Words which I had always known but which had not the same traditional hold upon me as upon many of my countrymen presented themselves to me with a power which I had never dreamed was in them' (*Sacrifice*, p. xxi).

When he began to study the articles 'for the purpose of discovering their theological method', he was struck by the contrast between them and the Reformed confessions, particularly the Scots Confession of John Knox. Whereas Knox begins with the fall of man, dealing with it in his second article, the Church of England does not mention the fall until the ninth article – and even then, Maurice points out, it deals with it not historically but morally, as serving to account for the present existential condition of every human being. And this was no mere academic quibble: the divergence of approach was grounded in different pastoral methods. The Church of England's method, as embodied in the Catechism, was to call Christians to live up to their true standing in Christ, to become what they are in reality. The Catechism, taught to all baptised children, 'tells them that they are members of Christ, children of God, inheritors of the kingdom of heaven'.

> The prayers framed for all the motley body which frequents our churches assume that all may call upon God as a reconciled Father. Here was the article translated into life. Human beings were treated as redeemed – not in consequence of any act that they had done, of any faith that they had exercised; their faith was to be grounded on a foregone conclusion; their acts were to be the fruit of a state they already possessed (*Sacrifice*, p. xxii; *Kingdom*, II, pp. 303f).

But once this 'catholic foundation' has been laid, the articles go on to grapple with the issues that had come to the forefront of controversy in the sixteenth century – freewill, election, justification – and on all these points the language of the articles was 'as distinct and definite as it can be'.

> The Calvinistic and Lutheran principles are plainly and distinctly asserted; there is no hint or prophecy of Arminianism; the Romish system in every point wherein it is opposed to the distinct affirmations of the Reformers . . . is repudiated.

Just as the 'catholic foundation' provides an essential basis for the affirmations of evangelical theology that follow, so these 'principles of the Reformation are asserted . . . not as necessary qualifications, but as indispensible conditions of the great catholic truths' (*Kingdom*, II, pp. 303f). So for Maurice, the significance of the articles lies in the fact that they do not constitute a system but reveal a method. He will not allow any single theological tenet to be developed into a system – not even justification, though he wants to affirm it 'in all its integrity and fulness' (ib., I, p. 95).

Maurice believed, with Coleridge, that men are usually right in their positive convictions but wrong when they resort to condemning the sincere convictions of others. There is a living principle at the heart of every theological system to which that system bears witness, while at the same time that truth is distorted by being isolated and systematised. The Thirty-nine Articles, however, enable the Church of England to do better justice to these complementary truths than the protestant or Roman Catholic churches, simply because they continually frustrate the attempts of individuals or schools of thought to create a system of Anglican theology. It is this conviction that underlies Maurice's words when he says of the articles:

> See whether you will not find in them the justification of every part of . . . your opinions to which you really in your hearts cleave – of all those views which you could not abandon because they were part of your very life; and whether you will not find in them the detection and exposure of various superstitions which have hung as rags about you and which, because they were those which most grieved your brethren, your partisans have persuaded you were the most precious and sacred.

For example, while protestants had made a necessary protest on behalf of individual conscience, catholics had maintained a steady witness to the corporate nature of the Christian faith. But the church is not therefore to be half catholic and half protestant. She is to be 'most catholic when she is most protestant' (*Kingdom*, II, p. 304; *Subscription*, p. 110; *Three Letters*, p. 13; cf. *Reasons for not joining a party*).

Interpreting the Reformation

As the apostle of 'Christian socialism', Maurice could not be satisfied with Luther's emphasis on faith in the heart and liberty in the conscience of the individual. Luther failed to realise the social implications of his message. For the sixteenth-century peasant, deliverance from his burdened conscience was not enough, unless accompanied by the lifting of his other burdens – economic exploitation and social degradation. On the other hand, however, the Lutheran reform did contain the rudiments of a coherent social ethic in its protest against monasticism, its reinstatement of marriage as a holy estate for clergy and laity alike, and its sense of vocation within family and nation.

> The common earth was God's creation. Kings, fathers and husbands had been appointed by him and were spoken of in his word; the whole economy of his kingdom had been transacted through their means. The papists had treated the world as the devil's world, with their *touch not, taste not, handle not*; but there was no safety in such abstinence – the security was in serving God with a clean heart and giving him thanks for his gifts (*Kingdom*, I, p. 103).

To the Reformation was often attributed the rampant individualism of the modern world and the fragmentation of society. But Maurice points out that the Reformers did not create the spirit of individualism, but channelled it in constructive directions. They 'did not call forth the rebellious activity of the period in which they lived but, when it was seeking a refuge in infidelity, taught it to find one in faith' (*MMP*, II, pp. 120ff; *Kingdom*, I, p. 80).

Like Newman, Maurice made the doctrine of justification central to his approach to the Reformation. He set out to counter the Tractarian presentation of justification, to attack 'those who in our days are turning this great staff of life into a reed'. He accuses the Tractarians of 'perverse misinterpretation' of the connection between baptism and justification – 'turning the permanent witness for it, to those who want it, into a momentary act by which it is conferred upon those who want it not'. For Maurice, as for Luther himself, justification is the *articulus stantis aut cadentis ecclesiae*; but it must be balanced by the complementary truths regarding membership of a body and a kingdom which have sometimes been neglected by the most zealous advocates of justification by faith (*Life*, I, pp. 262f).

Whereas Newman accused Luther of leaving Christians in bondage to their feelings and morbid cultivation of states of soul, Maurice correctly discerns that Luther's motive was a quest for the objective reality of divine grace. He gets to the heart of what the Reformers fought for when he points to 'the immeasurable difference whether the grace was supposed to be given to a man as so much stock which he might call his own or whether its effect was to induce him to disclaim all property in himself and to live entirely in Christ'. Putting words into Luther's mouth, Maurice makes him say:

> I do not . . . make . . . the grace of faith the ground of justification. I do not tell a man that he is to ask himself how much faith he has and, if he has so much, to call himself justified. What I tell him is precisely that he is not to do this . . . He is not to think or speculate about his faith at all. He is to believe and by believing to lose sight of himself and to forget himself (*Kingdom*, I, pp. 92f).

Maurice also dispatches the idea that justification by faith makes a man rely on his own opinion of what justification is – his faith is in a notion and ultimately in himself (as Coleridge once remarked, 'You do not really believe; you only believe that you believe'). But Luther, as Maurice reminds us, 'did not call upon men to acknowledge either a new doctrine or an old one, to believe either in a certain opinion concerning justification or in a certain opinion concerning the atonement. He called upon them to believe in God the Father Almighty, in Jesus Christ his only Son our Lord and in the Holy Ghost'. Luther repeatedly insisted that 'the *Credo* was justification'. By its very nature, faith 'is the act of going out of self, the act of entering into union with another from whom all our graces are to be derived' (*Kingdom*, I, pp. 94, 92).

Not that Luther exalted faith at the expense of the sacraments (in this case baptism); rather he established their true relation. The doctrine of baptismal regeneration was held by Luther (says Maurice), not alongside the doctrine of justification, but as its only adequate foundation. ' "Believe on the warrant of your baptism. You are grafted into Christ;

claim your position . . ." This was his invariable language; with this he shook the Seven Hills.' Of course this was exactly Maurice's language too and with it he hoped to shake English protestantism out of its degenerate state (*Kingdom*, I, p. 273).

Among the successors of the Reformation, claims Maurice, justification has been turned 'from a living principle into an empty shibboleth in which the divine election has lost its force, except as an excuse for doubting the existence of our own awful responsibilities'. In the *Theological Essays*, Maurice's manifesto against the debased religiosity of the age, he condemns the perversion of Luther's doctrine into its opposite. Legal fictions have supplanted a teaching which originally appealed to men's conscience and the moral character of reality. Against this 'popular protestantism', Maurice's language is as scathing as Newman's was against the Reformers. The difference is that Maurice hits the right target.

For Maurice, justification by faith means that men are set free from self-concern to become witnesses to the divine order in the world. Justification does not neutralise, but rather intensifies the great moral conflict between good and evil in both the individual and society. It is no mere forensic sleight of hand on the part of God but a personal relationship and commitment. In words that he applies to Luther, Maurice shows clearly his own understanding of the faith that justifies: 'Belief is that which carries him out of himself, above himself. It is no logical act, no process of the understanding. It must be awakened by a Person; it must have a Person for its object. All chains of logic, philosophy, divinity, must be broken that the man may assert his own right to breathe and to be' (*MMP*, II, p. 117).

Postive Protestantism

It is instructive to compare Maurice's view of later developments in Lutheran theology with Newman's. Maurice goes as far as to question the integrity of Newman's remarks. Referring to Newman's assertion, in the essay on development, that 'as is well known', Lutheranism had become simple heresy or unbelief, Maurice replies: 'This fact is not well known; Mr Newman does not know it himself; if he believes that Dr Pusey's work on Germany was the work of an honest eyewitness, he knows the contrary.' And in a parting thrust that reminds us that the Tractarians had no monopoly of moral seriousness, Maurice adds that by this and several other passages in the *Essay* 'among his other retractions', Newman 'has retracted his powerful and awful sermon "On Unreal Words"' (*Hebrews*, p. lxxvii). (We are reminded of Julius Hare's rebuke to the Tractarians, for their persecution of Hampden, under the title 'Thou shalt not bear false witness against thy neighbour'.) For Maurice, Newman's 'developments' are corruptions which would have succeeded in destroying the church, if

God had not raised up the Reformers to point men back to the true centre of the faith (*Hebrews*, p. lxii, lxxiv).

Maurice's *bête noir* is not, as with Newman, eighteenth-century rationalism, but seventeenth-century Lutheran scholasticism. Where Luther held that the foolishness of preaching would convey the living word of scripture to the hearts of the faithful, scholastic orthodoxy sponsored arid controversy over the fragmentary results of academic study of the Bible. Again, unlike Newman, Maurice does not regard subsequent developments in the rationalist criticism of the Enlightenment, followed by the critical method of Kant and the experiential theology of Schleiermacher, as a deepening spiral of apostasy. Kant, like Coleridge, made trial of his age and dug down to the solid foundations. His work remains a challenge that cannot be ignored. The existential approach of Schleiermacher is the equivalent in German protestantism of the Methodist rehabilitation of feeling in religion (*Kingdom*, I, pp. 172ff).

Maurice had to grapple with the Tractarian claim that protestantism was merely negative, a reaction to the permanent, positive catholic faith and parasitic on it. Maurice, however, always held that protestantism alone was not enough, that it was never meant to stand in isolation and that the Reformers did not intend a departure from the Christian tradition. The strongest protestantism is the sort that sustains and balances catholic principles. Here Maurice is anticipating ideas later developed by Tillich and specifically applied to Reformation ecclesiology by Jaroslav Pelikan – a dialectic of catholic substance and protestant principle (*Right and Wrong*, p. 18; cf. Tillich; Pelikan).

But Maurice makes no attempt to deny the predominantly negative form taken by some current versions of protestantism. 'Beginning in the spirit, the Reformation has . . . been made perfect in the flesh. Its principles have found no clothing but one of system which has stifled them, or one of state organisation which stifles the minds and energies of those who profess them.' While Newman claimed that the spirit of Luther was dead, Maurice admitted that the Lutheran, Calvinist and Zwinglian 'systems' 'have had their day and . . . the time of their extinction is at hand'. He deplores the 'meagre, negative, spurious protestantism of our day' which has become 'nothing but a fierce denunciation and contradiction of something else'. Those positive principles which Luther proclaimed are now regarded merely as symbols of our stand against Rome. We are in danger of proving the Tractarians right (*Kingdom*, I, pp. 123f; *Right and Wrong*, pp. 16, 13).

For Maurice true protestantism is a positive creative force, opposed to whatever is itself negative and destructive. Its principles of election, justification, the voice of scripture and the validity of national societies within the divine order are positive and permanent. Maurice holds that protestantism 'has a standing point of its own, that it is not merely condemnatory, merely negative; and that, so far as it keeps within its own proper and appointed province, it denounces and condemns only that which is itself negative and which sets at nought something that is needful for the life and being of man'. Protestant principles, 'though buried under notions and negations, are still vital and will rise again and will become united whenever protestants shall once more feel that they have a gospel from God and a gospel concerning God' to proclaim (*Kingdom*, I, p. 79; *Sacrifice*, p. xvi).

It would be highly anachronistic to try to assess Maurice in terms of modern theological trends. But at times he seems to anticipate the theology of revelation of the British theologian P. T. Forsyth and, overshadowing him, Brunner and Barth. But Maurice was no Barthian. As a disciple of Coleridge he reverences reason and has a place for speculative thought. It cannot be said that he develops a natural theology, as such, for in his thought natural theology and the theology of revelation are integrated and transcended in a message that, while received as the self-communication of God in Christ, remains fully in harmony with the nature of man and society. But in words that echo Calvin's statement at the beginning of the *Institutes* that theology consists in the knowledge of God and of ourselves, Maurice points forward to Barth's stress on the actuality of revelation when he says, 'We can know nothing of ourselves till we look above ourselves. We can see light only in God's light. The knowledge of man is possible because the knowledge of God is possible' (*Revelation*, p. 479).

17

Authority in Anglican Theology

At the end of a valuable essay on 'Tendencies of Religious Thought in England, 1688–1750', contributed to *Essays and Reviews* (1860), Mark Pattison focused on the question of authority in theology: 'Whoever would take the religious literature of the present day as a whole,' he wrote, 'and endeavour to make out clearly on what basis revelation is supposed by it to rest, whether on authority, on the inward light, on reason, on self-evidencing scripture, or on the combination of the four, or some of them, and in what proportions, would probably find that he had undertaken a perplexing but not altogether profitless inquiry' (p. 329). What were the reasons for this confused situation?

Building on the normative thought of Richard Hooker, the seventeenth-century divines had achieved a broad consensus on the question of authority (as on other matters) – a consensus that insisted on the paramount authority of holy scripture in all questions of faith and order, and as the only source of doctrines necessary for salvation; that acknowledged the place of tradition in the form of the consent of antiquity as our guide in interpreting the scriptures where their bearing was not readily apparent; and that allowed scope to reason, informed by experience and sound learning, to arbitrate in the formation of doctrine. As McAdoo has written, this consensus involved 'the centrality of scripture and the visibility and continuity of the church, both confirmed by antiquity, and illuminated by the freedom of reason and liberality of viewpoint' (p. 357).

That consensus had been challenged in the eighteenth century by several factors. First, radical protestant thought continued to challenge the consistency of the fathers. Already in the early seventeenth century, Chillingworth and the Tew Circle, influenced by Jean Daillé's critique of the fathers, had sat lightly to their authority, pointing out that there were fathers against fathers, councils against councils, a consent of one age

271

against a consent of another. The crypto-Arianism of such as Clarke and Hoadly in the eighteenth, showed that men were not willing to be browbeaten by mere assertion of patristic authority. As, in reply, such Anglican patristic scholars as Beveridge, Pearson and Bull burrowed into old folios of the fathers, the effect was to produce a disproportionate emphasis on antiquity (McAdoo, p. 405). Second, the so-called 'Usagers' among the nonjurors had exploited the potential of tradition to add liturgical flourishes such as the mixed chalice, prayers for the dead, the epiclesis and a prayer of oblation to the Prayer Book order of holy communion. Third, the concept of reason itself had degenerated from the intuitive, divine reason of the Cambridge Platonists, to the common, functional reason of the evidence mongers of the eighteenth century. By the time that Pattison wrote, the celebrated 'threefold cord' had become highly problematical: the authority of scripture was apparently being challenged by biblical higher criticism; historical research stemming from the late Enlightenment was emphasising the diversity of tradition; and reason was becoming an instrument of division rather than cohesion.

In this chapter we shall attempt to explore the impact of the Oxford movement on the developing understanding of authority in theology (rather than in church structures) within Anglicanism in the nineteenth and early twentieth centuries.

Scripture and Tradition

'The place and authority of scripture,' writes McAdoo, 'does not vary throughout the seventeenth century . . . It is the criterion in all writing on doctrine, ecclesiastical origins and polity, and the deciding factor in all disputed questions, appealed to by, and equally cogent for moderates, puritans and Laudians' (p. 309f). William Beveridge (1637–1708) wrote of the scope and limits of biblical authority:

> There is nothing necessary to be believed concerning God, nor done in obedience unto God by us, but what is here revealed to us; and therefore all traditions of men which are contrary to this word of God are necessarily to be abhorred, and all traditions of men not recorded in this word of God are not necessarily to be believed. What is here written we are bound to believe . . . and what is not here written we are not bound to believe.

But Beveridge adds a significant qualification:

> I say we are not bound to believe it, but I cannot say we are bound not to believe it; for there be many truths which we may believe, nay, are bound to believe, because truth, which notwithstanding are not recorded in the word of God.

This liberates the Anglican from a meagre and impoverished biblicism, but Beveridge is careful not to overstep the fundamental Reformation principle, insisted on in the sixth of the Thirty-nine Articles, that holy scripture contains all things necessary to salvation. He continues therefore:

Though there be many things we may believe, yet is there nothing we need believe in order to our everlasting happiness which is not here written; so that if we believe all that is here spoken, and do all that is here commanded, we shall certainly be saved, though we do not believe what is not here spoken, nor do what is not here commanded (*MC*, pp. 94f).

The place that classical Anglicanism allocates to tradition is then favourable though strictly circumscribed. Primitive tradition illuminated the biblical text. The mind of the fathers was assimilated into the Anglican way of thinking. Anglican scholars sacrificed great portions of their lives to the study of the fathers. Ussher devoted eighteen years to reading them systematically. In his *Discourse about Tradition* (1683) Simon Patrick refutes 'the calumny . . . that the Church of England rejects all tradition.'

> No, the scripture itself is a tradition; and we admit all other traditions which are subordinate, and are agreeable unto that; together with all those things which can be proved to be apostolical by the general testimony of the church in all ages: nay, if any thing not contained in scripture, which the Roman church now pretends to be part of God's word, were delivered to us, by as universal uncontrolled tradition as the scripture is, we should receive it, as we do the scripture (p. 48).

Patrick also upholds the authority of the inherited rule of faith in a way that would have won the approval of Keble, Newman or Manning. 'The sum and substance of the Christian religion,' he affirms, 'hath been delivered down to us, even from the apostles' days, in other ways or forms, beside the scriptures' – in the baptismal vows, the creed, in prayers and hymns (p. 18). Tradition confirms the interpretation of scripture (p. 22).

> The sense of the whole church . . . must be acknowledged also to be of greater or lesser authority, as it was nearer or farther off from the times of the apostles. What was delivered by their immediate followers ought to weigh so much with us, as to have the greatest humane authority, and to be looked upon as little less than divine (p. 7).

As McAdoo puts it, the appeal to antiquity 'was not an academic or antiquarian frame of reference nor was it primarily a method of doctrinal equation' (p. 318). Tradition provided a continuity essential to catholicity, but it was a continuity that was not merely external, a rigid straitjacket of enforced conformity to precedent, but internal and one of a common mind and felt spiritual affinity (ib., p. 319). It gave Anglicanism, uniquely among reformed churches, a profound sense of the Christian past and anchored it in history, while at the same time serving to counterbalance the more volatile elements of rational enquiry and liberality of discussion. It was owing to the balancing factors of reason, conscience and the Hookerian sense of what is appropriate to the circumstances, that tradition and antiquity were not permitted to become sources of authority, but were confined to the ancillary role of general guidance and sources of relevant evidence in doctrinal debate. The weakness of this position is, however, as McAdoo points out, that in some circumstances 'the appeal to antiquity can convey the impression of producing authorities rather than adducing evidence' (p. 407). It must be admitted that the Tractarians' crushing *catenae* of patristic precedents does tend to give precisely this impression.

Central to the Tractarian conception of the relation of scripture and tradition was the principle 'The church to teach, the Bible to prove.' Newman had learned it from Edward Hawkins, vicar of St Mary's and later provost of Oriel, who had opposed the plans of the Bible Society to issue copies of the scriptures without the Prayer Book bound in. As Newman recalled, Hawkins' sermon on this principle 'made a most serious impression upon me.' He added: 'He does not go one step, I think, beyond the high Anglican doctrine, nay, he does not reach it.' Hawkins' principle, 'self-evident as soon as stated, to those who have at all examined the structure of scripture,' was that 'the sacred text was never intended to teach doctrine, but only to prove it, and that, if we would learn doctrine, we must have recourse to the formularies of the church; for instance to the catechism and to the creeds . . . This view, most true in its outline, most fruitful in its consequences, opened upon me a large field of thought' (*Apol.*, p. 102). The doctrine is so crucial to Anglo-Catholic theology right up to and including Gore who frequently reiterates it, that it bears some underlining. It is implicit throughout Newman's work on *The Prophetical Office of the Church*, but finds expression also in the earlier work *The Arians of the Fourth Century*.

> Surely the sacred volume was never intended, and is not adapted to *teach* us our creed; however certain it is that we can prove our creed from it, when it has once been taught us, and in spite of individual produceable exceptions to the general rule. From the very first, that rule has been, as a matter of fact, for the church to teach the truth, and then appeal to scripture in vindication of its own teaching.

Heretics, on the other hand, in wilful pride, attempt to construct their own doctrine from scratch by 'eliciting a systematic doctrine from the scattered notices of the truth which scripture contains' (c. Chadwick, *Mind*, p. 146).

However, no disparagement of scripture was intended. Its supreme authority was affirmed, though in a qualified way. 'We agree with protestant sects in making scripture the document of ultimate appeal in matters of faith . . . though we consider scripture a satisfactory, we do not consider it our sole informant in divine truths,' explains Newman in the *Prophetical Office*. And 'we rely on antiquity to strengthen such intimations of doctrine as are but faintly, though really, given in scripture' (pp. 36f). Towards the end of the work he gives a balanced definition of the role and authority of scripture. He holds that holy scripture contains all things necessary to salvation, that is, either as being read therein or deducible therefrom; not that scripture is the only ground of the faith, or ordinarily the guide into it and teacher of it or the source of all religious truth whatever, or the systematiser of it, or the instrument of unfolding, illustrating, enforcing, and applying it; but that it is the document of ultimate appeal in controversy, and the touchstone of all doctrine (pp. 369f).

The true authority is to be found in the intimate correlation of scripture and tradition. Scripture is interpreted by tradition; tradition is verified by scripture. Tradition teaches, scripture proves. Tradition is vital because the Bible does not carry with it its own interpretation. Henry Manning's sermon *The Rule of Faith* (1838) consolidates the trend that had become apparent in the late 1830s. Because the Bible is not transparently clear, because Christians so easily go astray into private judgement, because the church is not infallible, a rule of faith over and above scripture is required, but one that is complementary to scripture. 'Scripture, then, being the proof of the creed, and the creed the interpreter of scripture, the harmony of these is the first rule of interpretation' (pp. 26, 35). For Keble, Newman, Pusey and Manning scripture could only be truly understood through the eyes of the fathers. For all their love for scripture, Newman and Pusey in particular (writes Owen Chadwick)

> believed the Bible could only be approached with the proper spirit of reverence when it was approached not with the fallen, objective, detached, intellectualist mind of the individual, but with the eyes of the ancient and undivided church for which the biblical texts were in fact written, and which selected some to be biblical and others not. For this reason they set out to make the fathers available to the English reader, with something of the same religious spirit in which the Reformers had sought to make the Bible available in the language of the people (*Mind*, p. 40).

This authoritative tradition, vital for the correct interpretation of scripture, was classically defined in the so-called Vincentian Canon, *quod semper, quod ubique, quod ab omnibus* – antiquity, universality, catholicity. In his sermon of 1836 *Primitive Tradition recognised in Holy Scripture*, Keble compared this to the common or customary law. The criteria of Vincent of Lerins are 'similar to those which jurists are used to apply to the common or unwritten laws of any realm. If a maxim or custom can be traced back to a time whereof the memory of man runneth not to the contrary; if it pervade all the different courts . . . and . . . if it be generally acknowledged in such sort, that contrary decisions have been disallowed and held invalid: then, whatever the exceptions to it may be, it is presumed to be part and parcel of our common law'. The church's acceptance of tradition depends 'on principles exactly analogous' (p. 33). Newman took this up in the following year when he rather tastelessly pointed out that 'murderers are hanged by *custom* . . . Tradition is uniform custom' (p. 39).

The Vincentian canon was abandoned by Newman when he wrote his *Development of Christian Doctrine*. Even in the earlier work *The Prophetical Office* he has difficulty with it. Gore, however, would continue to use it. As Owen Chadwick points out, the argument is circular – you are defining universality, catholicity etc. by means of a rule which assumes them to be already defined, a patently question-begging procedure. But the canon and the related doctrine of the *consensus patrum*, however unsuited to constructive or speculative theology, fulfilled to Keble's mind a practical purpose. It was a pastoral and pragmatic rule of thumb. This was not enough for Newman and he cast it aside as a broken reed.

For Manning, however, the Vincentian canon was a justification for going further: 'If things attested unanimously, universally and from the beginning, are not to be doubted,' he argues in *The Rule of Faith*, 'things which were early, and, though not everywhere traceable, yet prevalent and uncontradicted, have no small claim on our reception' (pp. 40f).

For Newman, tradition was the pulsating heart of the church's life, not merely a useful tool. It had to be probed and questioned until it yielded a firm foundation – which it could only do in some form of infallibility. But for Keble tradition was there to be used as a guide, not to bear a weight for which it was not intended. It was to provide a grid ('the system and arrangement') of fundamental articles of faith – the *regula fidei* – and to assist in the interpretation of scripture, particularly by means of allegory. It preserved down to the present time the polity of the early church – the three-fold ministry and apostolic succession, together with infant baptism which was obscure in scripture itself. But it was not merely preservative. Chadwick points out that Keble's doctrine of tradition differed from that of Hawkins and the old high churchmen, in that he made it reformative too. It puts upon us an obligation to obey and to follow (*Mind*, p. 39).

In *The Prophetical Office of the Church* Newman attempts a reconstruction of the *via media* of the Caroline divines; he tries to bind together again a three-fold cord – the formal supremacy of scripture, the material guidance of tradition, together with a place for reason and private judgement. On the last, he writes, the Anglican church takes a middle course between the protestant tendency to let private judgement run riot, and the Roman discipline of repressing it and compelling assent.

> The English church takes a middle course between these two. It considers that on certain definite subjects private judgement upon the text of scripture has been superseded, not by the more authoritative sentence of the church, but by its historical testimony delivered down from the apostles. To these definite subjects nothing more can be added (*Via Media*, p. 128).

But Newman really finds it difficult to accommodate private judgement at all and he devotes considerable space to exposing its abuses – all part of

Newman's lifelong quarrel with the 'popular protestantism' that had imparted to him saving faith but denied him the maternal nurture of the church.

In this work, *The Prophetical Office*, Newman attempts a new synthesis on the question of authority. Though it bears strong verbal resemblances to the classical Anglican position, it in fact departs significantly from it. In *The Arians of the Fourth Century* Newman had postulated an unwritten apostolic tradition, a summary of the essential Christian message – 'granting that the apostles conversed and their friends had memories'. Though subordinate to scripture, it amounted to a 'traditional system of authority, consistent with, though independent of scripture' (c. Lash, p. 123). In his sermon on primitive tradition (1836) Keble had emphasised that the rule of faith was a mostly unwritten sacred deposit which, if it could be authenticated as apostolic, demanded the same reverence as scripture. This rule of faith was the touchstone of scripture in the formation of the canon, though, once written, scripture became the 'sole and paramount' rule of faith. Nevertheless, where scripture is silent or ambiguous, the 'consent of the fathers is a probable index of apostolic tradition' (pp. 14ff, 26ff, 29ff). The Tractarian emphasis on tradition was not merely an understandable reaction to the popular protestant vulgarisation of scripture by rampant private judgement, but was also a reassertion of the dogmatic principle against liberal enquiry. It was a complacent return to the *consensus patrum* as the seventeenth-century scholars had deployed it, as though the rise of historical method and the challenge to all unquestioned traditional authorities by the Enlightenment had never taken place.

It is then in the light of the Tractarian reassessment of tradition and fear of (secular, liberal) reason that Newman attempts his synthesis. First he lays it down that 'scripture, antiquity and catholicity cannot really contradict one another'. Second, the supremacy of scripture is secured and the claims of reason depressed: 'When the moral sense or reason seems to be on one side and scripture on the other, we must follow scripture.' Third, where scripture seems to contradict tradition, scripture must give way: 'When the sense of scripture, as interpreted by reason, is contrary to the sense given to it by catholic antiquity, we ought to side with the latter.' Fourth, where fundamentals are concerned, our loyalty is to antiquity before the magisterium of the present church.

But then Newman turns to the other side of the coin, invoking the old high church plea of passive obedience: when antiquity contradicts the magisterium in unimportant matters, we are to defer to the teaching of the church. Furthermore: 'When the present church speaks contrary to our private notions and antiquity is silent, or its decisions unknown to us, it is pious to sacrifice our own opinions to that of the church.' But if, in spite of our efforts to agree with the church, we still differ from it, antiquity being silent, we must avoid causing any disturbance, recollecting that the church, and not individuals, 'has authority in controversies of faith' (*Proph. Off.*, pp. 160f).

Keble and Pusey maintained this attitude of passive obedience: it was the old ideology of the 'erastian paradigm' carried over to the new 'apostolic paradigm' – though actually they succeeded in creating quite considerable disturbance while at the same time claiming the virtues of longsuffering and submission to authority. But the strength of their position was that they refused to break communion with a church that they could not deny possessed the fundamentals of the faith – trinitarian doctrine, the dominical sacraments and the three-fold ministry with apostolic succession. Newman, however, provoked by the hostile reaction to *Tract 90*, and coming to believe the Church of England to be no true church, and salvation not assured within her, hitched the old Anglican teaching of passive obedience to the wagon of authoritarian Roman catholicism, overcoming, both in 1845 and in 1870, his reservations about the papacy. Underlying the movement of Newman's mind was a dissatisfaction with the quintessentially Anglican teaching on probability as the guide of life, and an insatiable craving for certitude. Soon after his secession, Newman wrote: 'Now it need not be denied that those who are external to the church must begin with private judgement; they use it in order ultimately to supersede it; as a man out of doors uses a lamp in a dark night, and puts it out when he gets home' (*Loss and Gain*, p. 143).

Richard Whately who at Oriel had taught Newman an Aristotelian logic and the concept of a divine society independent of the state connection, was a robustly protestant Anglican. As archbishop of Dublin, he opposed what he regarded as the dangerous nonsense of the Oxford movement. Whately was almost a survivor from the previous century – a physically impressive, energetic and domineering figure, a great shambling bear of a man; a defender of the Reformation from a broad church not an evangelical position. In his two essays, *The Kingdom of Christ Delineated*, he attacks, though not by name, Newman and the principles he stood for in the late 1830s. He will have no truck with 'the pretensions of supposed "antiquity" and "tradition"'. Holy scripture alone is the supreme authority in the church. He argues that 'the implicit deference due to the declarations and precepts of holy scripture, is due to *nothing else*, and that it is not humble piety, but profane presumption, either to attribute infallibility to the traditions or decision of an uninspired man or body of men, (whether church, council, fathers, or by whatever other title designated), or, still more, to acknowledge in these, *although fallible*, a right to fix absolutely the interpretation of scripture, to be blended therewith, and to supersede all private judgement' (pp. 277f, vii). Tradition and the voice of the church are thus made subordinate to, and dependent on scripture in the same way that parasite plants depend on the trees that support them. 'The parasite at first clings to, and rests on the tree, which it gradually overspreads with its own foliage, till, by little and little, it weakens and completely smothers it' (p. 197). Whately's was the voice of down to earth, no nonsense eighteenth-century Anglicanism, but it was not untrue to the tradition, and moreover, it was astonishingly prophetic of what was to come.

The Authority of Reason

Richard Hooker was the first to formulate on the basis of first principles the typical appeal of classical Anglicanism to scripture, reason (or experience) and tradition (or antiquity). At the hands of the Caroline divines, Hooker's method – albeit with some differences of emphasis between the liberals such as Hales and Chillingworth who endorsed Hooker's placing of reason above tradition, and the high churchmen who tended to reverse Hooker's order – created the finest flower of Anglican divinity, a monumental theological achievement. Hooker established the place of reason, as competent to interpret scripture, adjudicate on tradition and instruct the church as to what was and what was not binding in both, in Anglican theological method. Against exaggerated forms of nominalism, Hooker declares with Aquinas that God's being is a law unto his working, that the structures of the world are rational and operate according to divinely ordained laws in their proper spheres, and that reason is God's highest gift to humanity. The later divines, following Hooker, 'had firmly grasped the truth that reason was the human characteristic and that its sphere was not simply speculation but the whole range of human activities' (McAdoo, p. 312).

In his essay 'Of the Reverence Due to Antiquity' (*Misc. Works*, pp. 218–40), Clarendon, who as Edward Hyde had been a member of the Tew Circle and of one heart and mind with Falkland, insisted that 'the too frequent appeal and the too supine resignation of our understanding to antiquity' was the greatest obstacle to truth and knowledge. It is false modesty that holds back from questioning the wisdom of the fathers. No one follows them in everything. In particular their cosmology – angels, devils and the millenium – is obsolete. 'He who will profess all the opinions which were held by the most ancient fathers, and observe all that was practised in the primitive times, cannot be of the communion of any one church in the world.' Parties who differ most in their opinions and practices appeal with equal confidence to the so-called 'sense of antiquity' in support of their 'mutual contradictions'. We should indeed 'stand upon the old paths' – inform ourselves of what was said and done – but not lie down in them! This does not mean that Clarendon advocates a simplistic appeal to scripture. No current controversy, he asserts, could be settled by scripture. It is sufficient for its purpose but no guide to untangling fruitless controversies. 'It informs us sufficiently of all that we are obliged to think or to do; and whatsoever is too hard for us there to understand, is in no degree necessary for us to know.' It is clear that where there is this recognition of the plurality of interpretations of scripture and tradition, reason must be the arbiter.

However, just as the authority of scripture and tradition respectively were discriminatingly defined and restricted to their proper province, so too the role of reason was carefully limited. It was not so much constructive as critical, and hermeneutical of scripture and tradition. As Chillingworth argues against his Jesuit opponent, in the Roman church tradition has acquired a disproportionate authority, eclipsing not only scripture but reason:

> Following your church I must hold many things not only above reason, but against it, if any thing be against it; whereas following the scripture I shall believe many mysteries, but no impossibilities; many things above reason, but nothing against it; many things which had they not been revealed, reason could never have discovered, but nothing which by true reason may be confuted; many things which reason cannot comprehend how they can be, but nothing which reason can comprehend that it cannot be. Nay I shall believe nothing which reason will not convince that I ought to believe it (*MC*, pp. 105f).

The appeal to reason was by no means the preserve of one particular tradition within the Church of England. Jeremy Taylor, a liberal catholic, asserts: 'Scripture, tradition, councils and fathers are the evidence in a question, but reason is the judge' (c. McAdoo, p. 74). Simon Patrick, in the late seventeenth century, opposes reason to the mere assertion of authority, particularly an authority claiming infallibility for itself. God 'hath given us the use of reason, which if we will blindly resign to any pretended authority, what is it but to shut our eyes when we should open them' (*A Sermon*, p. 25). Gilbert Burnet, a liberal protestant, writes: 'We naturally have a faculty of private judgement which we use in all things. Has God revealed that we are to renounce it here?' (*Exposition*, p. 202). Burnet assumes the mantle of the Cambridge Platonists when he announces 'Reason is God's image in us' (ib., p. 211). Among high churchmen, Laud has it that the light of grace 'clears the eye of reason; it never puts it out' (c. McAdoo in Evans, ed., p. 273). But Henry Hammond, though he wrote *Of the Reasonableness of the Christian Religion*, restricts the role of reason to natural and moral questions, denying that it is competent to judge supernaturally revealed truth (Packer, pp. 56f).

Daniel Whitby and Joseph Butler go further than this. Whitby, a latitudinarian, wrote in 1714 of reason (albeit 'feeble reason': pp. 6f) as 'the only faculty which God hath given you, whereby to judge of truth and falsehood, or of the sense of his revealed words' (p. 35). Butler echoes this in his *Analogy of Religion* (1736): reason is 'the only faculty we have wherewith to judge concerning anything, even revelation itself' (p. 219). And Butler insists that 'reason can, and it ought to judge, not only of the meaning, but also of the morality and the evidence of revelation.'

> First. It is the province of reason to judge of the morality of the scripture ... whether it contains things plainly contradictory to wisdom, justice or goodness; to what the light of nature teaches us of God ... Secondly. Reason is able to judge, and must, of the evidence of revelation, and of the objections urged against that evidence (pp. 229ff).

Butler's is a critical reason; its role is discriminatory, even judicial, its task is to assess the evidence. But it knows its limitations, it serves an overriding moral purpose, and it has the apprehension of transcendent truth. Under the steadily advancing influence of Locke's empiricism, however, a more restricted, less elevated conception of reason began to prevail, one that was diffident about transcendental aspirations.

The century and a half leading up to *Essays and Reviews* (1860) in which Mark Pattison published his celebrated essay on religious tendencies, witnessed the progressive disintegration of the synthesis of authority that had been forged by the Caroline divines. The Anglican consensus had fragmented into parties standing for one component against another: reason against tradition, antiquity against private judgement, the Bible against both reason and tradition, and so on. But the rational tendency had been the dominant one in the eighteenth century. As Pattison put it:

> Throughout all discussions, underneath all controversies, and common to all parties, lies the assumption of the supremacy of reason in matters of religion ... Rationalism was not an anti-Christian sect outside the church making war against religion. It was a habit of thought ruling all minds, under the conditions of which all alike tried to make good the peculiar opinions they might happen to cherish ... The title of Locke's treatise, *The Reasonableness of Christianity*, may be said to have been the solitary thesis of Christian theology in England for great part of a century (pp. 257f).

This hardly does full justice to the high churchmen, but as a broad generalisation it is valid.

According to Pattison, theology had sunk to its lowest level, not because it was rational, but because it was mere 'common reason' – an appeal to educated common sense – which governed theological discussion, rather than, say, speculative reason or the intuitive reason of the Cambridge Platonists later to be revived by Coleridge.

> Dogmatic theology had ceased to exist; the exhibition of religious truth for practical purposes was confined to a few obscure writers. Every one who had anything to say on sacred subjects drilled it into an array of argument against a supposed objector. Christianity appeared made for nothing else but to be 'proved'; what use to make of it when it was proved was not much

thought about. Reason was at first offered as the basis of faith, but gradually became its substitute. The mind never advanced as far as the stage of belief, for it was unceasingly engaged in reasoning up to it. The only quality in scripture which was dwelt upon was its 'credibility' (pp. 259f).

While Butler shares some of these assumptions this was partly due to his method of meeting his adversaries on their own ground. His moral concern and his use of the doctrine of probation help to lift the work to a new level. And, as Henry Scott Holland pointed out in *The Optimism of Butler's 'Analogy'* (1908), Butler's idea of probability is not, as might appear, an attempt to settle upon the lowest common denominator in the argument with deism, but rather to find the highest common factor. It is not a negative argument but a positive one, for, to Butler's mind, probability is moral certainty. Butler holds together the rational and the moral.

The moral element or the authority of conscience – the idea that the practice of a Christian life validates the belief on which it is based – is found equally strongly in the high churchmen and nonjurors, with whom, however, it is united not with reason but with tradition and the authority of the church. 'You will not be able, by all the strength of reason,' declared bishop Wilson of Sodor and Man – later to become virtually a patron saint of the Tractarians – 'to subdue one lust, or support your mind under any great affliction'. But we are reminded not to play off the high churchmen against the rationalisers with whom they shared the spirit of the age, when we read in Wilson's *Maxims*: 'The mysteries of Christ are above our reason; but we believe them, because we have all the proofs necessary to convince any reasonable man that God has revealed them as certain truths' – words that are a distinct echo of Chillingworth (p. 119). The greatest high church moralist of the period, the nonjuror William Law (whose *Serious Call to a Devout and Holy Life* Keble later was to keep in a drawer for reverence's sake) achieved fame by his brilliant attack on Hoadly the latitudinarian bishop of Bangor. In his *Three Letters to the Bishop of Bangor* (1717–19), Law defended the authority of tradition and the power of the church's jurisdiction against Hoadly's spiritualising of the text, 'My kingdom is not of this world'. In 1893 Gore was to issue a reprint of these famous but little read letters. For these high churchmen and later for the Tractarians, the authority of tradition and of conscience would work together against reason and its interpretation of scripture, so that tradition and conscience became allies against reason. But it is a remarkable feature of Gore's mind that it was precisely on grounds of *conscience* that he sometimes could not accept tradition. In his thought there is the break-up and reconstruction of the Anglican synthesis of authorities (Avis, *Gore*).

Under the influence of Kant which in England slightly antedates the rise of the Oxford movement, the ethical approach to authority was intensified. Now it is not linked with tradition but with scripture.

Scripture and the practical reason – these are the supreme authorities for Coleridge, and through him for Maurice, although he, more so than Coleridge, has a place for tradition: anyone who accepts the creed accepts tradition, Maurice points out to the sectarians. For Maurice, too, the fathers have their place, but as witnesses to the living reality of God, not as the authoritative source of notions about him. The church and the Bible should be regarded as mutually illuminating (*Kingdom*, II, pp. 29, 32, 178; McLain, pp. 84, 96). Here is the promise of a synthesis such as Gore was to develop, but though the Mauricean theology was being formulated concurrently with the Tractarian theology, it was the latter which exerted the greater influence both on the age itself and upon later Anglicanism.

Probability in Authority

Rocking the cradle and tending the sheep on his glebe obviously did not stop Richard Hooker making a shrewd assessment of the world around him. He is an acute observer of human nature. The human mind, he comments, craves 'the most infallible certainty which the nature of things can yield'. But in many things divine, he points out, infallible certainty is not given us: we must allow ourselves to be guided by 'probable persuasions' (I, pp. 322ff). The disruption of the Anglican method in the matter of doctrinal authority in the nineteenth century can be interpreted as the result of a parting of the ways between the moderate Tractarians such as Keble who remained faithful to the doctrine of probability that they had inherited from classical Anglicanism via Butler, and those such as Newman whose craving for 'infallible certainty' led them beyond the Anglican fold.

Hooker set the direction of seventeenth-century Anglican thought in this matter. In *The Liberty of Prophesying*, Jeremy Taylor echoed him. In things not necessary to salvation, where we are 'left to our liberty', Taylor wrote, we rely upon 'right reason proceeding upon the best grounds it can, viz. of divine revelation and human authority, and probability is our guide' (c. McAdoo, p. 74). Here Taylor is merely representative of a point of view that surfaces constantly during the seventeenth century (ib.).

At the end of the century the Anglican layman John Locke gave it philosophical formulation in his *Essay Concerning Human Understanding* (1690). Locke has Hooker's realistic sense of the nature of things as they are, not as we fancy them to be in our pet ideologies. He echoes Hooker's teaching on the degrees of certainty and his insistence on proportioning assent to the strength of the evidence. Locke sets the key note of his work in the introduction when he remarks that if we can come to a just appreciation of both the extent and the limitations of our knowledge, 'we may learn to content ourselves with what is attainable by us in this state.' This knowledge, though limited, is enough to guide us in all the essential questions of life: 'The candle that is set up in us shines bright enough for all our purposes' (I, p. 7). The degree of assurance that probability affords 'is as great as our happiness or misery' requires, 'beyond which we have no concernment to know or to be' in this life (II, p. 144). The human condition is a state of moral probation, in which certitude is largely denied us. We are called to make our pilgrimage in the search for practical truth with 'only the twilight . . . of probability' to light our way (II, pp. 274f).

Bishop Butler is merely paraphrasing Locke when in *The Analogy of Religion* (1736) he reminds us that 'probability is the very guide of life' and the assurance it provides, though limited, is appropriate to 'the very condition of our being' in our earthly state of moral probation (pp. 73, 315). Keble and the moderate Tractarians would take this from Butler, if not from Locke, for it was of the very ethos of their Anglicanism which believed in going on in faith, quietly and humbly serving the least of Christ's little ones, not growing weary in well doing, not prying into mysteries too deep for us, not presuming on any reward. Newman's pre-tractarian poem sums it up: 'Lead, kindly Light, amid the encircling gloom, Lead thou me on . . . I do not ask to see the distant scene; one step enough for me.' Keble had learned from Butler that the natural world was a moral world; if not peopled with 'angel faces', it was certainly eloquent of religious truths and spoke of its 'divine original'. Sacramental of sacred meaning, it was full of homely lessons and parables. Newman, however, had lost those angel faces. When he looked out at the human world, he met 'a sight which fills me with unspeakable distress.' 'If I looked into a mirror, and did not see my face, I should have the sort of feeling which actually comes upon me, when I look into the living busy world and see no reflection of its creator . . . The sight of the world is nothing else than the prophet's scroll, full of "lamentations and mourning and woe"' (*Apol.*, pp. 277f).

Through Keble, Butler's *Analogy* exerted a profound influence on the catholic movement in the Church of England through the nineteenth century. R. W. Church, in his sermon on Butler (1880), judged that 'this great book, with the sermons which illustrate it, has had perhaps, directly or indirectly, more to do with the shaping of the strongest religious and moral thought in England, in the generation which is now passing away, than the writings of anyone who can be named' (*Pascal*, p. 25).

In the postcript to the third edition of his sermon on apostolical tradition, Keble attempted to reply to those critics of the sermon who saw it as a flirtation with unprotestant and unanglican notions of the infallibility of the church. Reiterating Hooker and Butler, Keble insisted that probable assent not demonstrative proof remained our guide (p. 82).

After Keble, the most redoubtable defender of the Butlerian doctrine of probability in the nineteenth century was W. E. Gladstone. Gladstone had a lifelong devotion to Butler's thought and produced an edition of his work, together with subsidiary studies. At the end of his life (1896) Gladstone claimed that though the argument of Butler's *Analogy* retained its validity, its method was more important still. 'To know what kinds and degrees of evidence to expect or to ask in matters of belief and conduct,' Gladstone wrote, perhaps unconsciously echoing Locke, 'and to be in possession of an habitual presence of mind built upon that knowledge, is, in my view, the master gift which the works of Butler are calculated to impart' (*Studies*, pp. 1, 5f). Probability is the guide, Gladstone asserts (and here it is the veteran politician speaking, deeply initiated in the art of the possible) not only of belief but also of conduct and action. The providential law of our existence in this world is 'the law not of perfection but of sufficiency'. Though offensive to human pride (we cannot help recalling Gladstone's verdict, back in the mid 1840s, on the mixture of motives that led Newman to renounce the church of his baptism), probability is the divinely appointed law of life (pp. 7f, 10f).

The same principle, of sufficiency not perfection, informs Gladstone's assessment of biblical criticism in that other work of his great old age *The Impregnable Rock of Holy Scripture*:

> We are bound by the rule of reason to look for the same method of procedure in this great matter of a written provision of divine knowledge for our needs, as in the other points of the manifold dispensation under which providence has placed us. Now the method or principle is one of sufficiency, not of perfection; of sufficiency for the attainment of practical ends, not of conformity to ideal standards (p. 9).

In an essay of 1879, 'Probability as the Guide of Life', Gladstone defines probability thus: 'Probability may be predicated whenever, in answer to the question whether a particular proposition be true, the affirmative chances predominate over the negative, yet not so as (virtually) to exclude doubt' (*Studies*, p. 338). Gladstone perceptively brings out the connection between objective certainty (infallibility or inerrancy) and subjective certainty (certitude as a state of mind) – and what he says is a tacit commentary both on Newman's development in the 1840s and on the Vatican decree on papal infallibility of 1870. 'Even if a demonstration intrinsically perfect were presented to us,' Gladstone points out, 'the possibility of error would still exist in the one link remaining; namely, that subjective process of our faculties by which it has to be appropriated.' Probability could never, therefore, be circumvented except by the gift of 'inerrability' made to the individual mind (pp. 343f). Here Gladstone uncovers the inevitable logical progression that leads from a propositional understanding of revelation to the need for a (propositionally) infallible guide within the church. Newman had brought out the logic of this in his essay on development: Gladstone may be implying that it was inconsistent of Newman to oppose the promulgation of the dogma of papal infallibility in 1870.

In a note added to the earlier essay in 1896, Gladstone acknowledges the risks entailed in Butler's method for those who are either not clever or holy enough (Butler's deists?) or perhaps both too clever by half and holy overmuch (Newman?). Alluding to Pitt's comment that Butler's work suggested more doubts than it solved, Gladstone declares:

> No other work, written to promote belief, had then, or within my knowledge has now, been written, which before answering objections, brings them so fully and clearly into view ... The man who first propounded and brought home the idea that the system under which the world is governed is not ideally perfect, spoke, without doubt, a formidable word (p. 370)

In *The Prophetical Office*, Newman is still working with Butler's probabilistic assumptions, though racking them to breaking point. 'We for our part,' he confesses – and here he is speaking not merely in the impersonal first person but for Anglicanism and the Tractarians – 'have been taught to consider that in its degree faith, as well as conduct, must be guided by probabilities, and that doubt is ever our portion in this life' (*Via Media*, p. 128). In the essay on development, however, Newman is arguing remorselessly for an infallible defining authority in the church. He withdraws his earlier objection to infallibility – namely that it can never be more than probable that infallibility is granted. Newman's argument in the essay is classically Butlerian – inductive, cumulative and probabilistic – but he is using it to establish very unbutlerian conclusions. Newman writes:

> In proportion to the probability of true developments of doctrine and practice in the divine scheme, is the probability also of the appointment in that scheme of an external authority to decide upon them, thereby separating them from the mass of mere human speculation, extravagance, corruption, and error, in and out of which they grow (*Dev.*, p. 168).

This incidentally reveals that in Newman's ultimate perspective the so-called tests of true development are not only inadequate but superfluous: only an infallible authority can discriminate with certainty the true from the spurious.

Newman recalls his objection in *The Prophetical Office* that 'as all religious knowledge rests on moral evidence, not on demonstration, our belief in the church's infallibility must be of this character; but what can be more absurd than a probable infallibility, or a certainty resting on doubt?' How are individuals to know with certainty that Rome is infallible? What can '"bring home to the mind infallibly that she is infallible; what conceivable proof amounts to more than a probability of the fact; and what advantage is an infallible guide, if those who are to be guided have, after all, no more than an opinion ... that she is infallible?"' (*Dev.*, p. 169).

Newman's answer is twofold. First, there is nothing exceptional about infallibility that does not apply equally to all our other language about degrees of certainty: 'Why is it more inconsistent to speak of an uncertain infallibility than of a doubtful truth?' However, this is merely arguing *ad hominem*, for Newman was certainly not interested in an 'uncertain infallibility': he wanted a practical certainty. In the *Grammar of Assent* (1870) he spoke of 'probabilities founded on certainties' (pp. 239ff). Second, the objection counts against the infallibility of the Bible as much as against the infallibility of the pope (ib., p. 170). This second reply was effective then, but is hollow now that the infallibility of scripture (in the sense of inerrancy, which is what Newman meant) has been given up.

The objection of classical Anglicanism – of Hooker, Locke, Butler, Keble and Gladstone – to infallibility is one that Newman skates over. He alludes to it only to state it thus: 'Such a dispensation would destroy our probation, as dissipating doubt, precluding the exercise of faith, and obliging us to obey whether we wish it or no' (p. 170). But this is not the classical Anglican objection. That objection is surely that infallibility is out of keeping with all we know of the Christian economy; that it destroys the sacramental principle by predicating divine attributes of a human, created reality (just as docetism in Christology and transubstantiation in sacramental doctrine do); and that it is a speculative not a practical truth (as Newman revealingly put it: if 'the preponderating force of antecedent probability . . . is great, it almost supersedes evidence altogether': *Dev.* p. 179).

Newman's appreciation of these considerations was perhaps hampered by his emphasis on divine revelation as the communication of truths in propositional form (even if ultimately 'not of words'), of faith as assent and of 'the essence of all religion' as 'authority and obedience' (ib., p. 173). For Keble and the continuing Anglicans of the Oxford movement, on the other hand, authority and obedience, though certainly of the essence of Christianity, were interpreted in practical, not speculative terms – as prayer and fasting, patience in affliction, following the light we have, submitting personal preferences to the common good, and not dwelling on one's own rights, deserts and satisfactions. They detected a failure of these modest qualities in Newman; they saw him as headstrong, self-indulgent, and self-assertive – a maverick theologian. Their refusal to follow Newman in the matter of infallibility exhibited a well tried and distinctive view of the dispensation in which we are called to make our pilgrimage, walking by faith not by sight (see further, Avis, *Ecum.Theol.*, pp. 54–9).

The Voice of the Laity
At the accession of Elizabeth I, bishop Bonner presented to the queen, on behalf of the convocation of Canterbury, six resolutions: of these the fifth

specifically denied the right of the laity to handle or define matters touching the faith, sacraments and discipline of the church. It was the swansong of unreformed clericalism. The Elizabethan settlement of religion established a significant role for the laity in the Church of England. Elton called it 'the triumph of the laity'. The Anglican church which emerged from the vicissitudes of the sixteenth century was a lay Christian's church in which, provided outward conformity was satisfied, a large area of private opinion and practice remained free.

We have noted the rise of a lay voice in the theological ferment of the seventeeth century. But the laity really came into their own in the eighteenth. As Norman Sykes has written:

> The eighteenth century witnessed a steady and progressive laicisation of religion . . . Hostile critics have preferred to describe the process as the secularisation of the church; but it may be contended that the laicisation of religion is a more accurate phrase; for albeit the clerical order generally was characterised by a markedly unprofessional temper, the laity not only deemed themselves a proper and necessary part of the organisation of the Christian church, but acted upon that persuasion with vigour and conviction (*Church and State*, p. 379).

Geoffrey Best has delightfully characterised the affinity of educated clergy and laity in this period:

> The clergyman, unless he were seriously affected by evangelicalism, could farm, shoot and fish like his lay neighbours and relations. If he could afford it he took his family to London in the season, or to one of the spas. He married and begat children and shared with his lay contemporaries that sacred regard for the promotion of family interests which marked the generations of Walpole and the Pitts. He found his sons jobs in the church or out of it, as seemed most promising (p. 48).

At the end of the century Edmund Burke reiterated Hooker's doctrine of the single Christian commonwealth in which church and state, or clergy and laity comprised the two parts. (While for Hooker the sovereign was a third component, overarching both, for Burke the sovereign would presumably have been included among the laity.) Burke disliked the talk of an alliance of church and state that Warburton had made famous in 1736. 'An alliance between church and state in a Christian commonwealth,' Burke denounced as 'an idle and fanciful speculation,' for 'an alliance is between two things that are in their nature distinct and independent . . . But in a Christian commonwealth the church and the state are one and the same thing, being different integral parts of the same whole. For the church has always been divided into two parts, the clergy and the laity; of which the laity is as much an essential, integral part, and has as much its duties and privileges, as the clerical member; and in the rule, order and government of the church has its share' (c. N. Sykes, op.cit.).

This division of powers within the one Christian commonwealth was respected in the fact that no ecclesiastical ordinances could be binding on the laity without receiving the approval of parliament (ib., p. 380).

It was a characteristic of the high church movement of the eighteenth century, culminating in the Oxford movement, to seek to curtail or repress the role of the laity – so vigorously insisted upon by Hooker – in the government of the church. Before lay synodical representation as a result of the Enabling Act of 1919, this naturally took the form of an attack on the competence of parliament. ''Tis a little too much to suppose country gentlemen, merchants or lawyers to be nicely skilled in the languages of the Bible, masters of all the learning of the fathers, or the history of the primitive church' commented Francis Atterbury pointedly in his campaign for the rights of convocation (c. N. Sykes, *op.cit.*, p. 378). (The point was a little disingenuous, for how many of the clergy could meet all these qualifications?) We have seen how the Tractarians were consistently opposed to allowing the laity a voice in the government of the church. 'For Froude, no layman, then or now, ought to interfere in the affairs of holy church' (Rowlands, diss., p. 119). Gladstone showed his independence of the Oxford spirit in encouraging bishop Selwyn of New Zealand to involve the laity in his proposed synods. When the Church of England was seeking a degree of autonomy through the 'Life and Liberty' movement led by William Temple, it was Charles Gore who (unsuccessfully) fought for confirmation rather than merely baptism as the qualification for the lay franchise. Gore's aim was a gathered, pure church, a *societas perfecta*, and he would have achieved this by tighter doctrinal discipline over the clergy, including university teachers, and by restricting participation in the oversight of the church to the dedicated inner group. His vision was of a church modelled on the Twelve rather than the Seventy.

Others perceived this as charting the church's course in an essentially sectarian direction. Outstanding among the champions of the national, reformed and lay character of the Church of England was Herbert Hensley Henson. No mean church historian, Henson pointed out that the English Reformation was 'a national work in which the laity took their full share' and that then 'the broad principle of the layman's religious competence for the task of ecclesiastical reform was firmly established' (*Church and Parson*, pp. 41f; cf. *Anglicanism*, p. 36). The point for which Henson was contending has been well put recently by Lord Dacre:

> The church is the congregation of the faithful, clergy and laity alike, and it includes many who loyally adhere without pedantically subscribing . . . An established church has a particular duty towards the laity: a duty of tolerance and comprehension. The laity is not to be dragged unwillingly towards a particular road by a party of activists exploiting their customary loyalty and deference (c. Frank Field in Moyser, ed., p. 65).

Those of us in the Church of England who continue to defend parliamentary and crown involvement in the government of the church, including the appointment of bishops, as a salutary check on ecclesiastical 'bandwagoning' and the machinations of synodical activists and caucuses, draw satisfaction from the evident fact that the laity will never allow the principle of establishment to be decisively overthrown. The ultimate influence of Hooker, Burke and Gladstone shines through in the affirmation of Lambeth 1968 that recommended that 'no major issue in the life of the church should be decided without the full participation of the laity in discussion and decision.'

Stephen Sykes has recently asserted: 'The strength of Anglicanism lies, I believe, in its practical grasp of the principle that the laity have an authority of their own by means of their comprehending participation in the public worship of the church' (Bryant, ed., p. 189). The reference to 'comprehending participation' points us back to the Reformation principles of a vernacular liturgy and the universal priesthood: the liturgy is performed by the whole people of God, not by a priestly caste acting in the place of a spiritually unqualified laity. In practice, however, the suggestion that the congregation really do understand the meaning of all that they are saying and doing in the liturgy might raise a cynical smile from the hard-pressed parish clergy. But that is by no means to dismiss the point that Sykes is making: the laity may be said (to adapt terminology used by Coleridge and Polanyi) to comprehend more than they actually understand. As I have written elsewhere: 'The faith of most Christian people today – no less than in earlier ages of semi-literacy – is instinctive, intuitive, unthought-out and unarticulated. It is sustained by richness of imagery and association, by a sense of mystery and unexplored depths conveyed by the gospel story, the liturgy and Christian hymnody' (*Ecum.Theol.*, p. 127). The faithful do have what Newman called an 'illative sense', an instinct for the truth, though it is truth expressed in symbolic rather than propositional form and is compatible with a good deal of superstition, prejudice, blind conservatism and downright ignorance. In his work *On Consulting the Faithful*, Newman spoke of the laity's *sensus fidei*, which Owen Chadwick interprets as 'that profound understanding, hardly expressed in words, which is the church's immediate apprehension of the Christian way of life' (*Newman*, p. 42; see further, Avis, *Ecum.Theol.*, pp. 66ff).

A church that maintains what Newman called 'the dogmatic principle' and understands itself as a *societas perfecta*, endowed by divine right with the power to make laws of doctrine and discipline and to enforce them, will be reluctant to give the laity their full place and to acknowledge the doctrine of the universal priesthood, for the simple reason that the laity are not subject to discipline as the clergy are. Similarly, there will be resistance to opening up a celibate male priesthood to married men and to women, married or unmarried, for the more the clergy have in common with the laity, the more the concept of the universal priesthood seems an appropriate account of the ministry, and the more restricted the church's disciplinary power becomes. As Congar has pointed out (*Lay People in the Church*, p. 12), such an ecclesiology tends to see the church actualised in 'a priesthood without people', while at the opposite extreme the Reformation concept of the church as 'a congregation of faithful men' tends to see it as 'a people without a priesthood'. Anglicanism reveals once again its independence of both Tridentine Roman Catholicism and naked protestantism in its consentient concept of representative or ministerial priesthood, combining the threefold ministry with the doctrine of the universal priesthood – to adapt Congar's terms, a priesthood in the midst of a people.

The Authority of Scholarship

Mandell Creighton, historian of the papacy and bishop of London at the turn of the century, laid down that 'the formula which most explains the position of the Church of England is that it rests on an appeal to sound learning' (*Church & Nation*, p. 251). The reformed English church that emerged from the sixteenth century was the product of the New Learning of the Renaissance: the contribution of Christian humanism was more openly received in England than elsewhere (*Historical Lectures*, p. 150). The Church of England encouraged the pure, disinterested pursuit of truth. It gave sanctuary to 'the devout scholar . . . who reverenced liberty, who believed in progressive enlightenment, who longed for an intelligent order of things' (ib., p. 176). In the jubilee years of queen Victoria, Creighton looked back on several centuries of spreading enlightenment, intellectual progress and tolerance – in other words, he allowed himself to become the mouthpiece of what Herbert Butterfield has taught us all to call the Whig interpretation of history. But Creighton has a point. As archbishop Garbett claimed, 'Alone among the ancient churches, the Church of England has consistently made this appeal to sound learning' (pp. 25f). R. W. Church not only endorsed this interpretation but embodied it. In his essay on Lancelot Andrewes, he showed how historical learning and a sophistication of culture were added in the seventeenth century to the Reformation appeal to scripture and the primitive church (*Pascal*, pp. 52ff).

This rosy picture obviously needs to be heavily qualified. As Henson pointed out, 'something very different from a zeal for sound learning covered England with ruined monasteries, raised no less than three revolts, and added to our national history a long list of judicial murders . . . Neither sound learning nor a zeal for true religion swayed the Tudor sovereigns, but their personal predilections and the cold sagacity of their cynical statecraft' (*C. of E.*, pp. 58f). The operative principle in the formation of the Anglican ideology, according to Henson, was not merely the appeal to learning, but the critical application of it that blunted the edge of all forms of absolutism, whether divine right papalism, the puritans' totalitarian biblicism, or the erastian control of the church that Henry and Elizabeth, if unchecked, would have undoubtedly imposed.

> The principle of the English Reformation was not so much sound learning as such – for every Christian apologist claimed for his own church the support of sound learning – but a frank acceptance of sound learning as competent to revise the current tradition, both in interpreting afresh the sacred text, and by certifying through independent research the true verdict of Christian antiquity (ib., p. 59).

Anglicanism acknowledges the authority of scholarship: this qualifies its reformed catholicism as a *liberal* reformed catholicism. At its best this liberalism, or better, liberality, implies no casual attitude to Christian truth. It is not the same as Newman's 'liberalism' that reduced all dogma to mere opinion. It has a strong moral dimension: Anglicanism is committed to the pursuit of truth and not to the blind defence of traditional positions. It appears to follow that no reasonable question, however disconcerting, is out of order in the church's theological explorations. The debates surrounding *Essays and Reviews* (1860), *Lux Mundi* (1889), *Foundations* (1912) and Anglican 'modernism' may not have been conclusive as far as the contested questions of Christian belief are concerned, but they surely established one thing: this is modern Anglicanism and it is consistent with the claims of the sixteenth and seventeenth centuries for the competence of scholarship to modify tradition. Anglicanism is, and always has been hospitable to rigorous theological enquiry. It attempts the bold experiment of combining the traditional disciplines of personal piety, parish worship, and credal orthodoxy with the most radical questioning in pursuit of the truth. Anglicanism is committed to what Jeremy Taylor called 'the liberty of prophesying' (see further, Avis, 'The Church's One Foundation').

One of the most deplorable examples of the failure of sound learning, objective scholarship and self-criticism was the extreme Tractarians' interpretation of the Reformation and the new direction that it charted for Anglican ecclesiology. In my view, it is vital for the recovery of Anglican theological equilibrium and moral integrity that this influential aberration should be exposed and corrected. It is sometimes suggested that one of the persistent strengths of Anglicanism is its historical sense: it may have been weak in systematic theology, but at least it was able to capitalise on the achievements of the historical movement in the late Enlightenment and the nineteenth century. Alas, this cannot be said of the more extreme Tractarians. For Newman and Pusey in particular all forms of relativism were satanic delusions. Faithful to their 'dogmatic principle' the Tractarians operated with a medieval 'textual' notion of authority. The fathers had spoken; the case was closed.

The response of Tractarians and liberal Anglicans to their encounter with the Reformation was decided by more than simply theological or ecclesiastical factors. It reflected also the convergence or collision of strong ideological currents, including romanticism, liberalism and – most importantly – the historical movement, with its method of documentary analysis combined with attention to underlying social factors and its stress on historical empathy and imaginative reconstruction. While all periods of history received far-reaching reinterpretation as the historical movement ran its course, none so lent itself to historical partisanship and polemical bias as the Reformation. Macaulay commented that 'No portion of our annals has been more perplexed and misrepresented by writers of different parties than the history of the Reformation.'

This situation was not remedied all at once by acceptance of scientific historical method – ecclesiastical histories remained controversy in disguise – and two dominant views of the Reformation, the Tractarian and the liberal Anglican, contended for acceptance in the first half of the nineteenth century. Both sides of the argument were informed by romanticism with its changed feeling for the past. Newman was as much of a romantic as Arnold or Coleridge. Coleridge and Maurice reverenced the past, valued continuity and treasured tradition as much as Newman, Keble or Pusey. They were all disciples of Sir Walter Scott. Yet they arrived at totally opposed assessments of a crucial period in the formation of the English tradition, the protestant Reformation.

This intriguing situation is what gives the present study what significance it has in the broad history of ideas, as distinct from ecclesiastical history. To resolve it demands further research into the Tractarian and liberal Anglican philosophies of history. The evidence seems to suggest that it will not do to bracket Tractarians and liberal Anglicans together as 'romantics'. The concept of romanticism needs differentiation. As far as its historical aspect is concerned, romanticism can be somewhat crudely distinguished into what might be called 'pageant of the past' romanticism and philosophical romanticism. Broadly speaking, the Tractarians belong to the former; the liberal Anglicans to the latter; Newman is a special case and requires separate assessment.

Following their master, Sir Walter Scott, the Tractarians were touched with a deep feeling for the past, but it was for the changing pattern on the surface of human history, the social pageant of a romanticised middle ages and the patristic period of Christianity. They were not cured of anachronistic habits of thinking. They could not resist transporting themselves back in time to observe with distaste the uncouth antics of sixteenth-century Germans. Nor did they fail to imagine how things would have fared if Cranmer and Jewel had carried on their struggle in nineteenth-century Oxford. With an extraordinary historical naïvete they identified Oxford contemporaries, like Bulteel, with various Reformers. Froude seems to be asking himself how Keble would have taken to Jewel if introduced to him in an Oxford senior common room. The Tractarian appraisal of the Reformation was chronically lacking in historical perspective.

The liberal Anglicans were not above reproach in this respect. They too glamourised the past: the Reformers to them were larger than life heroic figures battling against the tide of darkness and ignorance. Arnold in particular is not above making anachronistic comparisons, but at least when he does so it is usually with the intention of inducing a sort of historical vertigo: to be confronted with the Tractarian programme, he suggested, was like a sudden visitation of the Black Death after a cessation of many centuries. It was an attempt to immerse the enlightened, liberal, progressive nineteenth century in the dark ages once again.

The liberal Anglicans were, as much as the Tractarians, disciples of Sir Walter Scott. But Scott's influence on them was disciplined and informed by the sophisticated philosophy of history associated with Giambattista Vico (d. 1744; see further Avis, *FMHT*), Herder and Niebuhr. They transcended mere pageant-of-the-past romanticism with a scheme of historical development in which the Reformation figured significantly as representing the maturity of the European nation-states. As Duncan Forbes has shown, they possessed

> a fully fledged philosophy of civilisation, according to which all nations go through cycles of progress according to the law of their nature, passing inevitably from childhood to manhood and old age, from bondage, intellectual, moral and social, to independence, from credulity to incredulity, from feeling to reflection, from imaginative states, dimly mental, in the bosom of nature, through stages of intellectual clarity and vigour, to the final scepticism and barren theorising, the second barbarism, of late periods (p. 38).

It is precisely this philosophical conception of an unfolding pattern in the life of nations that gave the liberal Anglicans their superior historical grasp, preserved them from the sort of crass anachronisms perpetrated by the Tractarians and gave them a just appreciation of the Reformation as a crisis in European civilisation, an awakening, a new birth, that it was futile to hope to reverse after three hundred years.

Among the liberal Anglicans, Thomas Arnold is notable for a philosophy of history that echoes Vico and anticipates Collingwood in its vision of historical method as an attempt to put oneself in the place of those who have gone before, thinking their thoughts and seeing things as they saw them. Not that he and the others are not more than a little tinged with what Herbert Butterfield has stigmatised as the Whig interpretation of history – an interpretation that treats one's own standpoint as history's ultimate destination and contrives to see all things conspiring together to lead up to it. They were Victorians after all.

On this approach Butterfield has pronounced judgement. True historical understanding, he reminds us, is not achieved by subordinating the past to the present, but rather by 'making the past our present', by trying to see with the eyes of another century than our own.

> It is not reached by assuming that our own age is the absolute to which Luther and Calvin and their generation are only relative; it is only reached by fully accepting the fact that their generation was as valid as our generation, their issues as momentous as our issues, and their day as full and vital to them as our day is to us (pp. 20f).

Benefit of hindsight is both the supreme privilege and the strongest temptation of the historian. To consciously exclude it from his thoughts as he exercises his craft is perhaps the hardest discipline. As G. M. Trevelyan has put it, the historian has to strip himself of the knowledge of what came after; to think, for example, of the men and problems of the first session of the Long Parliament in ignorance of the Grand Remonstrance and the Civil War; to see the problems of past generations as they appeared to them ('Bias', p. 77).

As far as the Reformation is concerned, these considerations drastically curtail the polemical significance of the assumptions, beliefs and decisions of the sixteenth century. As Butterfield has written,

> We can never assert that history has proved any man right in the long run. We can never say that the ultimate issue, the succeeding course of events or the lapse of time have proved that Luther was right against the pope or that Pitt was wrong against Charles James Fox. We cannot say that the ultimate consequences of Luther's action have justified his purpose or his conduct . . . (p. 58).

It would be as though, dropping a pebble into a pond, we were to try to follow the ever-widening ripples from the pond into the stream, the stream into the river and the river into the sea.

Sound historical method, as Butterfield puts it, recognises that the struggle between protestants and catholics in the sixteenth century was an issue of their world, not of our world. The only safe way is 'to count protestants and catholics of the sixteenth century as distinct and strange people – as they really were – whose quarrels are as unrelated to ourselves as the factions of Blues and Greens in ancient Constantinople' (pp. 33f).

Of course there is continuity too. *We* may be protestants or catholics; we may belong to a tradition that embodies a corporate memory and that memory may be very long indeed. We may see ourselves as standing in the succession of the Tractarians or the broad churchmen. But though the words and slogans of past battles may still reverberate today, their meaning has subtly changed. Does justification by faith mean the same *existentially* today when what primarily concerns us whether there *is* a God who will justify, when guilt before a holy God has been eclipsed by a sense of alienation from the transcendent source of our being? Does the supreme authority of scripture mean the same to us as it did to them, when critical study has transformed the way we understand the Bible?

The liberal Anglicans were among the first to become aware of these changes in our intellectual horizons. That is perhaps why they seem to stand up to Butterfield's strictures better than the Tractarians who shut their eyes to them. These reflections on the philosophy of history certainly undermine much of what the Tractarians had to say about the Reformation. And even the liberal Anglicans do not emerge unscathed. That is why it is salutary to be reminded that their struggle too was primarily 'an issue of their world not of our world'.

In its later stages the catholic movement in the Church of England swung back into equilibrium, recovering scholarly objectivity and in particular a sound historical sense. Against Tractarian excesses, R. W. Church insisted that Anglicanism appealed to 'reality, history and experience' (*Oxford Movement*, p. 346). The volume *Lux Mundi* edited by Charles Gore in 1889 was an attempt 'to put the catholic faith into its right relation to modern intellectual and moral problems' – 'to the modern growth of knowledge, scientific, historical, critical' (pp. vii, x). Gore's own distinctive method in his great works of apologetic, culminating in *The Reconstruction of Belief* trilogy, was ostensibly objective, inductive and critical, with the historical method dominant. In the symposium *Foundations* (1912), A. E. J. Rawlinson redefined authority inductively and historically as the corporate witness of the saints to the validity of their spiritual experience (p. 378). And in *Essays Catholic and Critical* (1926) Rawlinson wrote: 'The final appeal is to the spiritual, intellectual and historical content of divine revelation, as verifiable at the threefold bar of history, reason and spiritual experience' (p. 95). In his Gifford Lectures *The Faith of a Moralist* (1930), the catholic Anglican philosopher A. E. Taylor spoke of the meaning of authority as comprising a combination of humility and adventurousness. What Taylor calls 'a true humility of soul in the presence of the given' (II, pp. 221, 224), must inevitably acknowledge an authority in scholarship which attempts to describe what is the case.

With regard to the Reformation, however, the powerful momentum set up by Tractarian ignorance and prejudice carried through to the present century. Post-Tractarian Anglicanism was often insular and arrogant with regard to protestant Christianity. A third-generation Tractarian, Charles Gore, for example, echoing the obsession of his mentors in the Oxford movement with episcopacy, claims that 'the root principle of the Reformation on the continent was the repudiation of any necessary succession in the ministry' (*Basis*, p. 33). Little wonder that H. M. Gwatkin could describe the Anglo-catholic version of church history as 'a theory which actually turns the whole course of church history into an edifying romance and, in particular, perversely mis-interprets almost every fact and circumstance which bears on the character of the Reformation of England and elsewhere' (p. 4). However, the romanticism was not all on one side. As Gordon Rupp has written, 'As an antidote to an uncritical acceptance of the tradition of Foxe and Burnet, it was all to the good: the vitriolic essays with which S. R. Maitland castigated the early Reformers must have deflated a good deal of quite unhealthy romanticism. But the rabble of antinomian fanatics, time-serving cowards and perverted heresiarchs of the modern caricature are further from the truth' (*Studies*, p. xiii).

To take a detailed look, as we have done in this book, at the way the Tractarians handled – or mishandled – Reformation history and theology is a salutary exercise. No one can read Tractarian polemic against personalities, whether dead like Luther, or alive like Arnold, without being disturbed by its incongruity with the obtrusive aspirations to truth and holiness with which it is not infrequently juxtaposed. All too often, finding out what the Reformers actually believed and taught seems to be regarded as a dispensable piece of pedantry that ought not to be allowed to cramp the broad sweep of the argument. Even today one still finds it assumed that we need neither bother to work through the Reformers at first hand or to open the great confessional documents – it is enough to dip into the relevant chapter of Troeltsch's *Social Teaching of the Christian Churches* or some other superannuated compendium. In 1932 the Anglican modernist H. D. A. Major assessed contemporary attitudes to the Reformation. 'Today', he wrote, 'Martin Luther, the greatest protagonist of the Reformation, is viewed as a vulgar, violent and mistaken man, as hostile to humanist culture as he was to social democracy. And the Reformation he achieved is regarded as the parent of a malign progeny which shattered the religious unity of western Europe and gave rise to a multitude of "Petulant, capricious sects, the maggots of corrupted texts"' (p. 225).

The free church authors of *The Catholicity of Protestantism* (1950) devoted a large proportion of their space to showing that the Anglo-catholic report *Catholicity*, to which theirs was a response, seriously distorted the teaching of the Reformers. This kind of shadow boxing is not merely a thing of the past. The central thesis of Louis Bouyer's *The Spirit and Forms of Protestantism* (1954) was accepted by E. L. Mascall in his *The Recovery of Unity* and has been reiterated in many of Mascall's subsequent books. The thesis is that, in so far as the Reformers diverged from catholic truth, they knew not what they did: they were merely the stooges of decadent scholasticism. Bouyer writes:

The negative, 'heretical' aspect of the Reformation neither follows from its positive principles, nor is it a necessary consequence of their development or vindication, but appears simply as a survival, within protestantism, of what was most vitiated and corrupt in the catholic thought of the close of the middle ages.

For Mascall, 'by far the most insidious and vicious' of these tendencies was the nominalism that had become dominant in philosophy and theology alike, with its 'barren and spectral extrinsecism'. The immediate theological consequence (as Bouyer, followed by Mascall, asserts) was that, according to Luther, justification makes no real change in a man's inward state (Bouyer, p. 198; Mascall, pp. 91, 25). To be sure, Luther left himself open to misunderstanding on this matter, but to try to conduct an ecumenical *rapprochement* on the basis of an interpretation of the fundamental doctrine of the Reformation, the *articulus stantis aut cadentis ecclesiae*, that no serious student of Luther would accept and that is inapplicable to Calvin in any case, is Quixotic in the extreme. And what is more, the Bouyer-Mascall thesis appears to be a mere tilting at windmills in the light of Gordon Rupp's criticism of it in *Protestant Catholicity*. Rupp attacks the notion that Luther and the other Reformers were imprisoned in the degenerate philosophical system of late medieval nominalism as containing 'major howlers' and as caricaturing the schoolmen. It is dispatched as a 'far-fetched and unscholarly hypothesis' (pp. 42, 45). The revival of Reformation studies in this century calls for a thorough revaluation of the thought of the Reformers. Their indebtedness to the *via antiqua* of Aquinas appears to be significantly greater than has been assumed in the past. The doctrine of natural law is one important area where surprising affinities can be detected between Luther and Aquinas. In any case, it is *prima facie* implausible to claim that, as products of an age of intellectual ferment like the fifteenth century, the Reformers could be definitively interpreted in terms of any one philosophical school.

It is deeply refreshing to turn in contrast to an exponent of Anglicanism who, while standing in the tradition of Newman and Gore, nevertheless brings a profound sympathy and insight to the study of the Reformation. In *The Gospel and the Catholic Church* (1936), Michael Ramsey set a new standard for Anglican engagement with the Reformation tradition. Luther's challenge, 'The true treasure of the church is the holy gospel of the glory and the grace of God' from the Ninety-five Theses of 1517, provides Michael Ramsey's essay in ecclesiology with a text and a refrain. In words that subvert all ecclesiastical party prejudice, he proclaims, *Catholicism always stands before the church door at Wittenberg to read the truth by which she is created and by which also she is judged* (p. 180, my emphasis).

In his work *Anglicanism in Ecumenical Perspective* (1962), the Roman Catholic (and former Anglican) H. W. Van de Pol called for urgent clarification of the Anglican attitude and relation to the Reformation.

Criticising the pronouncements of the Lambeth conferences hitherto for vague and ambiguous generalities, he insisted, 'What is needed is a complete and detailed clarification regarding the standpoint of doctrine and the real nature of the churches of the Anglican Communion' (p. 107). It is my hope that the resources provided in this book will assist the process of scholarly research and theological evaluation rightly desiderated by Van de Pol.

18

Towards an Authentic Paradigm for Anglicanism

The picture of Anglicanism that has emerged during the course of this survey is first and foremost of a communion that knows itself to be a branch of the Christian church. The Anglican church did not come into existence at the Reformation. What happened then was that an ancient church, with origins in the Celtic twilight, one that had had its delegates at early councils of the church catholic, reformed abuses and liberated itself from an oppressive foreign jurisdiction. It did so at the price of accepting 'state' interference and the ascendancy of lay rule – embodied in the sovereign – within the Christian commonwealth. The history of the Church of England needs to be construed under the 'erastian paradigm' until the Oxford movement. But when we speak of erastianism, we need to remember several qualifying factors.

(a) The term 'erastianism', while a useful catchphrase for a certain easily recognisable ecclesiological type, is technically inaccurate. It neither describes the doctrine of Erastus (Thomas Liebler) himself, nor the views of the sixteenth-century Reformers. For both these, however, the doctrine of magisterial responsibility within the church was intended as a safeguard against ecclesiastical tyranny: for Erastus, against the church's imposition of persecutory civil sanctions in excommunication; for the Reformers, against the heavy hand of Rome (see Avis, *CTR*, pp. 142ff).

(b) Any division into church and state in the formative period of Anglicanism is anachronistic. For the Reformers there was one Christian commonwealth, divided into clergy and laity, with the godly prince a sort of *tertium quid*, a sacred lay person. Provided he did not attempt to lay hands, so to speak, on the sacramental functions of the clergy, his ecclesiastical jurisdiction was no incursion into prohibited territory, but the proper exercise of his responsibilities for the welfare of all his subjects, clergy and laity alike.

(c) It is not clear to what extent the involvement of 'the state' in ecclesiastical affairs, exceeded that of medieval European monarchs from Constantine onwards, English kings before the Reformation, and modern governments operating under concordats with the Vatican. The erastian paradigm was not a product of the Reformation but was endemic both before and since and is intrinsic to the concept of Christendom. The history of Europe is the history of the rivalry, the power struggles, between kings and popes.

The Church of England was confident of its ecclesial integrity, its episcopal pedigree and its canonical competence. It was proud of its independence and confident of its theological position. The Act of Appeals of 1533 asserted that the English church 'always hath been reputed, and also found of that sort, that both for knowledge, integrity and sufficiency of number, it hath been always thought, and is also at this hour, sufficient and meet of itself without the intermeddling of any exterior person or persons, to declare and determine all such doubts, and to administer all such offices and duties as to their rooms spiritual doth appertain'. In his correspondence with divines of the Gallican church in the eighteenth century, archbishop William Wake refused to be dictated to or to have the Church of England treated on less than equal terms. The high church bishop of Exeter Sir Jonathan Trelawny, at his visitation in 1699 defended the integrity of the Anglican church against both protestant dissent and Roman imperialism:

> Our church is often compared to an isthmus between two great seas upon which the fury of both is constantly breaking. Then, surely, it ought to be our care to support the bounds; that neither the daily washing of either seas sap them, nor the violentest storms break through and force them. It may indeed, without vanity be owned that, on either hand, we have lost no ground; that as our first Reformers began the dispute successfully, so it has been continued, with the same good fortune, to this day, by answering our enemies in all things but slander and malice, in which they are both insuperable.

The mainstream Oxford movement, from Keble and Pusey to Gladstone, Church and Gore, far from calling in question the validity and integrity of the Church of England as a branch of the catholic church, upheld her integrity, independence and authority. When pope Leo XIII condemned Anglican orders as 'absolutely null and utterly void' in the bull *Apostolicae curae* in 1896, the archbishops of Canterbury and York acted in the spirit of their predecessors such as Laud and Wake in making a dignified, learned and crushing 'Responsio'. Regrettably, it cannot be said that more recent Anglican spokesmen have always maintained the standing ground of their church equally faithfully (see Avis, *Ecum.Theol.*).

The Reformers insisted on the right and duty of a 'particular' – by which they meant national – church to reform itself. That right and duty still stands. Anglicanism does not need to be constantly looking over its shoulder. It does not need to take its cue from Rome. Other churches have no veto, even a tacit one, over the Anglican Communion's conscience. Naturally Anglicans would prefer to work in harmony with other churches, but not at the price of one-sided restraints and concessions. Any such accommodation should be reciprocal.

Catholicity is not a quantitative concept. Newman and Gladstone were in the numbers game: they calculated the respective adherents of Roman Catholicism and Anglicanism. Newman conveniently left the Eastern churches out of account; Gladstone did not. But surely that is the wrong approach. There are two thousand Christian communions in the world: doubtless each has its own integrity after a fashion and each can appeal to the dominical promise, 'Where two or three are gathered together in my name, there I am in the midst'. Each must learn to regard the others as genuine expressions, albeit with limitations due to history, culture and other circumstances, of the mystical body of Christ. We need to work for greater mutual understanding in the context of total mutual acceptance on the basis of our baptism into Christ. This is the key to finding a new paradigm for Anglicanism, and indeed for ecumenical Christianity.

Christian identity is dependent on cultural norms. It settles into the shape determined by the available ideological receptacles. Christian identity is moulded not by pure theology, for there is no such thing, but by the assumptions, needs and demands of time and circumstance. In the medieval period, Christian or ecclesial identity took the mould of the relics of the Roman empire, to become a holy empire united, at least superficially and ostensibly, by allegiance to emperor and pope. In the sixteenth century, ecclesial identity was shaped to the demands of the emerging nation states. Particular churches were national churches. In the nineteenth century, ecclesial identity naturally flowed into the channels created by worldwide imperial power. Particular churches were provinces of the church catholic in its various branches. The historio-geographical situation was ripe for the formation of the Anglican Communion. In the twentieth century our sense of identity is paradoxically both macro-cosmic and microcosmic. The more we become aware of our status as citizens of the global community, the more our national heritage and local identity mean to us. Ours is the age of regional autonomy, devolution, the revival of ancient languages that had become almost extinct, and fierce national feeling on the part of oppressed racial or other groups. In the same way, the age of the ecumenical movement has seen the proliferation of Christian churches, sects and conventicles. The more we become aware of our common identity with Christians of other traditions, from whom we have been separated by political, geographical, linguistic and other cultural factors as much as by theological differences, the more we feel compelled to defend our own hard won way of living the Christian life together.

The constraints imposed by the need for identity maintenance in all societies are not always acknowledged. Van de Pol predicted a gradual merging of Christian identities in a homogeneous world church:

> The growth of Christian unification is . . . a process in which all churches individually and together grow in catholicity; in other words, a process in which they gradually embrace and express even more clearly and universally the whole fulness of Christ. All churches have fallen into one-sidedness and excesses in one or more theological, liturgical and spiritual aspects by a too exclusive emphasis on particular truths and values. By meeting one another and openness towards the contributions of others, the churches will assimilate and manifest externally in an ever wider, fuller and richer manner, all that Christ is and signifies. They will thereby become more and more alike; they will come closer to one another and become more conscious of their connection and communion. The more catholic a church becomes, the more ecumenical will be its thought and activity; and the more ecumenical a church's thought and activity, the more catholic it will appear to be (p. 237).

Van de Pol's vision of the ultimate fusion of cloned churches would spell the death of Christianity in the modern world which is strongly motivated by the quest for identity. Ecumenism surely need not mean that all churches come to resemble each other more and more until they are indistinguishable. An undifferentiated totality would be even more ideologically suspect than the present plurality of distinct communions with their patently defensive boundaries of identity. There must be another way of discovering our solidarity in Christ without sacrificing the identity constituted by our tradition, our time-tested way of being Christians together in a particular community.

The erastian paradigm is dead. In a secular and pluralistic culture there is no nostalgia for it. It never applied to the greater part of the Anglican Communion. The apostolic paradigm is divisive and, moreover, takes an aspect of catholicity for the whole. It makes the life of the whole body dependent on one particular instrument of that life – the ministry. It allows the tail to wag the dog. Newman and Manning found that there was no assurance of apostolicity outside of papal Romanism which recognised no other apostolic succession than the successive occupants of the *cathedra* of St. Peter. The apostolic paradigm presupposes that there is one true church, outside of which is no salvation. It is incompatible with any ecumenical theology. An alternative paradigm would be *baptismal* or *Christological*. To call it Christological might give the impression that the erastian and apostolic paradigms were not fundamentally Christological, when they were. The essential constituent of all genuine ecclesiologies is by definition Christological. So I would prefer to speak of a baptismal paradigm for the church and ecumenism. This has to do with our incorporation into the body of Christ through holy baptism, the faith that is presupposed in baptism and the credal profession that accompanies it. Baptism is the fundamental sacrament of Christianity: 'By one Spirit we were all baptised into one body' (I Corinthians 12: 13). Confirmation appropriates it, the eucharist presupposes it; ordination authorises the expression of the priesthood into which all the baptised are incorporated. Baptism constitutes the ground of our unity – the unity that exists and cries out to be realised in shared holy communion. The erastian and episcopal models have overlaid and concealed the true nature of the church – the fundamental Christological reality – that we are one body through our baptism into Christ. We do not deny one another's baptism; therefore we cannot deny our mutual status in Christ. This is the starting point for a journey of mutual understanding on the basis of unreserved mutual acceptance. We seek to be in communion with those who are already in communion with our Lord.

Anglicanism has never lost the baptismal paradigm; its official formularies and its classical divines have upheld it.

(a) The Reformers contended for the one thing needful, the true treasure of the church, the holy gospel whereby Christ was present with his people through word and sacrament (see Avis, *CTR*, pp. 3ff). Richard Hooker grounded the unity and integrity of the church on the 'one Lord, one faith, one baptism' of Ephesians 4.4ff, the baptismal faith that supernaturally appertained to the very essence of Christianity, as he put it. Building on the Erasmian distinction between things necessary for salvation and things indifferent, such Anglican divines as Hales, Hammond, Taylor, Stillingfleet, Burnet and Wake taught that the fundamentals of the faith required for salvation were also the only proper terms of communion within the church. The union of the catholic church, Stillingfleet perceived, depended on its making 'the foundation of its being to be the ground of its communion'.

(b) F. D. Maurice reiterates this ecclesiological principle when he insists in *The Kingdom of Christ* that 'the language that makes Christ known to us is the only language which can fitly make the church known to us' (II, p. 125). To belong to the church is to enter by baptism into a covenant relationship ('an eternal and indissoluble friendship') with God through Christ – a relationship of trust and obedience that it is incumbent upon us at all times to appropriate and to live by. It is our Christian duty to have faith in this baptismal union and to actualise it in every possible way. As we have seen, Maurice brought out the logic of Luther's theology that had grounded justification by faith on the objectivity of the sacrament of baptism: 'You are grafted into Christ; claim your position.' Baptism was the first of the six signs of the Kingdom of Christ, the church, enumerated by Maurice, the others being the creeds, forms of corporate worship, the eucharist, the ministry and scripture. These were the outward, visible manifestations of an inter-personal spiritual reality. The spiritual society did not abrogate and destroy natural channels of relationship and identity, but sanctified them and fulfilled them. Maurice believed that one of the positive principles of the Reformation was its recognition of the validity of national feeling and he linked this to the socio-political pyramid structure that incorporates family and local community into national life. Thus Maurice affirmed the value and identity of the particular components that make up the universal Kingdom of Christ (I, pp. 104, 258–288).

(c) William Reed Huntington's *The Church Idea* (1870), which contributed to the formation of the Chicago-Lambeth Quadrilateral (1886–88), was clearly influenced by Maurice, though he is not mentioned (see Wright, ed., pp. 24, 61–78). Huntington is a scathing critic of the erastian concept of Anglicanism. Anglicanism, he says, conjures up for many 'a flutter of surplices, a vision of village spires and cathedral towers, a somewhat stiff and stately company of deans, prebendaries and choristers'. This is the Anglican system. As a result of imposing the system in a 'take it or leave it' manner, the Church of England has alienated the majority of the English people. The true Anglican principle must be disentangled from the 'cloud of non-essentials'. It will be found to reside in the fourfold commitment to the holy scriptures as the word of God, the primitive creeds as the rule of faith, the dominical sacraments of baptism and the eucharist, and the episcopate as 'the keystone of governmental unity'. These are 'the primitive and catholic standards of unity' and remain the 'absolutely essential features of the Anglican position'. They qualify Anglicanism to become the basis of 'a church of the reconciliation'.

Huntington's fourfold scheme has been adapted and endorsed authoritatively on numerous occasions by both the American Episcopal Church and the whole Anglican Communion through the Lambeth Conferences. It is not of course a complete agenda for ecumenical dialogue: in that respect, Henry Chadwick's remark about the 'jejune theological content' of the Quadrilateral (in Wright, ed., p. 149) is misplaced. But it does constitute a platform of non-negotiable commitments – important for what they leave out as well as for what they include – that should serve as authoritative parameters for Anglicans in ecumenical conversations. The episcopate is insisted on, not in the sense of the apostolic paradigm, as the *sine qua non* of a Christian church, but (as the Lambeth Conference 1920 put it) as 'a ministry acknowledged by every part of the church as possessing not only the inward call of the Spirit, but also the commission of Christ and the authority of the whole body'. It is significant that the Quadrilateral does not have a fifth point on primacy, and in view of the endorsements that the Quadrilateral has received in Anglicanism, this omission presents a problem in the context of contemporary ecumenical engagement. Any attempt to develop a fifth dimension of ecclesial reality under the rubric of primacy is called into question by the Quadrilateral.

But that is not to say that a concept of primacy could not be accommodated within the fourth point of the Quadrilateral, though to achieve that it would have to remain subsumed under the episcopate and thus constrained by the principle *primus inter pares*.

Huntington's programme and the Chicago-Lambeth Quadrilateral based upon it is, like all expressions of the tradition of 'fundamental articles' (see Sykes in Sykes & Booty, ed., pp. 231–245), intentionally reductionist and minimalist. This curtailment of theological commitments is called for not only by the irenic and charitable spirit motivating this tradition, but by the fundamental conceptuality that distinguishes between things necessary and things indifferent (*adiaphora*). It was in keeping with the reconciling approach of this tradition that the Chicago convention of 1886, in adopting the Quadrilateral, expressed itself willing to forego its preferences in all human matters in order to achieve unity. In spite of the problems inherent in the appeal to fundamental articles (brought out by Sykes), it seems essential to pursue this approach as a counterbalance to undialectical notions of consensus. Consensus has been invoked in recent ecumenical discussion, but it is necessary to ask whether this appeal to consensus is compatible with the spiritual and intellectual liberty that modern Anglicanism has defended. As Macquarrie has pointed out, consensus cannot mean everyone thinking alike. 'Not only is that a state of affairs which will never come about; it would also mean the death of theology as a living exploration into truth. Theology is a dialectical science, so that every minority view, yes, even every heretical and schismatic view, has its elements of truth and justification, so that the majority view needs the constant stimulation and correction of the minority view if one is to move along the path that leads to deeper truth. [However] the liberty of pluralism is possible only where it is contained within wide areas of agreement' (p. 191; cf. 132; cf. Avis, *Ecum.Theol.*, ch. 4). It seems to me that the fundamental articles approach (perhaps more familiar to us as the question of the hierarchy of truths or of the essence of Christianity) is still essential to delineate those areas of deep agreement that provide the parameters within which theological argument can take place.

(d) A remarkable attempt to employ the very language that makes Christ known to us as the only language fit to make the church known to us (Maurice) or to make the foundation of the church's existence the ground of its communion (Stillingfleet) was the young Michael Ramsey's *The Gospel and the Catholic Church* (1936). It goes a considerable way towards overcoming the apostolic paradigm that Ramsey inherited from the catholic movement in the Church of England, but in the final analysis it does not go far enough. Ramsey takes Luther's words in the Ninety-five Theses as his text: 'The true treasure of the church is the holy gospel of the glory and grace of God.' He attempts to show, as Maurice had done before him, that the structures of catholicism – sacraments, canon, creed and episcopate – are strictly applications or expressions of the essential gospel. 'The gospel has created them, and in the gospel their meaning is to be found' (p.62). He asks: 'What is the place of this structure in essential Christianity?' and attempts to show that it is 'a development which grew in the gospel and through the gospel and which expresses the gospel and can be belittled only at the expense of the gospel' (p.57).

The course of the argument is predetermined by Ramsey's acceptance of the principle that there can be no abstraction of Christ and the gospel from the church and its structures: 'the only appeal back to Jesus which is logically and spiritually coherent is an appeal to the gospel of God uttered in the one body by its whole structure' (p.66). There is no denying the importance of what this principle stands for: we have no mandate for free-wheeling theological criticism of the church from outside the church. As Ramsey puts it: 'It we would draw near to the naked facts of Calvary and Easter, we can do so only in the one fellowship whose very meaning is death to self' (ib.). It is profoundly true that 'the catholicism . . . which sprang from the gospel of God is a faith wherein the visible and ordered church fills an important place' (ib.), that 'in telling of this one visible society the church's outward order tells indeed of the gospel' (p.50), and that only through the life of the church do we apprehend 'the whole meaning of the death and resurrection of Jesus' (p.180).

But these principles can, by no stretch of the imagination, be made to yield Ramsey's doctrine of apostolicity that insists that 'the structure of catholicism is an utterance of the gospel' (p.54), that episcopacy is 'part of the utterance of God's redemptive love' (p.67), that certain dispensations of grace are confined to bishops (p.83), that 'the episcopate is of the *esse* of the universal church' (p.84), and that 'the orders of protestant bodies are gravely deficient' (p.219). To claim that without the apostolic succession, we cannot have the gospel in its wholeness, is special pleading and smacks of the legitimation of ideology.

As we have abundantly seen in earlier chapters of this book, this is not a position that can claim the support of the founding fathers of the Church of England. Whitgift and Hooker contended precisely against the view of Cartwright and the puritans that a form of church government was contained in the gospel. Cartwright: 'As though matters of discipline and kind of government were not matters necessary to salvation and faith;' 'We offer to shew the discipline to be part of the gospel'; 'I speak of the discipline as of a part of the gospel.' Hooker replies: 'The mixture of those things by speech which by nature are divided, is the mother of all error.' As the puritans distinguish doctrine and discipline, he remarks, so the Church of England distinguishes faith and polity (Hooker, III, ii-iii; Avis, *CTR*, pp.115–127).

Michael Ramsey's profound and persuasive general model of the relation of the gospel and the church does indeed give us a principle of order, of transmitted authority, of apostolicity, but it does not establish, to my mind, that that can be achieved in only one way. It is one thing to say that the episcopate can bear witness to the corporate dimension of the gospel: it is quite another to reverse this and claim that the gospel entails the episcopate. *The Gospel and the Catholic Church*, as we have already noted, sets a new standard for Anglican engagement with Reformation ecclesiology. But the Reformers' notion of the *unum necessarium* did not include episcopacy. The historic episcopate is not of the essence of Christianity and cannot therefore be crucial to the identity of the Christian church. The true treasure is not as bulky as the young Michael Ramsey would have had us believe: more the grain of mustard seed than the spreading oak of catholic Christendom.

(e) It is a remarkable fact that the Lambeth Conferences of the Anglican Communion have succeeded in transcending the limitations of the 'apostolic paradigm'. They have grounded their successive messages to their communion and to the *ecumene* on the reality of the Christological foundation of the church in holy baptism and the baptismal faith. The Lambeth Conference of 1920 addressed its 'appeal to all Christian People' to 'all who believe in our Lord Jesus Christ and have been baptised into the name of the Holy Trinity, as sharing with us membership in the universal church of Christ, which is his body'. The 'Appeal' reached out to non-episcopal churches of the Reformation: 'There are the great non-episcopal communions, standing for rich elements of truth, liberty and life which might otherwise have been obscured or neglected. With them we are closely linked by many affinities, racial, historical and spiritual.' As Van de Pol points out, the Anglican churches have never made a negative declaration on the efficacy of non-episcopal ministries; Anglicanism's insistence on the threefold ministry with the historic succession is practical and not speculative (p. 147).

As so many of the divines treated in this book insisted, the Anglican church's adherence to episcopacy is in the interests of her own catholicity of order – an indispensable house-rule – but it does not imply any adverse judgement on the ministries of other communions. To their own Master they stand or fall. For the Anglican Reformers, episcopacy was ancient and perhaps apostolical, but above all it was the polity ordained by the magistrate, an *adiaphoron*. For Hooker, it was certainly apostolical but belonged to the (theoretically) mutable division of divine positive law and therefore could not be either of the essence of Christianity or the foundation of the church. For the Caroline divines, episcopacy was no longer a thing indifferent: it was apostolic and divine, but not the *sine qua non* of a true church. The ministries of foreign churches were deficient, not invalid. By the time of the Tractarians, the erastian paradigm was collapsing; the apostolic succession seemed all that was left. The Tractarians drew the inferences: apostolic succession was necessary for salvation; non-episcopal churches were no true churches and there was no assurance that salvation was to be obtained in them. More moderate and later high churchmen, such as Gladstone and Gore, felt the untenability of this position. They spoke vaguely of 'uncovenanted mercies'. They recognised that the Holy Spirit was not bound by rubrics. Bishops were the focus of unity, the only basis of unity and (in the young Michael Ramsey) of the essence of Christianity, integral to the gospel – though the later Ramsey came to regard Gore's uncompromising view of episcopacy as too fanatical – but not the only effectual channels of salvation.

However, the practical policy of the Anglican church, in its unity discussions with other churches, has been governed by the apostolic paradigm. The exclusion of the uniting churches of south India during the lengthy process of their assimilation of non-episcopal ministries into an episcopal structure, being the most notorious example (see Lampe). Here the apostolic ministry was allowed to become a fetish rather than a theologically defensible principle of transmitted authority and a focus of unity. It is perhaps this record that has provoked Stephen Sykes to comment that 'Anglicanism as it now exists is founded on an incoherent doctrine of the church and . . . its attempts to resolve or conceal this gross internal antinomy has repeatedly led it into a series of chronic conflicts from which it barely escapes with any integrity' ('Anglicanism and Protestantism', p. 127). It is indeed a tragic mistake to assume that the Anglican theological tradition will only permit *intercommunion* on the basis of episcopal orders. Anglicanism could not compromise on episcopacy as a condition of *structural union*, because the bishop is the *effective symbol* of unity (cf. Norris in Sykes & Booty, ed., pp. 300f). But in its right mind it could never dismiss the sacraments of non-episcopal communions as no sacraments, their ministers as no ministers and their churches as no churches, as the more extreme exponents of the apostolic paradigm did. Anglicanism's pioneering role in the formation of the World Council of Churches, with its quasi-baptismal confession of faith in Christ as God and saviour, shows that it has been committed in precisely the other direction. In its ecumenical discussions and relations with the protestant churches, Anglicanism has allowed itself to be guided by the *baptismal* paradigm. When Van de Pol wrote at the beginning of the 1960s he was able to point out that the Lambeth Conferences had approved agreements on the nature of the Christian ministry or priesthood with the (episcopal) Swedish Lutheran, eastern Orthodox and Old Catholic Churches (p. 144). Since then agreements on the ministry have been concluded between representatives of the Anglican church and non-episcopal Lutherans, Reformed churches, Methodists and others. Are these agreements all compatible? Is Anglicanism being consistent here? If so, is it prepared to act on the basis of these agreements? For inspiration it could do worse than to go back to the Lambeth Conference Appeal of 1920:

> The vision which lies before us is that of a church, genuinely catholic, loyal to all truth, and gathering into its fellowship all 'who profess and call themselves Christians', within whose visible unity all the treasures of faith and order, bequeathed as a heritage by the past to the present, shall be possessed in common, and made serviceable to the whole body of Christ.

The baptismal paradigm of ecclesiology, which is the assumption behind the Lambeth Appeal, may appear to be a formula for a reductionist doctrine of the church. Although it is confessedly a digging down to the foundations, to the bedrock of ecclesial reality, it is certainly not a compromise at the level of the lowest common denominator. The baptismal paradigm, as I understand it, involves a mystical perception of that fundamental ecclesial reality. It is response to the transcendent mystery of the God who may be loved but not thought, as *The Cloud of Unknowing* puts it. It takes that love of God in Christ as the central Christian phenomenon, and doctrines and dogmas as necessary and valid ways of discerning the mystery, provided we never forget that they are human productions, essentially personal and existential statements. The pluralism of belief and practice in world Christianity represents human perceptions of the many-faceted truth of God in Christ, as that is refracted through diverse cultures and life-forms. Where these come into conflict it is neither desirable nor possible for a central authority (magisterium) to pronounce on their authenticity. Instead, through the conflictual process itself – through argument, criticism and attempts to understand one another on the basis of respect and acceptance – beliefs may be refined and agreement perhaps discovered.

As a liberal reformed catholicism, marked by the principles of moderation, comprehensiveness and conservatism, with its dispersed sources of authority acting as mutual checks and balances, Anglicanism is particularly hospitable to this approach. Van de Pol suggested that the more the moderate type of Anglicanism, of the central churchmanship variety, develops, the more the Anglican Communion will grow into a prototype of reunited Christianity and will be recognised as such by other churches (p. 98). I would accept this only with the proviso that the central churchmanship element should be seen, not as driving more peripheral and extreme catholics, evangelicals and liberals out into the cold, but as providing the essential ballast and stability to enable them to continue to flourish and make their contribution to the ongoing debates about Christian belief, the nature of the church, Christian ethics and mission. I do not want to see a dominant liberal consensus, with its purely pragmatic attitude to truth, but genuine tripartite interaction. But this depends on the church learning to contain conflict and to enlarge the bounds of its diversity. We need an acceptance of the principle (inculcated so often by the classical Anglican divines) that there are no theological grounds for breaching communion over an issue, such as the ordination of women to the priesthood or the episcopate, that is not itself a condition of the church's communion. There is no cause for church authorities to suggest that those who are opposed to this reform (as I prefer to see it) might wish to seek a home elsewhere in the Christian church. But on the other hand, it would be retrograde to legislate that only bishops willing to ordain women should be consecrated in the future. The church can surely absorb clashes of conscience provided they do not lead to mutual excommunication. 'Excommunication' is a strong word, but that is exactly what those who break communion with those who are themselves in communion with our Lord – as well as those who stiffen terms of communion or terms of ministry – are engaging in.

As those who have been baptised by one Spirit into one body, our ultimate obligation is to be in communion with one another, otherwise we rend the body of Christ. But the right approach to unity in my view, is not to begin by attempting to reconcile the official doctrines and canonical superstructures of authority of respective churches, by one side accepting more than it ought and the other conceding more than it can deliver. Nor is it to lay such weight on the notion of consensus that minority groups become isolated, prophetic voices silenced, and a dull and lifeless uniformity takes over. In my view, the way ahead is to take the baptismal paradigm as our guide, to liberate the inner dynamic of Christian reality in the church – our incorporation into Christ through baptism by the word and the Holy Spirit – and to ask: What makes us Christians? What constitutes the church? What is essential to Christianity? How do historical determinants and canonical structures stand in relation to that? What is it that is enough to make us Christians and communicants in our own churches? And then to ask the further question: Is not that enough to provide the grounds for intercommunion? And is not intercommunion the only sound ecclesiological basis for further steps to unity?

Bibliography

JOURNALS AND COLLECTIONS

ATR	*Anglican Theological Review*
BC	*British Critic*
DNB	*Dictionary of National Biography*
ER	*Edinburgh Review*
HTR	*Harvard Theological Review*
JEH	*Journal of Ecclesiastical History*
JRH	*Journal of Religious History*
JTS	*Journal of Theological Studies*
LACT	*Library of Anglo-Catholic Theology*
MC	*See More and Cross (below)*
MC	*Modern Churchman*
PS	*Parker Society edition of the works of the English Reformers*
QR	*Quarterly Review*
SCH	*Studies in Church History*
SJT	*Scottish Journal of Theology*
Theol.	*Theology*

ADDLESHAW, G. W. O. *The High Church Tradition*, London 1941.

ALLEN, L. *John Henry Newman and the Abbé Jager*, Oxford 1975.

ANGLICAN - ROMAN CATHOLIC INTERNATIONAL COMMISSION *The Final Report*, London 1982.

ARNOLD, T. [on Niebuhr], *QR*, 32 (1825), pp. 67–92.

—— 'The Oxford Malignants,' *ER*, 63 (1836), pp. 225–239.

—— 'On the Social Progress of States,' in *Miscellaneous Works*, London 1845.

—— 'Preface to the Third Volume of the Edition of Thucydides,' *Miscellaneous Works*, London 1845.

—— *The Christian Life . . . Sermons . . . of Rugby School*, 3rd edn, London 1845.

—— *Fragment on the Church*, 2nd edn, London 1845.

—— *Introductory Lectures on Modern History with the Inaugural Lecture*, 6th edn, London 1874.

—— *Life*, see STANLEY, A. P.

AUBREY, J. *Brief Lives*, Harmondsworth 1972.

AVIS, P. D. L. 'The Shaking of the Seven Hills,' *SJT*, 32 (1979), pp. 439–455.

—— 'Richard Hooker and John Calvin,' *JEH*, 32 (1981), pp. 19–28.

—— [*CTR*] *The Church in the Theology of the Reformers*, London 1982.

—— *Ecumenical Theology and the Elusiveness of Doctrine*, London 1986.

—— [*FMHT*] *Foundations of Modern Historical Thought: From Machiavelli to Vico*, London 1986.

—— 'Coleridge on Luther,' *Charles Lamb Bulletin*, 56 (1986), pp. 249–255.

—— 'The Church's One Foundation,' *Theol.*, 89 (1986), pp. 257–263.

—— *Gore: Construction and Conflict*, with a foreword by Lord Ramsey of Canterbury, Worthing 1988.

—— 'What is Anglicanism?' in Sykes & Booty, eds, *The Study of Anglicanism*, London and Philadelphia 1988.

—— *Eros and the Sacred*, London 1989.

BAKER, W. J. 'The Attitudes of English Churchmen, 1800–1850, towards the Reformation,' Ph.D. diss., Cambridge 1966.

—— 'Hurrell Froude and the Reformers,' *JEH*, 21 (1970), pp. 243–259.

BANTOCK, G. H. 'Newman and Education', *Cambridge Journal*, 4 (1951), pp. 660–678.

BARNARD, L. W. 'The Use of the Patristic Tradition in the Late Seventeenth and Early Eighteenth Centuries', in Bauckham, R. and Drewery, B. eds, *Scripture, Tradition and Reason* (Essays in Honour of R. P. C. Hanson), Edinburgh 1988.

BELL, H. *Lutheri Posthuma or Luther's Last Divine Discourses*, London 1650.

BENNETT, G. V. 'William III and the Episcopate', in G. V. Bennett and J. D. Walsh, eds, *Essays in Modern English Church History*, London 1966.

—— *The Tory Crisis in Church and State 1688–1730*, Oxford 1975.

[BENNETT, G. V.] Preface (anon.) in *Crockford's Clerical Directory 1987–88*, London 1987.

BEST, G. *Temporal Pillars*, Cambridge 1964.

BEVERIDGE, W. *Works (LACT)*, Oxford 1846.

BIRT, H. N. *The Elizabethan Religious Settlement*, London 1907.

BOKENKOTTER, T. S. *Cardinal Newman as an Historian*, Louvain 1959.

BOOTY, J. E. *John Jewell as Apologist of the Church of England*, London 1963.

BOSHER, R. S. *The Making of the Restoration Settlement*, London 1951.

BOUYER, L. *The Spirit and Forms of Protestantism*, London 1963.

BRAMHALL, J. *Works (LACT)*, Oxford 1842.

BRANDRETH, H. R. T. *The Oecumenical Ideals of the Oxford Movement*, London 1947.

BRENDON, P. *Hurrell Froude and the Oxford Movement*, London 1974.

BRILIOTH, Y. *The Anglican Revival: Studies in the Oxford Movement*, London 1925.

BROOK, V. J. K. *Archbishop Parker*, Oxford 1962.

BROSE, O. *F. D. Maurice: Rebellious Conformist*, Ohio 1971.

BROWNE, T. *Religio Medici*, Oxford 1909.

BRYANT, M. D. (ed.) *The Future of Anglican Theology*, New York and Toronto, 1984.

BURGON, J. W. *Lives of Twelve Good Men*, London 1891.

BURNETT, G. *History of the Reformation*, Oxford 1829.

—— *An Exposition of the Thirty-nine Articles*, Oxford 1845.

—— *History of His Own Time*, London 1850.

BUTLER, J. *The Analogy of Religion, Natural and Revealed*, London 1889.

BUTLER, P. (ed.) *Pusey Rediscovered*, London 1983.

BUTTERFIELD, H. *The Whig Interpretation of History*, Harmondsworth, 1973.

BAUMEISTER, R. F. *Identity: Cultural Change and the Struggle for Self*, New York 1986.

CALVIN, J. *Institutes of the Christian Religion*, trans. H. Beveridge, London n.d.

CARGILL THOMPSON, W. D. J. 'The Philosopher of the Politic Society' in W. Speed Hill, ed., *Studies in Richard Hooker*, Cleveland, Ohio 1972.

[CATHOLICITY] *Catholicity: A Study of the Conflict of Christian Traditions in the West*, London 1947.

—— *The Catholicity of Protestantism*, ed. R. N. Flew and R. E. Davies, London 1950.

CHADWICK, W. O. *From Bossuet to Newman*, London 1957.

—— *The Mind of the Oxford Movement*, London 1960.

—— 'Catholicism', *Theol.*, 76 (1973), pp. 171–180.

—— *Newman*, Oxford 1983.

CHILLINGWORTH, W. *Letter Touching Infallibility*, London 1662.

—— *The Religion of Protestants a Safe Way to Salvation*, London 1846.

CHURCH, R. W. *The Oxford Movement*, London 1891.

—— *Pascal and Other Sermons*, London 1896.

CLARENDON *Life* (3 vols), Oxford 1827.

—— *Miscellaneous Works*, London 1751.

CLEBSCH, W. A. 'The Elizabethans on Luther' in Pelikan, J. ed., *Interpreters of Luther*, Philadelphia 1968.

—— *England's Earliest Protestants 1520–1535*, Westport, Connecticut 1980.

[CLOUD] *Cloud of Unknowing, The*, Harmondsworth, 1961.

COLERIDGE, S. T. *Aids to Reflection*, 5th edn, London 1843.

—— *Notes: Theological, Political and Miscellaneous*, London 1853.

—— *Letters of S. T. Coleridge*, ed. E. L. Griggs, IV, Oxford 1959.

—— *Table Talk*, ed. H. Morley, London 1884.

—— *Anima Poetae*, London 1895.

—— *Philosophical Lectures*, ed. K. Coburn, London 1949.

—— *Coleridge on the Seventeenth Century*, ed. R. F. Brinkley, Durham, North Carolina 1955.

—— *The Friend*, ed. B. E. Rooke (*Collected Works*, IV), Princeton and London 1969.

—— *On the Constitution of Church and State*, London 1972 (Everyman edn).

COLLINSON, P. *The Religion of Protestants: The Church in English Society 1559–1625*, Oxford 1982.

CONGAR, Y. *Lay People in the Church*, London 1959.

CONYBEARE, W. J. 'Church Parties' (1853), *Essays Ecclesiastical and Social*, London 1855.

COULDON, J. and ALLCHIN, A. M. (ed.) *The Rediscovery of Newman*, London 1967.

CREIGHTON, M. *The Church and the Nation*, London 1901.

—— *Historical Lectures and Addresses*, London 1903.

CROSS, C. *The Royal Supremacy in the Elizabethan Church*, London 1969.

—— *Church and People 1450–1660: The Triumph of the Laity in the English Church*, Hassocks, Sussex 1976.

CROSS, F. L. *The Oxford Movement and the Seventeenth Century*, London 1933.

DAVIES, D. 'Social Groups, Liturgy and Glossolalia,' *Churchman*, 90 (1976), pp. 193–205.

DAWLEY, P. M. *John Whitgift and the Reformation*, London 1955.

D'ENTRÈVES, A. P. *The Medieval Contribution to Political Thought: Aquinas, Marsilius, Hooker*, New York 1959.

DICKENS, A. G. *The German Nation and Martin Luther*, London 1974.

DISTAD, N. M. *Guessing at Truth: The Life of Julius Charles Hare (1795–1855)*, Shepherdstown 1979.

DIXON, R. W. *History of the Church of England from the Abolition of the Roman Jurisdiction*, London 1878.

[DOCTRINE] *Doctrine in the Church of England*, London 1938.

DRAPER, J. (ed.) *Communion and Episcopacy: Essays to mark the centenary of the Chicago-Lambeth Quadrilateral*, Oxford 1988.

ELTON, G. R. *The Tudor Constitution: Documents and Commentary*, Cambridge 1972.

[EMMAUS] *The Emmaus Report*, London 1987.

ERIKSON, E. H. *Identity: Youth and Crisis*, London 1983.

[ESSAYS] *Essays and Reviews*, London 1860.

EVANS, G. R. (ed.) *Christian Authority: Essays in Honour of Henry Chadwick*, Oxford 1988.

EVERY, G. *The High Church Party 1688–1718*, London 1956.

FALKLAND. *Of the Infallibility of the Church of Rome*, [Oxford 1645], ?edn, n.d.

FARLEY, E. *Ecclesial Reflection*, Philadelphia 1982.

FIELD, R. *Of the Church*, Edinburgh 1847.

FORBES, D. *The Liberal Anglican Idea of History*, Cambridge 1952.

FORRESTER, D. W. F. 'The Intellectual Development of E. G. Pusey 1800–1850,' D.Phil., diss., Oxford 1967.

FRAPPELL, L. O. 'Coleridge and the "Coleridgeans" on Luther,' *JRH*, 7 (1973), pp. 307–23.

FREUD, S. *Group Psychology and the Analysis of the Ego, Pelican Freud Library*, XII, Harmondsworth, 1985.

GARBETT, C. *The Claims of the Church of England*, London 1947.

GILBERT, A. D. *The Making of Post-Christian Britain*, London 1980.

GILL, R. *Prophecy and Praxis*, London 1981.

GILLEY, S. 'Nationality and Liberty, Protestant and Catholic: Robert Southey's Book of the Church', *SCH*, 18 (1982), pp. 409–432.

GLADSTONE, W. E. *Church Principles considered in their Results*, London 1840.

—— *The State in its Relations with the Church*, 4th edn, London 1841.

—— *A Chapter of Autobiography*, London 1868.

—— *Gleanings of Past Years*, London 1879.

—— *The Impregnable Rock of Holy Scripture*, London 1896.

—— *Studies Subsidiary to the Works of Bishop Butler*, Oxford 1896.

—— *Later Gleanings*, 2nd edn, London 1898.

GLADSTONE, W. E. *Correspondence on Church and Religion*, ed. D. C. Lathbury, London 1910.

GORE, C. *The Church and the Ministry*, 2nd edn, London 1889.

—— (ed.) *Lux Mundi*, London 1889.

—— *The Basis of Anglican Fellowship in Faith and Organisation*, London 1914.

—— *The Reconstruction of Belief*, London 1926.

GREAVES, R. W. 'Golightly and Newman 1824–1845,' *JEH*, 9 (1958), pp. 209–228.

GREEN, V. H. H. 'Mark Pattison and the Tractarians,' Friends of Lambeth Palace Library Annual Report 1985, pp. 9–23.

GREENFIELD, R. H. 'The Attitude of the Tractarians to the Roman Catholic Church 1833–1850,' D.Phil. diss., Oxford 1956.

GRIFFIN, J. R. *The Oxford Movement: A Revision*, Virginia 1980.

GWATKIN, H. M. *The Bishop of Oxford's Open Letter*, London 1914.

HAIGH, C. (ed.) *The English Reformation Revised*, Cambridge 1987.

HALES, J. *Golden Remains*, London 1688.

—— *A Tract Concerning Schism and Schismaticks*, London 1700.

—— *Works*, Glasgow 1765.

HALL, B. 'The Early Rise and Gradual Decline of Lutheranism in England (1520–1600),' *SCH*, Subsidia 2, *Reform and Reformation: England and the Continent, 1500–1715*, ed. D. Baker, Oxford 1979, pp. 103–131.

HALL, J. *Works*, Oxford 1837.

HAMMOND, H. *Works (LACT)*, Oxford 1849.

HANSON, A. T. and R. P. C. *The Identity of the Church*, London 1987.

HANSON, R. P. C. *The Attractiveness of God*, London 1973.

HARE, J. C. *The Contest with Rome*, London 1852.

—— *Vindication of Luther*, London 1855.

HARE, J. C. and AUGUSTUS *Guesses at Truth*, with a memoir by E. H. Plumtre, London 1866.

HARE, J. C. *The Victory of Faith*, 3rd edn with introductions by F. D. Maurice and A. P. Stanley, ed. E. H. Plumtre, London 1874.

—— *The Mission of the Comforter*, 3rd edn, London 1876.

HAUGAARD, W. P. *Elizabeth and the English Reformation*, Cambridge 1968.

—— 'A Myopic Curiosity: Martin Luther and the English Tractarians,' *ATR*, 66 (1984), pp. 391–401.

HENSON, H. H. *Anglicanism*, London 1921.

—— *Church and Parson in England*, London 1927.

—— *The Church of England*, Cambridge 1939.

HILL, C. *Antichrist in Seventeenth Century England*, Oxford 1971.

HOADLY, B. *The Nature of the Kingdom or Church of Christ: a sermon preached before the King*, 8th edn, London 1717.

HOLLAND, H. S. *The Optimism of Butler's 'Analogy'*, Oxford 1908.

HOLTBY, R. T. *Daniel Waterland 1683–1740*, Carlisle 1966.

HOOK, W. F. *The Three Reformations, Lutheran, Roman, Anglican*, 2nd edn, London 1847.

HOOK, W. F. *A Church Dictionary*, London 1854.

HOOKER, R. *Works*, ed. J. Keble, Oxford 1845.

HORKHEIMER, M. and ADORNO, T. W. *Dialectic of Englightenment*, London 1973.

HORT, F. J. A. 'Coleridge' in *Cambridge Essays*, Cambridge 1856.

HOWE, J. *Highways and Hedges: Anglicanism and the Universal Church*, London 1985.

HUNTINGTON, W. R. *The Church Idea: An Essay Towards Unity*, 4th edn, New York 1899.

HUNTLEY, F. L. *Bishop Joseph Hall 1574–1656*, Cambridge 1979.

JENSON, R. W. *The Triune Identity*, Philadelphia 1982.

JORDAN, W. K. *The Development of Religious Toleration in England: II (1603–1640)*, London 1936.

KEBLE, J. *Primitive Tradition recognised in Holy Scripture*, 4th edn, London 1839.

—— 'The State in its Relations with the Church,' *BC*, 26 (1839), pp. 355–397.

KNOX, R. B. *James Ussher, Archbishop of Armagh*, Cardiff 1967.

LAMPE, G. W. H. 'The Limuru Principle and Church Unity,' *Churchman*, 88 (1974), pp. 25–37.

LASH, N. L. A. *Newman on Development*, London 1975.

LAUD, W. *Works (LACT)*, 6th edn, Oxford 1849.

LAW, W. *Defence of Church Principles: Three Letters to the Bishop of Bangor 1717–1719*, ed. Gore and Nash, London 1893.

LIDDON, H. P. *Life of Edward Bouverie Pusey*, London 1893–97.

LIGHTFOOT, J. B. *St. Paul's Epistle to the Philippians*, London 1898.

LIVINGSTON, J. C. *The Ethics of Belief: An Essay on the Victorian Religious Conscience*, Tallahasee, Florida 1974.

LOCKE, J. *Works*, London 1801.

—— *Essay Concerning Human Understanding*, London 1961.

LUTHER, M. *Luther's Works*, St. Louis and Philadelphia, 1955–.

MAJOR, H. D. A. 'The Reformation: Old and New', *MC*, 22 (1932), pp. 225–228.

MANNING, H. E. *The Rule of Faith*, London 1838.

—— *The Unity of the Church*, 2nd edn, London 1845.

MARSHALL, J. S. *Hooker and the Anglican Tradition*, London 1963.

MARTIN, D. and MULLEN, P. *No Alternative: The Prayer Book Controversy*, Oxford 1981.

MATTHEW, H. C. G. 'Edward Bouverie Pusey: From Scholar to Tractarian,' *JTS*, NS 32 (1981), pp. 101–124.

MCADOO, H. R. *The Spirit of Anglicanism*, London 1965.

MACAULAY, T. B. 'Gladstone on Church and State,' in *Essays*, London 1905.

—— *History of England*, London 1906.

MCCLAIN, F. M. *Maurice: Man and Moralist*, London 1972.

MCCONICA, J. K. *English Humanists and Reformation Politics under Henry VIII and Edward VI*, Oxford 1965.

MACDOUGALL, H. A. *The Acton – Newman Relations*, New York 1962.

MCDOUGALL, W. *The Group Mind*, 2nd edn, Cambridge 1927.

MCNEILL, J. T. *Unitive Protestantism*, New York 1930.

MACQUARRIE, J. *Theology, Church and Ministry*, London 1986.

MASCALL, E. L. *The Recovery of Unity*, London 1958.

MAURICE, F. *The Life of F. D. Maurice*, London 1884.

MAURICE, F. D. *Subscription No Bondage*, Oxford 1835.

—— *Reasons for not joining a Party in the Church: a letter to the Ven. Samuel Wilberforce*, London 1841.

—— *Three Letters to the Rev. W. Palmer*, London 1842.

—— *Right and Wrong Methods of Supporting Protestantism: a letter to Lord Ashley*, London 1843.

—— *Thoughts on the Rule of Conscientious Subscription*, Oxford 1845.

—— *The Epistle to the Hebrews*, London 1846.

—— *What is Revelation?*, Cambridge 1859.

—— *MMP: Moral and Metaphysical Philosophy*, London 1872.

—— *The Doctrine of Sacrifice*, London 1879.

—— *Theological Essays*, London 1957.

—— *The Kingdom of Christ*, ed. A. R. Vidler, London 1958.

—— *Sketches of Contemporary Authors*, ed. A. J. Hartley, Archer Books 1970.

MAYER, T. F. 'Starkey and Melanchthon on Adiaphora,' *Sixteenth Century Journal*, 11 (1980), pp. 38–49.

METZ, J. B. *Faith in History and Society*, London 1980.

MEYER, C. S. 'Melanchthon's Influence on English Thought in the Sixteenth Century,' *Miscellaneae Historiae Ecclesiasticae II*, Louvain 1967, pp. 163–185.

MILL, J. S. *Autobiography*, London 1873.

MILMAN, H. H. 'The Reformation in England,' *QR*, 33 (1826), pp. 1–37.

MOBERLY, R. C. *Ministerial Priesthood*, London 1969.

MOL, H. *Identity and the Sacred*, Oxford 1976.

MOORE, P. (ed.) *The Synod of Westminster: Do We Need It?*, London 1986.

MORE, P. E. and CROSS, F. L. *Anglicanism*, London 1935.

MOYSER, G. (ed.) *Church and Politics Today: The Role of the Church of England in Contemporary Politics*, Edinburgh 1985.

MOZLEY, J. B. 'Luther,' *Essays Historical and Theological*, London 1878, I.

—— 'Dr Arnold,' *Essays . . .* , II.

NEILL, S. *Anglicanism*, Harmondsworth, 1958.

NEWMAN, J. H. *Lectures on Justification*, 2nd ed., London 1840.

—— *Lectures on Justification*, 3rd edn, London 1874.

—— *The Prophetical Office of the Church*, 1st edn, London 1837.

—— *The Prophetical Office of the Church*, 2nd edn, London 1838.

—— *The Prophetical Office of the Church*, 3rd edn (*The Via Media*), London 1877.

—— *Essays Critical and Historical*, London 1895.

—— *The Arians of the Fourth Century*, London 1897.

—— *Essay in Aid of a Grammar of Assent*, London 1903.

—— *Certain Difficulties Felt by Anglicans in Catholic Teaching*, London 1901.

—— *Lectures on the Present Position of Catholics in England* (1851), London 1903.

—— *On University Education*, London 1915 (Everyman edn).

—— *Essays and Sketches*, ed. F. C. Harrold, New York 1948.

—— *Apologia Pro Vita Sua*, London 1959 (Fontana edn).

—— *An Essay on the Development of Christian Doctrine*, 2nd edn (1878), London 1960.

—— *On Consulting the Faithful in Matters of Doctrine*, London 1961.

—— *University Sermons*, London 1970.

—— *An Essay on the Development of Christian Doctrine* (1845), Harmondsworth, 1974.

—— *Loss and Gain* Oxford 1986.

—— *Theological Papers on Faith and Certainty*, ed. H. M. de Acheval and J. D. Holmes, Oxford 1976.

NEWSOME, D. *The Parting of Friends*, London 1966.

NIJENHUIS, W. *Adrianus Saravia* (c. *1532–1613*), Leiden 1980.

NOCKLES, P. B. 'Continuity and Change in Anglican High Church-manship in Britain 1792–1850,' D.Phil. diss., Oxford 1982.

NORMAN, E. R. *Church and Society in England 1770–1970*, Oxford 1976.

NUTTALL, G. F. and CHADWICK, O. (ed.) *From Uniformity to Unity 1662–1962*, London 1962.

OAKELEY, F. 'Bishop Jewel: His Character, Correspondence and Apologetic Treatises,' *BC*, 30 (1841), pp. 1ff; 32 (1842), pp. 211ff.

O'HALLORAN, B. C. 'R. H. Froude: his influence on J. H. Newman and the Oxford Movement,' Ph.D. diss., Columbia University 1965.

ORR, R. R. *Reason and Authority: The Thought of William Chilling-worth*, Oxford 1967.

OVERTON, J. H. *The Nonjurors*, London 1902.

PACKER, J. W. *The Transformation of Anglicanism 1643–1660, with special reference to Henry Hammond*, Manchester 1969.

PALMER, W. *A Treatise on the Church of Christ*, 2nd edn, London 1839.

—— *A Compendious Ecclesiastical History from the earliest period to the Present Time*, new edn, London 1852.

—— *A Narrative of Events Connected with the Publication of the 'Tracts for the Times'*, London 1883.

[PRAYER BOOK] *The First and Second Prayer Books of Edward the Sixth*, ed. E. S. C. Gibson (Everyman edn), London 1910.

PATRICK, S. *A Sermon Preached before the King*, London 1678.

—— *A Discourse about Tradition*, London 1683.

PATTISON, M. 'Antecedents of the Reformation,' [*Frasers' Magazine*, 1859], *Essays*, I, ed. H. Nettleship, Oxford 1889.

—— *'Calvin at Geneva,' Essays*, II.

—— *Memoirs*, Fontwell, Sussex 1969.

PELIKAN, J. *Obedient Rebels: Catholic Substance and Protestant Principle in Luther's Reformation*, New York and London 1964.

PERRY, J. F. 'Newman's Treatment of Luther in the Lectures on the Doctrine of Justification,' Ph.D. diss., St. Mary's University, Halifax, Nova Scotia.

PETERS, R. 'John Hales and the Synod of Dort', *SCH*, 7, ed. G. J. Cuming and D. Baker, Oxford 1971, pp. 277–288.

PINNINGTON, J. E. 'Anglican Openness to Foreign Protestant Churches in the Eighteenth Century,' *ATR*, 51 (1969), pp. 133–148.

PUSEY, E. B. *An Historical Enquiry into the probable causes of the Rationalist Character lately predominant in the Theology of Germany*, London 1828.

—— *The Royal Supremacy not an arbitrary authority but limited by the laws of the church of which kings are members*, Oxford 1850.

—— *Daniel the Prophet*, Oxford 1864.

—— 'The Rule of Faith as Maintained by the Fathers and the Church of England' (1851), *Nine Sermons Preached before the University of Oxford*, 1865.

—— *An Eirenikon: The Church of England a Portion of Christ's One Holy, Catholic Church, and a means of restoring visible Unity*, Oxford 1865.

—— *What is of Faith as to Everlasting Punishment?*, 3rd edn, Oxford 1879.

RAMSEY, A. M. *The Gospel and the Catholic Church*, London 1936.

—— *F. D. Maurice and the Conflicts of Modern Theology*, Cambridge 1951.

ROSE, H. J. *The State of Protestantism Described*, 2nd edn, London 1829.

ROSE, H. J. *Letter to the Lord Bishop of London in reply to Mr. Pusey's Work*, London 1829.

—— *The Study of Church History*, London 1837.

ROUSE, R. and NEILL, S. C. *A History of the Ecumenical Movement 1517–1948*, London 1954.

ROWELL, G. *The Vision Glorious: Themes and Personalities of the Catholic Revival in Anglicanism*, Oxford 1983.

—— (ed.) *Tradition Renewed: The Oxford Movement Confer-ence Papers*, London 1986.

ROWLANDS, J. H. L. 'Church, State and Society: The Attitudes of John Keble, Richard Hurrell Froude and John Henry Newman, 1827–1845,' M.Litt. diss., Durham 1986.

RUPP, E.G. *Studies in the Making of the English Protestant Tradition*, Cambridge 1949.

—— *The Righteousness of God: Luther Studies*, London 1953.

—— *Protestant Catholicity*, London 1960.

—— *Religion in England 1688–1791*, Oxford 1986.

SCARISBRICK, J. J. *Henry VIII*, Harmondsworth 1971.

—— *The Reformation and the English People*, Oxford 1984.

SEELEY, J. R. *Ecce Homo*, London 1865.

SELWYN, E.G. (ed.) *Essays Catholic and Critical*, London 1926.

SMITH, M. G. [*Trelawny*] *Fighting Joshua . . . Sir Jonathan Trelawny . . . Bishop of Bristol, Exeter and Winchester*, Redruth 1985.

—— 'Toleration and Pastoral Ministry, Some Long-term Effects of James II's Religious Policy,' *Churchman*, 97 (1983), pp. 141–153.

SMITH, P. 'English Opinion of Luther', *HTR*, 10 (1917), pp. 129–158.

SOMMERVILLE, M. R. 'Richard Hooker and his Contemporaries on Episcopacy: An Elizabethan Consensus,' *JEH*, 35 (1984), pp. 177–187.

SOUTHGATE, W. M. *John Jewel and the Problem of Doctrinal Authority*, Cambridge, Mass. 1962.

STANLEY, A. P. *Life of Arnold*, London 1891.

STEPHEN, J. *Essays in Ecclesiastical Biography*, London 1875.

STILLINGFLEET, E. *Irenicum: A Weapon–Salve for the Church's Wounds*, 2nd edn, London 1662.

—— *A Rational Account of the Grounds of the Protestant Religion*, London 1665.

STRANKS, C. J. *Jeremy Taylor*, London 1952.

STREETER, B. H. (ed.) *Foundations*, London 1912.

STROUP, G. W. *The Promise of Narrative Theology*, London 1984.

STRYPE, J. *Life of Whitgift, II*, Oxford 1822.

STUNT, T. C. F. 'John Henry Newman and the Evangelicals,' *JEH*, 21 (1970), pp. 65–74.

SYKES, N. *Church and State in the Eighteenth Century*, Cambridge 1934.

—— *William Wake, Archbishop of Canterbury: 1657–1735*, Cambridge 1957.

—— *Old Priest and New Presbyter*, Cambridge 1956.

SYKES, S. W. *The Integrity of Anglicanism*, London 1978.

—— 'The Ministry and the Episcopal Office: An Anglican Approach to the Confessio Augustana,' *LWF Report* 6 (1979), pp. 29–59.

—— 'Anglicanism and Protestantism' in Sykes, ed., *England and Germany: Studies in Theological Diplomacy*, Frankfurt am Main and Bern 1982.

—— (ed.) *Authority in the Anglican Communion*, Toronto 1987.

SYKES, S. W. and BOOTY, J. (ed.) *The Study of Anglicanism*, London and Philadelphia 1988.

TAYLOR, A. E. *The Faith of a Moralist*, London 1951.

TAYLOR, J. *Works*, London 1839.

TEMPLE, W. *William Temple and his Message*, ed. A. E. Baker, Harmondsworth 1946.

THIRWALL, C. *Remains, Literary and Theological, I. Charges*, London 1877.

THIRWALL, J. C. *Connop Thirwall: Historian and Theologian*, London 1936.

THOMAS, P. H. E. 'The Lambeth Conference and the Development of Anglican Ecclesiology 1867–1978,' Ph.D. diss., Durham 1982.

THORNDIKE, H. *Works (LACT)*, Oxford 1844.

THURMER, J. A. 'Henry of Exeter and the Later Tractarians,' *Southern History*, 5 (1983), pp. 210–220.

TILLER, J. *A Strategy for the Church's Ministry*, London 1983.

TILLICH, P. *The Protestant Era*, Chicago 1948.

TJERNAGEL, N. S. *Henry VIII and the Lutherans: A Study in Anglo-Lutheran Relations from 1521–1547*, St. Louis 1965.

TOON, P. *Evangelical Theology 1833–1856, A Response to Tractarianism*, London 1979.

[TRACTS] *Tracts for the Times*, Oxford 1833–1841.

TREVELYAN, G. M. *Clio: A Muse and Other Essays*, London 1930.

—— 'Bias in History' in *Autobiography and Other Essays*, London 1949.

TREVOR-ROPER, H. *Catholics, Anglicans and Puritans*, London 1987.

TROELTSCH, E. *The Social Teaching of the Christian Churches*, trans. O. Wyon, London 1931.

TULLOCH, J. *Rational Theology and Christian Philosophy in England in the Seventeenth Century, I, Liberal Churchmen*, London 1874.

TYRRELL, G. *Christianity at the Crossroads*, London 1910.

USHER, R. *The Reconstruction of the English Church, I*, London 1910.

USSHER, J. *Works*, Dublin 1864.

VAN DE POL, W. H. *Anglicanism in Ecumenical Perspective*, Pittsburgh 1965.

VARGISH, T. *Newman: The Contemplation of Mind*, Oxford 1970.

VERKAMP, B. J. *The Indifferent Mean: Adiaphorism in the English Reformation to 1554*, Athens, Ohio 1977.

VIDLER, A. R. *F. D. Maurice and Company*, London 1966.

WAKE, W. *An Exposition of the Doctrine of the Church of England*, London 1686.

—— 'An Exhortation to Mutual Charity and Union among Protestants,' *Sermons and Discourses on Several Occasions*, London 1716.

WALLACE, D. D. 'The Anglican Appeal to Lutheran Sources: Philipp Melanchthon's Reputation in Seventeenth Century England,' *Historical Magazine of the Protestant Episcopal Church*, 52 (1983), pp. 355–367.

WALSH, J. D. 'Joseph Milner's Evangelical Church History,' *JEH*, 10 (1959), pp. 174–187.

WALTON, I. *Lives*, Oxford 1966.

WARD, W. G. 'A Few Words in Support of No. 90 of the Tracts for the Times,' Oxford 1841.

—— 'Arnold's Sermons,' *BC*, 60 (1841), pp. 298–364.

—— *The Ideal of a Christian Church*, 2nd edn, London 1844.

WARD, WILFRED *William George Ward and the Oxford Movement*, 2nd edn, London 1890.

WATERLAND, D. *Works*, Oxford 1823.

WELSH, P. J. 'Anglican Churchmen and the Establishment of the Jerusalem Bishopric,' *JEH*, 8 (1857), pp. 193–204.

WHATELY, R. *The Kingdom of Christ Delineated in Two Essays*, 3rd edn, London 1842.

WHITBY, D. *Dissuasive from Enquiring into the Doctrine of the Trinity*, 5th edn, London 1714.

WILLIAMS, I. *Autobiography*, 3rd edn, London 1893.

WILSON, T. *Maxims of Piety and of Christianity*, London 1898.

WOODHOUSE, H. F. *The Doctrine of the Church in Anglican Theology 1547–1603*, London 1954.

WORMALD, B. *Clarendon*, Cambridge 1951.

WRIGHT, J. R. (ed.) *Quadrilateral at One Hundred: Essays on the Centenary of the Chicago-Lambeth Quadrilateral 1886/88–1986/88*, Cincinnati 1988.

ZEEVELD, W. G. *Foundations of Tudor Policy*, Cambridge, Mass. 1948.

Index of Subjects

Index of Names

(Excluding Secondary Sources)